BUSINESS SPELLING AND WORD POWER

BUSINESS SPELLING AND WORD POWER

THIRD EDITION

Rosemarie McCauley

Professor, Department of Business Education and Office Systems Administration
Montclair State College
Upper Montclair, New Jersey

Keith Slocum

Associate Professor, Department of English
Montclair State College
Upper Montclair, New Jersey

GLENCOE

Macmillan/McGraw-Hill

Lake Forest, Illinois   Columbus, Ohio
Mission Hills, California   Peoria, Illinois

The manuscript for this book was processed electronically.

Business Spelling and Word Power, Third Edition

Imprint 1992
Copyright © 1991, 1983, 1961 by the Glencoe Division of Macmillan/
McGraw-Hill School Publishing Company. All rights reserved. Printed
in the United States of America. Except as permitted under the
United States Copyright Act of 1976, no part of this publication may
be reproduced or distributed in any form or by any means, or stored
in a database or retrieval system, without the prior written permission
of the publisher. Send all inquiries to: Glencoe Division, Macmillan/
McGraw-Hill, 936 Eastwind Drive, Westerville, Ohio 43081.

ISBN   0-02-678291-X

3 4 5 6 7 8 9 10 11 12 13 14 15   RRD-C   00 99 98 97 96 95 94 93 92

CONTENTS

PREFACE

The third edition of *Business Spelling and Word Power* updates the previous edition and yet retains the features that have made the development of spelling proficiency and word power both interesting and stimulating for many years. The organization, tone, workbook format, and business-related vocabulary emphasis and practice that have successfully been identified with the previous edition can again be found in this edition.

With this book improved spelling and vocabulary skill can be achieved through practice in a meaningful context. *Business Spelling and Word Power, Third Edition,* offers you the opportunity to:

1. Work toward improving spelling skill.
2. Focus attention on the correct use of homonyms and words often confused.
3. Develop and extend vocabulary understanding.
4. Reinforce the skills associated with word division, capitalization, and plurals formation.
5. Use the dictionary effectively.
6. Take part in business-related composing and editing activities.

The text is organized to promote effective learning. There are 24 chapters. The first chapter presents an intensive coverage of how to use a dictionary. Subsequent chapters highlight spelling rules and related language arts skills. A generous number of practice exercises reinforce learning. The final chapter provides a comprehensive experience, challenging you to apply your skill in a series of officelike situations.

Homonyms are presented, with practice exercises following, in Chapters 1 to 12, and words often confused are addressed and reinforced with practice exercises in Chapters 13 to 22.

Review Exercises appear at the end of every fourth chapter beginning with Chapter 4. These Review Exercises contain both sentences and formatted material for editing.

Throughout the text a number of words are asterisked for special study. A convenient dictionary section at the back of the book enables you to verify and develop your competence in understanding the meaning of these key words.

Vocabulary Enrichment exercises appear at the end of Chapter 3 and in each succeeding fourth chapter. These exercises selectively review the vocabulary words that are asterisked, engage you in composition practice, and introduce you to business vocabularies related to the following business practices: using banking services, recognizing the role of computers, maintaining accounting records, understanding telecommunications services, managing information, and making travel arrangements.

In keeping with the business-orientation focus, you are called upon to serve as an employee of High Tech World, a fictitious magazine publishing enterprise. Intermittently in the concluding part of each Review Exercise and then finally in the 12 editing exercises in Chapter 24, you have the opportunity to transfer learning to actual business formats used in the High Tech World office.

The appendix, which contains number usage rules, common prefixes and suffixes, foreign words and phrases, and abbreviations in common use, is a handy reference section.

The goal of effective written communication is error-free copy and the correct use of words. *Business Spelling and Word Power* will help you to reach that goal.

We thank the instructors who have used previous editions of this book and especially those who responded to a survey of users during the development of this edition. We have incorporated their suggestions into this edition to benefit both students and instructors.

Rosemarie McCauley
Keith Slocum

BUSINESS SPELLING AND WORD POWER

Uses of the Dictionary

Most people consult a dictionary for two reasons: (1) to find out how to spell a word and (2) to find out what a word means. While the definition and correct spelling of a word are certainly the primary information the dictionary provides, a good dictionary offers a great deal more. This chapter illustrates the wealth of information available to you in the dictionary. As you will see, the dictionary can be one of the most useful books at your disposal. Used properly, it can be an indispensable tool in your reading, writing, and speaking—at home, in school, and on the job.

The actual dictionary entries on the following pages are from *Webster's New World Dictionary of American English, Third College Edition.*

DEFINITION

When you see an unfamiliar word or are uncertain of the precise meaning of a word, you turn to the dictionary for a definition. For example, what is a **prospectus**?

pro·spec·tus (prō spek′təs, prə-; *also* prä-) *n.* ⟦L: see PROSPECT⟧ a statement outlining the main features of a new work or business enterprise, or the attractions of an established institution such as a college, hotel, etc.; often, specif., a document, made available to investors, containing detailed information about a stock issue, mutual fund, etc.

Many words, of course, have more than one meaning. Look at this entry for **coy**.

coy (koi) *adj.* ⟦ME, still, quiet < OFr *coi*, earlier *quei* < LL *quetus* < L *quietus*: see QUIET⟧ **1** orig., quiet; silent **2** *a)* shrinking from contact or familiarity with others; bashful; shy *b)* primly reserved; demure **3** affecting innocence or shyness, esp. in a playful or coquettish manner **4** reticent or evasive in making a commitment **5** [Archaic] inaccessible; secluded **6** [Obs.] disdainfully aloof —*vi.* [Archaic] to behave in a coy way —*vt.* [Obs.] to pet or caress — **coy′ly** *adv.* —**coy′ness** *n.*

original definition

There are eight separate definitions of **coy**, six as an adjective and two as a verb. Note that the first definition given is **coy**'s original sense of *quiet, silent*. That is because the definitions in *Webster's New World Dictionary* (and some others) are arranged from those most nearly associated with the origin of the word up to more recent meanings. In this way the reader can see how the word developed. In other dictionaries the most common meanings of a word are listed first. These dictionaries would begin with the definition of **coy** as *shy, demure*.

In order to use your dictionary most effectively, be sure you know how the definitions are arranged. This and a great deal of other information can be found in the user's guide at the beginning of your dictionary.

A *synonym* is a word that means the same, or almost the same, as another word. Sometimes the entry for a word contains a list of synonyms and a comparison of the slight differences in their meanings. Notice how the entry for **plan** makes distinctions among various synonyms.

synonym

> **plan** (plan) *n.* ⟦Fr, plan, plane, foundation: merging of *plan* (< L *planus:* see PLAIN¹) with MFr *plant* < It *pianta* < L *planta*, sole of the foot: see PLANT⟧ **1** a drawing or diagram showing the arrangement in horizontal section of a structure, piece of ground, etc. **2** *a*) a scheme or program for making, doing, or arranging something; project, design, schedule, etc. *b*) a method of proceeding **3** any outline or sketch **4** in perspective, any of several planes thought of as perpendicular to the line of sight and between the eye and the object — *vt.* **planned, plan'ning 1** to make a plan of (a structure, piece of ground, etc.) **2** to devise a scheme for doing, making, or arranging **3** to have in mind as a project or purpose — *vi.* to make plans
> *SYN.*—**plan** refers to any detailed method, formulated beforehand, for doing or making something *[vacation plans]*; **design** stresses the final outcome of a plan and implies the use of skill or craft, sometimes in an unfavorable sense, in executing or arranging this *[it was his design to separate us]*; **project** implies the use of enterprise or imagination in formulating an ambitious or extensive plan *[a housing project]*; **scheme**, a less definite term than the preceding, often connotes either an impractical, visionary plan or an underhanded intrigue *[a scheme to embezzle the funds]*

A word that means the opposite of another word is an *antonym*. Sometimes an entry includes one or more antonyms. The entry for **safe** provides both synonyms and antonyms.

> **safe** (sāf) *adj.* **saf'er, saf'est** ⟦ME *sauf* < OFr < L *salvus*, akin to *salus*, health, sound condition < IE base **solo-*, whole, well-preserved > Gr *holos*, whole, Sans *sarva*, unharmed, whole⟧ **1** *a*) free from damage, danger, or injury; secure *b*) having escaped danger or injury; unharmed **2** *a*) giving protection *b*) involving no risk *c*) trustworthy **3** no longer dangerous; unable to cause trouble or damage *[safe in jail]* **4** taking no risks; prudent; cautious: said of persons ☆**5** *Baseball* having reached a base without being put out — *n.* ⟦altered (after the adj.) < earlier *save* < SAVE¹⟧ **1** a container or box, capable of being locked and usually of metal, in which to store valuables **2** any compartment, box, etc. for storing or preserving food, etc. *[a meat safe]* **3** [Slang] a condom —**safe'ly** *adv.* —**safe'-ness** *n.*
> *SYN.*—**safe** implies freedom from damage, danger, or injury or from the risk of damage, etc. *[is it safe to leave?]*; **secure**, often interchangeable with **safe**, is now usually applied to something about which there is no need to feel apprehension *[he is secure in his job]* —*ANT.* **dangerous, precarious, unsure**

antonym

You can also find synonyms and antonyms for individual words in a specialized reference book called a *thesaurus*. However, while the thesaurus offers a more complete listing of synonyms and antonyms than the dictionary does, it does not offer the information on shades of meaning that the dictionary provides.

SPELLING

When you are uncertain how to spell a word, you turn to the dictionary to find out. How many **g**'s are there in **exa—erate**? Is it superintend**a**nt or superintend**e**nt?

ex·ag·ger·ate (eg zaj′ər ăt, ig-) *vt.* -at′ed, -at′ing ‖ < L *exaggeratus*, pp. of *exaggerare*, to increase, exaggerate < *ex-*, out, up + *aggerare*, to heap up < *agger*, a heap < *aggerere*, to bring toward < *ad-*, to + *gerere*, to carry: see GESTURE ‖ **1** to think, speak, or write of as greater than is really so; magnify beyond the fact; overstate **2** to increase or enlarge to an extreme or abnormal degree; overemphasize; intensify —*vi.* to give an exaggerated description or account — **ex·ag′ger·at·ed·ly** *adj.* —**ex·ag′ger·a′tion** *n.* —**ex·ag′ger·a′tive** *adj.* —**ex·ag′ger·a′tor** *n.*

su·per·in·tend·ent (-in ten′dənt) *n.* ‖ < LL(Ec) *superintendens*, prp. of *superintendere*, to superintend ‖ **1** a person in charge of a department, institution, etc.; director; supervisor **2** a person responsible for the maintenance of a building; custodian —*adj.* that superintends

Some words have more than one correct spelling. In such instances the dictionary lists both spellings. In some cases usage is about evenly divided between the two. In other cases one spelling occurs more often than the other. This is the spelling that is given first. Look at these entries for **judgment** and **theater**, for example.

judg·ment (juj′mənt) *n.* ‖ ME *jugement* < OFr < ML *judicamentum* < L *judicare:* see JUDGE, *v.* ‖ **1** the act of judging; deciding **2** a legal decision; order, decree, or sentence given by a judge or law court **3** *a)* a debt or other obligation resulting from a court order *b)* a document recording this obligation **4** a misfortune looked on as a punishment from God **5** an opinion or estimate **6** criticism or censure **7** the ability to come to opinions about things; power of comparing and deciding; understanding; good sense **8** *Bible* justice; right **9** [J-] short for LAST JUDGMENT Also sp. **judge′ment**

the·a·ter or **the·a·tre** (thē′ə tər) *n.* ‖ ME *theatre* < OFr < L *theatrum* < Gr *theatron* < base of *theasthai*, to see, view < IE base *dhāu-*, to see > Gr *thauma*, miracle ‖ **1** a place where plays, operas, films, etc. are presented; esp., a building or outdoor structure expressly designed for such presentations **2** any place resembling a theater, esp. a lecture hall, surgical clinic, etc., having the floor of the seating space raked **3** any place where events take place; scene of operations *[journalists in the SE Asian theater]* **4** *a)* the dramatic art or dramatic works; drama *b)* the theatrical world; people engaged in theatrical activity *c)* the legitimate theater, as distinguished from films, TV, etc. (often with *the*) **5** theatrical technique, production, etc. with reference to its effectiveness *[a play that is good theater]*

Many people believe that the first spelling of the word in an entry is the "preferred" spelling, or the spelling that is more correct, and that other variant spellings are less correct. This is not so. Either **theater** or **theatre** is acceptable; **judgement** is no less correct than **judgment**.

However, the dictionary entry does indicate the more common spelling of a word. While usage between **theater** and **theatre** is fairly evenly divided, as shown by the joint boldface entry, **theater** is listed first as the more common spelling. Since **judgement** appears at the end of the entry on **judgment**, it is used much less frequently; **judgment** is by far the more common spelling.

Most American business writers would write **theater** and **judgment** because it is standard business practice to follow the more common spelling of a word. Accordingly, while some of the words in the following chapters have more than one acceptable spelling, we always list the more common spelling because that is the spelling used in business.

In order to look up a word, of course, you need to know what letters it begins with. Usually, this presents no problem, since most words begin with the vowel or consonant you usually associate with the sound that begins the word.

Some consonant sounds, however, can be spelled in more ways than one. In these cases it is helpful to know what other letters or letter combinations can depict the same sound. The following chart indicates initial consonant sounds that can be spelled in more than one way.

Sound	The Word Usually Begins With	The Word May Begin With
f	f(fish)	ph(physician)
g	g(get)	gh(ghost)
		gu(guide)
h	h(hat)	wh(whole)
j	g(giant)	j(jump)
k	c(cat)	k(king)
		ch(chemistry)
		kh(khaki)
kw	qu(quiet)	
n	n(nickel)	kn(knife)
		gn(gnat)
		pn(pneumonia)
r	r(rust)	wr(wrist)
		rh(rhyme)
s	s(silent)	c(citizen)
		ps(psalm)
		sc(science)
		sw(sword)

DIVISION INTO SYLLABLES

By using a dot (sometimes, a hyphen), the dictionary tells you exactly where a word may be split into syllables. If, for example, you had to divide the word **fascinate** at the end of a line, where would you place the hyphen? Consult your dictionary to find out.

> **fas·ci·nate** (fas′ə nāt′) ***vt.*** **-nat′ed, -nat′ing** ‖ < L *fascinatus*, pp. of *fascinare*, to bewitch, charm < *fascinum*, a charm < ? or akin to Gr *baskanos*, sorcerer ‖ **1** orig., to put under a spell; bewitch **2** to attract or hold motionless, as by a fixed look or by inspiring terror **3** to hold the attention of by being very interesting or delightful; charm; captivate **—SYN.** ATTRACT **—fas′ci·nat′ing·ly** *adv.*

Webster's New World Dictionary, Third College Edition, uses either a dot or a hairline [‖] to separate syllables. The dot indicates where a word may be acceptably divided; the hairline indicates where, if possible, the word should not be divided at the end of the line. For example, the entry for **fascinate** indicates that **fascinated** should not be divided immediately before **ed** and that **fascinatingly** should not be divided immediately before **ly**.

A discussion of rules regarding the hyphenation of words in business writing is included in Chapter 23.

PRONUNCIATION

Through the use of a stress mark ('), the dictionary tells you which syllable of a word is accented—that is, spoken a bit more strongly or forcefully than the other syllables. In many cases more than one syllable receives stress. In these cases a heavy stress mark following a syllable indicates a strong stress; a lighter stress mark indicates a weak, or secondary, stress.

The *diacritical* marks (a, ä, ô, etc.) tell you how to sound various vowels and consonants in the word. (The *key words* at the bottom of each page furnish a key to the use of diacritical marks. Each is to be pronounced as it is in these key words.) Some words have several acceptable pronunciations. The first one listed is the most common pronunciation, but the others listed are also acceptable.

Let's try a word like **attenuate**. What syllables are accented? The dictionary provides the answer.

> **at·ten|u·ate** (ə ten′yo͞o ất′; *for adj.,* -it, -āt′) **vt. -at|ed, -at|ing** ⟦< L *attenuatus,* pp. of *attenuare,* to make thin < *ad-* to + *tenuare* < *tenuis,* THIN⟧ **1** to make slender or thin **2** to dilute or rarefy **3** to lessen in severity, value, amount, intensity, etc.; weaken **4** *Electronics* to reduce the strength of (an electrical impulse) **5** *Microbiol.* to reduce the virulence of (a bacterium or virus) usually to make a vaccine —**vi.** to become thin, weak, etc. —**adj. 1** attenuated **2** *Bot.* tapering gradually to a point, as the base of a leaf —**at·ten′|u|a′·tion** *n.* —**at·ten′|u|a′tor** *n.*

The second (**ten**) and fourth (**ate**) syllables are accented; **ten** receives the major stress, **ate** the secondary stress.

How are the individual syllables pronounced? The key words at the bottom of the page tell you.

> at, āte, cär; ten, ēve; is, ice; gō, hôrn, look, to͞ol; oil, out; up,
> fur; ə *for unstressed vowels, as* a *in* ago, u *in* focus; ′ *as in* Latin
> (lat′'n); chin; she; zh *as in* azure (azh′ər); thin, *the;* ŋ *as in* ring (riŋ)
> *In etymologies:* * = unattested; < = derived from; > = from which
> ☆ = Americanism   **See inside front and back covers**

| **Note** | The inside front cover provides a fuller pronunciation key. The inside back cover lists all the abbreviations and symbols used in the dictionary. |

The **a** in the first syllable, **at**, is pronounced like the **a** in **ago**. The second syllable is pronounced like the number **ten**. The **u** is pronounced like **yoo**, where the **oo** sounds like the **oo** in **tool**. Finally, the **a** in the fourth syllable, **ate**, has the long sound as in the word **ate**.

Notice that while this final syllable is pronounced a̅t̅ when a̅t̅t̅e̅n̅u̅a̅t̅e̅ is used as a verb, when it is used as an adjective, the pronunciation can change to ĭt (the ĭ has the short sound as in ĭs).

What is the most common pronunciation of **advertisement? comparable? inquiry? pianist?**

> **ad·ver·tise·ment** (ad′vər tiz′mənt; ad′vər tiz′-; ad vur′tiz-, əd-; -tis-)
> **n. 1** the act of advertising **2** a public notice or announcement, usually paid for, as of things for sale, needs, etc.

com·pa·ra·ble (käm′pə rə bəl; *often* kəm par′ə bəl) *adj.* ⟦ME & OFr < L *comparabilis*⟧ **1** that can be compared **2** worthy of comparison —**com′pa·ra·bil′i·ty** or **com′pa·ra·ble·ness** *n.* —**com′pa·ra·bly** *adv.*

in·quir·y (in′kwə rē, -kwor ē; in kwir′ē, -kwī′rē; *also* in′kwir′ē; -kwī′rē, -kwī′rē) *n., pl.* **-quir·ies** ⟦earlier *enquiry* < ME *enquere*⟧ **1** the act of inquiring **2** an investigation or examination **3** a question; query

pi·an·ist (pē′ə nist; pē an′ist, *often* pyan′ist) *n.* ⟦Fr *pianiste*⟧ a person who plays the piano, esp. a skilled or professional performer

---

DERIVATIONS

Your dictionary is the first place to turn to learn the origins of words. For example, where did the words **boycott** and **dunce** originate?

boy·cott (boi′kät′) *vt.* ⟦after Capt. C. C. *Boycott,* land agent ostracized by his neighbors during the Land League agitation in Ireland in 1880⟧ **1** to join together in refusing to deal with, so as to punish, coerce, etc. **2** to refuse to buy, sell, or use [to *boycott* a newspaper] —☆*n.* an act or instance of boycotting

dunce (duns) *n.* ⟦after John Duns Scotus: his followers, called *Dunsmen, Dunses, Dunces,* were regarded as foes of Renaissance humanism⟧ **1** a dull, ignorant person **2** a person slow at learning

While **boycott** and **dunce** are derived from proper names, most words in English are derived from other languages. Your dictionary tells you from which language a word comes and what it originally meant in that language. From what language does **biography** come?

bi·og·ra·phy (bī äg′rə fē; *also,* bē-) *n.* ⟦Gr *biographia*: see BIO- & -GRAPHY⟧ **1** the histories of individual lives, considered as a branch of literature **2** *pl.* **-phies** an account of a person's life, described by another; life story

Gr means *Greek*. If you check the two cross-references **bio-** and **-graphy**, you learn that the two Greek roots are *bios*—life and *graphein*—to write.

bi·o- (bī′ō, -ə) ⟦Gr < *bios*, life < IE base *gwei-,* to live > QUICK, L *vivere*, to live, *vita*, life, OIr *biu*, living, Gr *bioun*, to live, *zōion*, animal⟧ *combining form* life, of living things, biological [*biography, biochemistry*]

-gra·phy (grə fē) ⟦L *-graphia* < Gr, writing < *graphein*, to write: see GRAPHIC⟧ *combining form forming nouns* **1** a process or method of writing, recording, or representing (in a specified way) [*calligraphy, photography*] **2** a descriptive science or a treatise dealing with such a science [*geography*]

Other common language abbreviations are as follows:

Fr	French	L	Latin
Ger	German	ME	Middle English
Heb	Hebrew	OE	Old English
IE	Indo-European	Sp	Spanish
It	Italian		

You will find these abbreviations and many others in a list of abbreviations and symbols at the back of your dictionary.

Knowing the origin of words is interesting, and it can also help you spell them correctly and determine their meanings. If you know a foreign language, recognizing that a word is similar to a word in that language can help you remember both how to spell it and what it means.

For example, you are unlikely to forget the **e** in **mathematics** if you know the French equivalent, **mathématiques**, in which the **e** carries an accent mark. Nor will you forget the silent **b** in **debt** if you know that **debt** derives from the Latin **debitum**. Perhaps you find it difficult to remember the distinction between **psychiatry** and **psychology**. But if you have studied Latin and know that **-logy** refers to science and theory whereas **-iatry** refers to medical treatment, you will remember that **psychology** is a science dealing with mental and emotional processes, whereas **psychiatry** is a branch of medicine concerned with the study, treatment, and prevention of mental disorders. You will also remember that a **psychiatrist** is a doctor of medicine, but a **psychologist** need not be.

CAPITALIZATION

Should you capitalize **first aid? hispanic? r.s.v.p.?** Check your dictionary.

> **first aid** emergency treatment for injury or sudden illness, before regular medical care is available —**first-aid** (furst'ād') *adj.*
>
> **His·pan|ic** (hi span'ik) *adj.* ⟦L *Hispanicus*⟧ **1** Spanish or Spanish-and-Portuguese **2** of or relating to Hispanics —*n.* a usually Spanish-speaking person of Latin American origin who lives in the U.S. —**His·pan'|i·cism** (-i siz'əm) *n.* —**His·pan'|i·cist** *n.*
>
> **R.S.V.P.** or **r.s.v.p.** ⟦Fr *répondez s'il vous plait*⟧ please reply Also **RSVP** or **rsvp**

In addition to providing information about capitalization under individual entries, most dictionaries include a separate discussion of the rules governing capitalization in an appendix.

ABBREVIATIONS

Consult your dictionary to find the meaning of abbreviations like **e.g.** and **i.e.**

> **e.g.** ⟦L. *exempli gratia*⟧ for the sake of example; for example
> **i.e.** ⟦L *id est*⟧ that is (to say)

Some dictionaries alphabetize such abbreviations among the main entries. Others include them in a separate list.

GRAMMAR AND USAGE

Your dictionary contains much of the information found in a grammar textbook. Many questions you might have concerning proper grammar and usage can be answered by your dictionary.

For example, which is correct?

The mumps (is, are) unpleasant.

> **mumps** (mumps) ***n.pl.*** ⟦pl. of obs. *mump,* a grimace: prob. from patient's appearance⟧ [*with sing. v.*] an acute communicable disease, usually of childhood, caused by a virus and characterized by swelling of the salivary glands, esp. the parotid, and, in adults, often complicated by inflammation of the testes, ovaries, etc.

Even though **mumps** is a plural noun, it takes a singular verb. Hence the correct answer is:

The mumps is unpleasant.

You know that the plural of **goose** is **geese**. What is the plural of **mongoose?** Is it **mongeese**?

> **mon·goose** (mäŋ′gōōs′, män′-) ***n.,*** *pl.* **-goos′es** ⟦Marathi *mangūs*⟧ any of various civetlike, Old World carnivores (family Viverridae); esp., any of a sometimes domesticated genus (*Herpestes*) noted for their ability to kill poisonous snakes, rodents, etc.

MONGOOSE

No. The dictionary says *pl.* **-gooses**, so the plural of **mongoose** is **mongooses**.

How about the plurals of **basis? handful? notary public?**

> **ba·sis** (bā′sis) ***n.,*** *pl.* **ba′ses′** (-sēz′) ⟦L < Gr, a base, pedestal < *bainein,* to go < IE base **gwem-,* COME⟧ **1** the base, foundation, or chief supporting factor of anything **2** the principal constituent of anything **3** the fundamental principle or theory, as of a system of knowledge **4** *a*) a procedure or timed plan */paid on a weekly basis]* *b*) a specified attitude *[a friendly basis]* **—*SYN.*** BASE[1]
>
> **hand·ful** (hand′fŏŏl′) ***n.,*** *pl.* **-fuls′** ⟦ME < OE *handfull*⟧ **1** as much or as many as the hand will hold **2** a relatively small number or amount *[a mere handful of people]* **3** [Colloq.] as much as one is able to manage; someone or something hard to manage
>
> **notary public** *pl.* **notaries public** or **notary publics** an official authorized to certify or attest documents, take depositions and affidavits, etc.

Many words call for one preposition and not another in order to express their intended meanings clearly. Your dictionary will tell you which preposition is correct. For example, which preposition should you use with **comply**?

We must comply _____ many new regulations.

> **com·ply** (kəm plī′) ***vt.*** **-plied′, -ply′ing** ⟦ME *complien* < OFr *complir* < L *complere:* see COMPLETE⟧ to act in accordance (*with* a request, order, rule, etc.)

The dictionary indicates that the appropriate preposition is **with**. The sentence should read:

We must comply with many new regulations.

Now look at the entry for **correspond**.

> **cor·re·spond** (kôr′ə spänd′, kär′-) *vi.* [MFr *correspondre* < ML *correspondere* < L *com-*, together + *respondere*, to RESPOND] **1** to be in agreement (*with* something); conform (*to* something); tally; harmonize **2** to be similar, analogous, or equal, (*to* something) **3** to communicate (*with* someone) by exchanging letters, esp. regularly —**SYN.** AGREE —**cor′re·spond′ingly** *adv.*

Proper usage requires that you use several different prepositions depending on the context. For instance, when two things are similar or equal to each other, you say that they correspond **to** each other; when two people write letters to each other, you say that they correspond **with** each other.

Their newest copier corresponds to our older model.
Bernice corresponds with relatives in South America.

With the exception of names and places, every entry in the dictionary is identified by one or more of the following parts-of-speech labels:

n.	noun
vt.	transitive verb (the verb takes an object)
vi.	intransitive verb (the verb does not take an object)
adj.	adjective
adv.	adverb
prep.	preposition
conj.	conjunction
pron.	pronoun
interj.	interjection

If you need to know what part of speech a word is, or what part or parts of speech it can be used as, the dictionary will tell you. For example, look at the entry for **hello**.

> **hel|lo** (he lō′, hə lō′; hel′ō′) *interj.* [var. of HOLLO] an exclamation *a*) of greeting or of response, as in telephoning *b*) to attract attention *c*) of astonishment or surprise —*n.*, *pl.* **-los′** a saying or exclaiming of "hello" —*vi.* **-loed′, -lo′ing** to say or exclaim "hello" —*vt.* to say "hello" to

Hello is most often used as an *interjection* (**Hello!** Is anyone here?). It can also be used as a *noun* (The owner welcomed all new employees with warm **hellos**). On some occasions **hello** is used as a *verb*, though such usage is awkward and thus infrequent (They shouted to us, and we **helloed** back).

These kinds of information are found under the main entries in any good dictionary. Many dictionaries also provide other information about grammar and usage in one or more appendixes.

LEVELS OF USAGE

Many times your choice of words—your diction—depends on the situation. For instance, in talking about your job, you would be more likely to use slang in casual conversation with a friend than in an employment interview with a personnel director.

The dictionary indicates levels of usage for many entries. You can consult your dictionary to determine whether a particular word is appropriate for a given situation. Here are the typical labels you will find identifying and describing levels of usage. Words not identified by one of these labels are considered part of standard English and hence appropriate for any occasion.

colloquial	characteristic of informal writing and conversation
slang	not conventional or standard; used in very informal contexts
obsolete	occurs in earlier writings but is no longer used
archaic	occurs in earlier writings but is rarely used today
poetic	term or sense used chiefly in poetry, especially earlier poetry
dialect	term or sense is used only in certain geographical parts of the United States
British, Canadian, Scottish, etc.	characteristic of Great Britain, Canada, Scotland, etc.

What levels of usage are **ain't, methinks, wacky**?

ain't (ānt) ⟦early assimilation, with lengthened and raised vowel, of *amn't*, contr. of *am not*; later confused with *a'nt (are not), i'nt (is not), ha'nt (has not, have not)*⟧ [Colloq.] am not: also a dialectal or substandard contraction for *is not, are not, has not,* and *have not*: see also AN'T *Ain't* was formerly standard for *am not* and is still preferred to *amn't I* or *aren't I* by some literate speakers as the proper colloquial contraction for *am not* in an interrogative construction ⟦I'm right, *ain't* I?⟧

me·thinks (mē thiŋks') **v.impersonal** *pt.* **me·thought'** ⟦ME *me thinketh* < OE *me thyncth* < *me*, me, to me + *thyncth,* it seems < *thyncan*, to seem: see THINK² ⟧ [Archaic] it seems to me

wack·y (wak'ē) **adj. wack'i·er, wack'i·est** ⟦ < ? WHACK + -Y²: cf. SLAP-HAPPY⟧ ☆[Slang] erratic, eccentric, or irrational —**wack'i·ly adv.** —**wack'i·ness n.**

The correct answers are: **ain't** is colloquial; **methinks** is archaic; and **wacky** is slang.

IDIOMS

Phrases that have a meaning different from their apparent literal meaning are called *idioms*. Idioms and idiomatic expressions are defined in most large dictionaries. What is meant by **crocodile tears**? an **ivory tower**? a **red herring**?

crocodile tears insincere tears or a hypocritical show of grief: from an old belief that crocodiles shed tears while eating their prey

ivory tower figuratively, a place of mental withdrawal from reality and action: used as a symbol of escapism

red herring 1 a smoked herring **2** something used to divert attention from the basic issue: from the practice of drawing a herring across the trace in hunting, to distract the hounds **3** *Finance* [Colloq.] a preliminary prospectus, subject to amendment, for an issue of securities: from the notice printed on the front in red ink

---

SPECIAL INFORMATION

Information about famous people and places, both real and fictional, is found in all good dictionaries. In some dictionaries such information is included in special appendixes; in others it is included among the main entries. For example, identify the following: **Babbitt, The Hague, Laputa, Malthus**.

☆**bab·bitt**[1] (bab'it) **n.** Babbitt metal —**vt.** to line or cover with Babbitt metal

☆**bab·bitt**[2] or **Bab·bitt n.** ⟦ after George *Babbitt*, title character of a satirical novel (1922) by Sinclair Lewis ⟧ a smugly conventional person interested chiefly in business and social success and indifferent to cultural values; Philistine —**bab'bitt|ry** or **Bab'bitt|ry n.**

Hague (hāg), **The** city in W Netherlands: capital of South Holland province: seat of the government (cf. Amsterdam): pop. 672,000: Du. name 's Gravenhage

La·pu|ta (lə pyōōt'ə) in Swift's *Gulliver's Travels*, a flying island inhabited by impractical, visionary philosophers who engage in various absurd activities —**La·pu'tan adj., n.**

Mal·thus (mal'thəs), **Thomas Robert** 1766-1834; Eng. economist
Mal·thu·si|an (mal thōō'zhən, -zē ən) **adj.** of Malthus and his theory that the world population tends to increase faster than the food supply with inevitable disastrous results unless natural restrictions, such as war, famine, and disease reduce the population or the increase is checked by moral restraint —**Mal·thu'sian·ism n.**

OTHER VALUABLE FEATURES

In addition, the dictionary offers a wealth of other material, including lists of colleges and universities, historical and geographical information, a list of proofreading symbols, and rules for punctuation. Of course, the smaller the dictionary you use, the less likely it is to contain all of this information. So be sure to have with you at home, at school, and on the job a complete and authoritative dictionary. You will find it your most useful aid to correct writing, spelling, and vocabulary building.

A sample of a complete dictionary page follows. Study this sample carefully, and note the many different types of information it contains.

labyrinth

lab·y·rinth (lab′ə rinth′) *n.* ⟦ME *laborintus* (altered by folk etym. by assoc. with L *labor*, LABOR + *intus*, into) < L *labyrinthus* < Gr *labyrinthos*, of pre-Hellenic orig.⟧ **1** a structure containing an intricate network of winding passages hard to follow without losing one's way; maze **2** a complicated, perplexing arrangement, course of affairs, etc. **3** *Anat.* the inner ear: see EAR[1] —[L-] *Gr. Myth.* the labyrinthine structure built by Daedalus for King Minos of Crete, to house the Minotaur

lab·y·rin·thine (lab′ə rin′thin, -thēn′, -thin′) *adj.* **1** of or constituting a labyrinth **2** like a labyrinth; intricate; complicated; puzzling: also **lab′y·rin′thian** (-thē ən) or **lab′y·rin′thic**

lap joint a joint made by lapping one piece or part over another and fastening them together Also **lapped joint** —**lap′-joint′** *vt.*

La·place (lä pläs′), Marquis **Pierre Si·mon de** (pyer sē môn′ də) 1749-1827; Fr. mathematician & astronomer

Lap·land (lap′land′) region of N Europe, including the N parts of Norway, Sweden, & Finland, & the NW extremity of the U.S.S.R., inhabited by the Lapps

LAP JOINT

lb 1 *Football* linebacker **2** ⟦L *libra*, pl. *librae*⟧ pound; pounds

lib·er·tar·i·an (lib′ər ter′ē ən) *n.* ⟦LIBERT(Y) + -ARIAN⟧ **1** a person who believes in the doctrine of the freedom of the will **2** a person who believes in full individual freedom of thought, expression, and action —*adj.* of or upholding either of these principles —**lib′er·tar′i·an·ism** *n.*

li·ber·té, é·ga·li·té, fra·ter·ni·té (lē ber tā′ ā gà lē tā′ frà ter nē tā′) ⟦Fr⟧ liberty, equality, fraternity: the motto of the French Revolution of 1789

lik·able (līk′ə bəl) *adj.* having qualities that inspire liking; easy to like because attractive, pleasant, genial, etc. —**lik′able·ness** or **lik′a·bil′i·ty** *n.*

like[1] (līk) *adj.* ⟦ME *lik*, aphetic for *ilik* < OE *gelic*, similar, equal, lit., of the same form or shape, akin to Ger *gleich* < PGmc **galika-* < **ga-*, prefix of uncert. meaning + **lika*, body, (ON *līk*, Goth *leik*, OE *līc*): for IE base see LICH⟧ **1** having almost or exactly the same qualities, characteristics, etc.; similar; equal /a cup of sugar and a *like* amount of flour/ **2** [Rare] alike **3** [Dial.] likely —*adv.* [Colloq.] likely /*like* as not, he is already there/ —*prep.* **1** similar to; somewhat resembling /she is *like* a bird/ **2** in a manner characteristic of; similarly to /she sings *like* a bird/ **3** in accord with the nature of; characteristic of /not *like* her to cry/ **4** in the mood for; desirous of /to feel *like* sleeping/ **5** indicative or prophetic of /it looks *like* a clear day tomorrow/ **6** as for example /fruit, *like* pears and peaches, for dessert/ *Like* was originally an adjective in senses 1, 3, 4, 5, and an adverb in sense 2, and is still considered so by conservative grammarians —*conj.* [Colloq.] **1** in the way that; as /it was just *like* you said/ **2** as if /it looks *like* he is late/ —*n.* a person or thing regarded as the equal or counterpart of another or of the person or thing being discussed /did you ever see the *like* of it?/ —*vt.* **liked, lik′ing** [Obs.] to compare; liken —*vi.* [Dial.] to be on the verge; be about (*to* have done something) /he *like* to broke the door down/ *Like* is also used without meaning or syntactic function, as in casual talk, before or after a word, phrase, or clause /it's *like* hot/ —**and the like** and others of the same kind —**like anything** [Colloq.] very much; exceedingly —**like blazes** (or **crazy** or **the devil, mad,** etc.) [Colloq.] with furious energy, speed, etc. —**nothing like** not at all like; completely different from —**something like** almost like; about

like[2] (līk) *vi.* **liked, lik′ing** ⟦ME *liken* < OE *lician* (akin to Goth *leikan*) < base of *lic*, body, form (see prec.): sense development: to be of like form—be like—be suited to—be pleasing to⟧ **1** [Obs.] to please **2** to be so inclined; choose /leave whenever you *like*/ —*vt.* **1** to have a taste or fondness for; be pleased with; have a preference for; enjoy **2** to want or wish /I would *like* to see him/ **3** [Colloq.] to favor and support as the probable winner /I *like* Cleveland in the Series/ —*n.* [*pl.*] preferences, tastes, or affections —**more like it** [Colloq.] closer to being what is wanted —**lik′er** *n.*

-like (līk) ⟦< LIKE[1]⟧ *suffix* **1** *forming adjectives* like, characteristic of, suitable for /doglike, manlike, homelike/ **2** *forming adverbs* in the manner of /coward-*like*/ Words formed with *-like* are sometimes hyphenated and are always hyphenated when three *l*'s fall together /bull-*like*/

like·a·ble (līk′ə bəl) *adj.* LIKABLE

Webster's New World Dictionary of American English, Third College Edition. Copyright 1988 by Simon & Schuster, Inc. Reprinted by permission of Simon & Schuster, Inc.

like·ly (līk′lē) *adj.* **-li·er, -li·est** ‖ME *likly,* prob. aphetic < OE *gelic̄l̄* (or < ? ON *likligr*): see LIKE[1] & -LY[1] ‖ **1** apparently true to the facts; credible; probable *[a likely story]* **2** seeming as if it would happen or might happen; reasonable to be expected; apparently destined *[it is likely to rain]* **3** such as will probably be satisfactory or rewarding; suitable *[a likely choice for the job]* **4** having good prospects; promising *[a likely lad]* **5** [Dial.] attractive; agreeable --*adv.* probably *[she will very likely go]*

———— inflected forms, comparative and superlative

SYN. --*likely* suggests probability or an eventuality that can reasonably be expected *[he's not likely to win]*; **liable** and **apt** are loosely or informally used equivalents of **likely,** but in strict discrimination, **liable** implies exposure or susceptibility to something undesirable *[you're liable to be killed if you play with firearms]* and **apt** suggests a natural or habitual inclination or tendency *[such people are always apt to be fearful]*; **prone** also suggests a propensity or predisposition to something that seems almost inevitable *[she's prone to have accidents]* --*ANT.* unlikely, indisposed

———— synonym

———— antonym

lis·some or **lis·som** (lis′əm) *adj.* ‖altered < LITHESOME‖ bending or moving gracefully or with ease and lightness; lithe, supple, limber, agile, etc. --**lis′some·ly** or **lis′som·ly** *adv.* --**lis′some·ness** or **lis′som·ness** *n.*

———— variant spellings

———— run-in derived entries

lo·ci (lō′sī′) *n. pl. of* LOCUS

lock[1] (läk) *n.* ‖ME < OE *loc,* a bolt, bar, enclosure, prison, akin to Ger *loch,* a hole, ON *lok,* a lid, prob. < IE base **leug-,* to bend > Gr *lygos,* supple twig, L *luctāri,* to struggle‖ **1** a mechanical device furnished with a bolt and, usually, a spring, for fastening a door, strongbox, etc. by means of a key or combination **2** anything that fastens something else and prevents it from opening, turning, etc. **3** a locking together; jam **4** an enclosed part of a canal, waterway, etc. equipped with gates so that the level of the water can be changed to raise or lower boats from one level to another **5** the mechanism of a firearm used to explode the ammunition charge; gunlock **6** AIR LOCK (sense 1) **7** *Wrestling* a hold in which a part of the opponent's body is firmly gripped *[armlock]* --*vt.* **1** to fasten (a door, trunk, etc.) by means of a lock **2** to keep from going in or out; shut *(up, in or out)*; confine *[locked in jail]* **3** to fit closely; link; intertwine *[to lock arms]* **4** to embrace tightly **5** to jam or force together so as to make immovable *[locked gears, locked brakes]* **6** to put in a fixed position *[a throttle locked in the idle position]* ☆**7** to equip (a canal, etc.) with a lock or locks **8** to move or pass (a ship) through a lock **9** *Printing* to fasten (type elements) in a chase or on the bed of a press by means of quoins: often with *up* --*vi.* **1** to become locked **2** to be capable of being locked **3** to intertwine or interlock; link together **4** to close tightly and firmly *[his jaws locked]* **5** to jam, as gears **6** to pass through the locks of a canal --**lock away** to store or safeguard in a locked box, container, etc. --**lock on** *Aeron.* to track and automatically follow a target, as by radar --**lock out 1** to shut out by or as by locking the door against **2** to keep (workers) from a place of employment in seeking to force terms upon them --**lock, stock, and barrel** [Colloq.] completely; entirely --**lock up 1** to fasten the doors of (a house, etc.) by means of locks **2** to enclose or store in a locked container **3** to put in jail **4** to make certain to have the result one wants *[to have an election locked up]* --**under lock and key** locked up; safely put away

———— etymology, traced back to the Indo-European base

———— irregular plural

———— field labels, showing special senses

———— idiomatic usage

———— idiomatic phrases

lock[2] (läk) *n.* ‖ME *lokke* < OE *loc* (akin to Ger *locke*): basic sense "a bend, twist": IE base as in prec.‖ **1** a curl, tress, or ringlet of hair **2** *[pl.]* [Old Poet.] the hair of the head **3** a tuft of wool, cotton, etc.

———— compound entry

☆**long green** [Slang] PAPER MONEY

———— cross-reference

☆**long-hair** (lôŋ′her′) *adj.* designating or of intellectuals or their tastes; specif., playing or preferring classical music rather than jazz or popular tunes Also **long′haired′** --*n.* [Colloq.] an intellectual; specif., a longhair musician Sometimes used disparagingly

———— usage labels

look-see (look′sē′) *n.* [Colloq.] a quick look or inspection

Louisiana Purchase land bought by the U.S. from France in 1803 for $15,000,000: it extended from the Mississippi to the Rocky Mountains & from the Gulf of Mexico to Canada

———— hyphenated word

Louis Napoleon (born *Charles Louis Napoléon Bonaparte*) 1808-73; president of France (1848-52) & as Napoleon III, emperor (1852-71): deposed: nephew of Napoleon I

Louis Phi·lippe (fi lēp′) 1773-1850; king of France (1830-48): abdicated in Revolution of 1848

———— spot map, showing location in relation to other places

LOUISIANA PURCHASE
(map showing CANADA, LOUISIANA PURCHASE, Mississippi R., U.S., GULF OF MEXICO)

———— biographical entries

at, āte, cär; ten, ēve; is, īce; gō, hôrn, look, tool; oil, out; up, fur; ə *for unstressed vowels, as* a *in* ago, u *in* focus; ' *as in* Latin (lat′n); chin; she; zh *as in* azure (azh′ər); thin, *the;* ŋ *as in* ring (riŋ) *In etymologies:* * = unattested; < = derived from; > = from which ☆ = Americanism   **See inside front and back covers**

———— key to pronunciation

13

NAME   **CLASS**   **DATE**   **SCORE**

Dictionary Assignments

1. In your business writing, you should follow this important advice: *Eschew obfuscation.*
    Look up each of these words in the Dictionary Section at the back of this book, and write
    a brief definition in the spaces provided below.

    eschew _to keep away from something harmful & dislike_

    obfuscation _to cloud over_

    Does this piece of advice illustrate what it tells you to do? How would you restate it?

    _____

2. On what level of usage (standard, colloquial, slang, archaic, etc.) is each of the following
    words? Write your answer in the space at the right of each word.

    a. goof _slang_

    b. OK _colloquial_

    c. erst _Archaic_

    d. ope (to open) _poetic_

    e. anon _Archaic_

3. Write the derivation of the following words in the spaces provided.

    a. anthology _Gr - Anthologia_   c. career _Fr - Carriere_

    b. chauvinism* _Fr - Chauvinisme_   d. robot _Czech - robota_

> **Note**   A number of words in each chapter are marked with an asterisk (*). You should
> be fully familiar with these words. They will be emphasized in the Vocabulary En-
> richment portions of the text. Full dictionary entries for each of these words are
> provided in the Dictionary Section at the back of the book.

4. Underline the incorrectly spelled word in each of the following pairs.

    a. bankrupcy   bankruptcy

    b. develop   develope

    c. stubborness   stubbornness

    d. rememberance   remembrance

    e. centennial   centenial

5. What is the meaning of the prefix **tele** as in **telegraph**? _distant_

6. What is the meaning of the suffix **cracy** as in **democracy**? _____

7. Rewrite these words in the spaces provided, dividing them into syllables and marking the accented syllables.

    a. acumen* _____

    b. deference* _____

    c. dissolution* _____

    d. ignominy* _____

8. How do you pronounce the following words?

    a. erudite   _____   c. indefatigable   _____

    b. veracity   _____   d. indict   _____

9. Answer the following questions about the entry for the word **business**.

    a. What synonyms does the dictionary list for **business**? _____

    _____

    b. On the basis of the information in the entry, which word would be the best choice in the following sentence?

    The amount of _____ between the United States and Japan is enormous.

10. In the spaces provided, indicate which verbs should be used with the following nouns.

    a. economics (is, are) _____   c. civics (is, are)   _____

    b. thanks (is, are) _____   d. credentials (is, are) _____

11. The following words are misspelled. Spell them correctly in the spaces provided.

    a. fizeek _____

    b. kwell _____

    c. sensus _____

    d. sikoanalysis _____

12. Who was **Molière**? _____

13. When was **Henry Ford** born? _____

14. What is the capital of **New Jersey**? _____

15. Where is **Addis Ababa**? _____

16. What does **carpe diem** mean? _____

17. What is a **poison pill**? _____

18. Should **SOS** have periods? _____

19. For what does each of the following abbreviations stand?

 a. Anon _____

 b. GMAT _____

 c. COBOL _____

 d. Que._____

 e. Zn _____

spell¹ (spel) *n.* ‖ ME < OE, a saying, tale, charm, akin to Goth *spill,* tale < ? IE base *(s)pel-*, to speak loudly ‖ **1** a word, formula, or form of words thought to have some magic power; incantation **2** seemingly magical power or irresistible influence; charm; fascination **3** a trance —**cast a spell on 1** to put into, or as into, a trance **2** to win the complete affection of —**under a spell** held in a spell or trance; enchanted

spell² (spel) *vt.* **spelled** or **spelt, spell'ing** ‖ ME *spellen* < OFr *espeller,* to explain, relate < Frank **spellōn,* akin to prec. ‖ **1** to name, write, or signal the letters which make up (a word, syllable, etc.), esp. the right letters in the right order **2** to make up, or form (a word, etc.): said of specified letters **3** to signify; mean [hard work *spelled* success] —*vi.* to spell a word, words, etc.; esp., to do so correctly — **spell out 1** to read letter by letter or with difficulty **2** to make out, or discern, as if by close reading ☆**3** to explain exactly and in detail

spell³ (spel) *vt.* **spelled, spell'ing** ‖ ME *spelien* < OE *spelian,* to substitute for, akin to *spala,* a substitute ‖ **1** [Colloq.] to serve or work in place of (another), esp. so as to give a period of rest to; relieve **2** [Chiefly Austral.] to give a period of rest to —*vi.* [Chiefly Austral.] to take a turn of rest or relief —*n.* **1** a turn of serving or working in place of another **2** a period or turn of work, duty, etc. [a two-year *spell* as reporter] **3** a turn, period, or fit of something [a *spell* of brooding] **4** a period of a specified sort of weather [a cold *spell*] **5** [Colloq.] a period of time that is indefinite, short, or of a specified character ☆**6** [Dial.] a short distance **7** [Colloq.] a period or fit of some illness, indisposition, etc. **8** [Chiefly Austral.] a period of rest or relief from activity

spell·bind (spel'bīnd') *vt.* **-bound', -bind'ing** ‖ back-form. < SPELLBOUND ‖ to hold by or as by a spell; fascinate; enchant

☆**spell·bind·er** (-bīn'dər) *n.* a speaker, esp. a politician, who can sway an audience with eloquence

spell·bound (-bound') *adj.* ‖ SPELL¹ + BOUND² ‖ held or affected by or as by a spell; fascinated; enchanted

☆**spell·down** (spel'doun') *n.* SPELLING BEE

spell·er (-ər) *n.* **1** a person who spells words [a poor *speller*] ☆**2** a book of exercises for teaching spelling

spell·ing (-iŋ) *n.* **1** the act of one who spells words **2** the way in which a word is spelled; orthography

☆**spelling bee** a spelling contest, esp. one in which a contestant is eliminated after misspelling a word

spelling pronunciation a pronunciation of a word that is influenced by its spelling and does not follow standard usage [(fôr'kas·'l) is a *spelling pronunciation* of forecastle (fōk's'l)]

spelt¹ (spelt) *vt., vi. alt. pt. & pp. of* SPELL²

20. Study the above entries from *Webster's New World Dictionary,* and then answer the following questions.

 a. How many entries are there for the word **spell**? _____

 b. Which meaning of **spell** can be traced back to its Indo-European base? _____

c. What phrase using **spell** means *enchanted*? _____

d. What is the Old French origin of **spell**? _____

e. Is it correct to write, "He spelt four words incorrectly on his application"? _____

f. Is **spelt** an acceptable past tense form of **spell** when it means *to relieve*? _____

g. What level of usage is **spell** in the following sentence? _____

    Spell me while I take a break.

h. What two entries mean *a spelling contest*? _____

i. What part of speech is **spellbound**? _____

j. **Forecastle** is usually pronounced fōk's'l. What is the term given to the pronunciation fôr'kas'l? _____

k. Which came first, **spellbind** or **spellbound**? _____

l. How many distinct meanings are there for the phrase **spell out**? _____

m. Is **spelling** syllabicated **spell-ing** or **spel-ling**? _____

n. Does the verb **to spell** always take an object? _____

Homonyms

Look at the following sentences. In each, underline the word in parentheses that correctly completes the sentence:

1. I'm a little (horse, hoarse) today.
2. Are you familiar with the (principals, principles) of effective office management?
3. Our department is running low on (stationary, stationery).

Word pairs like these that are *pronounced* alike but have different spellings and meanings are called *homonyms*. The English language contains a large number of homonyms. Sometimes using the wrong one in a sentence can produce some comic results. For example, "I'm a little horse today" describes you as a small four-legged animal rather than someone in need of throat lozenges. The correct sentence is "I'm a little hoarse today."

Choosing the inappropriate homonym in the other two sample sentences would not result in sentences as humorous as this, but they would be equally incorrect. The correct sentences are:

Are you familiar with the principles of effective office management? (**Principal** means *main, most important*; **principle** means *rule*.)

Our department is running low on stationery. (**Stationary** means *standing still*; **stationery** means *writing materials*.)

Effective and accurate business communication demands that you become familiar with what each homonym means and that you learn how to tell homonyms apart and how to use them correctly. This is especially true for secretaries, who generally write such words with the same shorthand outline and transcribe in terms of their context.

In this text we have included a list of over four hundred of the most commonly used homonyms. We do not expect you to cover all the words in this list at once. That is not the best way to learn them. Instead, we have divided this big list into a series of small lists of 20 pairs or sets of words each. As you study each of the first 12 chapters, you will study one of these small groups of homonyms. Master each of these small lists, and by the time you complete Chapter 12, you will have mastered the entire list of homonyms.

ad	short form of *advertisement: Place the ad in tomorrow's paper.*
add	to combine to form a sum: *Add 2 and 2.*
adherence	a steady attachment, support, or approval: *The company requires a strict adherence to all health and safety procedures by its employees.*
adherents	loyal followers or supporters: *The new flextime policy has many adherents.*
aid	(verb) to help: *Will you aid us in this project?* (noun) help or assistance: *Your aid is appreciated.*
aide	an assistant: *He gained valuable experience working as a teacher's aide.*

air   the earth's atmosphere: *She opened the window for some fresh air.*
heir   one who inherits: *José is his uncle's sole heir.*

aisle   a passageway between seats in a theater or other meeting room: *Leave an aisle between these chairs.*
I'll   contraction of *I will*: *I'll be in conference all morning.*
isle   an island: *Gina is vacationing on a small isle in the Pacific.*

all   entirety, the whole of, things without exception: *All the conference rooms are occupied.*
awl   a pointed instrument used to pierce holes in leather: *The shoemaker used an awl to add two lace holes to my boots.*

allot   to assign a share, to allocate: *Because of the limited amount of time available, we can allot each speaker only five minutes.*
a lot   a piece of land: *In this town the price of a lot has doubled in less than one year;* a great many, a large number: *We received a lot of letters in response to our advertisement.*

Note	There is no such word as *alot*; it is a common misspelling of *a lot*. The phrase *a lot* is itself vague and colloquial. Try to choose words that are more precise: *We received more than two hundred letters in response to our advertisement.*

allowed   permitted: *No visitors are allowed in this section of the building.*
aloud   spoken at an audible level: *Abe practiced reading his speech aloud.*

altar   a raised structure used in religious ceremonies: *The bride approached the altar.*
alter   to vary, to modify: *The shortage of raw materials forced us to alter our production schedule.*

arc   part of a circle: *The plane flew in a wide arc around the mountain peak;* a high-voltage electric spark: *The arc leaped from one electrode to the other.*
ark   Noah's boat: *How large was Noah's ark?*

ascent   act of rising: *Phuong's ascent through the managerial levels was very rapid.*
assent   agreement, act of giving consent: *The Board of Directors has given its assent to the proposal.*

assistance   aid, help: *I need your assistance in setting up this new display.*
assistants   plural of *assistant,* helper: *Our new supervisor has hired two assistants who will give her all the assistance she needs.*

attendance   the act of being present or attending: *All committee members were in attendance for Thursday's important meeting.*
attendants   people who are present or who serve others: *The attendants parked our cars at the far end of the lot.*

bail (noun) security given to obtain release of a prisoner while awaiting trial: *Derek was released from jail after posting bail*; (verb) to use a bucket or other vessel to remove water from a flooded area: *They tried unsuccessfully to bail out the leaking boat.*

bale (noun) a large, closely pressed package of merchandise: *How much does a bale of cotton weigh?* (verb) to compress and tie up such merchandise: *Please bale up these newspapers for recycling.*

bald lacking hair on the top of the head: *Fred is prematurely bald*; lacking a natural or usual covering: *There is a bald spot on the lawn.*

bawled past tense of bawl (see below): *Al bawled out his subordinate for being late again.*

ball a spherical object: *Joe brought home a ball for his daughter*; a large, formal dance: *They bought tickets for the Annual Police Officers' Ball.*

bawl to yell or cry loudly: *When his new toy broke, the little boy began to bawl.*

bare naked: *It's too cold to go outside with your head bare*; empty: *After the sale the counters were virtually bare*; unadorned: *She always spoke the bare truth.*

bear (verb) to carry or support: *These two columns bear most of the weight of the second floor*; to give birth to: *The doctor told Mrs. Kleindienst that she is unable to bear children*; (noun) a large animal: *The store has a stuffed polar bear in the window.*

baron a nobleman: *Ms. Schneider has a relative in Germany who is a baron.*

barren incapable of producing offspring: *Because Mrs. Kleindienst is barren, she and her husband have decided to adopt a child*; having little or no vegetation: *The desert is barren*; unprofitable, empty: *This is a barren scheme.*

base (noun) the bottom, the foundation: *The base of the lamp is cracked*; (adjective) morally low: *He acted from base motives.*

bass a deep sound or tone: *Ed has a rich bass voice.*

beach the shore of an ocean, sea, or lake: *The oil spill washed onto the beach.*

beech a kind of tree: *The driveway was lined with beech trees.*

NAME	CLASS	DATE	SCORE

Homonym Assignments

A. Select from the following words the one that correctly fits the blank in each of the sentences below. Then write the word in the answer space provided.

adherence	heir	awl	arc	bale
adherents	aisle	allot	ark	bare
aid	I'll	a lot	attendance	bear
aide	isle	allowed	attendants	baron
air	all	aloud	bail	barren

1. With the coming of warm weather, sales of _____ conditioning units increase substantially.

1._____

2. The company nurse rushed to the _____ of the accident victim.

2._____

3. When you are ready to file the papers, _____ help you.

3._____

4. _____ to the nonsmoking policy was required.

4._____

5. The wind from the open window left the desk _____ of papers.

5._____

6. The new production manager will be _____ to the problems caused by the poorly operating equipment.

6._____

7. Juan was proud of his _____ record.

7._____

8. The sign said, "No smoking _____."

8._____

9. He forgot to _____ a parking space to the new supervisor.

9._____

10. There was too little _____ space between the rows of cabinets in the file room.

10._____

11. Reading _____ can be disturbing to others.

11._____

12. A(n) _____ is used to make a hole in leather, whereas a paper punch makes a hole in paper.

12._____

13. The travel agent suggested that she consider vacationing on a tropical _____.

13._____

14. The landscaper decided to arrange the trees in a(n)

_____.

14. _____

15. There was _____ of response to the new job
opening.

15. _____

B. In some of the following sentences, an incorrect word is used. Underline the incorrect
word, and write the correct word in the space provided. Where there is no error, write C
in the answer space.

1. Part of the publicity for the campaign included
hundreds of balloons, which made their assent when
the rally began.

1. _____

2. The accused was released on $10,000 bale.

2. _____

3. Proofreading statistics is often accomplished by having
one person read allowed to another.

3. _____

4. The architect was asked to altar the plans for the new
wing.

4. _____

5. To obtain an average, you must first add and then
divide.

5. _____

6. In the final vote, all the hands were raised, denoting
unanimous ascent.

6. _____

7. In the trademark, the company name was written in the
shape of a rainbow's ark.

7. _____

8. The bass discount figure was given on all sales.

8. _____

9. Higher property taxes are imposed on real estate near
the beach.

9. _____

10. The Christmas Ball was postponed because of the ice
storm.

10. _____

11. Dr. Franz looks older than he is because he is prematurely bawled.

11. _____

12. Her accountant advised her that it was more efficient to
bare the cost of the equipment by leasing it.

12. _____

13. The visiting dignitaries included a prince, a barren, and
a prime minister.

13. _____

14. He was sent abroad as a government aid.

14. _____

15. They danced on the bear wooden floor.

15. _____

C. Read the definition, and select the correct word from the second column to match that description. Write the word you selected in the answer space.

Definition	Word Choice	
1. to assist	aid, aide	1._____
2. helpers	assistance, assistants	2._____
3. to cry	ball, bawl	3._____
4. a structure often found in a religious ceremony	altar, alter	4._____
5. the shore of an ocean	beach, beech	5._____
6. permitted	allowed, aloud	6._____
7. act of rising	ascent, assent	7._____
8. a compressed package of something	bail, bale	8._____
9. to support or carry	bare, bear	9._____
10. a deep sound or tone	base, bass	10._____

D. Select the right word for the sentence shown, and write it in the answer space. Then compose a sentence for the homonym not selected, and write your sentence in the space provided.

1. The (base, bass) of the lamp needed repair.

1._____

_____

_____

_____

2. Did the (ad, add) appear in today's paper?

2._____

_____

_____

_____

3. Her (aid, aide) in collating made it possible for us to finish the job.

3._____

_____

_____

_____

4.   Be sure to (allot, a lot) enough time so you can arrive
     on time for an interview.   4. _____

     _____

     _____

     _____

5.   Getting the promotion was one more positive step in
     Albin's (ascent, assent) up the career ladder.   5. _____

     _____

     _____

     _____

6.   Be sure to clear the (aisle, isle) of any electric cords.   6. _____

     _____

     _____

     _____

7.   Please (bail, bale) up the scrap paper.   7. _____

     _____

     _____

     _____

8.   Everyone's (attendance, attendants) is required.   8. _____

     _____

     _____

     _____

9.   The forger tried to (altar, alter) the document.   9. _____

     _____

     _____

     _____

10. (I'll, Isle) call you in the morning.   10. _____

     _____

     _____

     _____

Twelve Easy Words Often Misspelled

In this chapter you will look at 12 words with which you are very familiar. All of them have only one syllable; yet all of them are misspelled or misused so frequently that they are perhaps the 12 most troublesome words in our language. Here they are:

its	their	to	whose	your
it's	there	too	who's	you're
	they're	two		

The following sentences are loaded with these words. Examine each sentence, cross out each misspelled word that you find, and write it correctly above the line.

1. Its to bad that there not coming to you're office today.

2. Whose taking charge of they're account now that it's importance has been recognized?

3. Its unlikely that their going to be there with all the facts at their disposal.

4. Your the salesperson whose customers are not to pleased with the service there getting.

5. They're accountants sat for too days trying to discover who's error caused your recent problems.

Compare your corrected sentences with those below. Those words which have been changed from the original sentences appear in boldface.

1. **It's too** bad that **they're** not coming to **your** office today.
2. **Who's** taking charge of **their** account now that **its** importance has been recognized?
3. **It's** unlikely that **they're** going to be there with all the facts at their disposal.
4. **You're** the salesperson whose customers are not **too** pleased with the service **they're** getting.
5. **Their** accountants sat for **two** days trying to discover **whose** error caused your recent problems.

If you are not always sure when to use each of these familiar words, this chapter will help you make the correct decisions with confidence.

its–it's.   Look at the first pair: **it's** and **its**. **It's** = **it is**. **It's** is a contraction—two words in one. In a contraction the apostrophe is used to indicate that one or more letters are missing, in this case the letter **i**. Thus **It's raining** = **It is raining**.

It's can also mean **it has**: **It's (It has) been nearly two weeks since she phoned**.

Its is a pronoun and indicates possession: **The company wanted to increase its profits**. (The profits belong to the company.)

If you remember that **it's** = **it is** or **it has**, you will have no trouble in determining whether a sentence calls for **it's** or **its**.   Simply write out the sentence substituting **it is** or **it has**.   If the sentence sounds correct, then use the contraction **it's**.   If the sentence does not sound right, use the possessive pronoun **its**.   For example, in the sample sentence above, you would not say, **The company wanted to increase it is** (or **it has**) **profits**.   Hence **its** is correct.

Look at this example: **(It's, Its) important that the company increase profits**.   Substitute **it is**: **It is important that the company increase profits**.   This sentence makes sense, so the contraction **It's** is correct.

Now try this one: **(It's, Its) taken us almost a month to complete this deal**.   Substitute **it is**: **It is taken us almost a month to complete this deal**.   That does not sound right.   But **it has** does: **It has taken us almost a month to complete this deal**.   Hence the contraction **It's** is still the correct choice here.

your–you're.   The same technique can be employed to determine which word to use from another pair of frequently confused words.

You're = **you are**.   Here again we have a contraction, two words in one.   **"You're fired!"** = **"You are fired!"**

Your is a pronoun indicating possession: **Is this your typewriter?**   (Does this typewriter belong to you?)   Here, too, if you are undecided whether a sentence calls for **you're** or **your**, try writing out the sentence using **you are**.   **Is this you are typewriter?** is clearly incorrect, so **Is this you're typewriter?** is incorrect.   The sentence should read **Is this your typewriter?**

Which is correct?   **Let me know when (you're, your) ready to leave**.   Since **Let me know when you are ready to leave** makes sense, the correct choice is **you're**.

whose–who's.   Use the same test to determine whether a sentence calls for **who's** or **whose**.

Who's = **who is** or **who has**:   **Who's going to lunch now?   Who's taken the dictionary from my desk?**

Whose indicates possession: **Whose friend are you?**   Look at this example: **(Who's, Whose) your friend?**   Substitute **who is**: **Who is your friend?**   Thus **Who's your friend?** is correct.   **Whose your friend?** would be wrong.

their–there–they're.   **They're** = **they are**.   **They're late** = **They are late**.   If the sentence makes sense when you substitute **they are**, then **they're** is correct.

There indicates place. **Put the package down over there**. (Note the similar spelling of these words: **here, there, where**. All three refer to place.) **There** can also serve as an introductory word (known technically as an *expletive*) in such sentences as these:

There are four people on the committee.
There is something I must tell you.

Their is a pronoun indicating possession: **Their representative wishes to speak with you. This is their new distribution center**.

To determine whether to use **they're, there**, or **their**, follow the same procedure you used with the three pairs of words we have already discussed. Write out the contraction within the sentence. If it makes sense, then **they're** is the proper form. If it doesn't, use **their** if the sense calls for possession; use **there** if the sense calls for place or an introductory word.

to–too–two. **Two** is a number—2. **We received two separate shipments**. You probably never misuse **two**. But on occasion you may have trouble deciding whether a sentence calls for **to** or **too**. Here's how to decide.

Too means *very, also,* or *more than.* **I'm coming too. The workers found the factory too hot**.

To (which is technically either a preposition or part of the infinitive form of a verb) is used for all cases not covered by **two** or **too**:

Go to the bank.
I want to speak to the personnel director.

If you are uncertain whether to use **to** or **too**, think of the double **o** in **too** as adding more or intensifying the meaning. When you want to intensify the meaning, use **too**. Otherwise, use **to**.

NAME	CLASS	DATE	SCORE

Spelling Assignments

A. In each of the blanks in the following sentences, insert the proper word from the following list. (*Note:* In some instances more than one word may be correct.)

its	there	too	who's
it's	they're	two	your
their	to	whose	you're

1. _____ entirely up to you _____ decide _____ products _____ going to buy.

2. _____ are _____ many products competing for such a limited market.

3. Do _____ members understand _____ responsibility for helping the community?

4. Labor representatives will meet tomorrow to present _____ problems _____ management representatives.

5. _____ about time you learned to check _____ own records _____.

6. Is it true _____ the receptionist _____ place I'm taking?

7. _____ staff will have _____ stay _____ until the van is repaired.

8. _____ covering the assignment for the employee _____ child is ill?

9. Each company should choose _____ advertising agency very carefully.

10. Will _____ be any of the new models on display at _____ exhibit next month?

B. In the following sentences, underline the word in parentheses that makes the sentence correct.

1. (It's—Its) been almost a year since we received (your—you're) last order.

2. When we call, we find (their—there—they're) always (to—too—two) busy.

3. (Who's—Whose) going (to—too—two) take her place in (your—you're) organization?

4. (Your—You're) reports (to—too—two) the buyers do not meet with (their—there—they're) approval.

5. After studying (their—there—they're) financial reports, we feel that (your—you're) right to question the way (their—there—they're) managing (their—there—they're) affairs.

6. You'll find all (your—you're) personal effects over (their—there—they're).

7. (Your—You're) the kind of person (who's—whose) well suited for personnel work.

8. The supervisors' group will inform you when (your—you're) application is brought (to—too—two) (their—there—they're) attention.

9. (Who's—Whose) been reading my mail?

10. (It's—Its) much (to—too—two) late for the members of (your—you're) staff to correct (their—there—they're) errors now.

11. If (your—you're) going to return the machine, please ship it in (it's—its) original carton.

12. (It's—Its) clear (who's—whose) advertising campaign is more effective.

13. (Their—There—They're) are (to—too—two) principal reasons why (their—there—they're) the leaders in the field.

14. The person (who's—whose) responsibility it is to make the final arrangements will be (their—there—they're) (to—too—two).

15. (Your—You're) proposal has (it's—its) advantages (to—too—two).

Homonyms

beat	(verb) to hit repeatedly: *The child beat her toy drum in time with the music;* to defeat: *Paul was always trying to beat the system;* (noun) a repeated sound or motion: *At the start of the interview, Joyce could hear the loud beat of her heart.*
beet	a vegetable: *Borscht is a soup made from beets.*
beer	a mildly alcoholic drink made from malt and hops: *Omar drives a delivery truck for a beer distributor.*
bier	a coffin: *The bearers carried the bier to the cemetery.*
berry	small juicy fruit with many seeds: *Her favorite berry is the raspberry.*
bury	to place a body or an object into the earth or a tomb: *We can bury most of this garbage at the new landfill.*
berth	job or position: *Nina deserves a berth on our team;* place to sleep on a ship or train: *Alex reserved a lower berth for the trip.*
birth	act of being born: *Kathleen's birth gave them great joy;* beginning: *Her invention gave birth to a whole new industry.*
billed	past tense of *bill,* submit an unpaid account: *We've been billed twice for this shipment.*
build	to make, establish: *It is very expensive to build a house these days. It takes years to build a good reputation.*
blew	past tense of *blow,* move air: *The wind blew all night.*
blue	the color: *Jane has blue eyes.*
bloc	group of persons united for a common purpose: *The powerful bloc opposed the strike settlement.*
block	(noun) a rectangular solid: *She used a small block of marble for a paperweight;* a city square: *The new building covers an entire city block;* (verb) to obstruct or blockade: *Some shareholders want to block plans for a merger;* to shape: *George asked the cleaners to block his hat.*
boar	a male pig: *The head of a wild boar hung in the office.*
bore	to drill a hole: *Can you bore through concrete with that drill?*
board	piece of wood: *He used a board for a makeshift desk;* meals provided for pay: *The fee includes room and board;* group of persons managing a firm: *The board of directors meets every Wednesday;* on a ship or train: *How many people are on board this train?*
bored	uninterested, wearied by something dull or tiresome: *The audience was bored by the speech.*

boarder   person who receives a room and meals regularly for pay: *Who is the new boarder?*

border   dividing line between two countries: *The Mexican border is ten miles from our plant*; an edge: *Her collar has a lace border.*

bolder   more forward, more courageous: *The bolder of the two girls got the job.*

boulder   a large rock: *A large boulder marks the entrance to the mall.*

born   (verb) past participle of *bear: My oldest son was born in August*; (adjective) able by nature: *Julia is a born athlete.*

borne   carried: *The entire responsibility was borne by one person*; given birth to: *She had borne three children.*

bough   (baú) branch of a tree or shrub: *She hung the birdfeeder from the bough of a tree.*

bow   (baú) (noun) the front part of a ship: *They stood near the ship's bow;* (verb) to bend from the waist to show respect: *You should bow when you are introduced to royalty.*

Note	bow (bō) (noun) anything curved or bent; a device for shooting arrows; a decorative knot with two or more loops

brake   (noun) device for slowing or stopping a machine or vehicle: *The brake on the bicycle needs to be repaired*; (verb) to slow down or stop: *The new government policy will brake the inflationary trend. If you brake too suddenly, the car's wheels may lock up.*

break   (verb) to separate into parts by force, smash: *If you lean on the counter, you may break the glass*; (noun) an opening or interruption: *There was a break in the contract negotiations.*

breach   failure to observe the terms of a law or agreement: *The manufacturer was sued for breach of contract*; an opening made by breaking something: *The workers entered through a breach in the wall.*

breech   the part of a firearm behind the barrel: *He held the rifle by the breech.*

bread   food made from flour or meal: *Laura prefers rye bread to whole wheat.*

bred   past tense of *breed,* to be the source of, produce: *In that case familiarity bred contempt. The rancher bred longhorn cattle.*

brewed   past tense of *brew,* to prepare by steeping, boiling, or fermenting: *Murray brewed a pot of tea before the meeting.*

brood   (noun) the young of an animal: *The hen cared for her brood of chicks*; (verb) to meditate, worry: *They continued to brood about the declining sales figures.*

bridal   pertaining to a bride or wedding: *The bridal party arrived at the reception late.*

bridle   (noun) the head part of a horse's harness: *Attach the reins to the horse's bridle*; (verb) to hold back, curb: *Ray tried to bridle his temper;* to hold the head high to express scorn, anger, pride: *The attorney bridled in anger at the judge's remarks.*

but except, otherwise, yet, only, just: *I'd like to buy this, but I don't have the money.*

butt (noun) the thick end of anything: *Put the butt of the gun on the floor;* the stub or stump: *There is a cigarette butt on the rug*; an object of ridicule or criticism: *Rick was often the butt of a joke*; (verb) to thrust or strike against: *It is against the rules for boxers to butt with their head.*

buy to purchase: *I have to buy a new printer.*

by next to, near at hand: *The water cooler is by the window*; through the medium of: *All of our furniture is made by hand.*

bye as in goodbye: *She said goodbye to her staff before leaving.*

NAME	CLASS	DATE	SCORE

Homonym Assignments

A. Select from the following words the one that correctly fits the blank in each of the sentences below. Then write the word in the answer space provided.

beat	bury	blew	bored	bough
beet	berth	blue	boarder	bow
beer	birth	bloc	border	buy
bier	billed	block	bolder	by
berry	build	board	boulder	bye

1. My employer prefers an upper _____ when traveling by train.

   1._____

2. The _____ of the dead hero was draped with a flag.

   2._____

3. The wind from the fan _____ the papers onto the floor.

   3._____

4. The convention expenses included both room and _____.

   4._____

5. The advertisement had an attractive _____ design.

   5._____

6. As the speaker droned on, the audience became _____ and restless.

   6._____

7. Stop _____ as soon as you can to pick up your free gift.

   7._____

8. A _____ and more aggressive policy sometimes helps increase business.

   8._____

9. Our investigation revealed that all the customers were _____ in error for the service charge.

   9._____

10. This month's sales _____ our all-time record.

    10._____

11. A charter is a corporation's _____ certificate.

    11._____

12. Attractive displays usually tempt people to _____ more merchandise.

    12._____

13. A falling _____ can do serious harm.

    13._____

14. The _____ of the boat was severely damaged in the collision.

14. _____

15. A small group of citizens tried to _____ the plan.

15. _____

B. In some of the following sentences, an incorrect word is used. Underline the incorrect word, and write the correct word in the space provided. Where there is no error, write C in the answer space.

1. Harry was the but of all their jokes.

   1. _____

2. The heavy-duty drill was able to boar through the rock.

   2. _____

3. Faulty brakes on the delivery truck caused the accident.

   3. _____

4. A smoldering cigarette but left by one of the employees was the cause of the fire.

   4. _____

5. They were guilty of breech of contract.

   5. _____

6. The papers need to be signed bye June 30.

   6. _____

7. The repair costs were born by the insurance company.

   7. _____

8. When he learned that he did not get the promotion he expected, he began to brewed.

   8. _____

9. The preholiday sale was expected to brake all records.

   9. _____

10. The tourists must show their passports at the boarder.

  10. _____

11. Poor service made the boarder seek new lodgings.

  11. _____

12. Despite what you think, Jane was well-bread.

  12. _____

13. The bridal business thrives in early spring and late summer.

  13. _____

14. During the Christmas season, the office is usually decorated with bows of holly.

  14. _____

15. A feeling of guilt was born by the entire staff.

  15. _____

C. Read the definition, and select the correct word from the second column to match that description. Write the word you selected in the answer space.

Definition	Word Choice	
1. a small juicy fruit	berry, bury	1. _____
2. a dividing line	boarder, border	2. _____
3. a male pig	boar, bore	3. _____
4. to separate into parts	brake, break	4. _____

5.	carried	born, borne	5._____
6.	meals provided for pay	board, bored	6._____
7.	failure to observe the terms of a law or agreement	breach, breech	7._____
8.	a food made from flour	bread, bred	8._____
9.	to meditate or worry	brewed, brood	9._____
10.	to hold back, curb	bridal, bridle	10._____

D. Select the right word for the sentence shown, and write it in the answer space. Then compose a sentence for the homonym not selected, and write your sentence in the space provided.

1. Jan tried to (billed, build) an effective team of workers.   1._____

_____

_____

_____

2. Bill was sometimes the (but, butt) of jokes.   2._____

_____

_____

_____

3. Ed made the phone call on his (brake, break).   3._____

_____

_____

_____

4. The policy changes (bread, bred) discontent.   4._____

_____

_____

_____

5. (Beats, Beets) are my favorite vegetable.   5._____

_____

_____

_____

6. Claire was (born, borne) on Valentine's Day.   6. _____

   _____

   _____

   _____

7. Sue used the graphics software package to make an at-
    tractive (boarder, border) for the flier.   7. _____

   _____

   _____

   _____

8. David needed a large (bloc, block) of wood for his
    project.   8. _____

   _____

   _____

   _____

9. They decorated the office in shades of (blew, blue).   9. _____

   _____

   _____

   _____

10. She yawned, so we thought she was (board, bored).   10. _____

   _____

   _____

   _____

Words Misspelled Because They Are Mispronounced

There are a number of misspelled words in the following sentences. Cross out each misspelled word that you find, and write it correctly above the line.

1. If you and your partener are hungery, prehaps you'd like to send out for sanwiches.

2. It would be a great privlege to meet the canidate who has done so much to ensure the portection of the enviornment.

3. Jules attackted the views presented in this pamplet on the role of mathmatics in modren business education.

4. We waited at the enterance to the libary for the goverment represenative, who arrived promptly at 8 p.m.

5. I was suprised to learn that our new secertary will probaly be leaving in Febuary.

Each of these five sentences contains four misspelled words. Here is the correct spelling of each one.

1. partner	hungry	perhaps	sandwiches
2. privilege	candidate	protection	environment
3. attacked	pamphlet	mathematics	modern
4. entrance	library	government	representative
5. surprised	secretary	probably	February

These words—and many like them—are misspelled mainly because they are mispronounced. Correct pronunciation will not *always* lead you to the correct spelling of a word because, as you know, a great many English words are not spelled as they sound. But some words, like those above, are misspelled mainly by people who do not pronounce them correctly. These people make the following types of pronunciation errors.

Add syllables or letters
Drop syllables or letters
Switch syllables or letters
Mispronounce syllables or letters

Here is a list of words commonly misspelled because of mispronunciation. The trouble spot in each word is underlined. Study this list, and pronounce each word carefully. If you pronounce these words correctly, you should have little difficulty in spelling them correctly.

Added syllables or letters

athletics	(3 syllables, *not* 4)	hindrance*	(2 syllables, *not* 3)
attacked	(2 syllables, *not* 3)	hungry	(2 syllables, *not* 3)
barbarous	(3 syllables, *not* 4)	jewelry	(*not* jewelery)
burglar	(2 syllables, *not* 3)	laundry	(2 syllables, *not* 3)
chimney	(2 syllables, *not* 3)	lightning	(2 syllables, *not* 3)
corsage	(*not* corsarge)	marinate	(3 syllables, *not* 2)
disastrous*	(3 syllables, *not* 4)	militarism	(5 syllables, *not* 6)
drowned	(1 syllable, *not* 2)	mischievous*	(3 syllables, *not* 4)
entrance	(2 syllables, *not* 3)	monstrous	(2 syllables, *not* 3)
exercise	(*not* excercise)	partner*	(2 syllables, *not* 3)
garage	(*not* gararge)	remembrance	(3 syllables, *not* 4)
grievous*	(2 syllables, *not* 3)	umbrella	(3 syllables, *not* 4)
height	(no **th** at the end)		

Dropped syllables or letters

accuracy	(4 syllables, *not* 3)
arctic	(Pronounce the **c**)
aspirin	(3 syllables, *not* 2)
authentic	(Pronounce the **t**)
auxiliary	(Don't forget the second **i**)
bachelor	(3 syllables, *not* 2)
boundary	(3 syllables, *not* 2)
camera	(3 syllables, *not* 2)
candidate	(Pronounce both **d**'s)
chocolate	(3 syllables, *not* 2)
criminal	(3 syllables, *not* 2)
diamond	(3 syllables, *not* 2)
different	(3 syllables, *not* 2)
environment	(Pronounce the **n**)
experiment	(4 syllables, *not* 3)
familiar	(Don't forget the second **i**)
February	(Pronounce the **r** after **b**)

forward	(Pronounce the **r**)
government	(Pronounce the **n**)
hundredth	(Pronounce the **d**)
identical	(Pronounce the **t**)
laboratory	(5 syllables, *not* 4)
library	(Pronounce the **r** after **b**)
literature	(4 syllables, *not* 3)
luxury	(3 syllables, *not* 2)
mathematics	(4 syllables, *not* 3)
memory	(3 syllables, *not* 2)
miniature	(4 syllables, *not* 3)
postpone*	(Pronounce the **t**)
prejudice*	(3 syllables, *not* 2)
privilege*	(3 syllables, *not* 2)
probably	(3 syllables, *not* 2)
promptly	(Pronounce the **pt**)
quantity	(Pronounce the **t**)
recognize	(Pronounce the **g**)
representative*	(Pronounce the **t**)
sandwich	(Pronounce the **d**)
scenery	(3 syllables, *not* 2)
secretary	(Pronounce the **r**)
sophomore	(3 syllables, *not* 2)
strictly	(Pronounce the **t**)
surprise	(Pronounce the **r** after **u**)
temperament*	(4 syllables, *not* 3)
temperature	(4 syllables, *not* 3)
Wednesday	(Don't forget the **d**)

Switched syllables or letters

environment*	perspiration
introduce	perspire
irrelevant*	precipitate*
modern	propose*
pattern (**er** as in **baker**)	strategic*
perform	tragedy
perhaps	

Mispronounced syllables or letters

accumulate*	divine (**i** as in **pit**)n
champion	hundred (**dred**, not **derd**)
divide (**i** as in **pit**)	pamphlet (**ph** = **f**)

pronunciation   separate
protection   similar
regular   —   tremendous

Spelling aids.   These sentences may help you remember the correct spelling.

1. A good **secret**ary keeps an employer's **secrets**.
2. The job of a **govern**ment is to **govern**.
3. Scientists **labor** in the **labor**atory.
4. Some people say "**congrats**" for **congrat**ulations.
5. At the beach, keep the **sand** out of your **sand**wich.
6. There is **a rat** in sep**arat**e.
7. **I** feel privi**l**eged to be here.
8. **Br**, it's cold in Fe**br**uary.
9. There's an **ant** in relev**ant**.
10. You get an **A** for spelling temper**a**ment and temper**a**ture correctly.

NAME   CLASS   DATE   SCORE

Spelling Assignments

A. There are misspelled words in some of the following sentences. Underline each misspelled word, and write the correct spelling in the space provided. If there are no misspelled words, write C in the space next to the sentence.

1. For the first few days on the job, a new office worker is more of a hinderance than a help.

   1._____

2. So far, only two canidates have been invited back for a second interview.

   2._____

3. Learning to operate a postage meter is a rather easy task to perform, but one must be very accurate.

   3._____

4. It is necessary to be familar with government regulations and requirements.

   4._____

5. All rules must be strictly observed in a laboratory envirnment.

   5._____

6. Many larger law firms maintain their own law libary.

   6._____

7. By this time you have probably had a chance to go over the figures.

   7._____

8. The regilar interoffice mail pickups are at 10 a.m. and 4 p.m.

   8._____

9. Much of the information in the report was irrelavant.

   9._____

10. What do you propose we do about the lag in production?

    10._____

11. The pamplets were not permitted to accumulate; they were delivered promptly.

    11._____

12. The new product was interduced by a massive advertising campaign.

    12._____

13. Modren offices rely on electronic equipment of all types.

    13._____

14. As a strategic measure, the committee meeting was posponed for the third time.

    14._____

15. One of the pardners in the firm was thinking about retiring.

    15._____

16. The chair could be adjusted easily to several diffrent heights.

16. _____

17. Videotape cameras are used in banks to improve security.

17. _____

18. The building temperture was controlled by means of a master control panel.

18. _____

19. Anyone who answers a business telephone automatically becomes a represenative of the company.

19. _____

20. John is taking courses in literture and mathmatics this semester.

20. _____

21. Please accept our congradulations on the success of your new business venture.

21. _____

22. There is an opening for an executive secretary in our company.

22. _____

23. The goverment filed crimnal charges against the bank robber on Wensday.

23. _____

24. The burgaler attempted to escape down the laundary chute.

24. _____

25. The selection of sanwiches from the cafeteria vending machines is limited.

25. _____

26. It was a tradegy to learn of the damage caused by the lightning.

26. _____

27. The value of dimonds has increased tramendously in today's economy.

27. _____

28. Every hundredth customer was given a special prize during the store's anniversary celebration.

28. _____

29. The booklets that you ordered are being sent to you in a seperate mailing.

29. _____

30. A tickler or follow-up file aids rememberance.

30. _____

B. Underline out the misspelled word or words in each of the following groups of four. Spell the word or words correctly in the space at the right. If there are no errors in the group, write C.

1.	hundredth	postpone	accracy	diamond	1. _____
2.	probably	secretary	temprament	boundary	2. _____
3.	monsterous	heighten	athletics	chimney	3. _____
4.	envirment	introduce	perform	recognize	4. _____
5.	partner	aspirin	labratory	prejudice	5. _____

6.	pattern	hundred	modern	separate	6._____
7.	percipitate	promptly	tradegy	surprise	7._____
8.	accumalate	February	divide	divine	8._____
9.	pamphlet	protection	similar	goverment	9._____
10.	champion	mischievious	familar	jewelry	10._____
11.	enterance	hungry	garage	corsage	11._____
12.	library	grievious	arctic	attacked	12._____
13.	disasterous	Wednesday	privilege	excercise	13._____
14.	candidate	sandwich	tremendous	temperture	14._____
15.	barbarous	prespire	pronunciation	perhaps	15._____
16.	drownded	marinate	luxery	umbrella	16._____
17.	perspiration	militaryism	authentic	experiment	17._____
18.	choclate	bachelor	criminal	foward	18._____
19.	memory	miniature	diffrent	idenical	19._____
20.	sophmore	scenery	auxilary	quantity	20._____

Homonyms

callous lacking in pity or mercy, unfeeling, insensitive: *The new supervisors were very callous in their treatment of department personnel.*

callus a thick, hardened place on the skin: *Ernie developed a large callus on his right thumb.*

cannon a large weapon of war: *There is a cannon in front of the VFW hall.*

canon a law or body of laws of a church: *Are you familiar with the Anglican canon?*; an established standard, principle, or rule: *I think their behavior violates the canons of good taste.*

canvas strong cloth widely used to make sails and tents: *These canvas tote bags are among our bestsellers.*

canvass to go through a district or area soliciting votes for a candidate or orders for a product: *McFadden's supporters will thoroughly canvass the Eighth District to obtain every possible vote for him. Girl Scouts canvass their neighborhoods every year to sell boxes of cookies.*

capital city where the government of a country or state is located: *Washington, D.C., is the capital of the United States*; money or property a company uses in carrying on business: *Initial capital of $50,000 was required*; an uppercase letter: *Begin every sentence with a capital.*

capitol building in which a state or national legislature meets. (*Note:* When you refer to the building where the U.S. Congress meets, use a capital C.): *After her election victory, she moved her office from the state capitol building to the Capitol in Washington, D.C.*

carat unit of weight for precious stones: *Juan gave his fiancée a two-carat diamond.*

caret a proofreading mark (∧) to show where something has been left out: *Sara inserted a caret and wrote in the missing letters.*

carrot a vegetable: *Carrots are a good source for vitamin A.*

cast (verb) to throw or fling with a quick motion: *They cast their fishing lines into the stream*; (noun) the players in a theatrical company: *The cast had a party following the opening-night performance*; that which is formed in a mold or from plaster: *The parts of some wood stoves are formed in a cast. The broken ankle is in a cast.*

caste exclusive social system having class distinctions based on birth, rank, wealth, position: *Each caste in India has existed for centuries.*

ceiling the top of a room: *The cartons were stacked almost to the ceiling*; an upper limit: *Should the government impose a price ceiling on gasoline?*

sealing fastening or closing tightly: *Plaster is used for sealing cracks.*

cell a small, bare room: *Each prison cell is designed for two inmates*; unit of living matter: *Diana examined the blood cell under the microscope*; a small electric battery: *Stephen bought a dry cell at the hardware store*; a small unit of a group: *Alberta was once a member of a Communist cell.*

sell to exchange for money or other payment: *It is difficult to sell a house when interest rates are high.*

cellar underground room: *Ms. Nguyen has a wine cellar in her home.*

seller one who exchanges property or goods for payment: *Both the buyer and the seller signed the contracts.*

censer an incense burner: *The priest covered the censer at the start of the ceremony.*

censor (noun) a person who examines material for portions deemed objectionable or harmful: *Mr. Kahn once served as a censor for the military*; (verb) to examine for objectionable or harmful material: *They may censor some of her correspondence from the Middle East.*

cent a coin (penny): *She did not have a single cent in her purse.*

scent an odor: *The scent of violets filled the room.*

sent past tense of *send*, mail, dispatch: *The office staff sent him a sympathy card.*

cents the plural of *cent: The daily paper now costs thirty cents.*

sense one of the specialized functions of hearing, sight, smell, taste, and touch: *The constant noise from the machines damaged his sense of hearing*; the point or meaning of something: *The paragraph doesn't make sense;* the ability to reason or think soundly: *Common sense will lead you to the correct answer.*

cereal food made from grain: *Oatmeal is a cereal.*

serial story published or broadcast one part at a time at regular intervals: *"The Lone Ranger" was a popular radio serial for years.*

chased past tense of *chase,* run after or cause to run away: *Mr. Abdelhady chased the bus for several blocks.*

chaste virtuous, modest: *A chaste person is to be admired.*

cheap not expensive, not worth much: *Merle always wears cheap clothes.*

cheep (verb) to make a sound like a young bird: *A bird cheeped from the bushes*; (noun) the short, shrill sound of a young bird: *The cheep of the bird startled them.*

choir a group of singers, most commonly in a church: *The boys' choir held rehearsals on Saturdays.*

quire a set of 24 or 25 sheets of paper of the same size and stock: *Maria took a quire of Lindcroft stationery with her.*

chord a combination of musical notes in harmony: *She played an A-major chord on the piano*; an emotional response: *Eileen's appeal struck a sympathetic chord with the listeners.*

cord thick string: *Tie a cord around this package*; a measure of wood cut for fuel: *One cord of wood equals 128 cubic feet;* a small, insulated electric wire fitted with a plug: *The cord on this clock is too short.*

chute an inclined passage to slide things down: *Orolyn slid the envelopes down the mail chute.*

shoot (verb) to let fly: *How accurately can you shoot an arrow with that crossbow?*; to photograph: *Bob wanted to shoot a picture of the party*; (noun) a young outgrowth from a shrub or tree: *She cut a bamboo shoot for decoration.*

cite to quote as an authority: *Economists cite statistics to support their theories*; to mention as an example: *Let me cite Joanne's experience as production supervisor.*

sight one of the five senses: *Jim lost the sight in his left eye*; something seen or worth seeing: *The tour guide pointed out the major sights of the city.*

site the seat or scene of any specific thing: *The site of a major Civil War battle is only four miles from here*; the location of a building, the land where a building stands or is to stand: *The board met to select a site for the new plant.*

clause a separate section of a formal document: *Mr. Cruz wanted to strike the second clause from the contract*; a group of words containing a subject and verb: *The main clause of a sentence is called the independent clause.*

claws sharp, curved nails on an animal's toes: *The cat's claws damaged the sofa.*

NAME	CLASS	DATE	SCORE

Homonym Assignments

A. Select from the following words the one that correctly fits the blank in each of the sentences below. Then write the word in the answer space provided.

canvas	caret	seller	serial	cite
canvass	carrot	cent	cheap	sight
capital	cast	scent	cheep	site
capitol	caste	sent	chord	clause
carat	cellar	cereal	cord	claws

1. Before authorizing the development of a new product, the firm decided to _____ the market. 1._____

2. The contract did not contain an escape _____. 2._____

3. An understudy is a _____ member who has to be ready as a substitute when called upon. 3._____

4. Quite often inactive files are stored in a basement or _____. 4._____

5. The biography was published as a _____ in three consecutive issues of the magazine. 5._____

6. An extension _____ was necessary in order to use the equipment in the new location. 6._____

7. The billboard was located on a prominent _____. 7._____

8. *Vendor* is another term for _____. 8._____

9. A _____ is a proofreading mark that is used to indicate where something has been left out. 9._____

10. A heading is usually typed with all _____ letters. 10._____

11. His sympathetic and caring attitude struck a responsive _____ among the employees. 11._____

12. Sam _____ the bonds by registered mail. 12._____

13. In summertime the garden is a very pleasant _____ . 13._____

14. She saved every _____ she could toward the
purchase of a new car.

14. _____

15. Her birthstone ring contained a ruby that weighed at
least one _____.

15. _____

B. In some of the following sentences, an incorrect word is used. Underline the incorrect
word, and write the correct word in the space provided. Where there is no error, write C
in the answer space.

1. Some years ago ceiling wax was used to fasten envelopes.

1. _____

2. It's not easy to cell luxury items in times of depression.

2. _____

3. One of the most popular breakfast foods is cereal.

3. _____

4. Have the seasonal orders been cent in yet?

4. _____

5. The duplicating job will require at least five choirs of
paper.

5. _____

6. I wanted to believe them, but their story just didn't
make sense.

6. _____

7. Only stamped mail should be placed in the shoot.

7. _____

8. The sent of the lilacs outside the window filtered into
the office.

8. _____

9. Mr. Wells had a collection of miniature canons on the
bookcase in his office.

9. _____

10. With the ceiling on the interest rate fluctuating dramati-
cally, potential home buyers are exercising caution.

10. _____

11. It was routine procedure to have the Public Relations
Department censor news releases before they were
given to the media.

11. _____

12. They were scheduled to chute the commercial at 3
p.m. in the studio.

12. _____

13. The dog wandered into the bank and was chaste by
the security guard.

13. _____

14. Washington, D.C., is the capital of the United States.

14. _____

15. By keeping her money in a savings account, Mary
could earn a few cents of interest each day.

15. _____

C. Read the definition, and select the correct word from the second column to match that description. Write the word you selected in the answer space.

Definition	Word Choice	
1. location	cite, sight, site	1._____
2. vegetable	carat, caret, carrot	2._____
3. an incense burner	censer, censor	3._____
4. an exclusive social system having class distinctions based on birth, rank, wealth, or position	cast, caste	4._____
5. to make a sound like a young bird	cheap, cheep	5._____
6. virtuous and modest	chased, chaste	6._____
7. sharp, curved nails on an animal	clause, claws	7._____
8. to mention as an example	cite, sight, site	8._____
9. a law or body of laws of a church	cannon, canon	9._____
10. city where the government of a country or state is located	capital, capitol	10._____

D. Select the right word for the sentence shown, and write it in the answer space. Then compose a sentence for the homonym not selected, and write your sentence in the space provided.

1. (Cereal, Serial) is my favorite breakfast food.   1._____

   _____

   _____

   _____

2. We were unable to open the mail (chute, shoot).   2._____

   _____

   _____

   _____

3. A burning (cent, scent) filled the air.

3. _____

_____
_____
_____

4. What a happy (cite, sight) it was—a payroll check including a large commission.

4. _____

_____
_____
_____

5. The movers placed a (canvas, canvass) over the furniture that was to be moved.

5. _____

_____
_____
_____

6. She got a (callous, callus) on her foot because her shoes were tight.

6. _____

_____
_____
_____

7. Brian's (cast, caste) kept him from moving quickly.

7. _____

_____
_____
_____

8. Each prisoner was kept in a separate (cell, sell).

8. _____

_____
_____
_____

9. Their idea was a good one in every (cents, sense).

9. _____

_____
_____
_____

10. Jorge did so well in the audition that he was chosen for the (cast, caste).

10. _____

_____
_____
_____

NAME	CLASS	DATE	SCORE

Vocabulary Enrichment

Chapters 1-3

A. You should now be familiar with the meaning of each of the words below. In the space provided to the right, write the word that best completes the meaning of the sentence. Cross out each word in the list as you use it.

accumulate	disastrous	hindrance	postpone	propose
acumen	dissolution	irrelevant	precipitate	representative
chauvinism	environment	mischievous	prejudice	strategic
deference	grievous	partner	privilege	temperament

1. A fiery _____ does not lead to success in on-the-job relationships.

   1._____

2. Typographical errors in a contract can have _____ results.

   2._____

3. It is an indication of laziness to _____ to a later date any work you can do today.

   3._____

4. Unable to reconcile their differences, the two businesswomen agreed to the _____ of their partnership.

   4._____

5. Ms. Ferelli is an intelligent manager with a remarkable _____ in sales techniques.

   5._____

6. _____ leads to bitterness, misunderstanding, and unhappiness; it is better to have an open mind.

   6._____

7. Your childhood _____ has a great deal to do with shaping your personality.

   7._____

8. Although George was initially opposed to the merger, he agreed to support it in _____ to Ms. Jacobson's convincing arguments.

   8._____

9. Various equipment problems were a _____ to our meeting the deadline.

   9._____

10. The art collector has been able to _____ a valuable collection of paintings.

    10._____

B. For this exercise you must refer to the list of words given for assignment A above. For each of the ten words you did not use in completing assignment A, compose a meaningful sentence on a separate sheet of paper.

C. Choose the word from the list below that is closest in meaning to the numbered word or words in the paragraph. Write the word you selected from the list in the answer space. Use each word only once.

analyzes	deposit	purpose
borrow	emergency	record
common	equal	representative
currency	installment	verifled
debt	intervals	withdrawals

Using Banking Services

Participating in business transactions at a local bank is
1. ORDINARY practice whether you are acting for yourself or
as a(n) 2. AGENT for a business firm. When you open a new
account, you provide a 3. SAMPLE of your handwriting so
that your signature can be 4. CHECKED when you make
5. DEDUCTIONS.

When you 6. ADD money to an account, you prepare a form
listing the total amount of the 7. CASH and/or checks you
are depositing. Individuals often have both a checking account
and a savings account because each serves a different 8. GOAL.

Sometimes individuals or businesses need to 9. GET A LOAN for
special purposes or projects—possibly even for 10. UNFORESEEN
circumstances. Before a bank will give a loan, it 11. EXAMINES
the borrower's credit rating to be certain that the 12. LOAN will be
paid back. Usually, loans are repaid in 13. EVEN amounts at
stated 14. TIME PERIODS. For this reason the loans are known
as 15. EQUAL PAYMENT loans.

1. _____

2. _____

3. _____

4. _____

5. _____

6. _____

7. _____

8. _____

9. _____

10. _____

11. _____

12. _____

13. _____

14. _____

15. _____

Doubling the Final Consonant

Which word in each of the following pairs is spelled correctly?

occu<u>rr</u>ed	ope<u>nn</u>ed	shi<u>pp</u>ed	diffe<u>rr</u>ed
occu<u>r</u>ed	ope<u>n</u>ed	shi<u>p</u>ed	diffe<u>r</u>ed

The correct spellings are **occurred, opened, shipped**, and **differed**. Did you get all four right? Did you know, or did you guess?

The most frequent type of spelling decision you have to make is whether to double the final consonant in situations like these. The wrong decision means spelling errors. There is a rule that tells you when to double the final consonant, and it is a rule with very few exceptions. Once you learn what is undoubtedly the most useful spelling rule of all, you will be able to solve thousands of spelling problems like these confidently and correctly. This is the rule:

Rule

When adding a suffix (word ending) that begins with a *vowel,* double the final consonant if:

1. The word ends in a *single* consonant (except *w, x,* or *y*), and
2. This consonant is preceded by a *single* vowel, and
3. The word is pronounced with the accent on the *last* syllable.

Do *not* double the final consonant unless all three conditions (1, 2, and 3) are met. This rule may seem complicated—but it is really easy if you take it step by step.

Remember that the rule applies *only* when you are adding a word ending that begins with a *vowel* (**a, e, i, o, u**), such as **able, ance, ary, ed, ence, er, est, ish, ing, ion, ize, ism, ory**. The rule does *not* apply when you are adding a word ending that begins with a *consonant*, such as **less, ly, ment, ness**.

Let's work through the word **occur** as an example.

1. **Occur** ends in a single consonant (**r**), and
2. This consonant is preceded by a single vowel (**u**), and
3. **Occur** is pronounced with the accent on the last syllable (you say **oc-cur′**).

Therefore: **occur, occurred, occurrence, occurring**.

Let's use the word **bid** as a second example.

1. **Bid** ends in a single consonant (**d**), and
2. This consonant is preceded by a single vowel (**i**), and
3. **Bid** is accented. (Since **bid** has only one syllable, it must be accented. When using this rule with one-syllable words, ignore the accent requirement. *All* one-syllable words meet this requirement automatically.)

Therefore: **bid, bidder, bidding**.

Now *you* work through the next example. Take the word **regret**.

1. Does it end in a single consonant? Yes, **t**.
2. Is this consonant preceded by a single vowel? Yes, **e**.
3. Do you pronounce **regret** with the accent on the final syllable? Yes, you say **re-gret′**.

Since all three conditions are met, you double the final consonant when adding a word ending beginning with a vowel. Therefore: **regret, regrettable, regretted, regretting**. Simple, isn't it?

Now take the word **plan**.

1. Does **plan** end in a single consonant? Yes, **n**.
2. Is this consonant preceded by a single vowel? Yes, **a**.
3. Is **plan** accented? Yes, it is automatically accented, since it consists of only one syllable.

Therefore: **plan, planned, planner, planning**.

Now try **relax**. Does **relax** end in a single consonant? Yes, **x**. And the rule tells us *not* to double the final consonant when that consonant is *w, x,* or *y.* Therefore: **relax, relaxed, relaxing, relaxation**. Even though **relax** satisfies conditions 2 (the final consonant is preceded by a single vowel) and 3 (it is pronounced with the accent on the last syllable), it does not satisfy all three conditions. Because *all three* conditions have *not* been satisfied, you do *not* double the final consonant.

As a final example, try the word **parallel**.

1. Does **parallel** end in a single consonant? Yes, **l**.
2. Is this consonant preceded by a single vowel? Yes, **e**.
3. Is **parallel** pronounced with the accent on the last syllable? No, you say **par′-al-lel**.

Thus, because *all three* conditions have *not* been satisfied, you do *not* double the final consonant. Therefore: **parallel, paralleled, paralleling**.

Remember, **relax** and **parallel** are not exceptions to the rule. They *follow* the rule that says not to double the final consonant if a word does not satisfy all three conditions: 1, 2, and 3.

Note | When **qu** precedes a vowel, as in the word **acquit**, the **u** is not considered a vowel because it has the sound of **w**. Since **acquit** ends in a single consonant (**t**) that is preceded by a single vowel (**i**), and it is pronounced with the accent on the last syllable (**ac-quit′**), the rule for doubling the final consonant applies. Therefore: **acquit, acquitted, acquittal, acquitting**.

Now, analyze each of the following words to see why the final consonant is doubled. Take each word slowly. Write it out on a piece of paper, and note how the rule applies at each step.

abhor*	abhorred	abhorring	abhorrence
admit	admitted	admitting	admittance
allot	allotted	allotting	allotment
annul	annulled	annulling	annulment
begin	beginner	beginning	
blot	blotted	blotter	blotting
can	canner	canning	canned
commit	committed	committing	commitment
compel	compelled	compelling	
control	controlled	controlling	controller
cut	cutter	cutting	
deter*	deterred	deterring	deterrent
dispel*	dispelled	dispelling	
drug	drugged	drugging	druggist
equip	equipped	equipping	equipment
excel	excelled	excelling	excellent[1]
expel	expelled	expelling	expellable
forget	forgettable	forgetting	forgetful
hot	hotter	hottest	hotly
occur	occurred	occurring	occurrence
omit	omitted	omitting	
permit	permitted	permitting	
plan	planned	planning	planner
propel*	propelled	propelling	propeller
regret	regretted	regretting	regrettable
remit*	remitted	remitting	remittance
rob	robbed	robbing	robber
ship	shipped	shipping	shipment
stab	stabbed	stabbing	
star	starred	starring	
stir	stirred	stirring	
stop	stopped	stopping	stoppage
submit	submitted	submitting	

[1]Exception to rule, since the accent is on the first syllable (ex′-cel-lent).

thin	thin<u>nn</u>ed	thin<u>nn</u>ing	thin<u>nn</u>er
war	war<u>rr</u>ed	war<u>rr</u>ing	war<u>rr</u>ior

As you saw at the beginning of this chapter, you do not double the final consonant for **open** and **differ**. Each of these words is pronounced with the accent on the first syllable: **o'-pen, dif'-fer**. Since they do not satisfy all three conditions (1, 2, and 3) of the rule, the final consonants are not doubled. You write **opened, opening, opener,** and **differed, differing**. Now analyze each of the following words to see why the final consonant is *not* doubled. Remember, these words are not exceptions to the rule. They simply do not satisfy all three conditions (1, 2, and 3). Why not?

act	acted	acting	actor
affix*	affixed	affixing	
alter	altered	altering	alteration
appeal	appealed	appealing	
balloon	ballooned	ballooning	balloonist
band	banded	banding	bandage
bank	banked	banking	banker
benefit	benefited	benefiting	
board	boarded	boarding	boarder
calm	calmed	calmness	calmly
cheer	cheered	cheerfulness	cheery
climb	climbed	climbing	climber
concoct*	concocted	concocting	concoction
condemn	condemned	condemning	condemnation
correspond	corresponded	corresponding	correspondence
credit*	credited	crediting	creditor
curb	curbed	curbing	curbstone
debit*	debited	debiting	
debt	debtor	indebted	
defend	defended	defending	defendant
deposit	deposited	depositing	depositor
despair	despaired	despairing	
differ	differed	differing	difference
disappear	disappeared	disappearing	disappearance
edit	edited	editing	editor
enter	entered	entering	
fear	feared	fearing	fearless
gain	gained	gaining	gainful
grant	granted	granting	grantor
green	greener	greenest	
greet	greeted	greeting	greeter
guard	guarded	guarding	guardian
index	indexed	indexing	
instill*	instilled	instilling	
kind	kindest	kindness	kindly
libel	libeled	libeling	libelous
parallel*	paralleled	paralleling	parallelogram
pertain*	pertained	pertaining	
point	pointed	pointing	pointer

post	posted	posting	postage
print	printed	printing	printer
profit	profited	profiting	profitable
prohibit	prohibited	prohibiting	prohibitive
prompt	promptly	prompting	promptness
register	registered	registering	
revolt	revolted	revolting	
short	shortly	shortness	shortsighted
snow	snowed	snowing	snowy
solicit*	solicited	soliciting	solicitation
strain	strained	straining	strainer
strict	strictly	strictness	strictest
suit	suited	suiting	suitor
sweet	sweeter	sweetly	sweetness
talk	talked	talking	talkative
tax	taxed	taxing	taxable
visit	visited	visiting	visitor
wish	wished	wishing	
wreck	wrecked	wrecking	wreckage

Now look at these words:

confer	conferred	conferring	conference
defer*	deferred	deferring	deference
infer*	inferred	inferring	inference
prefer	preferred	preferring	preference
refer	referred	referring	reference

At first glance **conference, deference, inference, preference,** and **reference** seem to be exceptions—but look again. Pronounce **reference** aloud. The accent has shifted to the first syllable. You say:

con'-fer-ence
def'-er-ence
in'-fer-ence
pref'-er-ence
ref'-er-ence

Since the accent of the root word is no longer on the last syllable, the rule tells us not to double the final consonant. Thus **conference, deference, inference, preference,** and **reference** are not exceptions to the rule.

Note

Overstep is really two words joined together: **over + step**. It is known as a *compound word*. When adding suffixes to compound words, concentrate on the final word, in this case **step**, and follow the rule for one-syllable words. Hence: **overstep, overstepped, overstepping**.

The following words are governed by the same principle:

countersign*	countersigned	countersigning	countersignature
eavesdrop	eavesdropped	eavesdropping	eavesdropper
handicap	handicapped	handicapping	handicapper
horsewhip	horsewhipped	horsewhipping	
offset	offsetting	offsetter	
outfit	outfitted	outfitting	outfitter
undersign	undersigned	undersigning	
understand	understanding	understandable	understandably

Exceptions There are a few exceptions to the doubling principle. Here are some of the more important ones:

cancellation	gaseous	tranquility
chagrined	programmed	transferable
crystallize	questionnaire	transference
excellent		

NAME   **CLASS**   **DATE**   **SCORE**

Spelling Assignments

A. Mentally add the suffix **ed** to each of the following words. Then write the complete word in the space provided.

1.	rob	____	16.	disturb ____
2.	occur	____	17.	develop ____
3.	benefit	____	18.	box ____
4.	control	____	19.	concoct ____
5.	profit	____	20.	dispel ____
6.	travel	____	21.	deter ____
7.	compel	____	22.	submit ____
8.	admit	____	23.	chagrin ____
9.	prefer	____	24.	render ____
10.	regret	____	25.	censor ____
11.	mat	____	26.	indent ____
12.	undersign	____	27.	index ____
13.	infer	____	28.	spark ____
14.	demur	____	29.	expel ____
15.	defect	____	30.	conduct ____

B. Each column contains a word and a suffix. Mentally add the suffix to the word. Then write the complete word in the space provided.

1.	transmit + al	____	7.	visit + or ____
2.	permit + ed	____	8.	edit + ing ____
3.	administer + ing	____	9.	fit + ing ____
4.	prohibit + ed	____	10.	benefit + ing ____
5.	profit + ing	____	11.	regret + able ____
6.	refer + ence	____	12.	regret + ing ____

13. merit + ed _____
14. omit + ed _____
15. subsist + ing _____
16. debit + ed _____
17. acquit + al _____
18. commit + ed _____
19. commit + ment _____
20. forget + ing _____
21. allot + ed _____
22. blur + ed _____
23. stop + age _____
24. thin + er _____
25. quiz + ed _____
26. tax + ed _____

27. drum + ed _____
28. credit + ing _____
29. market + ing _____
30. diagram + ed _____
31. transfer + ence _____
32. cancel + ing _____
33. equal + ity _____
34. prefer + able _____
35. appoint + ment _____
36. descend + ant _____
37. interrupt + ion _____
38. equip + ing _____
39. equip + ment _____
40. propel + ant _____

C. Mentally add the suffix **er** to each of the following words. Then write the complete word in the space provided.

1. begin _____
2. broadcast _____
3. control _____
4. travel _____
5. blot _____
6. ship _____
7. run _____
8. transmit _____
9. plan _____
10. rivet _____

11. hot _____
12. propel _____
13. outfit _____
14. eavesdrop _____
15. point _____
16. climb _____
17. bank _____
18. handicap _____
19. talk _____
20. defend _____

D. Each column contains a word and a suffix. Mentally add the suffix to the word. Then write the complete word in the space provided.

1. meter + ed _____
2. parallel + ing _____
3. crystal + ize _____

4. begin + ing _____
5. defer + ing _____
6. confer + ence _____

7.	critic + ism	_____	24.	inhabit + able	_____
8.	stir + ed	_____	25.	claim + ant	_____
9.	falter + ed	_____	26.	cancel + ation	_____
10.	gas + eous	_____	27.	red + ish	_____
11.	entrap + ed	_____	28.	sad + ly	_____
12.	recur + ing	_____	29.	regret + fully	_____
13.	exceed + ing	_____	30.	ton + age	_____
14.	exist + ence	_____	31.	wit + y	_____
15.	refer + ed	_____	32.	bag + age	_____
16.	forbid + en	_____	33.	system + atic	_____
17.	program + ed	_____	34.	can + ery	_____
18.	mix + ed	_____	35.	cut + lery	_____
19.	excel + ent	_____	36.	flat + ness	_____
20.	shrug + ed	_____	37.	knit + ed	_____
21.	outrun + ing	_____	38.	net + work	_____
22.	abhor + ence	_____	39.	libel + ous	_____
23.	vacation + ing	_____	40.	knot + y	_____

E. Write the proper form of the word in parentheses in the answer space.

1. How many dollars were (commit) to the project? — 1._____
2. Mr. Jacobs just (submit) the report a few minutes ago. — 2._____
3. Your (prompt) in filling this order is greatly appreciated. — 3._____
4. (Countersign) a traveler's check is necessary when you are ready to cash it. — 4._____
5. When (register) for a workshop, be sure to sign up well before the deadline. — 5._____
6. What secretarial (refer) books did you find most helpful? — 6._____
7. All the employees would have (benefit) from the terms of the new contract. — 7._____
8. When (travel) for business or pleasure, plan carefully. — 8._____
9. The witnesses (affix) their signatures to the will yesterday. — 9._____

10. The student's parent or legal (guard) must sign the application.

10. _____

11. Martha's (cheer) was one of her prime assets.

11. _____

12. During the night two employees were (rob).

12. _____

13. Please submit your invoice with your (remit).

13. _____

14. Victor's (excel) reputation preceded him.

14. _____

15. (Omit) the ZIP Code may delay the correspondence.

15. _____

16. The accident report carefully detailed the (occur).

16. _____

17. Keisha faced the interviewers (calm).

17. _____

18. Items that are (tax) vary from state to state.

18. _____

19. It is better to have good habits (instill) than bad ones.

19. _____

20. Please complete the (question), and return it in the enclosed envelope.

20. _____

Homonyms

coarse   unrefined, crude: *They used coarse language*; not fine in texture, rough: *This towel feels coarse.*

course   a way, path, or channel taken: *Which course of action should we take? The company has a nine-hole golf course for its employees*; direction taken: *The ship's course was due north*; regular mode of action or development: *The course of true love never did run smoothly*; part of a meal: *A complimentary dessert course was served with each meal*; a series of studies in school: *Betty took an accounting course last semester.*

colonel   (kur' nel) a high-ranking Army officer: *Mr. Rath was a colonel in the army.*

kernel   a grain or seed: *The cereal advertisement showed a kernel of corn*; an essential part: *There is a kernel of truth in the story.*

complement   (verb) to supply a lack, supplement: *Our new word processing equipment will complement our secretarial services*; (noun) that which fills up or completes: *With the arrival of this new shipment, we have reached our complement of fall merchandise.*

compliment   (noun) praise, commendation: *Olga received a compliment on a job well done*; (verb) to praise, to commend: *We often compliment Mr. Perez on the way he keeps his books.*

core   the central or most important part: *How to improve morale was the core of the discussion. The core of the apple contains the seeds.*

corps   a group of people having a common activity or occupation: *The press corps surrounded the President*; a branch of the armed forces having some specialized function: *Tom joined the Marine Corps last month.*

correspondence   communication by letters: *They were in frequent correspondence with their London office*; the letters exchanged: *We keep a file of all our correspondence.*

correspondents   plural of *correspondent,* one who communicates by letter: *Our correspondents have written us about foreign market conditions*; newspeople: *The European correspondents reported on the current strikes in France and Germany.*

council   group of people selected, appointed, or elected to make laws, settle questions, give advice: *The town council reported its findings and recommendations to the mayor.*

counsel   (verb) to advise: *We counsel you not to make any further investments in this company*; (noun) a lawyer: *Vicky conferred with counsel before answering the question.*

creak (verb) to move with a harsh, squeaky, grating noise: *I heard his bones creak*; (noun) harsh noise: *The creak in that door annoys me.*

creek a small stream, somewhat larger than a brook: *A creek runs through the property.*

crews plural of *crew,* a group of people working together: *The shop steward gave directions to both maintenance crews.*

cruise (noun) a journey by ship: *We have scheduled a one-week cruise to the Bahamas*; (verb) to take such a trip: *We will cruise throughout the Caribbean*; to move randomly from place to place: *The investigators will cruise the area in search of clues.*

cue a stick used to play pool or billiards: *The sporting goods store has a special on pool cues this week*; a hint, reminder or prompting: *When the personnel director closed the folder, John took that as his cue that the interview was over.*

queue (noun) a waiting line: *We saw Mr. Sovisky in a queue at the ticket window*; a collection of messages waiting to be processed by a computer: *Hundreds of messages were stacked on the queue*; (verb) to get in line: *They queue up for concert tickets*; to form items in a line for computer processing: *The computer queues up messages and processes them in order of priority.*

currant a berry: *The currant jelly is in the refrigerator.*

current (adjective) now in progress: *Read the current market analysis*; (noun) a body of water flowing in a definite direction: *The Gulf Stream is a warm current*; the flow of electric force: *This hair dryer can be used with either direct or alternating current.*

days the plural of *day,* a 24-hour period: *This special sale will last only three more days.*

daze To dazzle or stupefy: *Elena was in a daze due to her new-found wealth.*

dear beloved: *Children are dear to their parents*; costly, expensive: *These days the best cuts of meat are too dear for most people*; a polite form of address: *Dear Ms. Alfieri.*

deer an animal: *Our neighbor likes to feed the deer.*

dependence the quality or state of being supported by or subject to another: *Bill got a job in order to reduce his dependence on his father;* reliance, trust: *Carole's dependence on her assistant was absolute.*

dependents those who rely on another for support: *Nicholas listed his dependents on his tax return.*

dew the moisture that condenses after a warm day and appears during the night: *Their shoes were wet from the morning dew.*

do to carry out, perform: *Bianca had to do three separate jobs.*

due owed as a debt: *The bill is now due*; expected by a certain date: *The report was due at the end of the month;* owing (to): *The conflict is due to their stubbornness.*

die   (verb) to stop living: *Many people who die unexpectedly have not left a will;* (noun) a tool or device for stamping, cutting, molding, or shaping: *A rectangular die is used to stamp out license plates;* singular of *dice: Some board games are played by rolling a single die.*

dye   (verb) to change the color of anything by saturating it with a coloring substance: *Alfredo decided to dye his hair;* (noun) any substance used to color fabric, hair, etc.: *The manufacturer failed to use a colorfast dye in these shirts.*

discreet   showing good judgment, confidentiality: *The attorney was always discreet in handling delicate matters.*

discrete   separate and distinct: *Divide the files into eight discrete units.*

done   past participle of *do,* completed or ended: *We have done all the work assigned to us;* sufficiently cooked: *The hot dogs are done, but the hamburgers need to cook a little longer.*

dun   to ask a debtor repeatedly for payment: *Two of Mr. Parker's creditors have begun to dun him for payment.*

dual   having or composed of two parts: *Cars for people learning how to drive have dual controls.*

duel   a contest fought between two persons: *Alice and Marcia were in a constant duel over who would manage the department.*

faint   (adjective) not clear: *I see a faint light in the distance;* feeble, without strength: *I feel faint with hunger;* (verb) to lose consciousness temporarily: *Did she faint from the shock?*

feint   (noun) a movement intended to deceive, a pretended blow: *The boxer's feint drew down his opponent's guard;* (verb) to deliver such a pretended blow: *The boxer feinted with his left and then punched with his right.*

fair   (adjective) impartial: *Everyone accused of a crime is entitled to a fair trial;* reasonable: *We offer our services at a fair price;* light, clear, beautiful: *We can expect fair weather for the sale;* (noun) a festival at which goods and livestock are displayed: *The county fair attracts thousands of people.*

fare   (noun) sum of money paid for travel: *The airline lowered the plane fare between New York and Detroit;* a range of food: *The restaurant offers an extensive bill of fare;* (verb) to dine: *We fare like kings on lobster and steak;* to get along: *How did you fare at the meeting?*

NAME	CLASS	DATE	SCORE

Homonym Assignments

A. Select from the following words the one that correctly fits the blank in each of the sentences below. Then write the word in the answer space provided.

coarse	corps	cue	deer	due
course	correspondence	queue	dependence	discreet
complement	correspondents	days	dependents	discrete
compliment	crews	daze	dew	dual
core	cruise	dear	do	duel

1. When the last three styles are completed, we shall have our full _____ of spring fashions ready for market.

        1._____

2. Many a business deal is transacted on the golf _____.

        2._____

3. Good supervisors know that one _____ is worth a thousand criticisms.

        3._____

4. For tax purposes you must complete a form stating how many _____ you have.

        4._____

5. Sometimes it takes a fraction of a second to _____ up data for the computer.

        5._____

6. If the terms of an invoice are 2/10, n/30, then the discount period is only 10 _____ long.

        6._____

7. She is a _____ friend of mine.

        7._____

8. The nod of his head was the _____ to begin negotiations.

        8._____

9. She took a _____ for her vacation.

        9._____

10. The _____ courses in her program were in business administration.

        10._____

11. The note was _____ on May 23.

        11._____

12. Since the typewriter was capable of both pica and elite spacing, it was referred to as a _____-pitch machine.

        12._____

13. Frank and Pete were so competitive that in the olden days they would have challenged each other to a

    _____.   13. _____

14. Fred was rewarded with a raise for his _____ and efficient follow-through on job-related matters.   14. _____

15. A _____ file contains a copy of each outgoing letter and memo in chronological order.   15. _____

B. In some of the following sentences, an incorrect word is used. Underline the incorrect word, and write the correct word in the space provided. Where there is no error, write C in the answer space.

1. We divided the project into discreet parts.   1. _____

2. Always wear accessories that complement your outfit.   2. _____

3. Alice's many awards and certificates of achievement were very deer to her.   3. _____

4. We had a duel purpose for holding this sale on the weekend.   4. _____

5. The swollen stream with its swift currant caused many homeowners to make damage claims.   5. _____

6. The stairs were slippery from the morning dew.   6. _____

7. Can I trust you to be discrete about the handling of this problem?   7. _____

8. We must reduce our dependents on foreign oil.   8. _____

9. The shipping delay was do to the strike.   9. _____

10. The committee had to consult the Army Core of Engineers about the proposed project.   10. _____

11. It took Mr. Peterson over an hour to dictate replies to all of the day's incoming correspondents.   11. _____

12. The creaking door was reported to the maintenance crew.   12. _____

13. The project developed from his remark, which served as the colonel of the idea.   13. _____

14. When you are on a cruise, there are many coarses at the main meal.   14. _____

15. She took the queue from others in her department and organized her desk.   15. _____

C. Read the definition, and select the correct word from the second column to match that description. Write the word you selected in the answer space.

	Definition	Word Choice	
1.	to change the color	die, dye	1._____
2.	to advise	council, counsel	2._____
3.	a berry	currant, current	3._____
4.	a way, path, or channel	coarse, course	4._____
5.	groups of people working together	crews, cruise	5._____
6.	the central or most important part	core, corps	6._____
7.	a high-ranking Army officer	colonel, kernel	7._____
8.	to ask a debtor repeatedly for payment	done, dun	8._____
9.	showing good judgment	discreet, discrete	9._____
10.	praise, commendation	complement, compliment	10._____

D. Select the right word for the sentence shown, and write it in the answer space. Then compose a sentence for the homonym not selected, and write your sentence in the space provided.

1. When the (correspondence, correspondents) arrives, please sort it.

    1._____

    _____

    _____

    _____

2. The medication was so strong that she felt as though she were in a (days, daze).

    2._____

    _____

    _____

    _____

3. The accountant sent out letters to (done, dun) customers who had not yet paid their bills.

    3._____

    _____

    _____

    _____

4. Our (currant, current) fiscal status is good.

4. _____

_____

_____

_____

5. Sometimes you need to have the exact (fair, fare) to take a bus.

5. _____

_____

_____

_____

6. It is important to meet the date that the article is (do, due).

6. _____

_____

_____

_____

7. My photocopy of the report is very (faint, feint).

7. _____

_____

_____

_____

8. She analyzed the sentence by determining the (discreet, discrete) "part of speech" for each word.

8. _____

_____

_____

_____

9. When the interviewer looked at his watch, Helene took this as a (cue, queue) that the interview would soon be over.

9. _____

_____

_____

_____

10. Representatives from each department were asked to participate on an advisory (council, counsel).

10. _____

_____

_____

_____

NAME	CLASS	DATE	SCORE

Review Exercises

A. There are misspelled words in some of the following sentences.   Underline each misspelled word, and write the correct spelling in the space provided.   If there are no misspelled words, write C in the space next to the sentence.

1. Beginning office workers should be receptive to helpful suggestions.   1._____

2. By enabling us to respond more quickly to customers, the new computer has already repaid it's original cost.   2._____

3. A new bookcase was instaled to provide more shelf space.   3._____

4. Accracy is increased by the use of modren computers.   4._____

5. To protect your credit rating, you should repay loans promptly.   5._____

6. Its easy to open a checking account.   6._____

7. A refund will be made as soon as you're account is credited for the returned merchandise.   7._____

8. Most electronic typewriters come equiped with automatic centering and automatic underscoring capability.   8._____

9. You are to be congradulated for your initiative in handling the Martone case.   9._____

10. If you are not familar with acceptable formatting styles, check a secretarial reference book.   10._____

11. Their not interested in the new shiping plan.   11._____

12. You will be able to complete the report by simply refering to last year's copy as a guide.   12._____

13. The new policy on sick leave pertains to employees in all departments.   13._____

14. Thank you for you're letter in reference to our new product line.   14._____

15. When I left the publishing company, I found a similiar position with an advertising agency.   15._____

16. The cardboard boxes were reinforced with gumed tape. 16. _____

17. Both Maria and her employer benefited when she took evening courses in office procedures. 17. _____

18. This booklet describes the comfort you will experience when vacationning at one of our hotels. 18. _____

19. Did you submit your budget figures for the replacement equippment yet? 19. _____

20. Five years ago the company transferred its main office to New York. 20. _____

21. The company has both common and prefered stocks on the market. 21. _____

22. The listing, of coarse, is strickly confidential. 22. _____

23. Has it ever occured to you that you are a valued employee? 23. _____

24. Opportunities for employment in office work are excelent. 24. _____

25. Abdul was sited by the other supervisors for his discrete handling of a very difficult situation. 25. _____

B. Underline each error in the following letter, and write the correct spelling or usage in the space provided to the right of the line. If there are no errors in the line, write C in the space.

1 Febuary 16, 19--

2 Mr. William Olsen
3 Admistrative Assistant
4 Twenty-two Ridge Road
5 Bolder, CO 05505

6 Dear Mrs. Olsen:

7 As you probaly know, our firm recently sent you an introductory
8 copy of a new magazine, High Tech World, which has been designed
9 especially for busy office workers such as office assistance,
10 secertaries, and other office professionals. We hope that you
11 have had time to read some of it's interesting articles. They're
12 full of facts, tips, and surprizes. Some of the articles have
13 reference value, while others offer suggestions for ways to
14 improve your planing. Finally, there are some cheery articles
15 meant to brighten your day.

16 You can accummulate a wealth of information by reading our new
17 publication on a regular basis. Take advantage of a termendous
18 money-saving offer by signning up now for a two-year subscription.
19 A one-year subscription is also available if you prefer. This
20 special offer is not transferrable and expires at the end of this
   month.

21 If you include your remittance with your subscription, you will
22 receive two extra issues without charge. Keep High Tech World
23 coming without interruption. Order immediately! Ad your name
24 to our subscription list today.

25 Sincerly yours,

Ann Simmons
Publications Board

ly

1. _____
2. _____
3. _____
4. _____
5. _____
6. _____
7. _____
8. _____
9. _____
10. _____
11. _____
12. _____
13. _____
14. _____
15. _____
16. _____
17. _____
18. _____
19. _____
20. _____
21. _____
22. _____
23. _____
24. _____
25. _____

Dropping the Silent **e**

Chapter 5

Very few people would ever misspell words such as **write, move, come, hope, give**, and **please**. Although the **e** at the end of these words is not pronounced, few people would forget to put it there. Other forms of these words, however, are frequently misspelled.

Incorrect

writeing	moveing	comeing
hopeing	giveing	pleaseing

Correct

writing	moving	coming
hoping	giving	pleasing

There is a very simple rule to help you avoid such spelling mistakes. It covers even more words than the rule governing when to double the final consonant and, like that rule, permits you to solve countless spelling problems with ease and confidence.

Rule 1

Drop the final **e** when you add a suffix beginning with a vowel: **ing, able, er, ed, or,** etc.

---

accommodate	accommodated	accommodating	accommodation
accumulate	accumulated	accumulating	accumulation
achieve	achieved	achieving	
advertise	advertised	advertising	
advise	advisable	advising	advisory
allocate*	allocated	allocating	allocation
argue	argued	arguing	arguable
balance	balanced	balancing	
believe	believed	believing	believable
bicycle	bicycled	bicycling	
censure*	censured	censuring	censurable

choose		choosing		
commence*	commenced	commencing		
compensate*	compensated	compensating	compensation	
concede*	conceded	conceding		
concentrate	concentrated	concentrating	concentration	
criticize	criticized	criticizing		
delete*	deleted	deleting		
depreciate*	depreciated	depreciating	depreciation	
derive	derived	deriving	derivation	
designate	designated	designating	designation	
disburse*	disbursed	disbursing		
dissipate*	dissipated	dissipating	dissipation	
emerge	emerged	emerging	emergency	
endorse	endorsed	endorsing	endorsable	
enumerate*	enumerated	enumerating	enumeration	
exaggerate	exaggerated	exaggerating	exaggeration	
execute	executed	executing	execution	
exonerate*	exonerated	exonerating	exoneration	
facilitate*	facilitated	facilitating	facilitation	
fascinate	fascinated	fascinating	fascination	
finance	financed	financing	financial	
fluctuate*	fluctuated	fluctuating	fluctuation	
foreclose*	foreclosed	foreclosing	foreclosure	
guide	guided	guiding	guidance	
illuminate	illuminated	illuminating	illumination	
imagine	imagined	imagining	imagination	
imitate	imitated	imitating	imitation	
insinuate*	insinuated	insinuating	insinuation	
issue	issued	issuing	issuance	
italicize*	italicized	italicizing		
itemize	itemized	itemizing	itemization	
lease	leased	leasing		
license	licensed	licensing		
liquidate*	liquidated	liquidating	liquidation	
measure	measured	measuring	measurable	
move	moved	moving	movable	
note	noted	noting	notable	notation
notice	noticed	noticing		
owe	owed	owing		
persevere*	persevered	persevering	perseverance	
preserve	preserved	preserving	preservation	
pursue	pursued	pursuing	pursuant	
rate	rated	rating		
reconcile*	reconciled	reconciling		
recycle	recycled	recycling	recyclable	
reimburse*	reimbursed	reimbursing		
reiterate*	reiterated	reiterating	reiteration	
release	released	releasing		

reverse	reversed	reversing	reversible	reversal
sale	salable			
sample	sampled	sampling		
schedule	scheduled	scheduling		
seize	seized	seizing	seizure	
separate	separated	separating	separation	
supervise	supervised	supervising	supervisor	
transpose*	transposed	transposing	transposable	transposition
type	typed	typing	typist	
use	used	using	usage	
value	valued	valuing	valuable	
waste	wasted	wasting		

There are two groups of exceptions to the rule.

 Exception 1 Words ending in **ce** or **ge** do *not* drop the **e** before **able** and **ous**.

You need to retain the **e** to keep the **c** and **g** *soft*—like **s** and **j**. This is the way they sound in words like **noticeable, marriageable,** and **courageous**.

Because the vowels **e** and **i** indicate that when the consonants **c** and **g** precede them, they are to be pronounced with the soft **s** and **j** sounds, **e** and **i** are termed *softening vowels*.

Thus we can drop the final **e** of **notice** for **noticing**, but we must retain it for **noticeable**.

acknowledge	acknowledgeable	manage	manageable
advantage	advantageous	marriage	marriageable
change	changeable	notice	noticeable
courage	courageous	outrage	outrageous
damage	damageable	peace	peaceable
disadvantage	disadvantageous	pronounce	pronounceable
enforce	enforceable	replace	replaceable
exchange	exchangeable	service	serviceable
knowledge	knowledgeable	trace	traceable

Exception 2 A few words do not drop the final **e** because to do so would lead to mispronunciation or confusion.

Two of these words are **dye** and **singe**.

dye	dyeing	singe	singeing

Retaining the final **e** makes the distinction clear between **dye—dyeing** and **die—dying**, between **singe—singeing** and **sing—singing**. Other words that do not drop the final **e** are:

canoe	canoeing	shoe	shoeing
hinge	hingeing	tinge	tingeing
hoe	hoeing	toe	toeing

Other exceptions include **acreage, lineage, lineal**, and **mileage**.

Rule 2

Retain the final **e** when you add a suffix beginning with a consonant.

---

achieve	achievement	improve	improvement
advertise	advertisement	induce*	inducement
commence	commencement	like	likely
complete	completely	live	lively
definite	definitely	manage	management
encourage	encouragement	measure	measurement
enlarge	enlargement	move	movement
excite	excitement	noise	noiseless
forgive	forgiveness	require	requirement
hope	hopeful	safe	safety
		shame	shameless

The following words are exceptions:

abridge*	abridgment	judge	judgment
acknowledge	acknowledgment	nine	ninth
argue	argument	true	truly
awe	awful	whole	wholly
due	duly	wise	wisdom

NAME	CLASS	DATE	SCORE

Spelling Assignments

A. Mentally add the suffix **ing** to each of the following words. Then write the complete word in the space provided.

1.	please	_____	11.	judge	_____
2.	move	_____	12.	infringe	_____
3.	hope	_____	13.	eliminate	_____
4.	give	_____	14.	illuminate	_____
5.	depreciate	_____	15.	prepare	_____
6.	argue	_____	16.	commence	_____
7.	shoe	_____	17.	schedule	_____
8.	waste	_____	18.	aggravate	_____
9.	age	_____	19.	exaggerate	_____
10.	singe	_____	20.	believe	_____

B. Mentally add the suffix **able** to each of the following words. Then write the complete word in the space provided.

1.	dispose	_____	11.	value	_____
2.	argue	_____	12.	notice	_____
3.	move	_____	13.	marriage	_____
4.	desire	_____	14.	pleasure	_____
5.	like	_____	15.	knowledge	_____
6.	sale	_____	16.	manage	_____
7.	change	_____	17.	advise	_____
8.	charge	_____	18.	excuse	_____
9.	embrace	_____	19.	measure	_____
10.	pronounce	_____	20.	receive	_____

C. Mentally add the suffix **ous** to each of the following words. Then write the complete word in the space provided.

1.	courage	_____	6.	virtue	_____
2.	advantage	_____	7.	adventure	_____
3.	outrage	_____	8.	grieve	_____
4.	desire	_____	9.	fame	_____
5.	continue	_____	10.	nerve	_____

D. Underline the misspelled word or words in each of the following groups of three. Spell the word or words correctly in the space at the right. If there are no errors in the group, write C.

1.	linage	lively	safety	1.	_____
2.	sincerly	noiseless	hopeful	2.	_____
3.	completely	useage	argument	3.	_____
4.	comeing	hingeing	displacement	4.	_____
5.	discouragement	aweful	disbursement	5.	_____
6.	manageable	duly	ninth	6.	_____
7.	wisdom	salvageable	enforceable	7.	_____
8.	knowledgeable	wholly	quotable	8.	_____
9.	wasteful	enumerating	truly	9.	_____
10.	believable	irreplaceable	peacable	10.	_____
11.	accommodation	chargable	advisory	11.	_____
12.	loseing	interfered	facilitateing	12.	_____
13.	pursuant	noticeable	perseverance	13.	_____
14.	forgivness	achievement	compensation	14.	_____
15.	reiterateion	criticized	approval	15.	_____
16.	commencment	preservation	disciplining	16.	_____
17.	emergency	requirment	contributor	17.	_____
18.	dyeing	exercising	fascination	18.	_____
19.	dividing	realization	deriveing	19.	_____
20.	exaggeration	scarcly	imitation	20.	_____
21.	surely	enclosure	typeist	21.	_____

22. practicing	exonerating	imagineable	22._____
23. survival	separation	reimbursing	23._____
24. inducment	allocation	balancing	24._____
25. concentration	changable	definitely	25._____
26. communicative	italicized	liquidation	26._____
27. fluctuation	exhilaration	arrangment	27._____
28. acknowledgement	owed	surprised	28._____
29. likness	observance	accumulation	29._____
30. typewriting	canoeing	preparatory	30._____
31. infringment	slideing	elimination	31._____
32. reconciling	couragous	continuable	32._____
33. completion	congratulatory	dissipating	33._____
34. supervision	acrage	survival	34._____
35. standardization	superseding	censureable	35._____
36. advertising	packageing	sampled	36._____
37. transposition	endorsment	receiving	37._____
38. responsibly	citeing	insurable	38._____
39. serviceable	releasing	owing	39._____
40. foreclosure	outragous	announcing	40._____
41. pronouncement	tinging	tracing	41._____
42. deleted	leasing	noteable	42._____
43. reconciled	definable	issueance	43._____
44. valuing	exchangeable	dining	44._____
45. executing	guidance	traceable	45._____
46. disadvantagous	announcement	eliminating	46._____
47. reimbursement	insinuateing	improvment	47._____
48. recombining	imitating	mileage	48._____
49. shameless	likly	conceding	49._____
50. reversible	abridgement	acknowledging	50._____

Homonyms

fate destiny: *It was his fate to lose the election.*
fete (noun) a festival, especially one held out-of-doors: *The Mardi Gras is an annual fete held before Lent in New Orleans*; (verb) to celebrate an honor with festivities: *Her colleagues will fete Ms. Chin.*

feat an act or accomplishment showing great daring, skill, ingenuity: *Developing this new technology was a tremendous feat.*
feet plural of *foot,* terminal part of the leg, measurement: *Brent leaned back in his chair and put his feet on the desk, which is seven feet wide.*

find to discover: *Enrique tried to find the error in the checkbook.*
fined past tense of *fine,* to require to pay a sum of money as punishment for an offense: *The judge fined him $25.*

fir a type of evergreen tree: *A row of fir trees marks the far boundary.*
fur the skin and hair of an animal, garment made of such skins: *Ms. Wade bought a new fur coat last week.*

fisher one who fishes: *Leonard is a skilled fisher;* an animal similar to, but much larger than, a weasel: *At the lake last week we saw a fisher on the bank eating a trout.*
fissure crack in a wall or rock: *Moss grew in the fissure in the wall.*

flair a natural talent or aptitude: *Adrienne has a flair for creating effective window displays.*
flare to burn unsteadily: *The fire may flare up suddenly*; to express strong emotion: *He would flare up at the slightest provocation.*

flea (noun) a small parasitic jumping insect: *One flea can bite often.*
flee (verb) to run away: *The sudden storm forced us to flee to our cars.*

flew past tense of *fly,* to pass through the air: *The plane flew at an altitude of 30,000 feet.*
flu short for *influenza,* a virus disease: *Many people are off work with the flu.*
flue a pipe for conveying smoke: *Keep your chimney flue clean to avoid fires.*

flour ground grain used in baking: *Our company supplies flour to bakeries throughout the state.*
flower the bloom of a plant: *She placed a fresh flower on her desk every morning.*

for (preposition) *for* is used in various ways: *I have a message for the president. She left for home an hour ago. We are looking for a house to rent*; (conjunction) because: *I believe Iako will win, for he is better prepared.*

fore (noun) the front, toward the beginning: *Early in the meeting, the main issues were brought to the fore*; (interjection) in golf, a warning to those ahead of an errant shot that might hit them: *Fore!*

four the number (4): *Marjorie was one of four people to receive a promotion.*

forbear (fôr ber′) to hold back, refrain: *I will forbear responding to those remarks.*

forebear (fôr′′ ber′) ancestor: *Norman's forebears came to this country from Denmark.*

foreword an introduction or preface: *The annual report contains a foreword by the president of the company.*

forward at or near the front: *Ms. Jacobs requested one of the ship's forward cabins.*

fort a fortified building for military defense: *This old fort is a tourist attraction.*

forte something at which a person excels: *Marketing strategy is his forte.*

Note	forte (fôr′ tā) is a musical term meaning *loud*.

forth forward, onward: *Our sales have increased steadily from that day forth.*

fourth preceded by three others in a series: *Sales for the fourth quarter are up over 30 percent.*

foul disgusting: *There is a foul odor in the air today*; stormy: *Foul weather would spoil the company picnic*; unfair: *Our competitor is guilty of foul tactics in its sales campaign*; out of bounds in baseball: *He caught a foul ball at the game.*

fowl a bird used for food: *Turkey and chicken are fowl.*

gait the manner of walking or running: *Mr. Tanaka walked with a firm gait*; the various movements of a horse: *This horse has three gaits—walk, trot, and canter.*

gate a movable structure across an entrance or exit: *The gate to the supply yard is unlocked*; the total admission money paid by spectators to a performance: *The gate for the Sharkey-Mills fight was $1,000,000.*

gamble to bet, wager: *It is illegal to gamble in most states.*

gambol to skip about in play: *The children loved to gambol on the lawn.*

gild to overlay with a thin covering of gold: *Mr. Mucci wanted to gild the letters on his nameplate.*

guild an association of persons with similar interests or pursuits, a union: *Members of the local newspaper guild have voted to go on strike.*

gilt a thin layer of gold: *Ms. Wu's name was put on the office door in gilt letters.*

guilt state of having committed a wrong: *There was no doubt about the criminal's guilt.*

grate (verb) to have an unpleasant effect upon: *Loud noises grate on my nerves*; to grind into small pieces: *This gadget will grate cheese with ease*; (noun) a framework of iron bars to hold firelogs: *The fireplace grate is crooked.*

great large, important: *Great people can admit their mistakes.*

NAME	CLASS	DATE	SCORE

Homonym Assignments

A. Select from the following words the one that correctly fits the blank in each of the sentences below. Then write the word in the answer space.

fate	fined	four	forth	guild
fete	flair	foreword	fourth	gilt
feat	flare	forward	foul	guilt
feet	for	fort	fowl	
find	fore	forte	gild	

1. In all these years, the _____ on the trophy never tarnished.   1._____

2. Tony's answers indicated his _____.   2._____

3. The smoke alarm sounded as soon as the fire began to _____ up.   3._____

4. I assumed that Margaret was _____ in seniority because she followed Bob, who was third.   4._____

5. Working well with people is Ms. Mason's _____.   5._____

6. After the orientation meeting, each member went _____ with greater understanding about the planned changes.   6._____

7. Optical disk storage is in the _____ of the newly developing technologies.   7._____

8. When I discussed the banquet menu with the caterer, she indicated that the price of fish would be the same as the price of _____.   8._____

9. Salespersons in retail stores spend the greater part of a day on their _____.   9._____

10. It is better to plan than to leave things to _____.   10._____

11. To retrieve information is much the same as to _____ information.   11._____

12. His work was acknowledged in the _____ of the program.   12._____

13. The defendant was _____ for contempt of court.   13._____

14. Accepting the presidency and then never showing up for the meeting was a _____ move.   14. _____

15. The party was held to _____ Hector's promotion.   15. _____

B. In some of the following sentences, an incorrect word is used. Underline the incorrect word, and write the correct word in the space provided. Where there is no error, write C in the answer space.

1. The security officers at the gate checked her badge.   1. _____

2. When making an extreme product change, the manufacturer always takes a gambol.   2. _____

3. Following knee surgery, his gate seemed much slower.   3. _____

4. Mr. Evans, who is the current owner, inherited the business from his forebears.   4. _____

5. After a bout with the flue, Martine returned to work.   5. _____

6. The sound of the fire alarm caused the workers to flea the office in a hurry.   6. _____

7. Mavis tried to forebear crying.   7. _____

8. Because it was clogged, the flew pipe poured smoke out through the vents.   8. _____

9. Rudy's flair for drama makes him a dynamic, popular speaker.   9. _____

10. The architects were concerned with the fissure in the foundation.   10. _____

11. Betty never did wear her fir coat to work.   11. _____

12. The cheerful flower on the desk brightened up the otherwise drab décor.   12. _____

13. It was evident that the landscaper had a preference for fir trees.   13. _____

14. The ingredients included cornstarch, not flower.   14. _____

15. The building is of grate historic interest.   15. _____

C. Read the definition, and select the correct word from the second column to match that description. Write the word you selected in the answer space.

Definition	Word Choice	
1. small parasitic jumping insect	flea, flee	1. _____
2. one who fishes	fisher, fissure	2. _____

3. past tense of *fly*	flew, flu, flue	3._____
4. a fortified building for military defense	fort, forte	4._____
5. large, important	grate, great	5._____
6. the manner of walking or running	gait, gate	6._____
7. to express strong emotion	flair, flare	7._____
8. a warning in the game of golf	for, fore, four	8._____
9. plural of *foot*	feat, feet	9._____
10. a festival	fate, fete	10._____

D. Select the right word for the sentence shown, and write it in the answer space. Then compose a sentence for the homonym not selected, and write your sentence in the space provided.

1. Over 500,000 members belong to the newspaper (gild, guild).

    1._____

_____

_____

_____

2. A tremendous (feat, feet) was accomplished by the crew who worked overtime.

    2._____

_____

_____

_____

3. The (flew, flu) caused heavy absenteeism.

    3._____

_____

_____

_____

4. Moving the desks (foreword, forward) made the office appear more spacious.

    4._____

_____

_____

_____

5. My (fort, forte) is organizing conferences.

5. _____

_____

_____

_____

6. The Baxters' (fir, fur) tree was struck by lightning.

6. _____

_____

_____

_____

7. They shopped (for, fore) a birthday present.

7. _____

_____

_____

_____

8. In the (Foreword, Forward), the author thanked all those who had done research for the book.

8. _____

_____

_____

_____

9. It was Robin's job to (grate, great) the cheese.

9. _____

_____

_____

_____

10. The (Forth, Fourth) of July is a patriotic holiday.

10. _____

_____

_____

_____

ei and ie Words

Chapter 6

In the previous two chapters you have studied three very valuable rules that can help you decide whether to add or subtract letters when you change the form of a word. By knowing these three rules, you can spell thousands of words correctly and without hesitation. Knowing a fourth rule will guide you in spelling correctly hundreds of other words that contain either the **ei** or **ie** combination. This rule is expressed in the following verse:

Rule

Write **i** before **e**

Except after **c**

Or when sounded like **a**

As in **neighbor** or **weigh**.

There are three parts to this rule. Let's look at each one separately.

1. Write **i** before **e**. This is the general rule. The majority of **ei—ie** words contain the **ie** combination.

achieve	convenient	lien*	relieve
adieu	field	lieutenant	reprieve*
aggrieve*	fiend	mien	retrieve
alien*	fiery	mischief	review
audience	friend	niece	shield
belief	frontier	patient	shriek
believe	grief	piece	siege
besiege	grievous	pier	thief
brief	hierarchy*	pierce	tier
cashier	hieroglyphic*	priest	transient*
chandelier	hygiene	recipient*	unwieldy*
chief	lenient	relief	yield*
client			

2.   Except after **c**. After **c** use **ei**.

ceiling	deceit	inconceivable	receipt
conceit	deceitful	perceive*	receive
conceive	deceive	preconceive	

Exceptions   There are some exceptions to this part of the rule.

ancient	efficient	omniscient	society
conscience	financier	proficient*	species
conscientious	inefficient	science	sufficient
deficient	insufficient	scientific	

3.   Use **ei** when sounded like **a** as in **neighbor** or **weigh**. There are no exceptions to this part of the rule. It holds true in all instances.

beige	freight	obeisance	spontaneity
chow mein	heinous*	reign	surveillance*
deign*	heir	rein	veil
eight	inveigh	reindeer	vein
feign	neigh	skein	weigh
feint	neighbor	sleigh	weight

Exceptions   Now look at the exceptions to the general rule. Master these few exceptions, and you have mastered *all* **ei** and **ie** words. Any word that is not an exception follows the rule.

caffeine	foreign	neither	sleight
codeine	foreigner	protein	sovereign*
counterfeit*	forfeit*	seismograph	sovereignty
either	heifer	seize	surfeit*
Fahrenheit	height	seizure	their
feisty	leisure	sheik	weird

Spelling Assignments

A. Insert **ei** or **ie** (whichever is correct) in the spaces in the following words. Then rewrite the complete word on the line to the right.

1.   c_____ling   _____

2.   n_____ghbor   _____

3.   ach_____ve   _____

4.   bel _____ve   _____

5.   p_____r   _____

6.   d_____ gn   _____

7.   w _____ght   _____

8.   rel_____ve   _____

9.   rab_____s   _____

10.   s_____ze   _____

11.   w _____rd   _____

12.   r_____ gn   _____

13.   fr _____ nd   _____

14.   consc____nce   _____

15.   h_____ght   _____

16.   sl _____ght   _____

17.   f _____ry   _____

18.   h_____ rarchy   _____

19.   counterf ____t   _____

20.   forf _____t   _____

21.   for _____ gn   _____

22.   sover ____ gn   _____

23.   s_____ve   _____

24.   misch___vous   _____

25.   al _____ n   _____

B. Underline the misspelled word or words in each of the following groups of three. Spell the word or words correctly in the space at the right. If there are no errors in the group, write C.

1.	pierce	feind	chief	1._____
2.	chandelier	briefcase	freight	2._____
3.	deceit	ceiling	vein	3._____
4.	siege	sieze	surfiet	4._____
5.	leisure	either	protein	5._____
6.	neither	feign	rein	6._____
7.	veil	skien	eight	7._____

8. handkerchief	greif	cashier	8. _____
9. field	friend	neice	9. _____
10. piece	priest	Fahrenhiet	10. _____
11. aggrieve	ancient	cleint	11. _____
12. thievery	weild	neighbor	12. _____
13. frontier	reprieve	quotient	13. _____
14. greif	codeine	mien	14. _____
15. financier	surveillance	lein	15. _____
16. hygiene	deceitful	efficient	16. _____
17. proficient	review	reciept	17. _____
18. science	chow mien	caffiene	18. _____
19. besiege	recipient	transient	19. _____
20. achieve	yield	shiek	20. _____
21. society	thier	spontaneity	21. _____
22. theif	hiefer	scientific	22. _____
23. inconceivable	fiesty	inefficeint	23. _____
24. teir	shriek	omnisceint	24. _____
25. audience	conscientious	inviegh	25. _____

Homonyms

groan   to utter a deep sound expressing pain, distress, or disapproval: *The class greeted the announcement of a surprise quiz with a loud groan*; to make a creaking or grating sound as from great strain: *The shelves groaned from the weight of the heavy legal volumes.*

grown   the past participle of *grow*, to increase in size and develop toward maturity: *Mr. Montanya's daughter has grown a great deal since the last time I saw her.*

guessed   past tense of *guess*, form a judgment or estimate of something without actual knowledge: *We guessed what Mrs. Martinez had in mind.*

guest   a person entertained at the home of another, a visitor: *Mr. Patvin will be our guest next weekend.*

hail   (noun) frozen rain: *Hail pelted the roof*; (verb) to call loudly to: *It took twenty minutes to hail a cab*; to greet: *The band played "Hail to the Chief."*

hale   (adjective) strong, healthy: *Mr. Ortiz is hale and hearty*; (verb) to compel to go: *They want to hale him into court.*

hair   a threadlike outgrowth: *The barber is skilled at cutting hair.*

hare   a rabbitlike animal: *The hounds chased the hare.*

hall   passageway or corridor: *A narrow hall connects the two rooms*; a large room for gatherings: *Independence Hall is located in Philadelphia.*

haul   (verb) to move goods by wagon, truck, etc.: *We hired an independent trucking company to haul the supplies*; (noun) the distance over which something is transported: *It is a long haul from here to the new plant*; the amount gained at one time: *The boat brought in a good haul of fish.*

hangar   a shelter for airplanes: *The plane is in the hangar for repairs.*

hanger   one who hangs something: *Mr. Douglas once worked as a paper hanger*; a thing on which something is hung: *Put your coat on a hanger in the closet.*

hart   a male deer: *The hart bounded through the forest.*

heart   muscular organ: *Mrs. Jones suffered a heart attack*; the center or essential part of something: *The heart of the proposal is the freeze on hiring.*

heal   to bring back to health: *It takes time for such a wound to heal completely.*

heel   part of the foot: *Ray bruised his heel playing tennis*; part of a shoe: *Deena broke the heel on her shoe.*

hear   to perceive by ear: *I can't hear you.*

here   in this place: *Bring it here.*

heard   past tense of *hear: We heard from them yesterday.*

herd   a group of animals: *A herd of cows grazed in the field.*

hew to cut with an ax or knife: *The forest rangers proceeded to hew down the trees.*

hue a particular color: *The coat was a reddish hue.*

higher farther up: *Move the books to a higher shelf.*

hire to employ: *We need to hire someone to replace Mr. Farnaby.*

him objective case of the pronoun *he: Send him the bill.*

hymn song in praise or honor of God: *The choir sang a beautiful hymn.*

hoard to save greedily, store away: *Misers prefer to hoard their money rather than spend it.*

horde an overwhelming number of people: *A horde of shoppers waited for the doors to open.*

hoarse sounding rough and deep: *Nellie's voice is hoarse today.*

horse a four-legged animal: *Shirley owns a horse.*

hole an open, hollow place: *Rita stepped in a hole and twisted her ankle.*

whole having all its parts, complete: *The whole process takes less than an hour.*

holy sacred: *Helen keeps a copy of the Holy Bible on her night stand.*

wholly entirely: *I am not wholly satisfied with your report.*

hour sixty minutes: *The meeting lasted less than an hour.*

our belonging to us: *We believe our product is the best of its kind on the market.*

idle doing nothing, not busy, lazy: *The steel plant was idle for two months.*

idol any object worshipped as a god: *The golden idol was the highlight of the exhibit.*

incidence rate of occurrence: *This store has a high incidence of theft.*

incidents plural of *incident,* happening, event: *There were no violent incidents during the demonstration.*

NAME	CLASS	DATE	SCORE

Homonym Assignments

A. Select from the following words the one that correctly fits the blank in each of the sentences below. Then write the word in the answer space.

groan	hare	hews	horde	idle
grown	hall	hues	holy	idol
guessed	haul	higher	wholly	incidence
guest	hear	hire	hour	incidents
hair	here	hoard	our	

1. The person who _____ the closest number was the winner.

    1._____

2. Russ became Pete's _____ after Russ courageously defended the controversial proposal.

    2._____

3. The poor acoustics made it difficult to _____ the speaker.

    3._____

4. The truckers had to make a long _____ with the delivery.

    4._____

5. The office décor was in the autumn _____ of brown, gold, and orange.

    5._____

6. Each member was allowed to bring a _____ to the meeting.

    6._____

7. The use of computers in business has _____ immensely.

    7._____

8. Mrs. Chen was invited to serve as _____ speaker.

    8._____

9. The copier was placed in the outside _____ for easier access.

    9._____

10. To provide for better office coverage, we used a staggered lunch _____ plan.

    10._____

11. I was shocked by the increasing _____ of computer crime.

    11._____

12. The _____ of angry commuters charged onto the train, which was twenty-five minutes late.

    12._____

13. Mary and Jim remind me of the _____ and the tortoise in the way they go about their work.

13. _____

14. Consumers sometimes _____ products when they find out that there will be a price increase.

14. _____

15. I feel _____ responsible for her misfortune.

15. _____

B. In some of the following sentences, an incorrect word is used. Underline the incorrect word, and write the correct word in the space provided. Where there is no error, write C in the answer space.

1. It is about 225 miles from hear to Washington, D.C.

1. _____

2. The rancher sold the herd of sheep for a substantial profit.

2. _____

3. Within the our, I am expecting an important phone call.

3. _____

4. Lynn heard the rumor through the grapevine.

4. _____

5. Affirmative action laws are hailed by women, minorities, and older workers.

5. _____

6. The hymn books sold by the publisher were described as a collection of favorites.

6. _____

7. The hole food service system is currently under review.

7. _____

8. Claims for damage caused by hale are not valid for insurance purposes.

8. _____

9. She will be out of work for the next three weeks at least—or until her injuries heel.

9. _____

10. Please place the box on a higher shelf.

10. _____

11. Ms. Rodriguez said she wanted to hire someone as soon as possible.

11. _____

12. I felt wholly inadequate when I had to cover Marty's job without any training.

12. _____

13. A cold can make your voice horse.

13. _____

14. Some people feel that budget cutting is at the hart of curing inflation.

14. _____

15. I returned the hanger to the dry cleaner.

15. _____

C. Read the definition, and select the correct word from the second column to match that description. Write the word you selected in the answer space.

Definition	Word Choice	
1. a male deer	hart, heart	1._____
2. a shelter for airplanes	hangar, hanger	2._____
3. a large room for gatherings	hall, haul	3._____
4. to bring back to health	heal, heel	4._____
5. to cut with an ax or knife	hew, hue	5._____
6. to save greedily	hoard, horde	6._____
7. a group of animals	heard, herd	7._____
8. a rabbitlike animal	hair, hare	8._____
9. to employ	higher, hire	9._____
10. rate of occurrence	incidence, incidents	10._____

D. Select the right word for the sentence shown, and write it in the answer space. Then compose a sentence for the homonym not selected, and write your sentence in the space provided.

1. Martina hung her jacket on a (hangar, hanger).   1._____

   _____

   _____

   _____

2. The woodcutter was able to (hew, hue) down the
   bushes to clear a path.   2._____

   _____

   _____

   _____

3. Can you distribute (hour, our) report today?   3._____

   _____

   _____

   _____

4. He (guessed, guest) who would make the report for the
   committee.   4. _____

   _____

   _____

   _____

5. How did you (hear, here) about our product line?   5. _____

   _____

   _____

   _____

6. A three-(hole, whole) punch is a handy tool.   6. _____

   _____

   _____

   _____

7. The movers found it hard to (hall, haul) the heavy file
   cabinets.   7. _____

   _____

   _____

   _____

8. The (him, hymn) books were placed in the pews.   8. _____

   _____

   _____

   _____

9. Madelyn's (hoarse, horse) won the race.   9. _____

   _____

   _____

   _____

10. The (incidence, incidents) of error increased.   10. _____

   _____

   _____

   _____

Double Letters

Many words are misspelled because they contain double letters. Some have only one set of double letters, like **accustom** or **affirm**. Others have two sets of double letters, like **accommodate** or **embarrass**. A few have three sets of double letters, like **committee** or **bookkeeper**.

You will find the rule for doubling the final consonant helpful in spelling some of these words. Most of them, however, are not covered by any particular rule. These are the words stressed in this chapter. Study them until their correct spelling is firmly established in your mind. To help you concentrate on the difficult spots, these words are grouped according to the double letters they have in common.

cc

accede	accord	accurate	occupation
accept	accordingly	accuse	occupy
accident	accordion	accustom	occur
acclaim	account	eccentric	stucco
accolade	accredited	occasion	succumb*
accompany	accrue	occasional	tobacco
accomplish	accumulate	occupancy	vaccinate

ff

affected	affix	difficulty	offset
affection	affliction	diffuse	sheriff
affidavit*	chauffeur	effort	suffer
affiliate*	chiffon	effusive	sufficient
affirm	difference	offensive	suffocate
affirmative	different	offer	traffic

105

gg

aggravate	aggressive	exaggerate	luggage
aggregate*	baggage	haggard*	suggest

ll

allege*	bulletin	collision	metallic
allergic	bullion	collusion	millinery
alleviate*	cancellation	crystallize	million
alliance	cellophane	excellent	parallel
allocate	challenge	fallacy	poll
allot	chancellor	gallery	propeller
allow	collaborate	illusion	rebellion
allude	collateral*	illustrate	surveillance
ballast	colleague*	illustrious	tranquillity
billion	collect	intellect	villain
brilliant	college	intelligible	

mm

ammonia	commercial	dilemma	recommend
ammunition	commodity	grammar	rummage
command	communication	immediately	summary
commence	communism	immense	summer
comment	community	immortal	summons
commerce			

nn

annex	annuity*	cinnamon	innovation*
annihilate	annul*	connect	innumerable*
anniversary	antenna	connotation	questionnaire
annotate	beginner	flannel	tunnel
announce	centennial*	innocent	tyranny
annual			

pp

apparatus	appetite	appraisal*	opponent
apparel	applause	appreciate	opportunity
apparent	apples	approach	oppose
appear	application	appropriate	opposite
append	apply	approve	support
appendicitis	appoint	approximate	suppose

rr

arrange	corrupt	hurricane	irritate
arrears*	currency	interrupt	mirror
arrive	curriculum	irrational	narrative
arrogance	errand	irregular	surrender
carry	error	irrelevant	surround
correlate	furrier	irresistible	terrestrial
correspond	horrendous	irresponsible	terrific
corridor	horrible	irrigate	territory
corroborate*	horror	irritable	warrant

ss

assail*	assurance	issues	permission
assembly	assured	losses	permissive
assets	dismissal	massacre	process
assimilate*	duress*	massive	profess
assistance	emissary	messenger	professional
associate	excess	mission	professor
assortment	glossary	misspell	promissory
assuage	glossy	molasses	recession*
assume	harass*	necessary	scissors
assumption	issuance	passive	tissues

tt

acquittal*	attire	battalion	mutton
attack	attitude	flattery	operetta
attend	attract	glutton	pattern
attention	attribute	lettuce	platter

Miscellaneous

access	bookkeeper	engineer	stubborn
accessory	career	indiscreet	succeed
accommodate	coffee	mattress	success
address	committee	occurrence	suppress
assessment*	embarrass	possess	vacuum
balloon	embezzle*	seethe*	

NAME	CLASS	DATE	SCORE

Spelling Assignments

A. Insert **c** or **cc** (whichever is correct) in the spaces in the following words. Then rewrite the complete word on the line to the right.

1. a____ omplish _____
2. a____ umulate _____
3. a_____ urate _____
4. a_____ tion _____
5. a_____tual _____
6. a____ustomed _____
7. o_____upy _____
8. a____ ording _____
9. o_____ ur _____
10. o_____ asion _____

11. a_____ ede _____
12. toba _____ o _____
13. stu _____ o _____
14. a___ommodate _____
15. va_____inate _____
16. a_____use _____
17. a_____ ept _____
18. fa _____tual _____
19. a_____ orn _____
20. su_____ umb _____

B. Insert **f** or **ff** (whichever is correct) in the spaces in the following words. Then rewrite the complete word on the line to the right.

1. a_____ idavit _____
2. a_____iliate _____
3. a_____ ter _____
4. re _____ er _____
5. a_____ection _____

6. chau_____eur _____
7. di _____ icult _____
8. de_____ er _____
9. su_____ icient _____
10. su_____ ocate _____

C. Insert **g** or **gg** (whichever is correct) in the spaces in the following words. Then rewrite the complete word on the line to the right.

1. a_____ ravate _____
2. lu _____ age _____
3. ba_____ age _____

4. di _____ est _____
5. a_____ regate _____
6. exa____ erate _____

7. a ____ ressive   _____   9. ha _____ ard   _____

8. a _____ ent   _____   10. su ____ estion   _____

D. Insert **l** or **ll** (whichever is correct) in the spaces in the following words. Then rewrite the complete word on the line to the right.

1. a _____ ege   _____   11. co ____ ateral   _____

2. a _____ ergy   _____   12. co ____ eague   _____

3. a _____ ot   _____   13. co _____ ect   _____

4. a ____ ternate   _____   14. co _____ ege   _____

5. a _____ most   _____   15. fa_____ acy   _____

6. a ___ together   _____   16. fa_____ter   _____

7. ba _____ ance   _____   17. inte ____ igent   _____

8. co _____ ision   _____   18. para_____ el   _____

9. bu _____ etin   _____   19. prope_____ er   _____

10. ce ___ ophane   _____   20. re_____ evant   _____

E. Insert **m** or **mm** (whichever is correct) in the spaces in the following words. Then rewrite the complete word on the line to the right.

1. co ____ petent   _____   6. dile _____ a   _____

2. co _____ and   _____   7. i_____ediately   _____

3. co _____ plete   _____   8. reco_____ end   _____

4. co _____ unity   _____   9. stu_____ ble   _____

5. co _____ erce   _____   10. su _____ er   _____

F. Insert **n** or **nn** (whichever is correct) in the spaces in the following words. Then rewrite the complete word on the line to the right.

1. a ____ iversary   _____   6. cente_____ ial   _____

2. a ____ otation   _____   7. i_____ ept   _____

3. a _____ uity   _____   8. i_____ ovation   _____

4. a _____ ul   _____   9. questio ___ aire   _____

5. begi_____ ing   _____   10. tyra _____ y   _____

G. Insert **p** or **pp** (whichever is correct) in the spaces in the following words. Then rewrite the complete word on the line to the right.

1. a_____ aratus _____
2. pur _____ose _____
3. su_____ose _____
4. o_____osite _____
5. o_____ortunity _____
6. a____roximate _____
7. a_____ologize _____
8. a_____ reciate _____
9. a_____ lication _____
10. a_____ lause _____

11. dis ____ osition _____
12. a_____ ear _____
13. a_____ arent _____
14. a_____ raisal _____
15. disa _____oint _____
16. su_____ ort _____
17. A _____ ril _____
18. re _____ ly _____
19. a_____ roach _____
20. a_____ etite _____

H. Insert **r** or **rr** (whichever is correct) in the spaces in the following words. Then rewrite the complete word on the line to the right.

1. a_____ ange _____
2. te___est___ial _____
3. te___ito____y _____
4. co___obo___ate _____
5. se_____iously _____
6. e_____ and _____
7. i _____elevant _____
8. i ____ esistible _____
9. i __ esponsible _____
10. i _____ onic _____

11. i _____ itate _____
12. su_____ender _____
13. a_____ogance _____
14. te _____ ific _____
15. hu_____ icane _____
16. i _____ ate _____
17. fu _____ or _____
18. fu _____ ier _____
19. wa _____ ant _____
20. cu_____ ent _____

I. Insert **s** or **ss** (whichever is correct) in the spaces in the following words. Then rewrite the complete word on the line to the right.

1. sci_____ors _____
2. po___e__ion _____
3. mi_____ion _____
4. me____enger _____
5. emi_____ary _____

6. a_____leep _____
7. ma___culine _____
8. hara_____ _____
9. nece_____ary _____
10. di___mi__al _____

J. Insert **t** or **tt** (whichever is correct) in the spaces in the following words. Then rewrite the complete word on the line to the right.

1. a _____ ire _____
2. A _____ lantic _____
3. a _____ ack _____
4. a ___ en ____ ion _____
5. a _____ ract _____

6. a ____ ribu ___ e _____
7. glu _____ on _____
8. pa _____ ient _____
9. pa _____ ern _____
10. fla _____ ery _____

K. Underline the misspelled word or words in each of the following groups of four. Spell the word or words correctly in the space at the right. If there are no errors in the group, write C.

1.	apparel	afiliate	assail	sheriff	1. _____
2.	assert	assimilate	conotation	acusation	2. _____
3.	appliance	assurance	suffocate	dismissal	3. _____
4.	excess	aportion	scissors	intelligible	4. _____
5.	appraisal	harass	millinery	masacre	5. _____
6.	indiscrete	messenger	approve	difference	6. _____
7.	molasses	profess	adress	supose	7. _____
8.	proffessor	apply	assumption	deference	8. _____
9.	accessory	seeth	appalling	rebellion	9. _____
10.	balloon	bookeeper	coffee	appetite	10. _____
11.	committee	asociate	mattress	summary	11. _____
12.	possess	suppress	vacuum	interupt	12. _____
13.	ammonia	dilemma	reccomend	promissory	13. _____
14.	roommate	irresistible	irritate	commerce	14. _____
15.	hurricane	irelevant	errand	summons	15. _____
16.	brilliant	disappeared	sugest	questionaire	16. _____
17.	challenge	embarrass	occasional	irregular	17. _____
18.	necesarily	disapointment	correspond	territory	18. _____
19.	comunity	commission	imediately	opportunity	19. _____
20.	intelligent	annotate	college	clipping	20. _____
21.	offset	chancellor	surveilance	acrue	21. _____

22.	affix	pollish	approximate	oponent	22._____
23.	antena	arrears	settlement	assured	23._____
24.	remitance	process	occurrence	tissues	24._____
25.	issues	attorney	assets	durress	25._____
26.	suffered	intelligible	occupational	erased	26._____
27.	tobaco	annex	appointment	refer	27._____
28.	accidental	polled	acountant	carried	28._____
29.	luggage	ammunition	acomodation	misspelled	29._____
30.	allergy	aggregate	ocupied	recession	30._____
31.	colleague	remited	billion	errors	31._____
32.	annihilate	apendicitis	ofensive	lettuce	32._____
33.	anual	flattered	attitude	imitate	33._____
34.	apparent	necessity	questionaire	applicant	34._____
35.	immense	career	stuborn	applause	35._____
36.	align	surender	provisional	sucess	36._____
37.	occurence	succeed	alter	patern	37._____
38.	annuity	flannel	accessories	losses	38._____
39.	gramar	massive	surrender	ecentric	39._____
40.	remittance	crystallize	tranquillity	afirm	40._____

L. There are misspelled words in the following sentences. Underline each misspelled word, and write the correct spelling in the space provided.

1. Mr. Sheridan's employer found his actions excesive, embarassing, and highly unprofessional.

1._____

2. The errors in the pressent recomendation correspond to those in the last one.

2._____

3. His ecentric behavior is so eratic that we believe him to be totaly irresponsible.

3._____

4. This buton will be an efective advertising gimick.

4._____

5. An agressive selling campaign will aleviate our current problem of excess inventory.

5._____

6. The chancelor praissed the new business education curiculum as a patern for others to folow.

6._____

7. I supose you can coroborate these asertions of corup-
    tion.   7. _____

8. We must alot at least one milion dollars to television ad-
    vertising if we are to win this ellection.   8. _____

9. What is the princippal reason for the dificulty in collect-
    ing payment on these overdue acounts?   9. _____

10. The members of the comittee confered privately to dis-
    cus the terms of the setlement.   10. _____

11. The atorney charged that press coverage of her client's
    embezlement trial was excesive and biased.   11. _____

12. Your failure to setle your acount, now six months in
    arears, leaves us no choice but to turn the mater over
    to a colection agency for apropriate action.   12. _____

13. We apreciate your support of this sumer's community
    job action program.   13. _____

14. The board needs assesment of the sittuation imediately.   14. _____

15. This vacume cleaner plus acessories has been
    reduced 20 percent for our anual apliance sale.   15. _____

16. The bank rejected her loan application because her
    colateral was insuficient.   16. _____

17. Do you opose or suport the propposal to increase the
    number of multiple-ocupancy dwellings?   17. _____

18. A multivehicle accident in the tunnel conecting the two
    cities has closed trafic in both directions.   18. _____

19. Full remmittance should acompany each order for fall
    apparrell.   19. _____

20. Juanita, a communications major, is seeking a chaleng-
    ing carreer in comodities with the opportunity for rappid
    advancement.   20. _____

Homonyms

invade   to enter by force, intrude: *When did the Russians invade Czechoslovakia?*
inveighed   past tense of *inveigh,* protest, complain: *Mr. Makato inveighed against the high insurance premiums.*

jam   (noun) jellylike preserves: *We sell more strawberry jam than any other flavor;* (verb) to press into a tight place: *The people were forced to jam together in the elevator;* to render unable to perform: *This kind of paper will jam the machine.*
jamb   a side post of a doorway or window frame: *The door slammed against the jamb.*

knead   to mix by pressing and squeezing: *Julia decided to knead the bread dough by hand rather than in the mixer.*
need   (noun) a necessity: *Their immediate need was food;* (verb) to require: *I need more money.*

knew   past tense of *know: I knew Inez would be promoted.*
new   having been in existence only a short time, opposite of *old: We are about to introduce a new line of cosmetics.*

knight   a mounted soldier of the British feudal period known to be noble and brave (often used to express a likeness to such a person): *Ralph fancies himself a knight in shining armor;* a contemporary British nobleman: *The Queen made him a knight for his service to the nation.*
night   the period of darkness between sunset and sunrise: *I do not want to work the night shift.*

knot   a fastening made by tying together pieces of rope or cord: *Be sure the rope has a strong knot in it;* a measure of speed at sea greater than 1 mile per hour: *The top speed of the ocean liner was over 30 knots.*
not   a negative: *I am not going to work overtime tonight.*

know   to have information about: *Do you know how the new tax laws will affect you?*
no   a negative: *No, there is no rebate on that model.*

lacks   is deficient in, is without: *Mr. Zapotocky lacks the drive necessary to be a successful salesperson with our firm.*
lax   loose, slack, not strict: *Many students were disruptive because the discipline in the classroom was lax.*

lead   a heavy metallic element: *The project will require an additional 50 feet of lead pipe.*

led past tense of *to lead,* guide, be foremost: *Viola led her division in sales again this month.*

lean (verb) to rest at an angle on something: *Lean the ladder against a wall*; to depend or rely upon: *I intend to lean on your advice*; (adjective) with little or no fat: *The local butcher sells choice lean meat.*

lien a legal claim on the property of another for the payment of a debt: *Which bank holds the lien on this property?*

lessen to make less, decrease: *These new security measures should lessen our losses due to shoplifting.*

lesson something learned or studied: *Michele was late for her music lesson*; an instructive experience: *This incident has been a painful lesson.*

lesser smaller or less important: *The decision to close the plant was seen as the lesser of two evils.*

lessor a person or company that rents property to another through a contract known as a lease: *Acme Enterprises is the lessor for this building.* (The person to whom the lease is given is called the lessee.)

levee an embankment for preventing flooding: *The swollen river overflowed the levee.*

levy to impose or collect a tax or fine: *The judge decided to levy a fine of $100 for each violation.*

lie (verb) to recline: *Lie down on the bed*; to tell an untruth: *Don't lie to me*; (noun) an untruth: *That is a lie.*

lye a strong alkaline solution used in making soap: *Lye can be used to clear clogged pipes.*

load (noun) a burden: *Jason brought in a load of wood for the fire*; a shipping unit: *A new load of kitchen gadgets is in the receiving area*; (verb) to place on or in something: *The boys watched the men load grain onto the truck.*

lode a major vein of metallic ore: *Miners found a valuable lode of copper ore.*

loan something lent: *Jacqueline applied for an automobile loan.*

lone standing by itself, solitary: *Ms. Polski submitted the lone bid for the proposed reconstruction project.*

made past tense of *make,* to form, perform: *The temporary employees made numerous errors.*

maid a girl or young, unmarried woman: *The word "maid" is a shortened form of "maiden"*; a female servant: *The maid cleaned our motel room.*

mail (noun) correspondence transported by the postal system: *The mail must go through*; armor worn by a knight: *Sir Galahad wore a vest of heavy mail*; (verb) to send by the postal system: *I forgot to mail this letter.*

male the masculine sex: *Each of our regional managers is male.*

main (adjective) chief in importance: *Write to our main office*; (noun) a large pipe: *A water main burst on Third Street.*

mane the long hair on the neck of a horse, lion, etc.: *The horse's mane flew in the wind.*

mall a shaded walk or promenade: *They walked down the mall in Central Park*; a shopping area closed to vehicles: *There are more than one hundred shops in the new mall.*

maul (verb) to handle roughly: *The mob tried to maul him*; (noun) a heavy hammer: *Aaron used a maul and a wedge to split the firewood.*

NAME	CLASS	DATE	SCORE

Homonym Assignments

A. Select from the following words the one that correctly fits the blank in each of the sentences below. Then write the word in the answer space.

jam	no	lean	levy	main
jamb	lacks	lien	load	mane
knead	lax	lessen	lode	
need	lead	lesson	loan	
know	led	levee	lone	

1. Rose did not _____ who got the promotion.   1._____

2. The hiring of two new employees helped to _____ the workload.   2._____

3. Ardith remained the _____ dissenter.   3._____

4. Those who lived closest to the _____ suffered the greatest amount of water damage.   4._____

5. Dana was absent for the introductory _____.   5._____

6. Those who came early _____ the in-person registration line.   6._____

7. Too many employees take advantage when a supervisor is _____ in checking tardiness.   7._____

8. He is repaying his car _____ in monthly installments.   8._____

9. No machine can _____ dough as effectively as the human hand.   9._____

10. The _____ entrance was locked.   10._____

11. State government has the right to _____ a sales tax.   11._____

12. When I carried the carton of paper, it felt as heavy as a block of _____.   12._____

13. You _____ the right diskettes to operate a computer.   13._____

14. The repairer said that the wrong paper will _____ the copier.   14._____

15. After their lengthy discussion, the lawyer prepared to take action against the _____ on his property.   15. _____

B. In some of the following sentences, an incorrect word is used. Underline the incorrect word, and write the correct word in the space provided. Where there is no error, write C in the answer space.

1. The loan survivor lead the rescue team to where the water flowed over the levee.   1. _____

2. It is not difficult to learn how to use this new word processing program.   2. _____

3. Everyone knew the names of those with poor credit ratings.   3. _____

4. She had the dress made to order.   4. _____

5. Each statement is, in my opinion, a lye.   5. _____

6. The personnel director preferred to hire someone with experience for the knight shift.   6. _____

7. As time goes by, the fear of the effects of automation will lessen.   7. _____

8. Caldwell's policy of reckless spending lead his company to the verge of bankruptcy.   8. _____

9. The movers proceeded to lode the furniture into the van.   9. _____

10. The proposal that was accepted was the lessor of two evils.   10. _____

11. It became necessary to levy a fee when someone used the copier for nonbusiness purposes.   11. _____

12. Until the final debt was paid, the finance company held a lean on the car.   12. _____

13. The local merchants inveighed against the new parking ordinance.   13. _____

14. The last employee hired was mail.   14. _____

15. The mane purpose of the student exchange program was to improve international relations.   15. _____

C. Read the definition, and select the correct word from the second column to match that description. Write the word you selected in the answer space.

Definition	Word Choice	
1. jellylike preserves	jam, jamb	1. _____

2. a necessity   knead, need   2._____

3. the long hair on a horse   main, mane   3._____

4. a measure of speed at sea   knot, not   4._____

5. an alkaline solution used
   in making soap   lie, lye   5._____

6. something learned or
   studied   lessen, lesson   6._____

7. to depend or rely upon   lean, lien   7._____

8. a nobleman   knight, night   8._____

9. heavy metallic element   lead, led   9._____

10. to enter by force   invade, inveighed   10._____

D. Select the right word for the sentence shown, and write it in the answer space. Then compose a sentence for the homonym not selected, and write your sentence in the space provided.

1. What Hugo (lacks, lax) in performance, he makes up
   with his personality.   1._____

   _____

   _____

   _____

2. She felt like a (made, maid) because she had to buy
   the refreshments for the office.   2._____

   _____

   _____

   _____

3. During the training session, Elena found out how much
   she did not (know, no).   3._____

   _____

   _____

   _____

4. The training session provided him with many techniques
   that he (kneaded, needed) to know.   4._____

   _____

   _____

   _____

5. Each payment on his car (loan, lone) comes due the first of each month.

5. _____

_____

_____

_____

6. Brenda was caught in a (lie, lye).

6. _____

_____

_____

_____

7. The bank held the (lean, lien) on that property.

7. _____

_____

_____

_____

8. The accounting department (lead, led) the firm in perfect attendance.

8. _____

_____

_____

_____

9. Samples of the (knew, new) product were distributed.

9. _____

_____

_____

_____

10. The customers (invade, inveighed) against the price increase.

10. _____

_____

_____

_____

NAME	CLASS	DATE	SCORE

Vocabulary Enrichment

Chapters 4–7

A. You should now be familiar with the meaning of each of the words below. In the space provided to the right, write the word that best completes the meaning of the sentence. Cross out each word in the list as you use it.

affiliate	assimilate	dissipate	hierarchy	recipient
aggregate	commence	duress	induce	reconcile
aggrieve	concoct	enumerate	infer	reiterate
allege	defer	facilitate	liquidate	remit
alleviate	delete	fluctuate	persevere	transient
assessment	deter	harass	pertain	yield

1. Major news developments often cause stock prices to
   _____.   1._____

2. Some hotels cater to both _____ and permanent
   guests.   2._____

3. By making one poor investment after another, Mel
   watched his inheritance _____.   3._____

4. She is pleased that the phone company will
   _____ each call on the monthly statement that it
   sends.   4._____

5. They _____ their study of accounting with the
   method of recording the opening balance.   5._____

6. Paula's new assistant helps to _____ her
   workload.   6._____

7. To _____ our prompt decision, we were offered a
   substantial discount on the purchase.   7._____

8. Once a month it is necessary to _____ the check-
   book balance with the bank statement balance.   8._____

9. As a result of the bankruptcy proceedings, the firm had
   to _____ all of its assets.   9._____

10. Using word processing software makes it easy to add
    or _____ words, sentences, and paragraphs.   10._____

11. We may _____ paying taxes on some income if
    we invest it immediately.   11. _____

12. Having a procedures manual available helps to
    _____ the work flow during vacation periods and
    absences.   12. _____

13. An organization chart depicts the corporate manage-
    ment _____.   13. _____

14. A feasibility study is a preliminary _____ of the
    needs and resources that affect a plan of action. 14. _____

15. Despite a lack of cooperation and support, the detec-
    tive continued to _____ in his investigation of the
    facts.   15. _____

B. For this exercise you must refer to the list of words given for assignment A above. Select any ten words that you did not use in completing assignment A. For each of the ten words you selected, compose a meaningful sentence on a separate sheet of paper.

C. Choose the word from the list below that is closest in meaning to the numbered word or words in the paragraphs on pages 125–126. Write the word you selected from the list in the answer space. Use each word only once.

ability	instantly
achievements	intelligently
benefits	literate
consequences	negative
definition	predict
devices	presented
dictated	proliferation
external	steps
heart	streamlining
housed	transfers
impact	vast
increased	weigh
influence	

Recognizing the Role of Computers

The computer is one of the most important 1. ACCOMPLISHMENTS   1. _____

of this century. Not only have computers assisted in the world of

business by 2. SIMPLIFYING accounting, marketing research,   2. _____

forecasting, recordkeeping, and information management practices,

but they have also had an 3. EFFECT on nonbusiness areas as well.   3. _____

They guide our astronauts on their travel in space; they help engineers

design bridges and airplanes; they count votes and 4. FORETELL   4. _____

election results; they affect military strategy, research, medicine,

education, aviation, communications, and governmental efficiency;

and the list could go on.

The impact of the computer has already been felt in our daily lives. It

follows, therefore, that everyone needs to be computer- 5. EDUCATED   5. _____

today.

A simple 6. DESCRIPTION of a computer is that it is an automatic   6. _____

device that computes, makes decisions, and has the capacity for storing

and 7. IMMEDIATELY recalling 8. LARGE amounts of information.   7. _____

Computers come in a variety of shapes, sizes, and capacities.   8. _____

There are five phases to processing computerized information. The

phases are input, processing, storage, output, and distribution. Input

9. UNITS convert keyboarded information into machine language   9. _____

formats. The central processing unit (CPU) is at the 10. CORE of the   10. _____

computer system and handles the processing of the information through

its two major parts: the logic unit and the control unit. All the processing

11. DIRECTIONS are monitored by a program of instructions, often   11. _____

called software.

Computer storage is of two types: main storage, which is for data

12. MAINTAINED within the computer's CPU, and 13. OUTSIDE   12. _____

storage, on mediums such as magnetic tapes and disks. In the output   13. _____

stage, information processed by the computer is 14. MADE AVAILABLE   14. _____

for use as printouts, visual display data, or microforms, to name just

a few forms. In the distribution phase, the computer has the
15. CAPACITY to send its output by a variety of means to local or
remote locations.

15._____

Among the 16. ADVANTAGES that the computer offers us are
improved banking, new job opportunities, electronic money
17. EXCHANGES, improved medical care and research,
sophisticated communication systems, and many more. Some
of the 18. UNSATISFACTORY effects or shortcomings of
computerization are the 19. RAPID INCREASE of databases, the
loss of self-reliance due to computer takeover, standardization,
computer crime, invasion of privacy, and rapid change
20. COMMANDED by the technology itself.

16._____

17._____

18._____

19._____

20._____

A balanced approach is necessary as our society becomes more
and more computer-oriented and -dependent. We should recognize
the benefits of 21. GROWING computer use, yet we also need to be
aware of the 22. RESULTS of dependency. We need to continuously
23. EVALUATE the positive and negative effects of the computer on
our society. Yes, computers are here to stay, and to make the most
of them, we need to learn to understand their 24. POWER so that
we can live with them 25. ASTUTELY.

21._____

22._____

23._____

24._____

25._____

Silent Letters

Chapter

8

In Chapter 5 you looked at words that end in silent **e** and saw that knowing two simple rules could solve countless spelling problems. In this chapter you will look at a number of words that contain other silent letters or letter combinations. Most people find these words more difficult to spell than those containing silent **e**. See if you can recognize all the misspelled words in the following sentences. Underline each one, and spell it correctly in the space provided.

1. Many people ofen confuse a sychologist with a sychiatrist. 1._____

2. I have no dout that Mr. Knutsen will have the anser regard-
    ing how to get the company out of det. 2._____

3. I brout my car in for a weel alinment. 3._____

4. Maureen renched her rist dragging the file cabinet out into
    the aile. 4._____

5. The copyriter received a plaq for his clever advertising ryme. 5._____

Here are the misspelled words, spelled correctly:

1. often, psychologist, psychiatrist
2. doubt, answer, debt
3. brought, wheel, alignment
4. wrenched, wrist, aisle
5. copywriter, plaque, rhyme

There is no rule to help you solve the spelling problems that words like these present. They simply must be memorized. To help you, the words that follow are arranged in groups according to the silent letters they contain. Notice how many of the words in each group are similar in nature. In nearly all the words containing a silent **b**, for instance, that **b** is preceded by **m**. All but one of the silent **w**'s is followed by an **r**, and all but one of the silent **g**'s is followed by an **n**. Watch for similar patterns in the other groups.

You are already familiar with the spelling of most of these words. Concentrate on the words you do not know and their relationship to those you do. Remember, you cannot rely on correct pronunciation to guide you in spelling these words correctly. You must visualize them — get a clear picture in your mind of how they should look—and learn to spell them accurately.

In the lists that follow, the silent letters are underlined. Look at each group of words carefully—and concentrate on the silent spots.

Silent b

bomb	debt	limb	succumb
catacomb	doubt	numb	thumb
climb	dumb	plumber	tomb
comb	indebted	subtle	womb
crumb	lamb		

Silent g

align*	gnarled*	gnaw	resign
alignment	gnash	malign*	sign
benign*	gnat	phlegm	vignette*
ensign			

Silent gh

although	dough	sigh	thorough
borough	furlough	thigh	through
bough	high		

Silent gh followed by t

blight	fight	naught	slight
bought	flight	naughty	sought
bright	fought	night	straight
brought	freight	ought	taught
caught	haughty*	right	thought
copyright	height	sight	tight
daughter	light	sleight	weight
eight	might		

gh pronounced f

cough	laugh	slough
enough	rough	tough

Silent h

aghast	ghoul	honor	rhinoceros
exhaust	heir	khaki	rhubarb
exhume	heirloom	rhapsody	rhyme
ghastly	hemorrhage	rhetoric	rhythm
ghetto	herb	rheumatism	rhythmic
ghost	honest	rhinestone	thyme

Silent h after w

whale	wheat	whether	whistle
wharf	wheel	which	white
what	when		

Silent k

knack	knee	knight	knot
knapsack	kneel	knit	know
knave	knell	knob	knowledge
knead	knife	knock	knuckle

Silent l

almond	calm	salmon	stalk
alms	caulk	salve	talk
balk	could	should	walk
balm	half	solder	would
calf	palm		

Silent n

| autum<u>n</u> | colum<u>n</u> | condem<u>n</u> | hym<u>n</u> | solem<u>n</u> |

Silent p

cor<u>p</u>s	<u>p</u>salm	<u>p</u>sychoanalysis*	<u>p</u>tomaine*
cup<u>b</u>oard	<u>p</u>seudonym*	<u>p</u>sychology	ras<u>p</u>berry
<u>p</u>neumatic*	<u>p</u>sychedelic	<u>p</u>sychosis*	recei<u>p</u>t
<u>p</u>neumonia	<u>p</u>sychiatry		

Silent s

| ai<u>s</u>le | debri<u>s</u> | i<u>s</u>land | i<u>s</u>le |

Silent t

chas<u>t</u>en	has<u>t</u>en	mois<u>t</u>en	of<u>t</u>en
fas<u>t</u>en	lis<u>t</u>en	mor<u>t</u>gage	sof<u>t</u>en
glis<u>t</u>en			

Silent ue

fatig<u>ue</u>	leag<u>ue</u>	rog<u>ue</u>	vag<u>ue</u>
harang<u>ue</u>	plag<u>ue</u>	tong<u>ue</u>	vog<u>ue</u>
intrig<u>ue</u>	plaq<u>ue</u>		

Silent w

ans<u>w</u>er	<u>w</u>rath	<u>w</u>retch	<u>w</u>rite
copy<u>w</u>riter	<u>w</u>reath	<u>w</u>retched	<u>w</u>rithe
play<u>w</u>right	<u>w</u>reck	<u>w</u>ring	<u>w</u>rong
<u>w</u>rangle	<u>w</u>rench	<u>w</u>rinkle	<u>w</u>rote
<u>w</u>rap	<u>w</u>restle	<u>w</u>rist	<u>w</u>ry

NAME	CLASS	DATE	SCORE

Spelling Assignments

A. Each of the following words contains one or more silent letters. There is a blank where those silent letters should be. Insert the letters, and then rewrite the entire word correctly in the space provided.

1.	plum_____ er	_____	16.	colum_____	_____
2.	num _____	_____	17.	solem_____	_____
3.	thum_____	_____	18.	beni _____ n	_____
4.	ag_____ ast	_____	19.	mali _____ n	_____
5.	hau_____ ty	_____	20.	_____ tomaine	_____
6.	strai _____ t	_____	21.	_____salm	_____
7.	r _____apsody	_____	22.	ai _____ le	_____
8.	ex_____ aust	_____	23.	tong _____	_____
9.	r ___eumatism	_____	24.	vog_____	_____
10.	r _____ythm	_____	25.	vag_____	_____
11.	_____ nee	_____	26.	rog _____	_____
12.	_____nell	_____	27.	leag _____	_____
13.	a_____ mond	_____	28.	_____ rithe	_____
14.	ba_____ k	_____	29.	play ____ right	_____
15.	cou_____ d	_____	30.	_____ rist	_____

B. Insert the silent letters or letter combinations missing from the following words; then rewrite the entire word in the space provided.

1.	_____nock	_____	6.	fli _____ t	_____
2.	frei _____ t	_____	7.	su_____tle	_____
3.	i _____ land	_____	8.	autum_____ _	_____
4.	_____ retched	_____	9.	de_____ t	_____
5.	_____sychosis	_____	10.	i _____ le	_____

11. _____ nit _____

12. _____ rath _____

13. ___ neumonia _____

14. lis _____ en _____

15. dou _____ t _____

16. mor ____ gage _____

17. sof _____ en _____

18. recei _____ t _____

19. ans _____ er _____

20. ras _____ berry _____

21. w _____ arf _____

22. ___ seudonym _____

23. _____ neel _____

24. _____ nob _____

25. wom _____ _____

26. of _____ en _____

27. _____ nash _____

28. nau _____ ty _____

29. condem _____ _____

30. _____ rench _____

31. clim _____ _____

32. thorou _____ _____

33. _____ now _____

34. wa _____ k _____

35. resi _____ n _____

36. thou _____ t _____

37. _____ rote _____

38. ___ nowledge _____

39. throu _____ _____

40. tou _____ _____

C. There are misspelled words in some of the following sentences. Underline each misspelled word, and write the correct spelling in the space provided. If there are no misspelled words, write C in the space next to the sentence.

1. Although Will lost his morgage receipt, he knew that his canceled check would be sufficient proof of payment. 1. _____

2. The project was plaged by doubts wich proved to be justified. 2. _____

3. Office automation has brought about enormous changes in office procedures. 3. _____

4. Piles of debri clogged the aisle. 4. _____

5. Someone once said, "Nowledge is power," and I agree. 5. _____

6. The top salesperson in the new campaign received an attractive bronze plaq. 6. _____

7. Do you know the seudonym this famous playright frequently uses? 7. _____

8. Woud you be kind enough to sin this petition? 8. _____

9. You should try to remain calm in an emergency. 9. _____

10. Anna is undecided wether to undergo sychoanalysis. 10. _____

D. Write the proper form of the word in parentheses in the answer space.

1. Beth (thumb) through the pages quickly.

2. Al's (indebt) prevented him from getting another loan.

3. The report was read (thorough).

4. She feverishly (knock) on the door.

5. Rico used (column) paper to make it easier to add up the figures.

6. Has the whole report been (write) yet?

7. I am (listen) to every word you say.

8. Can you (straight) out the files for me?

9. Lamar (laugh) when he saw the surprised look on my face.

10. For safety reasons (condemn) the property was the only alternative the building inspector had.

11. Everyone's anxiety (height) as the election day drew nearer.

12. (Align) copy in the typewriter once the paper has been removed takes skill.

13. Saying thank-you is always a (thought) gesture.

14. Joan (balk) at the prospect of working overtime for the third evening in succession.

15. My hobby is (knit).

16. The clothes in the garment bag were not as (wrinkle) as those in the suitcase.

17. The palm trees swayed in the (balm) breeze.

18. Make sure that you (tight) the cap on the bottle of paper cement so that the glue does not dry out.

19. Watching them vie to pay for lunch was almost as interesting as watching a (wrestle) match.

20. Everyone wants to be sure that a job provides further opportunity for (climb) the career ladder.

1. _____

2. _____

3. _____

4. _____

5. _____

6. _____

7. _____

8. _____

9. _____

10. _____

11. _____

12. _____

13. _____

14. _____

15. _____

16. _____

17. _____

18. _____

19. _____

20. _____

Homonyms

manner	a way of acting or of doing something: *I don't like the manner in which they were fired.*
manor	a mansion, a landed estate: *While traveling in France, Luis stayed at an old Norman manor.*
mantel	a shelf above a fireplace: *The painting hung over the mantel.*
mantle	something that envelops and covers: *The soldiers advanced under the mantle of darkness;* cloak: *The baron's mantle was tattered and soiled;* or may be used figuratively: *The mantle of authority was passed on to him.*
mean	(verb) to have in mind, intend, indicate: *Explain what you mean by that statement;* (adjective) bad-tempered, vicious: *Deliberately breaking that toy was a mean thing to do;* halfway between extremes, in a middle position: *The professor based the test grades on the mean score of all class members.*
mien	a way of carrying and conducting oneself, manner: *Ms. Ruenz displays a mien of absolute self-confidence.*
meat	the flesh of an animal: *A vegetarian will not eat meat.*
meet	to come together with: *Meet me in St. Louis.*
mete	to allot: *Dividends were meted out to stockholders in proportion to their investments.*
medal	small piece of engraved metal intended to honor and preserve the memory of an event or a person: *Kim won a gold medal for excellence in creative writing.*
meddle	to concern oneself with other people's affairs without being asked or needed: *It is not wise to meddle in the affairs of others.*
metal	substance such as iron, lead, gold, or silver: *These metal doors provide extra security.*
mettle	spirit, courage: *Carla displayed her mettle during this period of stress.*
mind	(noun) what a person thinks, an opinion: *Shondell always speaks her mind on any issue;* the intellect: *The mind is a terrible thing to waste;* (verb) to give heed to: *Please mind your manners;* to take care of: *Lisa will mind the store while I am at lunch.*
mined	past tense of *mine,* to dig ores, coal, etc., from the earth: *The playwright Eugene O'Neill once mined for gold in South America.*
miner	one who works in a *mine,* pit or excavation for digging coal, ore: *Joe's brother is a coal miner.*
minor	(adjective) smaller, less important: *There is a minor flaw in the glazing on this statue. The representative met with minor local officials;* (noun) a person under the legal age of responsibility: *Minors may not vote.*

missed	past tense of *miss,* to fail to hit, reach, or contact: *We missed the train.*
mist	a fog or vapor: *A heavy mist made driving difficult.*
morning	the early part of the day, ending at noon: *These packages must be delivered by tomorrow morning.*
mourning	sorrow for a person's death, showing of sorrow by observing certain rituals: *Black is often worn when one is in mourning for the loss of a loved one.*
muscle	a bundle of special tissues that function to move a part of the body: *Abduhl pulled a leg muscle.*
mussel	an edible, clamlike animal: *He ordered a plate of steamed mussels at the restaurant.*
mustard	yellow powder or paste used for seasoning food: *We supply individual packets of catsup and mustard to the fast-food restaurants in this area.*
mustered	past tense of *muster,* to gather together, assemble, collect: *She mustered all her arguments against the proposed price increase.*
naval	relating to the navy: *Trafalgar is the site of a famous naval battle.*
navel	small depression in the abdomen: *He has a birthmark near his navel.*
oar	a pole used to row a boat: *The oar struck a rock and shattered.*
or	conjunction denoting an alternative: *Either Ruth or Hugh will be promoted to department supervisor.*
ore	a mineral containing a metal: *The mine contains vast quantities of iron ore.*
oral	spoken: *We have an oral commitment on a new contract.*
aural	relating to the ear or to the sense of hearing: *Bill's aural faculties were impaired because of prolonged exposure to excessive noise.*
our	belonging to, made by, or done by us: *Our sales for the last quarter are down 20 percent.*
hour	sixty minutes: *Mr. Warde was more than an hour late for work today.*
overdo	to do too much, overwork, exhaust: *Do your work conscientiously and thoroughly, but do not overdo it.*
overdue	expected or due some time ago but not yet arrived, not yet paid: *The 6:45 train is an hour overdue. Payment on your account is a month overdue.*
pail	a bucket: *Drown campfires with a pail of water.*
pale	without much color, whitish: *Charlene was pale with fright. The walls were painted a pale blue.*
pain	suffering: *I have a severe pain in my neck.*
pane	a sheet of glass: *A pane in the window was accidentally shattered.*
pair	two of a kind: *Jim bought Catherine a pair of gloves for her birthday.*
pare	to trim or peel off the outer part: *This peeler can pare an apple in seconds. The office must pare expenses down to the bone.*
pear	a fruit: *She ate a pear with lunch.*

NAME	CLASS	DATE	SCORE

Homonym Assignments

A. Select from the following words the one that correctly fits the blank in each of the sentences below. Then write the word in the answer space.

manner	mien	meddle	morning	or
manor	meat	metal	mourning	ore
mantel	meet	mettle	mustard	
mantle	mete	missed	mustered	
mean	medal	mist	oar	

1. The founder's portrait hung over the _____ in the reception area.

    1._____

2. It was difficult for the judge to _____ out the harsh sentence that the law required.

    2._____

3. The workers in the accounting department _____ their energies to get the quarterly reports in on time.

    3._____

4. He responded to the charges under a _____ of silence.

    4._____

5. Lieutenant Vasquez received a _____ for his bravery.

    5._____

6. The standards set by the new manager tested the _____ of every member of the office staff.

    6._____

7. I could read the report today _____ wait until tomorrow.

    7._____

8. The _____ rush hour always seems worse than the evening one.

    8._____

9. Barbara did not _____ to be sarcastic.

    9._____

10. Can we _____ earlier tomorrow?

    10._____

11. Those who lost the election acted as though they were in _____.

    11._____

12. Louise always has a cheerful and friendly _____.

    12._____

13. The work sheet didn't balance because he
_____ including one account balance.

13. _____

14. The wealthy author, who was a recluse, lived in a
_____ outside the city limits.

14. _____

15. The _____ from the spray paint stained the nearby cabinet.

15. _____

B. In some of the following sentences, an incorrect word is used. Underline the incorrect word, and write the correct word in the space provided. Where there is no error, write C in the answer space.

1. Do you mind if I borrow your pen?

1. _____

2. One of the responsibilities of the Board of Directors is to meat out dividends.

2. _____

3. A miner problem, if not attended to, can develop into a major one.

3. _____

4. Winnie prepared detailed notes and mustered her courage to present her speech.

4. _____

5. Our child labor laws are designed specifically to protect minors in the workplace.

5. _____

6. Uranium is found in an oar called pitchblende.

6. _____

7. To prevent aural impairment of employees, most automated typewriters have an acoustical sound shield.

7. _____

8. What is sometimes needed is less discussion and more mussel.

8. _____

9. The government sanctioned navel maneuvers in response to the aggressive act.

9. _____

10. Oral agreements are not binding in courts of law.

10. _____

11. William sold the boat but not the oars.

11. _____

12. The new drapes were a mustard color.

12. _____

13. The salesperson was careful not to medal in the customer's private business.

13. _____

14. Enrique has been asked to mete with the accountants on Monday.

14. _____

15. People came from all over to view the naval display in the harbor.

15. _____

C. Read the definition, and select the correct word from the second column to match that description. Write the word you selected in the answer space.

	Definition	Word Choice	
1.	substance such as iron, lead, gold	metal, mettle	1._____
2.	the flesh of an animal	meat, meet, mete	2._____
3.	spirit, courage	metal, mettle	3._____
4.	past tense of the verb *to mine*	mind, mined	4._____
5.	lacking in color	pail, pale	5._____
6.	sixty minutes	hour, our	6._____
7.	less important	miner, minor	7._____
8.	something that envelops and covers	mantel, mantle	8._____
9.	an edible, clamlike animal	muscle, mussel	9._____
10.	past tense of *miss*	missed, mist	10._____

D. Select the right word for the sentence shown, and write it in the answer space. Then compose a sentence for the homonym not selected, and write your sentence in the space provided.

1. (Aural, Oral) reports are better when the speaker uses visuals.

   1._____

   _____

   _____

   _____

2. The display case contained all the (medals, meddles) won by the team.

   2._____

   _____

   _____

   _____

3. It is important to (meet, mete) deadlines.

   3._____

   _____

   _____

   _____

4. It is good to be cheerful, but you can (overdo, overdue) it.

4. _____

_____

_____

_____

5. Everyone was in (morning, mourning) at the loss of a coworker.

5. _____

_____

_____

_____

6. Everyone agrees that Mr. Hernandez displays a (mean, mien) of self-confidence.

6. _____

_____

_____

_____

7. According to the headlines, the trapped (miners, minors) were rescued.

7. _____

_____

_____

_____

8. The professor's casual (manner, manor) made her well liked by her students.

8. _____

_____

_____

_____

9. Mason did not feel comfortable when he had to (meet, mete) out negative comments.

9. _____

_____

_____

_____

10. There was an all-out effort to (pair, pare) down expenses.

10. _____

_____

_____

_____

NAME	CLASS	DATE	SCORE

Review Exercises

A. There are misspelled words in some of the following sentences. Underline each misspelled word, and write the correct spelling in the space provided. If there are no misspelled words, write C in the space next to the sentence.

1. Please send a written receit as soon as you receive our shipment.

    1._____

2. Customs agents were at the peir waiting to seize the illegal articles.

    2._____

3. Shortages at the hieght of a season can definitly be a tragedy to a manufacturer.

    3._____

4. A courageous person is never deterred by anger or lack of support.

    4._____

5. Light industry is moveing out of the city and into the suburbs, where acreage is less costly.

    5._____

6. The aggreement was terminated by mutual consent.

    6._____

7. The employees achieved increased productivity with the new equipment.

    7._____

8. I was the chairperson of the Nineth Annual Banquet.

    8._____

9. Most cashiers have been trained in recognizing counterfiet bills.

    9._____

10. When filling out an accident report, you must be accurate and thorough in stating the facts of the incidence.

    10._____

11. At the end of the day, the cashier was releived to learn that her cash drawer ballanced.

    11._____

12. The results of the questionnaire confirmed what we had guest at the outset.

    12._____

13. During the newspaper strike, citizens found out how much they really mist reading the newspaper.

    13._____

14. He delivered an aural address, but he supplied each person with a written copy of the speech as well.

    14._____

15. It is advantagous for a young physician to learn about areas of the country where there is a shortage of doctors.

15. _____

16. An endorsement citing the product's possible harmfulness to health was required by the FDA.

16. _____

17. Our new client had ocassion to visit our main office recently.

17. _____

18. Pursueing occupational success takes both perseverance and time.

18. _____

19. Standardized forms are used effectively in many offices.

19. _____

20. Good gramar is necessary for success.

20. _____

21. Employees usually appreciate feedback on thicr work.

21. _____

22. Finding desk space to accommodate the temporary employees was a dilemma.

22. _____

23. Paste-ups are prepared easily by using scissors and paper cement.

23. _____

24. Vague instructions are both confusing and discouraging.

24. _____

25. In accounting, a transposition error is suggested if the amount of the diference is evenly divisible by 9.

25. _____

B. Underline each error in the following letter, and write the correct spelling or usage in the space provided to the right of the line. If there are no errors in the line, write C in the space.

October 17, 19--

1 Mr. Warren Chisholm, Ofice Manager
2 Brandise Furnature Manufacturers
3 1417 Main Street
4 Bosten, MA 02116

Dear Mr. Chisholm:

5 Your office employees would be wellcome as regular readers of
6 High Tech World--a new monthly publication especialy for office
7 profesionals. For this reason we recently sent each of your
8 employees a sample copy of our pubblication.

9 You can put High Tech World on the reading list for each of your
10 employees by ordering a company subscription. The subscription
11 copy could be left in a conveneint place so that all of your staff
12 could have acess to it in order to browse through it or to read it
13 from cover to cover.

14 A special one-year suscription offer is presently available that
15 adds two extra isues without charge. This special offer expires
16 on November 30 and costs only a few penies per copy. Multiple
17 subscriptions, which are build to one firm, are also available at
18 further reduced rates.

19 Do your staff a favor today by orderring a subscription to High
20 Tech World. It will be a welcome site to your staff. Take the
21 cue from a number of other employers who have won confidence and
22 compliments from thier employees.

23 Your signature on the enclosed order form will asure you that High
24 Tech World will be at your office as soon as the next addition is
25 off the press.

Very truly yours,

Ann Simmons
Publications Board

ly
Enclosure

1. _____
2. _____
3. _____
4. _____
5. _____
6. _____
7. _____
8. _____
9. _____
10. _____
11. _____
12. _____
13. _____
14. _____
15. _____
16. _____
17. _____
18. _____
19. _____
20. _____
21. _____
22. _____
23. _____
24. _____
25. _____

Prefixes

A prefix is one or more syllables placed before a root or word to change the meaning of the root or word. **Dis, il,** and **un,** for example, are prefixes. When we add them to the words **approve, legal,** and **necessary,** we create new words.

dis + approve = disapprove
il + legal = illegal
un + necessary = unnecessary

Similarly, **suade** is the root of **persuade**. If we add **dis** to **suade**, we form the new word **dissuade**, which means the opposite of **persuade**.

There are a great many prefixes in English, many of which are derived from Latin or Greek prefixes. The prefixes **il, im,** and **ir,** for instance, all derive from Latin **in**, meaning *not*. For ease of pronunciation, **il** is usually used before words beginning with **l**; **im,** before words beginning with **b, m,** or **p**; **ir,** before **r**; and **in,** before everything else. The Appendix contains a list of various prefixes and their meanings.

Recognizing these prefixes can be of considerable help in spelling a great many words. However, you will not get involved in analyzing word origins and derivations here. Instead, you will focus on some potential spelling problems in common words involving double letter combinations. These problems can be avoided if you are familiar with these various prefixes. In each case the full prefix is added to the word. Do not drop any letters. Become familiar with the following prefixes and the words in which they occur. If you recognize the prefix, you should have no difficulty in spelling these words correctly.

dis meaning *fail, cease, do the opposite of*

Prefix + Word or Root	= New Word	Prefix + Word or Root	= New Word
dis + satisfy	= dissatisfy	dis + similar	= dissimilar
dis + sect	= dissect*	dis + simulate	= dissimulate*
dis + semble	= dissemble*	dis + sipate	= dissipate
dis + seminate	= disseminate*	dis + sociate	= dissociate
dis + sension	= dissension	dis + soluble	= dissoluble*
dis + sent	= dissent	dis + solute	= dissolute
dis + sertation	= dissertation*	dis + solve	= dissolve
dis + service	= disservice	dis + sonance	= dissonance*
dis + sident	= dissident	dis + suade	= dissuade

il meaning *not, in, to, onto*

Prefix + Word or Root	= New Word	Prefix + Word or Root	= New Word
il + legal	= illegal	il + logical	= illogical
il + legible	= illegible	il + luminate	= illuminate
il + legitimate	= illegitimate	il + lusion	= illusion
il + licit	= illicit*	il + lusive	= illusive
il + literate	= illiterate		

im meaning *not*

Prefix + Word or Root	= New Word	Prefix + Word or Root	= New Word
im + maculate	= immaculate	im + mobile	= immobile
im + material	= immaterial	im + moderate	= immoderate
im + mature	= immature	im + modest	= immodest
im + measurable	= immeasurable	im + moral	= immoral
im + mediate	= immediate	im + mortal	= immortal
im + mense	= immense	im + movable	= immovable
im + merse	= immerse	im + mune	= immune
im + migrate	= immigrate	im + mutable	= immutable

inter meaning *between, among*

Prefix + Word or Root	= New Word	Prefix + Word or Root	= New Word
inter + racial	= interracial	inter + rogate	= interrogate*
inter + relate	= interrelate	inter + rupt	= interrupt
inter + religious	= interreligious		

mis meaning *wrong, wrongly, bad, badly*

Prefix + Word or Root	= New Word	Prefix + Word or Root	= New Word
mis + sent	= missent	mis + spend	= misspend
mis + shape	= misshape	mis + state	= misstate
mis + speak	= misspeak	mis + step	= misstep
mis + spell	= misspell		

over meaning *above, excessive*

Prefix + Word or Root	= New Word	Prefix + Word or Root	= New Word
over + rate	= overrate	over + ride	= override
over + reach	= overreach	over + ripe	= overripe
over + react	= overreact	over + rule	= overrule
over + refined	= overrefined	over + run	= overrun

un meaning *not, the opposite of*

Prefix + Word or Root	= New Word	Prefix + Word or Root	= New Word
un + named	= unnamed	un + neighborly	= unneighborly
un + natural	= unnatural	un + nerve	= unnerve
un + naturalized	= unnaturalized	un + noted	= unnoted
un + navigable	= unnavigable	un + noticed	= unnoticed
un + necessary	= unnecessary	un + numbered	= unnumbered
un + needed	= unneeded		

under meaning *beneath, below standard*

Prefix + Word or Root	= New Word	Prefix + Word or Root	= New Word
under + rate	= underrate	under + ripe	= underripe
under + report	= underreport	under + run	= underrun
under + represent	= underrepresent		

There are hundreds of other words that may take the prefixes you have just examined. But these words present no special problems. Each one starts with a letter different from the letter at the end of the prefix.

Prefix + Word or Root	= New Word	Prefix + Word or Root	= New Word
dis + entangle	= disentangle	mis + hap	= mishap*
dis + taste	= distaste	mis + lead	= mislead
inter + vene	= intervene	mis + take	= mistake
mis + behave	= misbehave	over + done	= overdone
mis + demeanor	= misdemeanor*	over + zealous	= overzealous
mis + fortune	= misfortune	un + easy	= uneasy
mis + guide	= misguide	under + take	= undertake

NAME	CLASS	DATE	SCORE

Spelling Assignments

A. Insert **s** or **ss** (whichever is correct) in the spaces in the following words. Then rewrite the complete word on the line to the right.

1. di____approve_____
2. mi____pell   _____
3. mi___tatement_____
4. mi____tep   _____
5. di____appear_____
6. di____ection _____
7. mi____hap   _____
8. di____appoint _____
9. di____ent   _____
10. mi___construe_____
11. di____imilar _____
12. mi___behave_____
13. di____olve   _____

14. di____grace _____
15. di___reputable_____
16. di____credit _____
17. di___comfort _____
18. di____arm   _____
19. di___possess _____
20. di___atisfy _____
21. di___integrate _____
22. di____like   _____
23. mi__demeanor_____
24. di____onance _____
25. di____please _____

B. Underline the misspelled word or words in each of the following groups of three. Spell the word or words correctly in the space at the right. If there are no errors in the group, write C.

1. dissociate	ilegible	unnatural	1._____
2. mistake	misfit	mispeak	2._____
3. impartial	imperfect	illegitimate	3._____
4. interrogate	interrupt	interacial	4._____
5. unnecessary	uneasy	unneeded	5._____
6. underrepresented	ilusive	illogical	6._____
7. underrate	overreact	dissect	7._____

8.	immaterial	illogical	diservice	8. _____
9.	misshapen	immense	misent	9. _____
10.	disertation	overreaction	misguided	10. _____
11.	unnoted	dissident	overrule	11. _____
12.	immobile	dissent	interreligious	12. _____
13.	interrelate	dissolve	unnumbered	13. _____
14.	misplace	illicit	misslead	14. _____
15.	disemble	dissension	overcharge	15. _____
16.	ilumination	immoderate	immense	16. _____
17.	dissuade	disatisfaction	disfigure	17. _____
18.	underscore	undervalue	understate	18. _____
19.	undermine	imagine	immunity	19. _____
20.	impatient	impeccable	impertinent	20. _____
21.	imature	uneasy	overripe	21. _____
22.	unoccupied	unerve	impossible	22. _____
23.	overrun	impassive	imobile	23. _____
24.	mislay	immodest	dissable	24. _____
25.	invaluable	overrate	imoral	25. _____

Homonyms

passed	(verb) past tense of *pass*, to occur, go by: *The time for delay has passed*; approved: *The motion was passed unanimously.*
past	(adjective) gone by, ended: *Our troubles are past*; just gone by: *Sales during the past year have been excellent*; (noun) time gone by: *All this happened in the distant past.*
patience	willingness to wait or endure: *We must have patience while he learns the new procedures.*
patients	plural of *patient*, person being treated by a doctor or dentist: *Dr. Kim's patients praised her skill and compassion.*
pause	a temporary stop or hesitation, interruption: *We now take a pause for these commercial messages.*
paws	the feet of a four-footed animal with claws: *Gerald's cat is black with white paws.*
peace	calm, absence of fighting: *All I want is a little peace and quiet.*
piece	a part of something: *This piece of tubing needs to be replaced.*
peak	the top or highest point: *The antenna was mounted on the peak of the roof. Retail sales reach their peak in December.*
peek	to look quickly and furtively: *The secretary would peek into the room to see if the conference was still in session.*
pique	(verb) to arouse emotion, especially resentment: *The representative's rude behavior piqued Ms. Jones*; (noun) resentment: *Lauren showed her pique by refusing to talk to him.*
peal	a loud, long sound: *A peal of thunder broke the silence.*
peel	(noun) the skin of a fruit: *She accidentally dropped a banana peel on the floor*; (verb) to strip the skin from: *This kitchen gadget can peel most fruits and vegetables in seconds*; to remove by stripping: *After you soak the bottle, it should be easy to peel off the label.*
pedal	(noun) a lever operated by the foot: *Maurice had an accident when his foot slipped off the brake pedal*; (verb) to move by a pedal: *Maureen pedals her bicycle to work every day.*
peddle	to go from place to place with wares to sell: *In this town you must have a license to peddle in the streets.*
peer	(verb) to look at closely: *The children can peer through the toy store window*; to come out slightly: *We saw the sun peer from behind a cloud*; (noun) a person of the same rank, ability, or status: *In every respect, Ms. Jorgensen was Mr. Schmidt's peer as a financial analyst.*

pier   a structure built out over water and supported by pillars: *The Steel Pier at Atlantic City is a famous landmark.*

plain   (adjective) undecorated: *Maria wore a plain dress to the interview;* easy to understand: *Mr. Rourke's language was plain and sincere;* (noun) a flat stretch of land: *The Great Plains stretch east from the Rocky Mountains for hundreds of miles.*

plane   short for *airplane,* aircraft: *The company chartered a plane;* a carpenter's tool for smoothing surfaces: *The carpenter used a plane to fix the warped door;* level or grade: *The plane of the discussion was quite high;* in geometry, a flat surface: *In high school we studied plane geometry before solid geometry.*

pleas   plural of *plea,* a statement in defense or justification, an excuse: *The defendant entered pleas of not guilty to all charges;* urgent requests or appeals: *His pleas to be given one final chance were in vain.*

please   to give pleasure to, satisfy: *It would please me to hear you play the piano;* a term of politeness in requests: *Please come in and be seated.*

pole   a long, slender piece of wood: *He backed his car into a telephone pole;* either end of the earth's axis: *Mr. Adamson has flown over both the North Pole and the South Pole;* either of two parts where opposite forces are strongest: *The ends of a magnet are called the poles.*

poll   (verb) to take a vote: *You may poll the office staff on this issue;* (noun) a place where votes are cast: *The polls close at 8 p.m.;* a survey of public opinion concerning a particular subject: *What are the results of the latest Gallup Public Opinion Poll?*

populace   all the people in a country or region: *The candidates frequently poll the populace to determine their opinions on issues.*

populous   full of people, crowded: *The Northeast is a very populous area of the country.*

pore   (noun) an opening in the skin: *Ingrid washes her face twice daily to keep her pores clean;* (verb) to study intently: *The examiner pored over the bank's records.*

pour   to cause to flow in a steady stream: *Pour the gasoline into the funnel slowly.*

pray   to speak to God in worship: *Let us pray for peace;* to ask for by prayer: *They will pray for her speedy recovery.*

prey   (noun) an animal hunted by another animal: *Mice are the prey of owls;* a victim: *He was an easy prey for unscrupulous dealers;* (verb) to seize upon something as a victim: *The muggers in the city prey upon tourists.*

presence   the condition of being present in a place: *The audit was conducted in the presence of company officials;* a commanding appearance: *Ms. Rutherford has the presence of a diplomat.*

presents   gifts: *Joyce's arms were full of Christmas presents.*

pries   present tense of *pry,* to look closely, peer or snoop: *Ms. Parker frequently pries into other people's business.*

prize   (noun) something won in a game or contest, a reward: *Mr. Ojeida won the prize as top salesperson of the year;* (verb) to value highly: *I prize truth above all other things.*

principal   (adjective) main, most important: *Our principal store is in Paramus;* (noun) the governing officer of a school: *The principal of the school presided over the assembly;* sum of money on which interest is paid: *The bank paid 8 percent interest on the principal.* (*Spelling Aid:* principAL = mAin)

principle   a fundamental rule or doctrine of behavior or science: *The principle of supply and demand determines the price of the item. This toy works because of the principle of gravity.* (*Spelling Aid:* principLE = ruLE)

profit   financial gain from a business transaction: *Beth made a substantial profit when she sold her condominium.*

prophet   a person who speaks inspired religious truths: *John the Baptist was a prophet;* a person who foretells the future: *Malcolm was considered a financial prophet on Wall Street.*

rain   water falling in drops from the clouds: *They waited in the rain for nearly an hour.*

reign   (noun) period during which a ruler holds power: *The reign of Queen Elizabeth I lasted forty-five years;* (verb) to rule: *A king is soon to reign over these people;* to be prevalent: *Prosperity will reign over the land if these proposals are enacted.*

rein   part of an animal's bridle: *Pull on the left rein to turn the horse.*

raise   to lift up: *Raise your hand if you wish to say something;* to bring up: *It is not easy to raise children. I am reluctant to raise that issue;* to gather together, collect: *We must raise funds for this project;* to increase in level or amount: *This school must raise its standards. The landlord is going to raise the rent.*

rays   streams of light: *Prolonged exposure to X-rays can be dangerous.*

raze   to tear down and destroy completely: *They plan to raze the old factory to make way for the new industrial park.*

NAME	CLASS	DATE	SCORE

Homonym Assignments

A. Select from the following words the one that correctly fits the blank in each of the sentences below. Then write the word in the answer space.

passed	peek	plane	presence	prophet
past	pique	pole	presents	
patience	peer	poll	principal	
patients	pier	pore	principle	
peak	plain	pour	profit	

1. Although we consider Alex to be our _____, he lacks confidence in his abilities.

   1._____

2. The time for discussion has _____; we must act now.

   2._____

3. A _____ of customers revealed that a price rise would decrease sales.

   3._____

4. The discussion was maintained on a very high _____.

   4._____

5. I will be glad to repeat the accusation in the _____ of witnesses.

   5._____

6. Why did the auditor _____ over the books for such a long time?

   6._____

7. _____ is a virtue.

   7._____

8. She had to call all the _____ and cancel their appointments.

   8._____

9. At age 52 she was at the _____ of her career.

   9._____

10. At half _____ four, I will be ready to leave.

    10._____

11. His sarcastic remarks served to _____ her anger.

    11._____

12. If he had followed the correct mathematical _____, he would have gotten the right answer.

    12._____

13. Last month's _____ set an all-time record.

    13._____

14. The safety of his employees was his _____ concern.

14. _____

15. Before you leave, _____ into my new office to see the arrangement of furniture and equipment.

15. _____

B. In some of the following sentences, an incorrect word is used. Underline the incorrect word, and write the correct word in the space provided. Where there is no error, write C in the answer space.

1. The bank teller fell pray to temptation when he embezzled the funds.

1. _____

2. The new color scheme improved the appearance of the plane, drab room.

2. _____

3. In the summer ice cream sales reach their pique.

3. _____

4. Once you peel a pressure-sensitive label from its original backing, you can affix it without moistening it.

4. _____

5. You cannot go from door to door to pedal a product unless you have a license.

5. _____

6. The board of directors rains over the officers of the company.

6. _____

7. It was necessary to hire skillful contractors to raze the old brick building with care.

7. _____

8. Darren feared pier evaluation most.

8. _____

9. The principal of the high school stressed the importance of good study habits.

9. _____

10. To peek Betty, Mary called her by her nickname, which is Betts.

10. _____

11. At 5 p.m. we will hear the peal of the church bells.

11. _____

12. So many letters of complaint pored in that temporary help was needed to handle the replies.

12. _____

13. Since the equipment was modular, each piece could be purchased as needed.

13. _____

14. The hurricane caused severe damage to the peer.

14. _____

15. A beautiful gold charm was among the many retirement presence Grace received.

15. _____

C. Read the definition, and select the correct word from the second column to match that description. Write the word you selected in the answer space.

	Definition	**Word Choice**	
1.	long, slender piece of wood	pole, poll	1._____
2.	part of an animal's bridle	rain, reign, rein	2._____
3.	calm, absence of fighting	peace, piece	3._____
4.	crowded	populace, populous	4._____
5.	to value highly	pries, prize	5._____
6.	to look quickly	peak, peek, pique	6._____
7.	to communicate spiritually in worship	pray, prey	7._____
8.	a lever operated by foot	pedal, peddle	8._____
9.	sum of money on which interest is paid	principal, principle	9._____
10.	an opening in the skin	pore, pour	10._____

D. Select the right word for the sentence shown, and write it in the answer space. Then compose a sentence for the homonym not selected, and write your sentence in the space provided.

1. Amy is not well liked because she (pries, prize) into other people's business.

    1._____

_____

_____

_____

2. Leaders in business often need to have the vision of a (profit, prophet).

    2._____

_____

_____

_____

3. The (populace, populous) in beach areas is very concerned about doing away with pollution.

    3._____

_____

_____

_____

4. The auditor's (presence, presents) made the
   employees uncomfortable.   4. _____

   _____

   _____

   _____

5. Despite (pleas, please) to the contrary, John decided to
   change the procedures.   5. _____

   _____

   _____

   _____

6. The meeting began promptly at half (passed, past) two.   6. _____

   _____

   _____

   _____

7. They preferred (plain, plane) food to spicy food.   7. _____

   _____

   _____

   _____

8. The terms of the agreement included a plan to (raise,
   raze) the old factory.   8. _____

   _____

   _____

   _____

9. Because of the lack of (rain, reign), many crops were
   lost.   9. _____

   _____

   _____

   _____

10. It was necessary to take a (pause, paws) in the
    proceedings.   10. _____

   _____

   _____

   _____

Suffixes are syllables that are added to the end of words to change their form or meaning. For example, **ly** is added to the adjective **quick** to form the adverb **quickly**. The verb **advise** plus **ment** yields the noun **advisement**. The same verb plus another suffix, **or**, gives us **advisor**.

In each of the above illustrations the addition of the suffix changed the basic form of the word. Sometimes the suffix can significantly alter the meaning of the word. For example, when the suffix **less** is added, **thank** becomes **thankless**, **penny** becomes **penniless**, **profit** becomes **profitless**. The differences between **thankful** and **thankless** are the result of two different suffixes.

In the next seven chapters you will learn how to spell correctly words containing a variety of common suffixes. In this chapter you will study two common suffixes—**ly (ally)**, **ness**—that can pose double-letter spelling problems similar to those presented by the prefixes in the previous chapter. Learning a few simple rules, however, will help you solve these problems easily.

ly

The suffix **ly** means *like* or *in a specified manner*. Most words that end in **ly** are adverbs, which are usually created by adding **ly** to an adjective.

brave + ly = bravely	slow + ly = slowly
calm + ly = calmly	soft + ly = softly
rapid + ly = rapidly	

Few people have trouble spelling such words as these. The trouble comes when the word ends in **l**. Which of the following are correct?

accidentaly	annualy	incidentaly	usualy
accidentally	annually	incidentally	usually

The correct answers are **accidentally, annually, incidentally,** and **usually**.

<table>
<tr><td colspan="2">Rule</td></tr>
</table>

With very few exceptions, the suffix **ly** is simply added to the root word. If that word ends in **l**, the result is **lly**.

Here is a list of some of the common words that end in **l** and hence contain a double letter (**ll**) when **ly** is added.

Root or Word	+	Suffix	=	New Word
accidental	+	ly	=	accidentally
actual	+	ly	=	actually
annual	+	ly	=	annually
beautiful	+	ly	=	beautifully
beneficial	+	ly	=	beneficially*
biennial	+	ly	=	biennially*
careful	+	ly	=	carefully
cheerful	+	ly	=	cheerfully
classical	+	ly	=	classically
coincidental	+	ly	=	coincidentally*
comical	+	ly	=	comically
conditional	+	ly	=	conditionally*
confidential	+	ly	=	confidentially
continual	+	ly	=	continually
cool	+	ly	=	coolly
cruel	+	ly	=	cruelly
doubtful	+	ly	=	doubtfully
dual	+	ly	=	dually
economical	+	ly	=	economically
equal	+	ly	=	equally
especial	+	ly	=	especially
essential	+	ly	=	essentially
ethical	+	ly	=	ethically*
eventual	+	ly	=	eventually
exceptional	+	ly	=	exceptionally
external	+	ly	=	externally
factual	+	ly	=	factually
final	+	ly	=	finally
financial	+	ly	=	financially
formal	+	ly	=	formally
functional	+	ly	=	functionally
fundamental	+	ly	=	fundamentally
gainful	+	ly	=	gainfully
general	+	ly	=	generally

Root or Word	+	Suffix	=	New Word
grammatical	+	ly	=	grammatically
grateful	+	ly	=	gratefully
habitual	+	ly	=	habitually
helpful	+	ly	=	helpfully
historical	+	ly	=	historically
ideal	+	ly	=	ideally
identical	+	ly	=	identically
incidental	+	ly	=	incidentally
individual	+	ly	=	individually
industrial	+	ly	=	industrially
initial	+	ly	=	initially
intentional	+	ly	=	intentionally
internal	+	ly	=	internally
international	+	ly	=	internationally
legal	+	ly	=	legally
literal	+	ly	=	literally
local	+	ly	=	locally
logical	+	ly	=	logically
loyal	+	ly	=	loyally
manual	+	ly	=	manually
mechanical	+	ly	=	mechanically
medial	+	ly	=	medially
mental	+	ly	=	mentally
moral	+	ly	=	morally
natural	+	ly	=	naturally
occasional	+	ly	=	occasionally
oral	+	ly	=	orally
partial	+	ly	=	partially
personal	+	ly	=	personally
physical	+	ly	=	physically
practical	+	ly	=	practically
principal	+	ly	=	principally
professional	+	ly	=	professionally
psychological	+	ly	=	psychologically
racial	+	ly	=	racially
real	+	ly	=	really
respectful	+	ly	=	respectfully
restful	+	ly	=	restfully
royal	+	ly	=	royally
skillful	+	ly	=	skillfully
special	+	ly	=	specially
statistical	+	ly	=	statistically
successful	+	ly	=	successfully
total	+	ly	=	totally
truthful	+	ly	=	truthfully
universal	+	ly	=	universally
unusual	+	ly	=	unusually

Root or Word	+	Suffix	=	New Word
visual	+	ly	=	visual<u>ly</u>
wistful	+	ly	=	wistful<u>ly</u>
woeful	+	ly	=	woeful<u>ly</u>
wonderful	+	ly	=	wonderful<u>ly</u>

Exception 1   If a word ends in **ll**, drop one **l** before adding **ly**.

full + ly = fully (NOT fullly)   dull + ly = dully (NOT dullly)

Exception 2   In four words that end in silent **e—due, one, true, whole—**the final **e** is dropped before the **ly** suffix is added.

duė + ly = duly   truė + ly = truly
onė + ly = only   wholė + ly = wholly

Exception 3   Some adjectives—**incredible, notable, possible, visible,** etc.—that end in **ble** also deviate slightly from the standard rule. To change these adjectives to adverbs, simply change the final **e** to **y**.

incrediblė + l̸y = incredibly (NOT incrediblely)
notablė + l̸y = notably (NOT notablely)
possiblė + l̸y = possibly (NOT possiblely)
visiblė + l̸y = visibly (NOT visiblely)

ally

Rule

Adjectives ending in **ic** take the **ally** suffix to form adverbs.

Root or Word + Suffix	= New Word	Root or Word + Suffix	= New Word
Adjective	**Adverb**	**Adjective**	**Adverb**
academic + ally	= academically	erratic + ally	= erratically
artistic + ally	= artistically	fanatic + ally	= fanatically
automatic + ally	= automatically	fantastic + ally	= fantastically
basic + ally	= basically	prophetic + ally	= prophetically*
chronic + ally	= chronically	rhythmic + ally	= rhythmically
drastic + ally	= drastically	romantic + ally	= romantically ·
eccentric + ally	= eccentrically*	scholastic + ally	= scholastically
eclectic + ally	= eclectically*	specific + ally	= specifically
ecstatic + ally	= ecstatically	static + ally	= statically
emphatic + ally	= emphatically	systematic + ally	= systematically

> **Exception**   This rule has only one notable exception: **publicly**.

---

ness

Another common suffix, **ness** (a noun suffix used to indicate a state, quality, or condition— **greatness, sadness,** etc.), can present spelling problems when the root word ends in **n**. Is it **meaness** or **meanness, suddeness** or **suddenness?**

> ### Rule
>
> Add the suffix **ness** to the root or word. The root or word remains unchanged, even when it ends in **n**.

Root or Word + Suffix	= New Word	Root or Word + Suffix	= New Word
barren + ness	= barrenness	mean + ness	= meanness
common + ness	= commonness	plain + ness	= plainness
drunken + ness	= drunkenness	stubborn + ness	= stubbornness
even + ness	= evenness	sudden + ness	= suddenness
green + ness	= greenness	sullen + ness	= sullenness
keen + ness	= keenness	thin + ness	= thinness
lean + ness	= leanness	wanton + ness	= wantonness

NAME	CLASS	DATE	SCORE

Spelling Assignments

A. Insert **l** or **ll** or **all** (whichever is correct) in the spaces in the following words. Then rewrite the complete word on the line to the right.

1. actua _____ y _____
2. annua _____ y _____
3. rea _____ y _____
4. who _____ y _____
5. artistic _____ y _____

6. romantic ____ y _____
7. public _____ y _____
8. emphatic ___ y _____
9. extreme ____ y _____
10. sincere _____ y _____

B. Insert **n** or **nn** (whichever is correct) in the spaces in the following words. Then rewrite the complete word on the line to the right.

1. drunke ___ ess _____
2. mea _____ ess _____
3. kind _____ ess _____
4. sulle _____ ess _____
5. happi ____ ess _____

6. bitter _____ ess _____
7. like _____ ess _____
8. delightful _ess _____
9. timeless __ ess _____
10. tired _____ ess _____

C. Underline the misspelled word or words in each of the following groups of three. Spell the word or words correctly in the space at the right. If there are no errors in the group, write C.

1. beautifuly	legally	orally	1._____
2. duely	artistically	historically	2._____
3. systematically	biennialy	erratically	3._____
4. stubborness	basically	possiblely	4._____
5. automatically	realy	conditionally	5._____
6. formally	financialy	fully	6._____
7. truly	drasticaly	economically	7._____

8.	especialy	characteristically	suddenness	8. _____
9.	coincidentally	dually	only	9. _____
10.	terriblely	manually	initially	10. _____
11.	wholly	incredibly	mechanicly	11. _____
12.	totaly	principally	practically	12. _____
13.	worthlessness	medically	physically	13. _____
14.	forgiveness	factualy	helpfulness	14. _____
15.	carefully	specificly	cruely	15. _____
16.	intentionally	moraly	usually	16. _____
17.	usefulness	emphaticaly	meanness	17. _____
18.	dutifully	dullness	professionally	18. _____
19.	wistfuly	comically	commonly	19. _____
20.	royally	visually	loyally	20. _____

D. Write the proper form of the word in parentheses in the answer space.

1. The report was (statistic) correct.   1. _____

2. Mrs. Cheng's (thoughtful) was appreciated by the office staff.   2. _____

3. I said (hopeful) that I expected a raise.   3. _____

4. Financial statements are prepared (periodic).   4. _____

5. We were (true) delighted to learn of your recent promotion.   5. _____

6. To prepare a flowchart, one must first study the step-by-step procedures (logic).   6. _____

7. A (financial) sound business often has an AAA credit rating.   7. _____

8. Using a service bureau can reduce the regular staff's workload (tremendous).   8. _____

9. The commentator's personal remarks during the newscast were (public) retracted in the next day's telecast.   9. _____

10. The candidate was (visible) upset by his opponent's remarks.   10. _____

Homonyms

rap	to knock sharply: *Just rap on the door if you want to come in.*
wrap	to cover by folding something around: *Wrap the package carefully before shipping it.*
rapped	past tense of *rap: The neighbor rapped twice on the window.*
rapt	spellbound, engrossed: *The conventioneers gave rapt attention to the featured speaker.*
wrapped	past tense of *wrap: The clerk wrapped the parcels.*
real	existing as a fact, true, genuine, not made up: *This is not a real diamond. Brad is a real friend;* when describing money or economic matters, means the actual value of something after factors such as inflation or taxes are considered: *Real economic growth is essential for the welfare of this country. Our real income is less than you might think.*
reel	(noun) a spool: *I need another reel of cord to finish tying these packages;* a roller for film or the film itself: *The third reel of film is missing;* (verb) to move in a swaying or staggering manner: *We watched him reel down the hall.*
reek	to have a strong, unpleasant smell: *The streets reek because of the prolonged sanitation strike.*
wreak	to inflict vengeance or punishment: *Hamlet vowed he would wreak vengeance on the murderer of his father;* to bring about, cause: *This policy will wreak havoc with the housing industry.*
residence	a place where one lives: *Professor Vieira has a summer residence in Maine.*
residents	people who live in a place: *Residents in the community protested the closing of the local fire station.*
rest	(verb) to relax: *If you're ill, you should rest in bed;* to place on or against: *Rest it against the wall;* (noun) remainder: *Answer the rest of the letters tomorrow.*
wrest	to tear away by violent twisting: *The shoplifter tried to wrest her arm away from the security guard;* to gain with difficulty: *It will not be easy to wrest this market from our competitors.*
rights	just claims, privileges: *Citizens have both rights and responsibilities.*
rites	plural of *rite,* solemn ceremony performed in accordance with prescribed rule: *Funeral rites vary from one culture to another.*
writes	present singular of *write,* compose: *Ms. Battersby writes a column for the company newsletter.*
ring	(verb) to give forth a clear sound: *Ring the bell on the counter if you need help;* (noun) a circle of metal or other material generally worn on the finger: *Earl doesn't wear his wedding ring;* an exclusive group of persons working together for selfish or illegal purposes: *The police broke up a drug ring.*

wring to twist with force: *Wring out your wet clothes, and hang them up to dry.*

road street: *The township will widen this road next year.*
rode past tense of *ride,* to be carried on: *They rode the train to work.*

role an actor's part in a play: *Haruun played the title role in* Othello; a part played in real life: *Harkness played a major role in restoring public confidence.*
roll (verb) to move along by turning over and over: *The cart will roll down the aisle*; (noun) a list of names: *Call the roll*; a small loaf of bread: *Vanessa ordered ham and cheese on a seeded roll.*

roomers people who rent one or more rooms to live in, lodgers: *Three roomers share the bathroom at the end of the hall.*
rumors unconfirmed reports, gossip, hearsay: *There are rumors that the company will shift its headquarters to Atlanta.*

sail (verb) to travel by water: *Ms. Travers likes to sail on weekends*; (noun) cloth spread to the winds to make a ship move: *A canvas sail is very heavy when it's wet.*
sale exchange of goods for money: *This property has been for sale for over a year;* an offering of something at lower prices than usual: *Our store's Labor Day Sale is always a big success.*

scene the place where an event occurs: *A criminal always returns to the scene of the crime*; a division of a play: *The second scene of Act II is too long*; a view of people or places: *The scene from Mount Rainier is beautiful*; a display of strong emotion before others: *Michael made a scene at the party.*
seen past participle of *see,* to perceive by the eye: *I have not seen Carlotta this month.*

seam a line formed by sewing together two pieces of material: *The seam of the dress is ripped*; any line marking the joining of edges: *The only seam in this vinyl floor is in the closet.*
seem to appear to be, to be apparently true: *Maureen seems to be the candidate best qualified for the position.*

seas large bodies of salt water: *They sailed the seven seas.*
sees present singular of *see: The Senator sees the President regularly.*
seize to take hold of suddenly or violently: *The store detective was able to seize the shoplifter before she escaped*; to take possession by force: *Jim is not afraid to seize an opportunity when it presents itself.* (Note *ei* spelling.)

serge a kind of cloth with slanting lines on its surface: *Leon wore a blue serge suit to the interview.*
surge to rise and fall violently, to rush forward in a great wave: *During a clearance sale, shoppers surge to the rear of the store.*

sew to fasten with needle and thread: *Jack stopped to sew a button on his coat before leaving for work.*

so in this manner or in order that: *Hold your pen so*; to this degree: *Do not talk so fast;* very: *You are so considerate*; therefore: *Our costs are up, so we will have to increase prices.*

sow to scatter seed on the ground: *The farmer decided to sow the field with wheat rather than rye.*

shear to cut with shears or scissors: *How many sheep can they shear in one hour?*

sheer very thin, almost transparent: *Mrs. Condos bought a pair of sheer stockings*; not mixed with anything else, absolute: *Your proposal is sheer nonsense*; straight up and down: *It is a sheer drop of 1000 feet to the foot of the cliff.*

shone past tense or past participle of *shine*, to emit rays of light: *The moon shone brightly.*

shown past participle of *show*, to exhibit: *I have shown you our new line of merchandise.*

sighs plural of *sigh*, to take in and let out a deep breath: *There were many sighs of relief when a new agreement was reached before the strike deadline.*

size extent, magnitude, amount: *We have not yet determined the size of the loss.*

NAME	CLASS	DATE	SCORE

Homonym Assignments

A. Select from the following words the one that correctly fits the blank in each of the sentences below. Then write the word in the answer space.

rap	wreak	writes	role	so
wrap	rest	ring	roll	sow
real	wrest	wring	roomers	sighs
reel	rights	road	rumors	size
reek	rites	rode	sew	

1. The worker who was dismissed swore to _____ vengeance upon his immediate supervisor.

    1._____

2. A Certificate of Incorporation provides a company with the legal _____ to operate as a corporation.

    2._____

3. Betty Alders, the comptroller, played a leading _____ in securing passage of the rate increase.

    3._____

4. Despite his sore finger, Don still _____ legibly.

    4._____

5. Her dismissal started many _____.

    5._____

6. The construction crew began to widen the _____.

    6._____

7. The extension phone has a sharp, insistent _____.

    7._____

8. Often meeting rooms _____ of cigarette smoke after a conference.

    8._____

9. It was necessary to return the dress because it was the wrong _____.

    9._____

10. Mr. Sims _____ to the restaurant to have lunch with Mr. Forrestal.

    10._____

11. The new supervisor called the department meeting _____ she could address her staff all at once.

    11._____

12. My _____ income decreases each time the inflation rate increases.

    12._____

13. Would you please forward the _____ of my mail to my home address?

    13._____

14. When the elevator door would not open, Sue began to
_____ on it frantically.

14. _____

15. Chet would _____ his hands when he became
nervous.

15. _____

B. In some of the following sentences, an incorrect word is used. Underline the incorrect
word, and write the correct word in the space provided. Where there is no error, write C
in the answer space.

1. His summer residents was at a popular resort.

1. _____

2. The Annual Company Dinner can almost be compared
with a tribal right because of its formality.

2. _____

3. Nautical seens are her favorite.

3. _____

4. Victory was rested from his grasp at the very last moment.

4. _____

5. Many ill-treated employees would like to reek vengeance on their unfair employers.

5. _____

6. The property was shone by appointment only.

6. _____

7. The audience's rapped attention was a tribute to the
speaker's skill with words.

7. _____

8. Before you mail the package, be sure that it is wrapped
securely.

8. _____

9. Ineffective management is the reel reason that many
businesses fail.

9. _____

10. A special meeting was called to determine ways to rest
sales from the competition.

10. _____

11. Diana was ill for a long time, it seams.

11. _____

12. There was a serge in prices once the supply
decreased.

12. _____

13. To enhance his position, the treasurer used every opportunity to seas control of additional responsibilities.

13. _____

14. Wilma responded to the announcement of her promotion with sheer surprise.

14. _____

15. I have not been shown how to ring up sales on the
cash register.

15. _____

C. Read the definition, and select the correct word from the second column to match that description. Write the word you selected in the answer space.

Definition	Word Choice	
1. a kind of cloth with slanting lines	serge, surge	1._____
2. to cut with scissors	shear, sheer	2._____
3. people who live in a place	residence, residents	3._____
4. extent, magnitude	sighs, size	4._____
5. exchange of goods for money	sail, sale	5._____
6. a place where an event occurs	scene, seen	6._____
7. to be apparently true	seam, seem	7._____
8. large bodies of salt water	seas, sees, seize	8._____
9. to scatter seed onn the ground	sew, so, sow	9._____
10. spellbound	rapt, wrapped	10._____

D. Select the right word for the sentence shown, and write it in the answer space. Then compose a sentence for the homonym not selected, and write your sentence in the space provided.

1. In order to (rest, wrest) the property from his control, they had to have him declared incompetent.

   1._____

   _____

   _____

   _____

2. Please order another (role, roll) of labels for me.

   2._____

   _____

   _____

   _____

3. The Constitution defends the civil (rights, rites) of citizens.

   3._____

   _____

   _____

   _____

4. His favorite suit was his blue (serge, surge) one.

4. _____

_____

_____

_____

5. The summer furniture (sail, sale) begins tomorrow.

5. _____

_____

_____

_____

6. They tried to (sees, seize) control of the firm by buying many shares of stock.

6. _____

_____

_____

_____

7. "Don't try to do (sew, so) much," was the doctor's advice.

7. _____

_____

_____

_____

8. As a new employee, Lana had to be (shone, shown) all the new procedures.

8. _____

_____

_____

_____

9. What is your current (residence, residents)?

9. _____

_____

_____

_____

10. She was cold so she (rapped, wrapped) the blanket tightly around herself.

10. _____

_____

_____

_____

Words Ending in **cede—ceed—sede** and Words Adding **k** After Ending in **c**

Chapter 11

Words ending in cede—ceed—sede

Which word in each of the following columns is spelled correctly?

supersede	prosede	intersede
supercede	procede	intercede
superceed	proceed	interceed

The correct spellings are:

supersede	proceed	intercede

As this brief quiz indicates, these three different endings—**cede, ceed, sede**—all sound alike: *seed.* Choosing the right one, however, is not difficult. That is because only 12 words in the English language end in the sound **seed**, and not all of them are commonly used. Learn the following facts, and you will have mastered all the **seed** words:

1. Only one word in the entire language ends in **sede—supersede.***
2. Only three words end in **ceed—exceed, proceed, succeed**.
3. The remaining eight words end in **cede—accede, antecede, cede, concede, intercede,* precede, recede, secede.**

Of these eight words you are likely to use only four with any frequency—**concede, intercede, precede, recede**. **Antecede**, which means *to go before*, is very rarely used. The word **antecedent** (derived from **antecede**) is more common and is most often found in discussions of grammar, where it means a word that goes before a pronoun and is referred to by the pronoun.

175

Words adding k after ending in c

<table>
<tr><td>Rule</td></tr>
</table>

When adding suffixes that begin with softening vowels (**ing, er, ed, y**) to words ending in **c**, put a **k** after the **c** and then add the suffix.

Take the word **picnic,** for example. Very few people misspell **picnic.** But many people begin to have trouble when they add the suffixes **ing, er, ed,** and **y.** The natural tendency simply to add these suffixes to **picnic** leads to the following:

1. The final **c** in **picnic** is *hard.* It sounds like **k.**
2. If you merely added **ing** to **picnic,** you would soften the hard **c** to an **s** sound. (A vowel after **c** [for example, **i** in **ing**] almost always softens the **c** sound to **s.**) So **picnicing** would be pronounced **pik′-nis-ing.**

To retain the hard **k** sound of **c** when you add **ing,** simply put a **k** after the **c** and then add **ing.** So you have **picnicking.**

Here is how to deal with the words in this group.

colic		colicky	
frolic	frolicked	frolicker	frolicking
mimic	mimicked		mimicking
panic	panicked	panicky	panicking
picnic	picnicked	picnicker	picnicking
politic	politicked		politicking
shellac	shellacked		shellacking
traffic	trafficked	trafficker	trafficking

Notice that there is no **k** in **mimicry, frolicsome,** etc., because the suffix begins with a consonant, not a softening vowel. Similarly, there is no **k** in **political** because the suffix **al** does not begin with a softening vowel.

Note The word **arc,** meaning a curve or a type of welding, is an exception. The dictionary lists **arced** and **arcing** as correct spellings, with **arcked** and **arcking** as acceptable variants.

NAME	CLASS	DATE	SCORE

Spelling Assignments

A. In the following list, some words are misspelled. Underline each misspelled word, and write the correct spelling in the space provided. If the printed word is correctly spelled, write C in the space.

1.	acceed	_____	6.	recede	_____
2.	exceed	_____	7.	succeed	_____
3.	procede	_____	8.	interceed	_____
4.	supercede	_____	9.	preceed	_____
5.	concede	_____	10.	antecede	_____

B. Add **cede, ceed,** or **sede** (whichever is correct) to each of the following prefixes. Then rewrite the complete word on the line to the right.

1.	super _____	_____	6.	ac_____	_____
2.	ex_____	_____	7.	con_____	_____
3.	re _____	_____	8.	se_____	_____
4.	pre _____	_____	9.	suc_____	_____
5.	pro _____	_____	10.	inter _____	_____

C. Write the proper form of the word in parentheses in the answer space.

1. Garston was thought to be a (traffic) in stolen goods.   1._____
2. Emma's newborn baby was (colic) all evening.   2._____
3. The employees (picnic) on the company grounds yesterday.   3._____
4. Nan spent the weekend (shellac) the floor in her den.   4._____
5. Representatives of both (politic) parties were present for the meeting.   5._____
6. Neighborhood children (frolic) on the lawn.   6._____

7. Many people (panic) during the stock market crash of 1929.

7. _____

8. At the office party, Jake (mimic) his boss's manner of speech.

8. _____

9. They were known to be (traffic) in narcotics.

9. _____

10. The (picnic) ran to their cars when it began to rain.

10. _____

11. The painters have not yet (shellac) the floor.

11. _____

12. A lot of office (politic) took place prior to the election.

12. _____

13. (Frolic) children played on the company lawn.

13. _____

14. Periodic fire drills were held to prevent people from (panic).

14. _____

15. They are highly skilled in the art of (mimic).

15. _____

16. The suspect had (traffic) in narcotics.

16. _____

17. Fireworks (arc) high over the treetops.

17. _____

18. The staff members discussed (politic) over lunch.

18. _____

19. (Panic) depositors waited for the bank doors to open.

19. _____

20. Their plans to corner the market seemed almost (maniac).

20. _____

D. Write the words missing from the statements in the answer space.

The only word that ends in **sede** is ____1____.

1. _____

The only three words that end in **ceed** are ____2____, ____3____, and ____4____.

2. _____

3. _____

4. _____

A **cede** word that means *to give in* is ____5____.

5. _____

A **cede** word that means *to go between* is ____6____.

6. _____

A **cede** word that means *to go before* is ____7____.

7. _____

A **cede** word that means *to go back* is ____8____.

8. _____

A **cede** word that means *to say yes* is ____9____.

9. _____

A **cede** word that means *to withdraw formally* is ____10____.

10. _____

Homonyms

sleight	dexterity, skill: *The magician used sleight of hand to make the coin disappear.*
slight	(adjective) small, thin, meager: *Sue has a slight cold. He is slight of build;* (verb) to treat discourteously or indifferently: *We must be careful not to slight Ms. Lopomo at the reception.*
soar	to fly at a great height, fly upward: *Eagles soar to enormous altitudes.*
sore	(adjective) painful, aching: *Melissa has a sore throat;* (noun) a break in the skin: *Patrick has a festering sore on his leg.*
sole	(noun) bottom of a shoe or foot: *There is a hole in the sole of the shoe;* (adjective) one and only: *My sole purpose is to convince you of my innocence.*
soul	inner spirit: *Do you believe that the soul lives after the body dies?*
some	an unspecified number, quantity, etc.: *Ms. Zurich has been with the firm for some years now.*
sum	an amount of money: *The sum paid in reparation for the injury was excessive;* the whole amount, total: *The whole is the sum of its parts.*
staid	sedate, settled, steady, solemn: *Despite the disruptive behavior of some people in the auditorium, the committee members remained staid throughout the hearing.*
stayed	past tense of *stay,* to remain or dwell: *Professor Toynton stayed after class to answer additional questions. We stayed at an old country inn on our vacation.*
stairs	series of steps: *Ralph carried the package up four flights of stairs.*
stares	present singular of *stare,* to look long or directly at something with eyes wide open: *He often stares out the window during class.*
stake	(noun) a wooden post: *The tent collapsed when the stake pulled out of the ground;* (verb) to bet or hazard: *She was willing to stake her career on the correctness of her decision.*
steak	cut of meat: *Ruth ordered a steak sandwich for lunch.*
stationary	not moving, standing still, unchanging: *The wholesale price of eggs has been stationary for a year.*
stationery	writing materials—paper, cards, envelopes, etc.: *Please order two cartons of letterhead stationery.* (*Spelling Aid:* stationAry refers to plAce; stationERy refers to papER.)
steal	to rob: *The cashier tried to steal money from the register;* to move secretly: *Karl steals quietly into the office whenever he's late.*
steel	a metal made from iron: *These kitchen bowls are made of stainless steel.*

stile   a step or set of steps for passing over a fence or wall: *The farmer used the stile to walk from one field to the other.*

style   the way in which something is said or done: *Consult a manual of style for the correct format. Ms. Maring's style is too formal for modern business correspondence.*

straight   direct, not curved: *A straight line is the shortest distance between two points.*

strait   a narrow body of water: *The Bering Strait separates Alaska from Siberia;* usually plural, a distressing situation: *From a strictly financial point of view, we are in dire straits.*

tacks   short nails or pins with sharp points and large flat heads: *We need more tacks for the bulletin board.*

tax   a mandatory fee: *The sales tax in New Jersey is 6 percent.*

tail   the hind part: *The dog chased its tail. Tuck the tail of your shirt into your pants.*

tale   a story: *Dickens wrote* A Tale of Two Cities.

taught   past tense of *teach,* to train, impart knowledge to: *Della taught herself French and Spanish.*

taut   tight, not slack: *Pull the rope taut.*

tear   a droplet from the eye: *A tear trickled down his cheek.*

tier   a row, a layer: *Our seats are in the upper tier of the grandstand.*

threw   past tense of *throw,* to fling, hurl: *Carlos threw the packages onto the truck.*

through   (preposition) in one side and out the other: *She walked through the room;* to various places in: *We traveled through New England on our vacation;* (adjective) finished: *Jack is through with his work.*

throne   the chair on which a king or queen sits on formal occasions: *The king's throne was on a platform at the end of the hall.*

thrown   past participle of *throw,* to toss or hurl: *I have accidentally thrown out my copy of the report.*

tide   (noun) the daily rise and fall of a body of water: *We wanted to know the time of high tide;* change from one condition to the other: *The economic tide has shifted;* (verb: **tide over**) to help along for a time: *This money will tide you over until you find another job.*

tied   past tense of *tie,* to fasten, join: *Aaron tied a knot.*

timber   lumber: *The timber was shipped to the mill.*

timbre   distinctive tone or character: *Beverly's voice has a bell-like timbre.*

toe   a digit of the foot: *Larry broke his toe.*

tow   to pull along: *Our car is too small to tow a trailer.*

NAME	CLASS	DATE	SCORE

Homonym Assignments

A. Select from the following words the one that correctly fits the blank in each of the sentences below. Then write the word in the answer space.

soar	staid	stake	steal	tide
sore	stayed	steak	steel	tied
sole	stairs	stationary	throne	
soul	stares	stationery	thrown	

1. The cost-of-living index has remained _____ for
    the last three months.   1._____

2. We _____ at the newest hotel in the city.   2._____

3. An inexpensive carpet was _____ over the
    marble floor.   3._____

4. He felt a _____ of emotion swell within him as he
    faced the crowd to thank them.   4._____

5. Your supply of _____ should reach you in a few
    days.   5._____

6. Prince Charles is the heir to the British _____.   6._____

7. My _____ aim in life is to please my family.   7._____

8. Most people feel uncomfortable when someone
    _____ at them.   8._____

9. During the strike at the _____ mill, the price of
    metal soared.   9._____

10. She felt tongue-_____ because she was so
    shocked at the developments.   10._____

11. All of us have a great _____ in our federal and
    local governments.   11._____

12. The good news made our spirits _____.   12._____

13. The _____ dinner was the most expensive one
    on the menu.   13._____

14. Records show that shoplifters _____ an enor-
    mous amount of merchandise annually.   14._____

15. All the exercise at the company outing left many of the
employees _____ .   15. _____

B. In some of the following sentences, an incorrect word is used. Underline the incorrect word, and write the correct word in the space provided. Where there is no error, write C in the answer space.

1. Why did he steak a fortune on the outcome of the vote?   1. _____

2. Across the street is a shop where you can have the sole of your shoe repaired.   2. _____

3. He ordered his steak medium rare.   3. _____

4. I deposited a large some in my savings account.   4. _____

5. Even though she had the blouse for a number of years, it was right in stile.   5. _____

6. Manuel is sleight in stature, but he is very strong.   6. _____

7. The canvas was stretched so that it was taught.   7. _____

8. Two hundred dollars was advanced to Ms. Mendoza to tide her over until her reimbursement check for the convention expenses came through.   8. _____

9. News of the stock split through the stockholders into a jovial mood.   9. _____

10. Frieda kept everyone in suspense as she recounted the tale of her weekend experience.   10. _____

11. The increased price of timbre has had the effect of increasing the cost of homeownership.   11. _____

12. Instead of going through the appropriate administrative channels, Rosa went boldly straight to the top.   12. _____

13. Their leadership style was too authoritarian.   13. _____

14. They withheld too much tacks from Dana's paycheck.   14. _____

15. To accommodate the new set of manuals, we need another tear on the bookcase.   15. _____

C. Read the definition, and select the correct word from the second column to match that description. Write the word you selected in the answer space.

Definition	Word Choice	
1. a specified amount of money	some, sum	1. _____

2. short nails or pins with
    sharp points   tacks, tax   2._____

3. small, thin, meager   sleight, slight   3._____

4. a set of steps for passing
    over a wall   stile, style   4._____

5. a narrow body of water   straight, strait   5._____

6. in one side and out the other   threw, through   6._____

7. to pull along   toe, tow   7._____

8. distinctive tone or character   timber, timbre   8._____

9. sedate, solemn   staid, stayed   9._____

10. inner spirit   sole, soul   10._____

D. Select the right word for the sentence shown, and write it in the answer space. Then compose a sentence for the homonym not selected, and write your sentence in the space provided.

1. The (stationary, stationery) bike provided a lot of good
    exercise.   1._____

    _____

    _____

    _____

2. Mr. Winston was the (sole, soul) owner of the firm.   2._____

    _____

    _____

    _____

3. Linda had a seat in the second (tear, tier).   3._____

    _____

    _____

    _____

4. Madeline went (threw, through) the interview success-
    fully.   4._____

    _____

    _____

    _____

5. I put (some, sum) of my paycheck into the bank weekly. 5. _____

_____

_____

_____

6. The questioning was intensive during the trial; nevertheless, the defendant's composure remained (staid,
stayed) throughout. 6. _____

_____

_____

_____

7. If there is even a (sleight, slight) chance that we can
succeed, I want to try. 7. _____

_____

_____

_____

8. Be aware that the two-letter state abbreviation is the
proper (stile, style) to be used in typing an envelope address. 8. _____

_____

_____

_____

9. The young children (tide, tied) their shoes without any
help. 9. _____

_____

_____

_____

10. Mike was uncomfortable because of the (stairs, stares)
he got from those who opposed his plan. 10. _____

_____

_____

_____

NAME   **CLASS**   **DATE**   **SCORE**

Vocabulary Enrichment

Chapters 8–11

A. You should now be familiar with the meaning of each of the words below. In the space provided to the right, write the word that best completes the meaning of the sentence. Cross out each word in the list as you use it.

align	dissembled	ethically	malign	supersede
beneficially	disseminated	gnarled	misdemeanor	vignette
benign	dissertation	haughty	pneumatic	
biennially	dissoluble	illicit	prophetically	
coincidentally	dissonance	initially	pseudonym	
conditionally	eccentrically	intercede	psychosis	
dissect	eclectically	interrogate	ptomaine	

1. His _____ nature at all times made him well liked
    by coworkers and supervisors alike.   1._____

2. Following the bank robbery, the police began to
    _____ all of the personnel and customers who
    were present.   2._____

3. Mary's timesaving practices for handling the incoming
    mail were _____ in a special interoffice memo.   3._____

4. It was necessary to call in a mediator to _____ in
    the grievance action.   4._____

5. Having achieved so many successes so quickly in her
    career, she appeared to have a(n) _____ attitude
    in her relationships with others.   5._____

6. Scott was hired on a six-month trial basis; therefore, he
    was hired only _____.   6._____

7. To facilitate payments, there was a(n) _____
    tube conveyor system between the repair shop and the
    cashier's office.   7._____

8. Because Troy did not associate much with his
    coworkers, they felt that he acted _____.   8._____

9. In the history of our company, he was the only employee I know of who was fired because he had a(n) _____ influence on his coworkers.

9. _____

10. Affirmative action laws prohibit a prospective employer from asking questions regarding a previous arrest record for a(n) _____ .

10. _____

11. Miriam _____ her fears by pretending to be confident of success.

11. _____

12. Jean's constant gossiping created _____ among the other office employees.

12. _____

13. Writers often use a(n) _____ to keep their identity secret.

13. _____

14. Dr. Naylor gave an address based on his recently completed _____ .

14. _____

15. It is sometimes difficult to get printed or typed material to _____ properly on a form.

15. _____

B. For this exercise you must refer to the list of words given for assignment A above. Select any ten words that you did not use in completing assignment A. For each of the ten words you selected, compose a meaningful sentence on a separate sheet of paper.

C. Choose the word from the list below that is closest in meaning to the numbered word or words in the paragraphs on pages 187–188. Write the word you selected from the list in the answer space. Use each word only once.

assets	**periodic**
automated	**principles**
balances	**recorded**
changes	**records**
compared	**referred**
current	**regulations**
entry	**repeats**
environment	**sound**
figures	**status**
fiscal	**summarized**
interacts	**transaction**
manually	**worth**
owed	

Maintaining Accounting Records

Let's take a look at some basics in accounting. Orderly
records of the 1. MONETARY activities of a business or an   1._____
individual are called accounting records. Two factors dictate
the need for efficient accounting records in today's business
2. SETTING. In the first place, accounting information is   2._____
necessary as a basis for effective planning and decision
making. Secondly, 3. INTERMITTENT reports on financial status   3._____
are required outside the business as a result of government
4. REQUIREMENTS and because of business transactions with other   4._____
companies and institutions.

Every office worker 5. WORKS RECIPROCALLY with accounting   5._____
records of some type as part of a day's work. Sometimes these
records are processed 6. BY HAND, but the growing trend is to   6._____
process these records using 7. ELECTRONIC equipment.   7._____

A study of accounting traces the accounting cycle. A new
business starts its 8. SET OF BOOKS by preparing a balance   8._____
sheet, which shows the financial 9. CONDITION of the business   9._____
at the start of its first day. The balance sheet lists the
10. THINGS OF VALUE, what is owned; the liabilities, what is   10._____
11. OBLIGATED; and the capital, the business's 12. VALUE at a   11._____
given time.   12._____

Just as soon as one 13. BUSINESS EXCHANGE takes place, the   13._____
status on the beginning balance sheet is changed. Hundreds,
sometimes thousands, of these business exchanges take place in
a given business day. These day-to-day exchanges are 14. LISTED   14._____
in a book of original entry called a journal, which can be
15. LIKENED to the "diary" of a business.   15._____

Every 16. RECORDED ITEM in the journal is posted to an   16._____
appropriate ledger account so that all the 17. DEVIATIONS in   17._____
one particular item are 18. TOTALED in one place. At the end   18._____

of the fiscal period, which is normally monthly, quarterly, or
annually, the 19. AMOUNTS in the accounts are summarized on a   19. _____
work sheet. An income statement is prepared from the work sheet
20. NUMBERS, and a net income or loss for the period is   20. _____
shown. Income accounts are closed and a new balance sheet is
prepared at this time, reflecting the 21. PRESENT and updated   21. _____
fiscal status of the business. This cycle 22. RECURS in each   22. _____
fiscal period.

Understanding how debits and credits affect the various account
balances is the key to a 23. RELIABLE background in   23. _____
accounting 24. THEORY. Understanding the theory of debit and   24. _____
credit is sometimes 25. ALLUDED to as understanding the   25. _____
language of business.

Words Ending in **ar—er—or**

The three endings **ar, er,** and **or** have several different functions and meanings. The most common, **er,** of course, is used to form the comparative form of most adjectives (**harder, longer,** etc.). All three can be used to indicate an actor or doer (**beggar, employer, counselor**). While the choice of **er** as an adjective suffix never poses a spelling problem, there is no simple rule or memory aid that can help you with other words ending in **ar, er,** or **or.** Fortunately, you are probably already familiar with the proper spelling of most of the frequently used words that end with these three combinations. Look at the following lists, and focus your attention on the words you are not sure of. Learn these, and you will know the words ending in **ar, er,** or **or** that you would normally use. Consult your dictionary when you need the proper spelling of others.

Note	In some instances the endings of some words are not true suffixes (**cellar**, for example). We have included these words here because we are concerned more with correct spelling than we are with accurate word descriptions.

ar

angular	curricular	particular	similar
beggar	dollar	peculiar	singular
burglar	familiar	pillar	spectacular
bursar*	grammar	polar	sugar
calendar	insular	popular	vehicular
cedar	liar	registrar	vicar
cellar	lunar	regular	vinegar
circular	molar	scholar	vulgar
collar	muscular		

er

adjuster	consumer	lecturer	purchaser
administer	cosigner	ledger	receiver
advertiser	debater	manager	register
amplifier*	defender	manufacturer	retainer
announcer	designer	merger	shareholder
appraiser	diameter	messenger	shipper
arbiter	disaster	meter	soldier
beginner	employer	minister	stenographer
believer	eraser	observer	subscriber
boarder	examiner	officer	teacher
bookkeeper	farmer	order	teller
border	foreigner	partner	traveler
carrier	haberdasher	passenger	treasurer
caterer	interpreter	prisoner	voucher
character	jeweler	prompter	waiver
commissioner	laborer	proofreader	writer
comptroller*	lawyer	provider	

or

accelerator	contributor	inheritor	rigor
actor	counselor	inventor	rumor
administrator	creditor*	investigator	sailor
advisor	debtor*	investor	savor
aggressor	depositor	janitor	sculptor
ambassador	dictator	labor	senator
ancestor	director	legislator	solicitor
anchor	distributor*	manor	spectator
auditor*	doctor	minor	sponsor
author	duplicator	monitor	successor
aviator	editor	mortgagor	suitor
bachelor	educator	motor	superior
behavior	elevator	neighbor	supervisor
benefactor	emperor	odor	surveyor
bettor	escalator	operator	survivor
calculator	executor	orator	tabulator
censor	factor	predecessor	tailor
collector	governor	prior	tenor
commentator	harbor	professor	tractor
competitor	humor	proprietor*	traitor
conductor	impostor	protector	ventilator
conqueror	incinerator*	radiator	vigor
conspirator	indicator	realtor	visitor
contractor	inferior	refrigerator	word processor

NAME	CLASS	DATE	SCORE

Spelling Assignments

A. In the following list, some words are misspelled. Underline each misspelled word, and write the correct spelling in the space provided. If the printed word is correctly spelled, write C in the space.

1.	beggar	_____	16.	grammer	_____
2.	adjustor	_____	17.	familiar	_____
3.	advertiser	_____	18.	appraisor	_____
4.	aviator	_____	19.	beginner	_____
5.	accelerater	_____	20.	consumor	_____
6.	bursar	_____	21.	bookkeeper	_____
7.	calender	_____	22.	successer	_____
8.	solicitar	_____	23.	tractor	_____
9.	circuler	_____	24.	purchasor	_____
10.	similar	_____	25.	registrer	_____
11.	celler	_____	26.	peculiar	_____
12.	managor	_____	27.	polor	_____
13.	author	_____	28.	subscribor	_____
14.	auditer	_____	29.	collector	_____
15.	singuler	_____	30.	distributer	_____

B. Insert **ar, er,** or **or** (whichever is correct) in the spaces in the following words. Then rewrite the complete word on the line to the right.

1.	tabulat _____	_____	5.	calculat _____	_____
2.	design _____	_____	6.	duplicat _____	_____
3.	examin _____	_____	7.	eras _____	_____
4.	deposit _____	_____	8.	interpret _____	_____

9. legislat_____ _____
10. generat _____ _____
11. invent _____ _____
12. indicat _____ _____
13. investigat____ _____
14. lectur_____ _____
15. manufactur __ _____
16. contract_____ _____
17. passeng _____ _____
18. incinerat ____ _____
19. refrigerat ____ _____
20. observ_____ _____
21. petition _____ _____
22. janit_____ _____
23. invest _____ _____
24. radiat_____ _____

25. plaster_____ _____
26. offic_____ _____
27. receiv _____ _____
28. shipp_____ _____
29. visit_____ _____
30. protect_____ _____
31. spectat _____ _____
32. senat_____ _____
33. slipp _____ _____
34. stenograph __ _____
35. regist_____ _____
36. supervis ____ _____
37. govern_____ _____
38. counsel _____ _____
39. impost_____ _____
40. tell_____ _____

C. Underline the misspelled word or words in each of the following groups of three. Spell the word or words correctly in the space at the right. If there are no errors in the group, write C.

1. anguler	vehicular	tractor	1. _____
2. editor	popular	similar	2. _____
3. senater	indicator	subscribor	3. _____
4. odor	bordar	vigor	4. _____
5. spectaculer	voucher	purchaser	5. _____
6. stenographer	erasor	actor	6. _____
7. teacher	tailor	arbitor	7. _____
8. auditer	employer	announcer	8. _____
9. jeweler	character	ambassader	9. _____
10. counselor	humer	realtor	10. _____
11. escalator	doctor	professer	11. _____
12. aggresser	interpreter	executer	12. _____
13. scholar	dollar	vicar	13. _____

14.	luner	emperor	debter	14._____
15.	censor	minor	moter	15._____
16.	competitor	commentator	administrator	16._____
17.	disastor	superier	partner	17._____
18.	prior	proprietor	comptrollar	18._____
19.	ledger	copywriter	sponsor	19._____
20.	grammer	facter	caterer	20._____
21.	director	prisoner	merger	21._____
22.	amplifier	lawyer	operater	22._____
23.	burglar	vulgar	educator	23._____
24.	registrar	crediter	piller	24._____
25.	particular	travelor	waiver	25._____
26.	messengar	retainer	shareholder	26._____
27.	inferior	proofreader	foreignar	27._____
28.	commissioner	behavier	benefactor	28._____
29.	bursar	regular	contributor	29._____
30.	governor	collar	treasurer	30._____

Homonyms

tracked past tense of *track*, to trail, leave marks: *They tracked mud into the reception room.*

tract area or region not specifically bounded: *Our company has just purchased a large tract of land*; a pamphlet or leaflet: *Ms. Gross has written a tract on estate planning*; a system of living organs having a special function: *Dr. Sawyer specializes in diseases of the digestive tract.*

troop (noun) a body of soldiers or scouts: *Our company sponsors a Boy Scout troop*; a great number: *A troop of children toured the plant yesterday*; (verb) to go in large numbers: *The tour group may troop past the assembly line.*

troupe a group of performers: *A ballet troupe is in town.*

undo to unfasten: *Please undo this now*; to destroy: *This decision could undo all of our efforts.*

undue not fitting, not proper: *The lobbyists have exercised undue influence on legislators to win votes for certain bills*; too great, too much, unwarranted: *Many authorities condemn the undue rigor of some of our tax laws.*

vain having too much pride: *Doug is quite vain*; with *in*, of no use, without success: *Our efforts to save the company from bankruptcy were in vain.*

vane an indicator of wind direction: *The weather vane on the barn blew down.*

vein a blood vessel: *Linda accidentally punctured a vein in her wrist*; a large deposit of ore: *The engineers have located a large vein of copper;* the general disposition running through something: *The interview was conducted in a humorous vein.*

vary to change, alter, modify: *The new supervisor has not asked us to vary any of our procedures.*

very (adverb) to a great extent, extremely: *Our new phone system is very complicated*; (adjective) in the fullest sense, absolute: *She proceeded to do the very opposite of what she had promised*; being just what is needed or suitable: *Jan is the very person we need to head this operation.*

vial a small container for liquids: *I gave my secretary a small vial of perfume.*

vile foul, disgusting, offensive: *Anne will not tolerate vile language. A vile odor filled the room.*

viol a stringed instrument: *She played the bass viol in the community orchestra.*

vice evil conduct, corruption: *Gambling is a vice according to our state laws.*

vise tool used for holding an object firmly while it is being worked upon: *The hardware store has a carpenter's vise on sale this week.*

waist the circumference of the body between the ribs and the hips: *Rich has a narrow waist.*

waste (verb) to spend uselessly: *Any involvement in this project would waste both time and money*; (noun) useless or worthless material: *Our new manufacturing process eliminates most of the waste*; a desert, a wilderness: *These hundreds of square miles are little more than a barren waste.*

waive to give up a right or claim to something: *Mr. Garson was offered $400,000 to waive his rights to the Burton estate.*

wave (noun) a moving swell of water or any movement like it: *The bathers were engulfed by an enormous wave*; (verb) to move back and forth: *Wave your hand to attract their attention.*

waiver relinquishment of a right: *I accept your waiver of claim to the property.*
waver to be hesitant, indecisive: *He would often waver about which model to recommend.*

ware goods, a specified kind of merchandise: *The local department store has a kitchenware section.*
wear to carry on one's person for covering, ornament, defense: *It's not proper to wear clothes that are too informal for the business office*; to impair by constant use or friction: *Customer traffic will quickly wear away the shine on these floors*; to hold up in use: *These shoes wear well.*

way manner, method, path, means, direction: *This is the best way to invest your money.*
weigh to find the weight of: *Weigh these packages before you call the delivery service*; to consider: *Weigh all the evidence before making your decision.*

weak not strong: *The opposing party offers a weak economic recovery program.*
week seven successive days: *Sunday is the first day of the week.*

weather condition of the atmosphere: *What is the weather forecast for tomorrow?*
whether indicating a choice or alternative: *I don't know whether to adopt your proposal or theirs.*

wet (verb) to dampen: *Wet a sponge and wipe the table*; (adjective) damp: *Take off those wet clothes.*
whet to sharpen by rubbing: *Geoffrey will whet the knife before slicing the roast*; to stimulate: *Seasoned foods whet the appetite.*

which pronoun or adjective indicating choice: *Which is yours? Which way is out?*
witch evil woman with magical powers: *The Salem judges accused her of being a witch.*

while during the time that: *Mr. Ali phoned while you were at lunch.*
wile a trick or stratagem: *He used every wile to outwit his opponent.*

wrung past tense of *wring*, to squeeze, force out: *I wrung out the clothes by hand.*
rung past participle of *ring*: *The telephone has not rung all day*; (noun) a crosspiece of a ladder or chair: *I climbed up the ladder one rung at a time.*

wry   cleverly and ironically humorous: *Ms. Fakher made several wry remarks during the interview.*

rye   a cereal grass: *She preferred rye bread to white.*

you'll   contraction of *you will* or *you shall: You'll be moving to a new office.*

yule   Christmas: *Andy lighted the yule log.*

NAME	CLASS	DATE	SCORE

Homonym Assignments

A. Select from the following words the one that correctly fits the blank in each of the sentences below. Then write the word in the answer space.

tracked	vice	wave	way	whet
tract	vise	waiver	weigh	wrung
vain	waist	waver	weather	rung
vane	waste	ware	whether	you'll
vein	waive	wear	wet	yule

1. The auditor _____ the error from the date it was made up through the present.

   1._____

2. If the author signed the contract as it is presently written, he would _____ his rights to the copyright.

   2._____

3. Careless shoppers may _____ significant sums of money through foolish buying.

   3._____

4. The real estate sale included both the farm and a significantly large _____ of land.

   4._____

5. Choosing the right kind of clothing to _____ to work every day is important.

   5._____

6. The smell of coffee brewing does _____ our appetite for a break.

   6._____

7. Employment trends in some key industries often serve as the weather _____ of trends for the whole economy.

   7._____

8. At the present time, it is not certain _____ there will be a change in the fall prices.

   8._____

9. Lamar's recent promotion is another _____ on the ladder to success in business.

   9._____

10. _____ help to ensure your success if you plan to study and keep abreast.

   10._____

11. We argued in _____ for the increased funding.

   11._____

12. Sue was so scared that the grip she had on my hand felt like a _____.

   12._____

13. He would _____ about his decisions too
    frequently to be an effective leader.   13. _____

14. The grapevine is an informal _____ of com-
    munication.   14. _____

15. Their greatest _____ was their smoking.   15. _____

B. In some of the following sentences, an incorrect word is used. Underline the incorrect
word, and write the correct word in the space provided. Where there is no error, write C
in the answer space.

1. There was no official news yet that the drill had struck
   a gold vain.   1. _____

2. All of the employees rebelled because of the pressure
   under which they were forced to work.   2. _____

3. Her rye sense of humor made her very popular.   3. _____

4. Each time you move up a rung of the career ladder, it
   means greater responsibility.   4. _____

5. The signs of recovery from inflation are still very weak. 5. _____

6. Always be sure to way all the facts carefully before
   coming to a final decision.   6. _____

7. To get attention in the very crowded meeting hall, Mr.
   Warren began to wave his hand vigorously.   7. _____

8. Her popularity suffered because she had a habit of
   making vile remarks.   8. _____

9. A troop of union representatives went to the executive
   offices to dramatize their complaints.   9. _____

10. The chemist mixed the formula by carefully measuring
    each liquid in a vial first.   10. _____

11. Many companies recycle their scrap or waistpaper.   11. _____

12. One of the rules of our filing system is that no file
    should be kept out longer than a week.   12. _____

13. The sales for the quarter did not vary much.   13. _____

14. Kevin had to undue the damage his remarks had done.   14. _____

15. It doesn't matter weather I go or I stay.   15. _____

C. Read the definition, and select the correct word from the second column to match that description. Write the word you selected in the answer space.

Definition	Word Choice	
1. Christmas	you'll, yule	1._____
2. a cereal grass	rye, wry	2._____
3. a trick or stratagem	while, wile	3._____
4. to dampen	wet, whet	4._____
5. the circumference of the body between the ribs and the hips	waist, waste	5._____
6. goods, a specified kind of merchandise	ware, wear	6._____
7. condition of the atmosphere	weather, whether	7._____
8. a group of performers	troop, troupe	8._____
9. a stringed instrument	vial, vile, viol	9._____
10. evil woman with magical powers	which, witch	10._____

D. Select the right word for the sentence shown, and write it in the answer space. Then compose a sentence for the homonym not selected, and write your sentence in the space provided.

1. (Which, Witch) color do you prefer?   1._____

_____

_____

_____

2. Even though the figures were changed in the report, the final percentages did not (vary, very) much.   2._____

_____

_____

_____

3. (You'll, Yule) never regret doing the best that you can do.   3._____

_____

_____

_____

4. The scientist placed the chemical in a (vial, vile) for
   storage.   4. _____

   _____

   _____

   _____

5. The attorney was charged with having (undo, undue) influence on his client's testimony.   5. _____

   _____

   _____

   _____

6. Carmen tried not to appear (vain, vane) as she accepted the compliments on her new outfit.   6. _____

   _____

   _____

   _____

7. The dog entered the house and (tracked, tract) dirt on
   the kitchen floor.   7. _____

   _____

   _____

   _____

8. The company was uneasy about having a (troop,
   troupe) of visitors tour the plant.   8. _____

   _____

   _____

   _____

9. The keynote speaker aimed to (wet, whet) the
   audience's appetite for the program that was to follow.   9. _____

   _____

   _____

   _____

10. Which (way, weigh) should I format the report?   10. _____

    _____

    _____

    _____

Review Exercises

A. There are misspelled words in some of the following sentences. Underline each misspelled word, and write the correct spelling in the space provided. If there are no misspelled words, write C in the space next to the sentence.

1. The panickey woman slipped on the wet floor.
   1._____

2. The auditor and accountant had to mete for several hours to discuss the tax shelter strategy.
   2._____

3. The candidate found it difficult to consede the election, especially after the close vote.
   3._____

4. Terminals are often used to interrogate or query a computer for information.
   4._____

5. Illogical steps in a computer program need to be debugged.
   5._____

6. Announcements about new equipment developments seem to be erratic rather than systematic.
   6._____

7. The floors should be shellacked after the walls are painted.
   7._____

8. If a lease is broken, a tenant can be disspossessed.
   8._____

9. Efficient keyboarding cannot be measured rhythmically with a metronome.
   9._____

10. There has been a marked drop in sales as a result of the foriegn import competition.
    10._____

11. Manufacturers of ladies' apparel follow the fashion news conscientiously.
    11._____

12. Mr. Solas, formerly the president, is now the chairman of the board.
    12._____

13. Our sales for the month have risen at an apparently fantastic rate.
    13._____

14. A bank usualy insists on collateral for a large loan.
    14._____

15. Plastic packageing is very popular these days.
    15._____

16. Accessories should always complement an outfit.
    16._____

17. Reliable stores cheerfully refund money to customers who are dissatisfied with their purchases.
    17._____

18. Returns should be maid within ten days.
    18._____

19. The delegates voted to override the president's veto.
    19._____

20. The will was duely signed and witnessed.   20. _____

21. Many college students work on a part-time basis to
    help defray their academic expenses.   21. _____

22. The attorney for the defense started to interogate the
    witness.   22. _____

23. The terms of the new contract superseded those of the
    old one.   23. _____

24. The proceeds from the scholarship fund sponsored by
    our firm are distributed to high school graduates each
    June at commencement.   24. _____

25. The plan was financialy sound.   25. _____

B. Underline each error in the following memos, and write the correct spelling or usage in
the space provided to the right of the line. If there are no errors in the line, write C in the
space.

MEMO TO: Maria Hernandez, Personnel Department

FROM: Mary Jo Oliverio, Records Center

DATE: September 9, 19--

SUBJECT: December Conference Participation

1 I am enclosing a copy of a pamplet describing a Micrographics
2 Workshop that is going to be held in Washington, D.C., early
3 in December.

4 It sounds like it has much to ofer, and I would like you to
5 consider my request for some release time to attend the workshop
6 for the three daze.

7 Would you be interested in joinning me?

   mjo
   Enclosure

1. _____

2. _____

3. _____

4. _____

5. _____

6. _____

7. _____

8 MEMO TO: Mary Jo Oliverio, Records Centor

9 FROM: Maria Hernandez, Personal Department

10 DATE: September 11, 19--

11 SUBJECT: December Conference Paticipation

12 Thank you for sending allong the booklet on the Micrographics
13 Workshop to be held in Washington, D.C., on December 4 threw 6.
14 The topics do sound grate, and I especially like the idea of a
15 program permiting the participants the choice of which sessions
16 they wish to attend from a selection of three concurent sessions.

17 This time, however, I am afraid too have to say that I won't be
18 able to join you. It seems that I have already committed myself
19 to conduct an all-day orientation workshop on the Wednesday of
20 that week--which is one of the three daze of the Micrographics
21 Workshop.

22 Due keep me in mind should you receive any other similar
23 conference announcments. I'm really interested in learning more
24 about the topik, and going to a workshop together would make it
25 an evan more pleasant experience, I no.

   mh

8. _____

9. _____

10. _____

11. _____

12. _____

13. _____

14. _____

15. _____

16. _____

17. _____

18. _____

19. _____

20. _____

21. _____

22. _____

23. _____

24. _____

25. _____

Words Ending in **able—ible**

A large number of words end with either **able** or **ible**. These two suffixes are added to roots or words to form adjectives meaning *able to, capable of,* and *worthy to be*. For example, **acceptable** means *worthy to be accepted*; **visible** means *able to be seen*. The **able—ible** words illustrate the point made earlier—that the correct pronunciation of a word does not always help you with its spelling.

Because pronunciation does not indicate which suffix is correct, the **able—ible** words have troubled nearly everyone. While many people rely on which ending "looks" right, the following series of guidelines is more reliable and should help solve most of your **able—ible** problems.

These guides are not absolutely foolproof. There are exceptions, and a few words that meet the guidelines for one ending actually take the other one. Nevertheless, they are the best we have, and they are generally true. These guides apply to the vast majority of words you use or will come across.

Study them carefully.

Words ending in able

Rule 1

Words usually end in **able** when the *base, root,* or *stem* is a *complete* word.

Keep in mind the word *complete*. You will see its importance shortly.

accept<u>able</u>	avail<u>able</u>	detest<u>able</u>	perish<u>able</u>
account<u>able</u>	avoid<u>able</u>	fashion<u>able</u>	prefer<u>able</u>
adapt<u>able</u>	break<u>able</u>	favor<u>able</u>	profit<u>able</u>
adjust<u>able</u>	credit<u>able</u>	lament<u>able</u>*	question<u>able</u>
agree<u>able</u>	depend<u>able</u>	market<u>able</u>	recover<u>able</u>
alter<u>able</u>	detect<u>able</u>	pass<u>able</u>	tax<u>able</u>
ascertain<u>able</u>			

In each instance see what happens when you drop the **able**.

accept	avail	detest	perish
account	avoid	fashion	prefer
adapt	break	favor	profit
adjust	credit	lament	question
agree	depend	market	recover
alter	detect	pass	tax
ascertain			

You have a *complete* word left.

Rule 2

Words usually end in **able** when the root is a *complete* word from which the final **e** has been dropped.

admir<u>able</u>	debat<u>able</u>	excus<u>able</u>	not<u>able</u>
ador<u>able</u>	deplor<u>able</u>	imagin<u>able</u>	rat<u>able</u>*
advis<u>able</u>	describ<u>able</u>	lik<u>able</u>	receiv<u>able</u>
argu<u>able</u>	desir<u>able</u>	liv<u>able</u>	siz<u>able</u>
believ<u>able</u>	endur<u>able</u>	lov<u>able</u>	us<u>able</u>
compar<u>able</u>	excit<u>able</u>	mov<u>able</u>	valu<u>able</u>

Drop the **able**, and you have a *complete* word that *lacks* a final **e**.

admir(<u>e</u>)	debat(<u>e</u>)	excus(<u>e</u>)	not(<u>e</u>)
ador(<u>e</u>)	deplor(<u>e</u>)	imagin(<u>e</u>)	rat(<u>e</u>)
advis(<u>e</u>)	describ(<u>e</u>)	lik(<u>e</u>)	receiv(<u>e</u>)
argu(<u>e</u>)	desir(<u>e</u>)	liv(<u>e</u>)	siz(<u>e</u>)
believ(<u>e</u>)	endur(<u>e</u>)	lov(<u>e</u>)	us(<u>e</u>)
compar(<u>e</u>)	excit(<u>e</u>)	mov(<u>e</u>)	valu(<u>e</u>)

Note   Words ending in **ce** or **ge** do *not* drop the **e** before adding **able** in order to keep the **c** and **g** soft—like **s** and **j**.

changeable	enforceable	marriageable	pronounceable
chargeable	exchangeable	mortgageable	replaceable
damageable	knowledgeable	noticeable	serviceable
embraceable	manageable	peaceable	

Rule 3

Words usually end in **able** when the *base, root,* or *stem* ends in **i** or the original word ends in **y**.

This rule is especially easy to fix in your mind. If you did not follow this rule with roots ending in **i**, you would soon find yourself with such odd-looking words as **reliible** (which is clearly wrong). So it makes good sense to have **able** follow all roots ending in **i** or when **y** is changed to **i**.

applicable	(apply)	memorable	(memory)
certifiable	(certify)	pitiable*	(pity)
classifiable	(classify)	pliable*	(ply)
enviable	(envy)	reliable	(rely)
equitable*	(equity)	undeniable	(deny)
justifiable	(justify)		

Rule 4

Words usually end in **able** when the *base, root,* or *stem* takes other suffixes that begin with a long **a** sound as in **way**.

abominable	(abominate)	inseparable	(separate)
communicable	(communicate)	intolerable	(tolerate)
demonstrable	(demonstrate)	inviolable	(violate)
durable	(duration)	irritable	(irritate)
impenetrable	(penetrate)	negotiable	(negotiate)
implacable	(placate)	tolerable	(tolerate)
inimitable	(imitate)	venerable*	(venerate)

Rule 5

Words usually end in **able** when the *base, root,* or *stem* ends in hard **c** (sounded as in **cook**) or hard **g** (sounded as in **dig**).

amic<u>able</u>*	despic<u>able</u>*	indefatig<u>able</u>*	navig<u>able</u>
applic<u>able</u>	explic<u>able</u>	irrevoc<u>able</u>*	practic<u>able</u>

Note	**a—o—u** are hardening vowels. Hence the **g** and **c** before **a** (as in the words above) have the hard sound.

Exceptions	Some words end in **able** but do not fall into any of the above groups. Study the following carefully.

aff<u>able</u>*	formid<u>able</u>*	inexor<u>able</u>*	palp<u>able</u>*
amen<u>able</u>*	hospit<u>able</u>*	inflamm<u>able</u>	port<u>able</u>
cap<u>able</u>	indomit<u>able</u>*	inscrut<u>able</u>*	prob<u>able</u>
controll<u>able</u>	inevit<u>able</u>	malle<u>able</u>*	vulner<u>able</u>*

Words ending in ible

Rule 1
Words usually end in **ible** when the *base, root,* or *stem* is *not* a *complete* word.

Just a few examples will illustrate this point.

aud<u>ible</u>	feas<u>ible</u>*	indel<u>ible</u>*	plaus<u>ible</u>*
combust<u>ible</u>	horr<u>ible</u>	infall<u>ible</u>	poss<u>ible</u>
compat<u>ible</u>	impercept<u>ible</u>	intell<u>ible</u>	suscept<u>ible</u>
cred<u>ible</u>*	implaus<u>ible</u>	invis<u>ible</u>	tang<u>ible</u>
divis<u>ible</u>	imposs<u>ible</u>	neglig<u>ible</u>	terr<u>ible</u>
ed<u>ible</u>	incorrig<u>ible</u>	percept<u>ible</u>	vis<u>ible</u>
fall<u>ible</u>*	incred<u>ible</u>		

It is important to distinguish here between a *complete* word and one that is *not complete.* Under Rule 2 for **able** words, we discussed roots that lack only a final **e**. Consider the following:

desirable—desir(<u>e</u>)   likable—lik(<u>e</u>)

These roots are complete words except for one letter. The following **ible** words contain roots that are really not words. They are not recognizable as anything else but roots.

horrible—<u>horr</u>   indelible—<u>indel</u>   possible—<u>poss</u>

Rule 2

Words usually end in **ible** when the *base, root,* or *stem* is a *complete* word that can add **ion** without adding any letters in between the end of the word and the suffix **ion**.

For **exhaustible,** the root is **exhaust**—a *complete* word. You can add **ion** to **exhaust** without any intervening letters: **exhaustion**.

access*	accession	accessible
collect	collection	collectible
connect	connection	connectible
corrupt	corruption	corruptible
depress	depression	depressible
destruct	destruction	destructible
digest	digestion	digestible
express	expression	expressible
impress	impression	impressible
perfect	perfection	perfectible

Exceptions   Only a few words do not follow this rule.

adoptable	correctable	detectable	predictable

Rule 3

Words usually end in **ible** when the *base, root,* or *stem* ends in **ns** or **ss**.

accessible	expressible	irresponsible	reprehensible
admissible	incomprehensible*	ostensible*	responsible
compressible	indefensible	permissible	sensible
defensible	insensible		

Exception   One word in two forms is a notable exception.

dispensable   indispensable

This is covered by an **able** rule: If any form of a word can take a suffix with a long **a,** the word takes the **able** ending. **(In)dispensable** is related to **dispensation**.

Rule 4

Words usually end in **ible** when the *base, root,* or *stem* ends in soft **c** (sounded as in **force**) or soft **g** (sounded as in **giant**).

convincible	illegible*	intelligible	negligible
crucible	incorrigible*	invincible	producible
deducible	ineligible	irascible	reducible
eligible	intangible	legible	tangible*
forcible			

Exceptions   Here are other **ible** words that do not fall into any of the above groups. Study them carefully.

collapsible	discernible*	inflexible	resistible
contemptible	flexible	irresistible	reversible
convertible	gullible*		

NAME	CLASS	DATE	SCORE

Spelling Assignments

A. Insert **able** or **ible** (whichever is correct) in the spaces in the following words. Then rewrite the complete word on the line to the right.

1. agree _able_ _____
2. excit_able_ _excitable_
3. envi _able_ _____
4. toler _able_ _____
5. neglig _ible_ _____
6. navig _able_ _____
7. aff _ible_ _____
8. predict _able_ _____
9. respons _ible_ _____
10. permiss _ible_ _____
11. prob _able_ _____
12. indispens ____ _____
13. flex _ible_ _____
14. vis _able_ _____
15. irresist _ible_ _____
16. avail _able_ _____
17. lik _able_ _____
18. indel ____ _____
19. amic ____ _____
20. poss _ible_ _____
21. adapt _able_ _____
22. terr _ible_ _____
23. horr _ible_ _____

24. aud _ible_ _____
25. equit _ible_ _____
26. suscept _ible_ _____
27. formid _able_ _____
28. indomit _able_ _____
29. cred _ible_ _____
30. vulner ____ _____
31. perfect _ible_ _____
32. detest _ible_ _____
33. sens _ible_ _____
34. excus _able_ _____
35. practic _able_ _____
36. presum _ible_ _____
37. consider _able_ _____
38. damag _able_ _____
39. read _ible_ _____
40. perish ____ _____
41. insepar ____ _____
42. infall ____ _____
43. corrupt ____ _____
44. manag ____ _____
45. question ____ _____
46. not ____ _____

47. siz *i ble* _____   49. inscrut _____ _____

48. hospit *able* _____   50. ed *i ble* _____

B. In the following list, some words are misspelled. Underline each misspelled word, and write the correct spelling in the space provided. If the printed word is correctly spelled, write C in the space.

1.	acceptable	_____	11. incomprehensible	_____
2.	lamentable	_____	12. insensible	_____
3.	gullible	_____	13. durible	_____
4.	discernible	_____	14. fallable	_____
5.	plausable	_____	15. forcable	_____
6.	accountable	_____	16. visible	_____
7.	legible	_____	17. imperceptable	_____
8.	ineligible	_____	18. valueable	_____
9.	desirible	_____	19. explicable	_____
10.	enforceable	_____	20. indispensable	_____

C. Underline the misspelled word or words in each of the following groups of three. Spell the word or words correctly in the space at the right. If there are no errors in the group, write C.

1.	serviceable	profitable	questionnable	1. _____
2.	taxible	adviseable	justifiable	2. _____
3.	expressible	communicable	practicible	3. _____
4.	affable	feasable	amicable	4. _____
5.	palpable	laughable	imaginable	5. _____
6.	arguable	detectible	terrible	6. _____
7.	likable	knowledgable	presentable	7. _____
8.	despicable	controlable	implacable	8. _____
9.	inviolable	indelible	malleible	9. _____
10.	portible	ratible	exchangeable	10. _____
11.	certifyable	irritible	irrevocable	11. _____
12.	compatible	remarkable	describible	12. _____
13.	accessible	pronounceable	tangible	13. _____

14.	noticeable	insatiable	movable	14._____
15.	amenable	appreciable	divisable	15._____
16.	impossible	culpable	pliable	16._____
17.	passible	memorable	applicible	17._____
18.	useable	incorrigible	expendible	18._____
19.	debatable	indefatigable	undeniable	19._____
20.	correctible	incredible	receivable	20._____
21.	crucible	pitiable	collectible	21._____
22.	sociable	negligable	marketable	22._____
23.	reprehensible	probable	incorrigeable	23._____
24.	inevitible	collapsible	ostensable	24._____
25.	convertible	producible	predictable	25._____
26.	eligible	digestible	inflammible	26._____
27.	forcible	sensible	tangable	27._____
28.	venerible	inexorable	deductable	28._____
29.	traceable	illegible	capable	29._____
30.	inflexible	reversable	contemptable	30._____

Words Often Confused

In the first 12 chapters, you studied commonly used homonyms. Now you are going to study words that sound almost alike—words like **accept** and **except**, for example, or **adapt, adept,** and **adopt**. Like homonyms, these words are often written with the same shorthand outline and must be transcribed in terms of their context. And like homonyms, these words are often confused. Effective and accurate business communication requires that you become familiar with these words, their precise meaning, and their correct usage, as you have become familiar with the homonyms presented in the previous chapters.

The following chapters contain a list of approximately 300 of these frequently confused words. This large list is divided into smaller lists of 14 pairs or sets of words each. By studying one group of these words with each of the remaining chapters, you will have mastered all these frequently confused words when you have completed the text.

accede	(ak sēd′) to agree or consent, give in: *We will accede to your demands on this item in the contract.*
exceed	(ek sēd′) to go or be beyond a limit, surpass: *Sales this quarter will exceed even our most optimistic forecast.*
accelerate	(ak sel′ər āt′) to cause to go or happen faster: *We must accelerate our production schedule to meet the increased demand.*
exhilarate	(eg zil′ə rāt′) to stimulate, put into high spirits: *Crowds of holiday shoppers coming into her store exhilarate Esther.*
accept	(ak sept′) to receive, to take something that is offered: *I accept your job offer. We cannot accept any returns after ten days from the date of purchase.*
except	(ek sept′) (preposition) other than, but, leaving out: *Send us everything except the daisy wheels*; (verb) to exclude or leave out: *We except them from the punishment.*
access	admittance, way or approach, passage: *Which employees have access to the personnel files?*
excess	an amount or degree beyond what is normal or required: *Skim the excess fat off the top of the soup. Because Leon often drank to excess, he was fired. Moderation is preferable; it is better not to do anything to excess.*
adapt	to adjust, to make fit or suitable, to modify or alter for a different purpose or situation: *When you adapt to a new job, you adjust yourself to new conditions and demands. We can adapt these plans to suit your individual needs.*
adept	very skillful, expert: *She is adept in designing computer programs.*
adopt	to take for one's own: *Our company will adopt a new payroll plan next January*; to take a child of other parents and rear as one's own: *Bill and Mary decided to adopt a child*; to accept formally: *At its next meeting, the Executive Board may adopt the Finance Committee's report.*

addict   someone who is obsessively dependent on some habit: *Theo's casual use of cocaine led to his becoming an addict*; one who is devoted to a particular activity: *When it came to video games, Tom was an addict.*

edict   an order or command: *When was this edict issued?*

addition   the act, process, or result of increasing; something added: *Ms. Jones will be a valuable addition to our sales force.* (*Memory Aid: a* as in *add.*)

edition   all the copies of a book, newspaper, or magazine issued at the same time: *This text is the third edition of* Business Spelling and Word Power. (*Memory Aid: e* as in *editor.*)

adverse   (sound the *d*) unfriendly, unfavorable, harmful: *Ms. Maersk offered very adverse criticism of his proposal. The company was forced to operate under adverse government regulations.*

averse   opposed, unwilling: *We are averse to making any money available for mortgages at this time.*

advice   (ad vīs′) (noun) an opinion about what should be done: *I need your advice about which offer to accept.*

advise   (ad vīz′) (verb) to tell others what they should do or say, to offer advice, to counsel: *Please advise me about which offer to accept. The auditor will advise the company president not to cut salaries.*

affect   (verb) to influence: *The policies of the Federal Reserve Bank affect our entire economy*; to stir the emotions or the mind: *For this television commercial, we need music that will affect the viewers*; to pretend, to assume the character or the appearance of: *Ms. Rempell is very intelligent, but she frequently affects ignorance.*

effect   (noun) result, outcome, or consequence: *The effect of the new taxes was felt in every business*; accomplishment or fulfillment: *Every member of the staff must work hard to put the new payroll incentive plan into effect*; impression: *The slide presentation produced a startling effect on the audience.*

> **Note**   **Effects** (plural) also means *goods* or *possessions:* household effects, business effects, etc.

all ready   completely prepared: *The filing cabinets are all ready to be shipped.*
already   by this time, before the time, even now, by now: *When we called, we found that the package had already been shipped. I am already an hour late for the appointment.*

all together   collectively, in a group: *After a long separation, we were all together at last.*
altogether   entirely, completely, on the whole: *I am altogether certain that Ms. Goldberg is the best person for this position.*

alley   (al′ē) narrow, back street: *The delivery entrance is in the alley*; a place for bowling: *Ned Andrews manages the bowling alley across the street.*

ally (al′ī) (noun) person or nation united with another person or nation: *England was our ally in World War II.*

ally (əlī′) (verb) to unite by formal agreement as by a treaty or alliance: *A weak nation will naturally want to ally itself with a stronger nation.*

allude to mention casually, to refer to indirectly: *In the course of his talk, I heard Mr. Larkins allude to his European adventures.*

elude to avoid or escape by cunning or quickness: *The criminal successfully eluded the police dragnet*; to escape notice or detection: *The arithmetical error did not elude the bookkeeper.*

Words Often Confused Assignments

A. Select from the following words the one that correctly fits the blank in each of the sentences below. Then write the word in the answer space.

accelerate	access	adopt	averse	effect
exhilarate	excess	addition	advice	all ready
accept	adapt	edition	advise	already
except	adept	adverse	affect	

1. Mr. Chester tells me that we cannot _____ the terms you are offering.

1._____

2. When the _____ to our factory is completed, we shall be able to fill our orders more efficiently.

2._____

3. The mere thought that he was a candidate for promotion really did _____ him.

3._____

4. We do not permit our name brand products to be sold to anyone _____ licensed dealers.

4._____

5. The second _____ of the book was released today.

5._____

6. We _____ our clients to deal with reputable dealers only.

6._____

7. A drop in sales of durable goods such as automobiles usually reflects _____ economic conditions.

7._____

8. Did the recent change in federal tax laws _____ your company?

8._____

9. Now that I have accomplished what I intended to do, I am _____ to go.

9._____

10. Changes in the terms of the agreement had no _____ on retirement benefits.

10._____

11. When I finally reached the telephone, I found that it had _____ stopped ringing.

11._____

12. With practice, Paula became _____ at using our new collating device.

12._____

13. A special password was necessary to gain
_____ to certain computer files.   13. _____

14. My _____ about ordering 200 copies of the pro-
gram was carefully considered.   14. _____

15. The company planned to _____ its marketing
strategies in an effort to improve sales.   15. _____

B. In some of the following sentences, an incorrect word is used. Underline the incorrect word, and write the correct word in the space provided. Where there is no error, write C in the answer space.

1. The ally was closed because of construction.   1. _____

2. Please place the original and the copies of the report
all together on my desk.   2. _____

3. To exhilarate production does not automatically mean
to increase sales.   3. _____

4. She took my advise and applied for the job.   4. _____

5. The income did not accede the expenses.   5. _____

6. I considered Arlene an alley in my efforts to suggest
change.   6. _____

7. Our group went altogether on the chartered flight.   7. _____

8. Within ten days of purchase, we cheerfully accept any
used merchandise for exchange or credit.   8. _____

9. As Theo described his work experience, he could not
help but elude to his previous employers.   9. _____

10. I must accelerate my efforts to complete this task.   10. _____

11. Under present world conditions, we need every ally we
can get.   11. _____

12. We advise you to do whatever is possible to hold your
production costs down.   12. _____

13. The new typewriter enables us to change type styles
and adapt them to the dictator's preference.   13. _____

14. Although Britt tried to avoid it, she could not allude the
fact that her payment was overdue.   14. _____

15. The averse criticism that Mr. Engle received had an impact on his decision to resign.   15. _____

C. Read the definition and select the correct word from the second column to match that description. Write the word you selected in the answer space.

	Definition	**Word Choice**	
1.	other than, but, leaving out	accept, except	1._____
2.	an amount or degree beyond what is normal	access, excess	2._____
3.	all the copies of a publication issued at the same time	addition, edition	3._____
4.	to take for one's own	adapt, adept, adopt	4._____
5.	result, outcome, or consequence	affect, effect	5._____
6.	opposed, unwilling	adverse, averse	6._____
7.	completely prepared	all ready, already	7._____
8.	an order or command	addict, edict	8._____
9.	to mention casually	allude, elude	9._____
10.	surpass	accede, exceed	10._____

D. Complete each of the following sentences.

1. The addict _____

_____

2. Helen already _____

_____

3. The accountant was adept _____

_____

4. The excess _____

_____

5. Please accept _____

_____

6. My advice _____

_____

7. Except for the _____

_____

8. Adverse circumstances_____

_____

9. Please advise _____

_____

10. Ben was averse _____

_____

Words Ending in **ary—ery** and **efy—ify**

As you saw in Chapter 13, determining whether a word ends in **able** or **ible** can be difficult at times. Accurate pronunciation is of no help in choosing between these suffixes, and the guidelines available to help you decide which is correct are not foolproof.

In this chapter you are going to look at two more pairs of suffixes—**ary—ery** and **efy—ify**—but in each case deciding which to choose is comparatively easy. In each pair only a few common words end with one suffix; all the rest end with the other. Simply memorize these few words which end with the less common suffix, and your spelling problems involving **ary—ery** and **efy—ify** are solved.

Words ending in ary—ery

Of the words that end in **ery**, most pose no spelling problem. Correct pronunciation is your guide to correct spelling. You would be unlikely to spell any of the following, for example, with an **ary** ending:

artillery	bribery	flattery
bakery	finery	recovery

In a few words, however, the **ery** ending is pronounced **airy**. One of these words, **very,** you know well. In only six other common words is the **ery** ending pronounced **airy**.

cemet<u>ery</u>	dysent<u>ery</u>	monast<u>ery</u>
confection<u>ery</u>	millin<u>ery</u>	station<u>ery</u>
		writing paper

> **Note** Make the distinction between **stationery,** meaning *writing paper*, and **stationary,** meaning *standing in place*.

Memorize these six words, and you should have no difficulty in determining whether a word ends in **ery** or **ary**. Whenever you are in doubt about which of these two suffixes is correct, and the word is not one of these six words, the word will almost surely end in **ary**.

Here is a list of some common words that have the **ary** suffix.

actu<u>ary</u>*	disciplin<u>ary</u>	lumin<u>ary</u>*	second<u>ary</u>
advers<u>ary</u>*	discretion<u>ary</u>*	mission<u>ary</u>	secret<u>ary</u>
arbitr<u>ary</u>	element<u>ary</u>	moment<u>ary</u>	sedent<u>ary</u>
auxili<u>ary</u>	emiss<u>ary</u>*	necess<u>ary</u>	solit<u>ary</u>
benefici<u>ary</u>	exempl<u>ary</u>*	not<u>ary</u>*	subsidi<u>ary</u>
bound<u>ary</u>	heredit<u>ary</u>	prelimin<u>ary</u>	summ<u>ary</u>
comment<u>ary</u>	honor<u>ary</u>	prim<u>ary</u>	tempor<u>ary</u>
contempor<u>ary</u>	imagin<u>ary</u>	propriet<u>ary</u>	tribut<u>ary</u>
culin<u>ary</u>	infirm<u>ary</u>	pulmon<u>ary</u>*	vision<u>ary</u>
diction<u>ary</u>	judici<u>ary</u>*	salut<u>ary</u>	vocabul<u>ary</u>
diet<u>ary</u>	libr<u>ary</u>	sanctu<u>ary</u>	volunt<u>ary</u>
digni<u>tary</u>	liter<u>ary</u>	sani<u>tary</u>	

Words ending in efy—ify

When added to roots, the suffixes **efy** and **ify** create verbs meaning *to make* or *to form into* (**liquefy, modify, purify,** etc.). Here, too, while pronunciation will not help you to determine whether a word ends in **efy** or **ify**, knowing which suffix is correct is easy because only four words end in the suffix **efy**. Here they are:

liquefy	putrefy	rarefy	stupefy

> **Note**
> The word **defy** derives from the Old French word **defier**; the **efy** combination in **defy** is not a suffix.

When these words add suffixes or change their forms, the **e** is still retained before the **f**, even if the **y** is dropped.

lique<u>fy</u>*	putre<u>fy</u>*	rare<u>fy</u>*	stupe<u>fy</u>*
lique<u>fies</u>	putre<u>fies</u>	rare<u>fies</u>	stupe<u>fies</u>
lique<u>fying</u>	putre<u>fying</u>	rare<u>fying</u>	stupe<u>fying</u>
lique<u>fied</u>	putre<u>fied</u>	rare<u>fied</u>	stupe<u>fied</u>
lique<u>faction</u>	putre<u>faction</u>	rare<u>faction</u>	stupe<u>faction</u>

Memorize these four words, and you will have solved all problems about which suffix is correct. All other words in this group end in **ify**. Here are some of them:

class<u>ify</u>	ident<u>ify</u>	pac<u>ify</u>*	rect<u>ify</u>*
ed<u>ify</u>*	just<u>ify</u>	pur<u>ify</u>	spec<u>ify</u>
fals<u>ify</u>	mod<u>ify</u>	qual<u>ify</u>	test<u>ify</u>
fort<u>ify</u>	moll<u>ify</u>*	quant<u>ify</u>	vil<u>ify</u>*
glor<u>ify</u>	null<u>ify</u>*	rat<u>ify</u>	

NAME	CLASS	DATE	SCORE

Spelling Assignments

A. Insert **ary** or **ery** (whichever is correct) in the spaces in the following words. Then rewrite the complete word on the line to the right.

1. secret_____ _____	21. dysent _____ _____
2. diction _____ _____	22. advers _____ _____
3. cemet_____ _____	23. dignit _____ _____
4. sedent _____ _____	24. station _____ _____
	standing still
5. actu _____ _____	25. station _____ _____
	paper
6. millin _____ _____	26. confection __ _____
7. diet_____ _____	27. prelimin ____ _____
8. comment ___ _____	28. arbitr _____ _____
9. liter_____ _____	29. moment ____ _____
10. brib_____ _____	30. judici _____ _____
11. emiss_____ _____	31. benefici ____ _____
12. infirm _____ _____	32. tempor _____ _____
13. monast_____ _____	33. fin_____ _____
14. vocabul ____ _____	34. auxili _____ _____
15. distill _____ _____	35. element ____ _____
16. dispens ____ _____	36. not _____ _____
17. cel _____ _____	37. sanit_____ _____
18. bak_____ _____	38. recov _____ _____
19. flatt_____ _____	39. heredit _____ _____
20. artill _____ _____	40. prim _____ _____

B. Insert **efy** or **ify** (whichever is correct) in the spaces in the following words. Then rewrite the complete word on the line to the right.

1.	mod_____	_____	14.	putr _____	_____
2.	ed _____	_____	15.	test _____	_____
3.	glor _____	_____	16.	stup_____	_____
4.	myst _____	_____	17.	pac _____	_____
5.	liqu _____	_____	18.	cruc_____	_____
6.	qual_____	_____	19.	ampl _____	_____
7.	spec _____	_____	20.	d _____	_____
8.	fort_____	_____	21.	ident _____	_____
9.	rect _____	_____	22.	fals _____	_____
10.	pur_____	_____	23.	vil _____	_____
11.	rar _____	_____	24.	moll_____	_____
12.	class _____	_____	25.	null _____	_____
13.	rat _____	_____		

C. Underline the misspelled word or words in each of the following groups of three. Spell the word or words correctly in the space at the right. If there are no errors in the group, write C.

1.	rarify	vilify	codify	1.	_____
2.	mollify	stupifying	crucify	2.	_____
3.	liquify	signify	glorefy	3.	_____
4.	stupify	pacify	classefy	4.	_____
5.	beautify	certify	putrefy	5.	_____
6.	falsefy	verify	notefy	6.	_____
7.	diversefy	justefy	quantify	7.	_____
8.	exemplify	typefy	personefy	8.	_____
9.	gratefy	simplify	indemnify	9.	_____
10.	humidify	identify	terrify	10.	_____
11.	beneficiary	liqufying	ratify	11.	_____
12.	boundery	purify	monastary	12.	_____
13.	millinery	specify	edify	13.	_____

14.	recovery	proprietary	honorary	14._____
15.	secondary	stupefaction	luminary	15._____
16.	bakery	fortify	artillery	16._____
17.	vocabulery	dysentery	imaginery	17._____
18.	rarefied	confectionery	finery	18._____
19.	qualify	cemetary	celery	19._____
20.	exemplary	contemporary	liquified	20._____

D. There are misspelled words in some of the following sentences. Underline each misspelled word, and write the correct spelling in the space provided. If there are no misspelled words, write C in the space next to the sentences.

1. The auditer requested a summary of the monthly sales figures for our subsidary company. 1._____

2. The availible discretionary income our neighbors have to spend is much more than ours. 2._____

3. It was necessary to divide the sales territory because of the increase of new businesses in the area and the amount of milage involved. 3._____

4. The new office building had a contemporary design and was accessable from two majer highways. 4._____

5. We intend to apply for an adjustible-rate mortgage to finance our secondary residence. 5._____

6. Her conduct in the mater was exemplery in spite of the intolerable situation. 6._____

7. It was necessary to rectify the error imediately. 7._____

8. Serial numbers on office equipment are a desireable means by which to identify specific peaces of equiptment. 8._____

9. The stockholders hoped that the preliminary financial reports would reveal favorable earnings for the quarter. 9._____

10. An enviable and noteable acheivement was Mr. Marcum's appointment as the honorary chairperson of the Annual Charity Dinner Dance. 10._____

11. Most people who use the library are responsible, as atested to by the fact that the majority of library books are returned before the do date. 11._____

12. It was a grueling interview because every canidate was asked to take a stand on a debatable question and provide reasons to justafy his or her position.

12. _____

13. Please modify the terms of the contract so that it will be acceptible to all concerned parties.

13. _____

14. Can you make a list of the taxible items and the deductible items for me?

14. _____

15. In our vacinity, supermarkets often charge very different prices for comparible items.

15. _____

Words Often Confused

allusion   (from *allude*) a passing, casual, or indirect reference: *Mr. Larkins made a brief allusion to his European adventures.*

illusion   something that deceives by producing a false impression: *A mirage, seeing water in the desert where there is no water, is an illusion. It is an illusion to believe that sales will improve.*

angel   (soft **g** sounded like **j** in **jell** because it is followed by a softening **e**) a spiritual being, a heavenly messenger: *Our Christmas sale catalog has a picture of an angel on the cover;* a good, lovely, or innocent person: *Patients called her an angel of mercy because of her volunteer work at the hospital.*

angle   (hard **g** sounded like **g** in **good**) the geometric measurement of two intersecting lines: *These windows do not open beyond a 45° angle;* a point of view, an aspect, a phase of something: *Viewed from this angle, the house looks larger.*

annual   yearly: *I received a copy of the company's annual report last week.*

annul   to cancel, invalidate, abolish: *Legal complications forced us to annul the agreement.*

appraise   to estimate the value or quality of an object, to set or fix the value: *Evans and Deitz both appraise the property at $350,000.*

apprise   to give notice, to inform, to advise: *We will apprise you of any change in our prices. The owner should be apprised as soon as the appraisal is completed.*

ballad   (bal′əd) a romantic or sentimental song, a song or poem usually of unknown authorship: *His recording of old English ballads has been highly successful.*

ballet   (ba lā′) an intricate group dance using pantomime and stylized movements: *Dana danced the ballet with the grace of Pavlova.*

ballot   (bal′ət) a ticket or form by which a vote is registered, the act or method of voting: *Ms. Lisle cast her vote by absentee ballot.*

bazaar   a market, shop, or fair at which miscellaneous articles are sold: *We donated an old typewriter for the church bazaar.*

bizarre   strikingly unconventional, odd: *The street peddler's appearance was bizarre. How do you explain Mr. Lao's recent bizarre behavior?*

beat   (bēt) to defeat, to conquer: *Our new product is sure to beat anything our competitors can offer;* to strike repeatedly: *The baby beat the toy drum.*

bet   (bet) to wager: *Ms. Harcourt bet Mr. Jackson $100 that the stock market would rally next week.*

beside   at the side of: *Sit down beside the desk.*

besides   in addition to: *There will be others from our company at the convention besides us;* other than, except: *No one we know will be there besides Jim.*

biannual   occurring twice a year: *The biannual royalty statements are mailed in October and April.*

biennial   occurring once every two years: *The biennial election for the House of Representatives occurs in November.*

bibliography   a list of books or articles about a subject or person, or by an author: *Wanda compiled an extensive bibliography of current articles on flextime.*

biography   a story of a person's life written by someone else: *Have you read the new biography of Henry Ford?*
(*Note:* An *autobiography* is the story of a person's life written by that person.)

borough   a self-governing town or administrative unit in some states: *Queens is one of the five boroughs in New York City.*

borrow   to obtain something on loan: *I must borrow $20 until payday;* to adopt or use as one's own: *I'm going to borrow an idea from one of our competitors.*

burro   a small donkey: *She rode on a burro during her vacation in the West.*

burrow   (noun) a hole in the ground made by an animal for shelter: *The horse stumbled in a rabbit burrow;* (verb) to make or hide in a burrow: *The rabbit burrowed into the hillside to escape the dogs.*

breadth   (bredth) the distance from side to side: *This street has a breadth of 35 feet.* (*Spelling Aid:* Same **dth** as in *width.*)

breath   (breth) air taken in and given out by the lungs: *Mr. Ames took a deep breath before entering the room.*

breathe   (brēth) to take breaths, to inhale and exhale: *Breathe deeply to calm yourself.*

carton   (kärt″n) a cardboard box: *This carton is too flimsy to be useful.*

cartoon   (kär tōon′) an exaggerated, amusing, or humorous sketch or line drawing, sometimes satirizing people or events, or (plural) a regularly issued series: *The newspaper printed a political cartoon on the editorial page. The children love Saturday morning cartoons.*

casual   (kazh′oo əl) happening by chance: *We had a casual meeting last week;* offhand: *Stan did not know how to interpret her casual remark;* careless, informal, negligent: *Do not wear casual dress to a job interview.*

causal   (kôz′əl) bringing something about, effecting: *There is a causal connection between rising prices and rising profits and wages.*

NAME   **CLASS**   **DATE**   **SCORE**

Words Often Confused Assignments

A. Select from the following words the one that correctly fits the blank in each of the sentences below. Then write the word in the answer space.

allusion	annul	ballot	bibliography	breadth
illusion	appraise	beat	biography	breath
angel	apprise	bet	borough	breathe
angle	ballad	beside	borrow	casual
annual	ballet	besides	burro	causal

1. Economists are not sure about the _____ relationship between depressions and business policies.

    1._____

2. The light, modular furniture created the _____ of spaciousness.

    2._____

3. We feel that we should _____ you of all the facts before you make the decision.

    3._____

4. I did not know Jose well; he was a _____ acquaintance.

    4._____

5. After assessing the damage from every _____, the insurance adjuster settled the claim.

    5._____

6. Before jewels or furs can be insured, it is necessary to _____ them.

    6._____

7. A well-known historian was recently commissioned to write a _____ of the newly elected President.

    7._____

8. Bernice was so competitive that we all knew she would try to _____ her own sales record.

    8._____

9. As a result of his asthma, he found it hard to _____ without a humidifier.

    9._____

10. Mark was so sure of himself that he was willing to _____ that his idea would work.

    10._____

11. I did not recognize the person who was sitting _____ you.

    11._____

12. There was a _____ of related readings at the
end of each chapter in the text.

12. _____

13. Reading a company's _____ report prior to a job
interview is a good idea.

13. _____

14. In order to _____ money, a corporation sells
bonds.

14. _____

15. She tried to _____ the contract because there
was no witness to the signatures.

15. _____

B. In some of the following sentences, an incorrect word is used. Underline the incorrect
word, and write the correct word in the space provided. Where there is no error, write C
in the answer space.

1. Who is expected at the meeting beside the regular
members?

1. _____

2. Their presentation of the figures created an allusion of
high profits.

2. _____

3. The odor of tobacco on his breadth was offensive to
the other employees.

3. _____

4. After much consideration, the board cast a unanimous
ballad for Jim Huber as president.

4. _____

5. Sometimes causal friendships grow into lifelong
friendships.

5. _____

6. Some of the items sold at the bizarre were inexpensive.

6. _____

7. It is good practice to avoid burrowing office supplies
from co-workers.

7. _____

8. Beth compiled an extensive biography to support the information in the report.

8. _____

9. When reading the newspaper, my dad always turns to
the carton section first.

9. _____

10. The neighborhood has an annual yard sale.

10. _____

11. The property was appraised for tax purposes.

11. _____

12. Their bizarre behavior was the topic of conversation.

12. _____

13. On her vacation to Puerto Rico, Loretta took a ride on
a burro.

13. _____

14. The same object can look entirely different when
viewed from a different angel.

14. _____

15. Raul hoped to get a breathe of fresh air by opening the
window.

15. _____

C. Read the definition, and select the correct word from the second column to match that description. Write the word you selected in the answer space.

	Definition	Word Choice	
1.	strikingly unconventional	bazaar, bizarre	1._____
2.	a hole	borough, borrow, burro, burrow	2._____
3.	story of a person's life written by someone else	bibliography, biography	3._____
4.	occurring twice a year	biannual, biennial	4._____
5.	to wager	beat, bet	5._____
6.	distance from side to side	breadth, breath, breathe	6._____
7.	at the side of	beside, besides	7._____
8.	a passing, casual, or indirect reference	allusion, illusion	8._____
9.	a point of view	angel, angle	9._____
10.	a romantic or sentimental song	ballad, ballet, ballot	10._____

D. Compose a meaningful sentence for each of the following words.

1. carton_____

_____

2. biannual_____

_____

3. borough _____

_____

4. breathe _____

_____

5. biography_____

_____

6. angel _____

_____

7. beat _____

_____

8. casual _____

_____

9. besides _____

_____

10. illusion _____

_____

Words Ending in **ance—ence** and **ant—ent**

A great many words end with one of these four common suffixes. The first pair, **ance** and **ence**, are added to roots to form nouns. They indicate an action, quality, or state (**acceptance, importance, independence**). The suffixes **ant** and **ent** can be used to form nouns (**accountant, resident**) or adjectives (**elegant, ancient**). Unfortunately, there is no rule or set of rules that will guide you in correctly spelling words that end in these suffixes. You must memorize them.

Some of the most commonly misspelled words with these four suffixes are listed in the following pages. Study them until you are familiar with them and have a "feel" for their proper spelling. As you study them, note in particular the many words that have two forms (e.g., **relevance—relevant, confidence—confident**). In every single case the vowel is the same in both suffixes. Hence if you know how to spell one of these words, you automatically know how to spell the other.

ance

abeyance*	circumstance	hindrance	reliance
abundance	clearance	ignorance	reluctance
acceptance	compliance	importance	remembrance
accordance	continuance	inheritance	remittance
acquaintance	contrivance*	instance	repentance
admittance	conveyance*	insurance	repugnance
allegiance	defiance	irrelevance	resistance
alliance	deliverance	issuance	romance
allowance	distance	maintenance	significance
ambulance	elegance	nuisance	substance
annoyance	endurance	observance	surveillance
appearance	entrance	ordinance	sustenance*
appliance	extravagance	performance	temperance
arrogance	forbearance*	perseverance*	tolerance
assistance	fragrance	petulance	utterance
assurance	furtherance	predominance	variance
attendance	grievance	radiance	vengeance
balance	guidance	relevance	vigilance
brilliance			

ence

abhorrence
absence
abstinence*
acquiescence
adherence
adolescence
affluence
audience
benevolence
circumference
coherence
coincidence
commence
competence
concurrence
condolence*
conference
confidence
conscience
consequence
convalescence
convenience

corpulence*
correspondence
deference*
dependence
deterrence
difference
diligence*
dissidence
eloquence
eminence
essence
evidence
excellence
existence
experience
fraudulence
impatience
impertinence
impotence
imprudence
incidence
incompetence

independence
indulgence
inference
influence
innocence
insistence
insolence
intelligence
interference
irreverence
lenience*
magnificence
malevolence
negligence*
obedience
obsolescence*
occurrence
omnipotence
omniscience
opulence
patience
permanence

persistence
precedence
preference
presence
prevalence
prominence
prudence
quintessence*
recurrence
reference
reminiscence*
residence
resurgence
reticence
reverence
science
sentence
sequence
silence
subsistence
transference
violence

ant

abundant
accountant
applicant
arrogant
assailant
assistant
attendant
brilliant
buoyant
compliant*
conversant
covenant
defendant
defiant
descendant

disinfectant
distant
dominant
dormant
elegant
exorbitant*
extravagant
exuberant*
fragrant
gallant
grievant
hesitant
ignorant
important
inhabitant

insignificant
instant
irrelevant
lieutenant
malignant
observant
occupant
pageant
pennant
petulant*
pleasant
predominant
radiant
relevant*
reliant

reluctant
remnant
repentant
repugnant*
resistant
resonant
restaurant
significant
stimulant
tenant
tolerant
vagrant*
variant
vigilant*
warrant*

ent

abhorrent*
absent
accident
acquiescent
adjacent*
adolescent
affluent*
agent
ancient
apparent
belligerent*
benevolent*
client
coherent
comment
competent
component
concurrent
confident
consequent
consistent
constituent*
convalescent
convenient
corpulent
correspondent

current
deficient
delinquent
dependent
deterrent
different
diffident*
diligent
dissident
efficient
eloquent
eminent*
evident
excellent
existent
expedient*
experiment
exponent
fraudulent*
frequent
imminent*
impatient
impertinent
impotent
impudent*

incandescent*
incident
incoherent*
incompetent
inconsistent
incumbent*
independent
inherent
innocent
insistent
insolent*
insolvent*
insufficient
insurgent
intelligent
intermittent*
irreverent
magnificent
malevolent
obedient
obsolescent
omnipotent
omniscient
opponent
opulent

patent*
patient
permanent
persistent*
pertinent
potent
present
president
prevalent*
proficient
prominent
prudent*
quotient
recurrent
reminiscent
repellent
resident
respondent
resurgent
reticent
reverent
silent
superintendent
transparent
violent

NAME   CLASS   DATE   SCORE

Spelling Assignments

A. Insert **ance** or **ence** (whichever is correct) in the spaces in the following words. Then rewrite the complete word on the line to the right.

1. abhorr _____ _____	16. compet_____ _____
2. defer _____ _____	17. confid_____ _____
3. abund_____ _____	18. differ_____ _____
4. refer_____ _____	19. preval_____ _____
5. accept _____ _____	20. repent _____ _____
6. concurr_____ _____	21. deliver _____ _____
7. admitt_____ _____	22. persist _____ _____
8. confer_____ _____	23. toler _____ _____
9. prefer_____ _____	24. transfer ____ _____
10. occurr_____ _____	25. extravag____ _____
11. brilli _____ _____	26. subsist _____ _____
12. allow _____ _____	27. exist_____ _____
13. abs_____ _____	28. mainten ____ _____
14. assist_____ _____	29. promin _____ _____
15. clear_____ _____	30. issu _____ _____

B. Underline the misspelled word or words in each of the following groups of three. Spell the word or words correctly in the space at the right. If there are no errors in the group, write C.

1. compliance	excellance	defiance	1._____
2. fragrance	hindrance	irrelevance	2._____
3. insurence	audience	benevolence	3._____
4. diligence	eloquence	experience	4._____
5. remittance	substance	temperence	5._____
6. conveyance	interference	innocence	6._____

7.	irreverence	difference	reticence	7. _____
8.	annoyance	abeyance	obedience	8. _____
9.	entrence	sustenence	romance	9. _____
10.	coincidence	adherence	condolence	10. _____
11.	sequence	evidence	corpulance	11. _____
12.	recurrance	reverence	acquaintance	12. _____
13.	residence	contrivence	assurence	13. _____
14.	violence	alliance	allegiance	14. _____
15.	perseverence	ignorance	guidance	15. _____
16.	resistance	arrogance	vigilance	16. _____
17.	importance	affluance	consequence	17. _____
18.	quintessence	inference	reluctance	18. _____
19.	abstinence	leniance	precedence	19. _____
20.	reliance	dependence	existance	20. _____

C. Add **ant** or **ent** (whichever is correct) to the following roots. Then rewrite the complete word on the line to the right.

1.	account_____	_____	16.	intellig _____	_____
2.	benevol_____	_____	17.	innoc_____	_____
3.	abund _____	_____	18.	assist_____	_____
4.	resid _____	_____	19.	reluct_____	_____
5.	dilig _____	_____	20.	brilli_____	_____
6.	eloqu_____	_____	21.	exuber_____	_____
7.	descend ____	_____	22.	observ_____	_____
8.	defend_____	_____	23.	inhabit _____	_____
9.	independ____	_____	24.	afflu_____	_____
10.	superintend__	_____	25.	incompet____	_____
11.	presid _____	_____	26.	insol _____	_____
12.	excell_____	_____	27.	applic _____	_____
13.	ignor _____	_____	28.	assail_____	_____
14.	occup _____	_____	29.	perman _____	_____
15.	vigil _____	_____	30.	incumb _____	_____

D. Underline the misspelled word or words in each of the following groups of three. Spell the word or words correctly in the space at the right. If there are no errors in the group, write C.

1.	irreverant	defiant	disinfectant	1._____
2.	restaurant	existant	impatient	2._____
3.	hesitent	insignificant	stimulent	3._____
4.	pleasant	obedient	persistent	4._____
5.	prevalent	impudent	adjacent	5._____
6.	distant	important	vagrant	6._____
7.	deficient	extravagant	repentent	7._____
8.	malignent	intermittent	arrogant	8._____
9.	lieutenant	expedient	convalescant	9._____
10.	radiant	attendant	complient	10._____
11.	abhorrent	warrent	grievant	11._____
12.	repugnent	fragrant	instant	12._____
13.	irrelevent	tenent	efficient	13._____
14.	tolerent	reliant	resistent	14._____
15.	significant	petulant	variant	15._____
16.	opponant	absent	prominant	16._____
17.	competent	confident	respondent	17._____
18.	incoherent	permanent	insolvent	18._____
19.	fraudulant	apparant	constituent	19._____
20.	present	pertinent	reticent	20._____

Words Often Confused

cease   (sēs) to stop, discontinue: *We will cease production next week.*
seize   (sēz) to take hold of suddenly or violently: *He might angrily seize the phone and yank it from the wall*; to take possession by force: *An aggressive manufacturer will seize every opportunity to make a profit;* confiscate: *The Coast Guard prepared to seize the stolen cargo.*

censor   (sen'sər) (verb) to examine things like motion pictures, mail, etc., and to prohibit anything considered objectionable or harmful: *Some parents want to censor the books their children study in school*; (noun) a person who censors: *In wartime the censors read the mail of suspected persons.*
censure   (sen'shər) to blame, to condemn as wrong: *President Wharton will censure the entire department for the error.*

census   an official count of the population, usually done periodically: *The national census is taken every ten years.*
senses   the functions of sight, smell, hearing, touch, and taste: *When people lose one of their senses, the others usually become stronger.*

certain   (surt″n) sure, inevitable, without any doubt: *This advertisement is certain to get results*; some, but not very much: *I agree with what you say to a certain extent.*
curtain   (kurt″n) fabric that covers a window or conceals a stage: *They arrived at the theater just as the curtain was going up.*

charted   past tense of *chart,* to map, to plan in detail: *Lewis and Clark charted the Northwest Territory. The advertising agency carefully charted the promotion campaign for the new product.*
chartered   (verb) past tense of *charter,* to hire or lease a vehicle: *The company chartered a bus for the trip to Atlantic City*; (adjective) hired or leased: *The foreign ministers arrived by chartered plane.*

choose   to select, pick out: *We need to choose a design for the new company stationery*; to want, desire: *I do not choose to participate.*
chose   past tense of *choose: We chose this design for the new company stationery; I chose not to participate.*

climactic   (klī mak'tik) pertaining to the highest point: *In a climactic sequence, the most important point is withheld until the end. Dr. Hitachi was called to the phone during the climactic moment of the play.*
climatic   (klī ma'tik) pertaining to climate, weather: *We cannot conduct this experiment without ideal climatic conditions.*

clothes (klō*th*z) wearing apparel, such as suits, dresses, and skirts: *Ms. Deville's clothes are too casual to be worn in the business office.*

cloths (klôths) fabrics: *The yard goods section at the department store is showing its new line of cloths.*

collision violent contact, a crash: *Ten people died in the collision of a bus with a truck.*

collusion a secret understanding between two or more persons to cheat, defraud, or damage the interest of others, a conspiracy: *The two stockbrokers were indicted for collusion.*

coma (kō′mə) a state of prolonged unconsciousness caused by sickness or injury: *Mr. Filmore fell into a coma shortly after he was injured in an automobile accident.*

comma (käm′ə) a mark of punctuation (,): *It is incorrect to join two sentences with a comma.*

command (verb) to direct, order, be in control of: *General Wingate will command the First Army;* (noun) an order, directive, authority, power, control: *A soldier must learn to obey every command.*

commend to mention favorably, to praise: *The wise employer will commend his or her employees when their work merits recognition.*

comment a casual remark: *The speaker made a brief comment about the weather.*

compose to write, make up, create: *Some poets compose long odes. The whole is composed of its parts. Our company is composed of five separate divisions.*

comprise to include: *Those properties comprise thirty lots. The whole comprises its parts. Our company comprises five separate divisions.*

compromise (noun) a settlement in which each side makes concessions, or the result of such settlement: *The strike was settled when both sides agreed on a compromise;* (verb) to expose one's reputation to danger, suspicion, or disrepute, or weaken one's principles or ideals: *To alter my stand on civil liberties would compromise my reputation with the voting public.*

comprehensible understandable, intelligible: *These instructions are too technical to be comprehensible to the average layperson.*

comprehensive large in scope, inclusive: *Ruth has a comprehensive knowledge of the latest computer technology. He passed his comprehensive examinations with honors.*

confidant (kän′fə dant′) one to whom secrets are entrusted: *Mr. Polski was her confidant.*

confident (kän′fə dənt) assured, certain: *Betty was confident she would be promoted.*

NAME	CLASS	DATE	SCORE

Words Often Confused Assignments

A. Select from the following words the one that correctly fits the blank in each of the sentences below. Then write the word in the answer space.

cease	census	collision	command	comprise
seize	senses	collusion	commend	compromise
censor	choose	coma	comment	comprehensible
censure	chose	comma	compose	comprehensive

1. The operator's manual contained _____ instructions.

   1._____

2. A person's _____ can often provide a warning of physical danger.

   2._____

3. The advertising agency stopped making exaggerated claims for the product because it did not want a federal agency to _____ it.

   3._____

4. She seemed to _____ the opportunity to join us whenever she could.

   4._____

5. The software manual was so well written that it was _____ to a beginner.

   5._____

6. Many people have difficulty using the _____ correctly in sentences.

   6._____

7. Until he obtained a permit, he was told to _____ construction.

   7._____

8. National _____ reports are often used for planning purposes.

   8._____

9. The public relations director had the authority to _____ all advertising copy.

   9._____

10. It takes practice to _____ effective business letters.

    10._____

11. After weeks of deliberation, the workers were ready to offer a _____ on the terms of the contract.

    11._____

12. The doctors feared that the patient might never come out of the _____.

    12._____

13. To save money on his car insurance, Jim increased the deductible amount on his _____ coverage to $500.

13. _____

14. The insurance investigator tried to prove that there had been _____ between the heir to the estate and his lawyer.

14. _____

15. She _____ to retire early.

15. _____

B. In some of the following sentences, an incorrect word is used. Underline the incorrect word, and write the correct word in the space provided. Where there is no error, write C in the answer space.

1. Synthetic fibers can be woven into a variety of clothes, which are used by people who sew.

1. _____

2. Roger called to make certain that I would remember the meeting.

2. _____

3. The noise of the collision was heard several blocks away.

3. _____

4. Office workers should always dress in neat cloths.

4. _____

5. It takes skill to use the coma correctly in business correspondence.

5. _____

6. Bill was censored for revealing confidential information.

6. _____

7. Her comments on my report were favorable.

7. _____

8. Chartered flights usually cost less than commercial flights.

8. _____

9. I was given the opportunity to chose the paint color for my new office.

9. _____

10. The air conditioner did much to enhance climactic conditions in the office.

10. _____

11. Plans for the publicity campaign were chartered a while ago.

11. _____

12. Rita choose not to make the purchase at this time.

12. _____

13. His voice was so commending that it caused everyone to listen.

13. _____

14. At the climatic point of LuAnn's story, we were all in suspense.

14. _____

15. No comprise seemed possible between the parties.

15. _____

C. Read the definition, and select the correct word from the second column to match that description. Write the word you selected in the answer space.

	Definition	**Word Choice**	
1.	to select, pick out	choose, chose	1._____
2.	pertaining to climate	climactic, climatic	2._____
3.	to include	compose, comprise, compromise	3._____
4.	to mention favorably, to praise	command, commend, comment	4._____
5.	to prohibit anything considered unsuitable	censor, censure	5._____
6.	to take possession by force	cease, seize	6._____
7.	fabric that covers a window	certain, curtain	7._____
8.	one to whom secrets are entrusted	confidant, confident	8._____
9.	fabrics	clothes, cloths	9._____
10.	mapped	charted, chartered	10._____

D. Compose a newspaper headline using each of the words (or derivatives of the words) listed below. Try to keep your headlines informative but brief (4 to 8 words). They can represent real or fictitious events. Underline the vocabulary word in each headline.

charter   *<u>Chartered</u> Flight Lost at Sea*

coma   *Infant in <u>Coma</u> Following Fall*

1. collision _____

2. censure _____

3. comment _____

NAME	CLASS	DATE	SCORE

Vocabulary Enrichment

Chapters 12–15

A. You should now be familiar with the meaning of each of the words below. In the space provided to the right, write the word that best completes the meaning of the sentence. Cross out each word in the list as you use it.

adjacent	deference	gullible	mollify	reminiscences
adversary	discernible	illegible	notary	stupefy
amicable	exemplary	inexorable	obsolescence	tangible
auditor	expedient	insolent	ostensible	vigilant
belligerent	fallible	insolvent	persistent	vulnerable
benevolent	feasible	irrevocable	plausible	
bursar	formidable	lenience	prudent	
comptroller	fraudulent	liquefy	relevant	

1. Despite their attempts to change his mind, he stubbornly maintained that his decision was
   _____.

   1._____

2. As a result of his prior experiences, he was a(n) _____ opponent in the campaign.

   2._____

3. Because of the slowdown in production, the firm was _____ to criticism from its distributors.

   3._____

4. She was required to have her signature validated by a(n) _____.

   4._____

5. Land, buildings, and property are examples of fixed or _____ assets.

   5._____

6. Because all participants came from a 20-mile radius, New York City was the most _____ location for the meeting.

   6._____

7. The retiring president shared some _____ about her early days with the company.

   7._____

8. If computers and printers are networked, it is possible to print information at a printer that is not _____ to the computer.

   8._____

9. The sales representatives from two different com-
    panies found themselves in a(n) _____ relation-
    ship as each attempted to close the sale.   9. _____

10. A series of _____ decisions earned the new com-
    pany executive the respect of his peers.   10. _____

11. The firm had to declare bankruptcy because it had be-
    come _____.   11. _____

12. Rapid technological developments unfortunately
    promote _____.   12. _____

13. All the research conclusively supported the fact that
    the plan was _____.   13. _____

14. The tuition payments were sent directly to the office of
    the _____.   14. _____

15. Better Business Bureaus investigate _____ prac-
    tices.   15. _____

B. For this exercise you must refer to the list of words given for assignment A above. Select any ten words that you did not use in completing assignment A. For each of the ten words you selected, compose a meaningful sentence on a separate sheet of paper.

C. Choose the word from the list below that is closest in meaning to the numbered word or words in the paragraphs on pages 253–254. Write the word you selected from the list in the answer space. Use each word only once.

compatibility	locations
delayed	message
development	movement
device	occur
distant	parties
enables	shaped
expenses	simultaneously
images	specified
implement	split
improvement	stores
interactive	text
keyboarded	virtually
linking	

Understanding Telecommunication Services

Simply stated, telecommunications involves the use of any
technology that provides for the 1. TRANSMISSION of
information between two 2. SITES by electronic means.
Telecommunication technologies can take many forms, ranging
from those systems which have been in use for long periods of
time to those which are still in the developing stages.

1._____

2._____

The telephone is a telecommunication 3. APPARATUS that
enables voice communication to 4. TAKE PLACE. In a typical
telephone conversation, there is interactive communication
because the two 5. PARTICIPANTS listen and talk in turn.

3._____

4._____

5._____

Electronic voice mailboxes represent a more recent
technological 6. ACHIEVEMENT in which the computer
7. CAPTURES the voice message given by one person and
delivers the message to another person or to a group of people
according to 8. PRESCRIBED instructions.

6._____

7._____

8._____

In voice mail transactions, there can be interaction, but it
is 9. NOT IMMEDIATE. Taking voice mail one step further is
the technology known as electronic phone. This technology
enables two individuals to accomplish 10. BACK AND FORTH
communication — each on his or her own computer screen. In
this case each party has a 11. DIVIDED screen and views both
the sending and receiving 12. TEXT at the same time.

9._____

10._____

11._____

12._____

Teleconferencing is the ultimate form of telecommunications
in that two groups which are in remote locations can actively
interact 13. AT THE SAME TIME. They can see each other and
speak with each other with 14. ALMOST no time lapse.
Teleconferencing 15. PERMITS groups of people to hold a joint

13._____

14._____

15._____

meeting from remote locations. Although the technology is
costly to 16. <u>CARRY OUT</u>, it does save the travel 17. <u>COSTS</u>
that would typically be required if a number of people had to
go to a particular location for a meeting.

16. _____

17. _____

Other means of telecommunication include the following:
Telex transmission, which uses specialized equipment
with a keyboard. A telex unit can send 18. <u>TYPED</u> messages
to other telex units at 19. <u>REMOTE</u> locations.
Facsimile transmission, which permits the electronic
transfer of both 20. <u>PICTURES</u> and 21. <u>WORDS</u> from one location
to another in seconds.
Cellular phones, which have grown in popularity in recent years,
particularly due to 22. <u>BETTERMENT</u> in the quality of transmission.
Local Area Networks, involving the 23. <u>BRINGING TOGETHER</u>
of computers and peripheral equipment at the same and/or
distant locations.

18. _____

19. _____

20. _____

21. _____

22. _____

23. _____

The direction that telecommunications will take in the future
will be 24. <u>MOLDED</u> by trends in technology, competition,
regulation, and customer demand. 25. <u>WORKING TOGETHER</u>
<u>HARMONIOUSLY</u> is a desired goal of all newly developing
telecommunication systems. In any case, telecommunications
surely offers office workers "a new way with words."

24. _____

25. _____

Words Ending in **ise—ize—yze**

The three suffixes **ise, ize,** and **yze** are added to roots to form verbs. They carry a variety of meanings, including *to subject to* (**jeopardize, analyze**), *to make like* (**dramatize**), *to become like* (**crystallize**), *to treat like* (**idolize**), *to cause to acquire* (**modernize, legalize**), and *to engage in an activity* (**advertise**).

Over 400 words end in **ise, ize,** or **yze**. Since virtually all of them end with the same sound—*ize*—correct pronunciation will not help you decide which of these three spellings is correct. In the vast majority of cases, however, the correct suffix is **ize**. All you need to do is to become familiar with the relatively few words that end in either **ise** or **yze**, and your spelling problems involving words ending in these suffixes will be over.

Rule 1

Only two common words end in **yze—analyze** and **paralyze**.

It is unlikely that you will ever use such technical terms as **catalyze, dialyze,** or **electrolyze**.

Rule 2

A small number of words end in **ise**.

In some cases the **ise** ending is not truly a suffix but rather part of the root. The distinction is not important here, however, because you are concerned with correct spelling, not precise word derivations.

cise

circumcise
excise*

exercise
exorcise

incise*

Note	All other similar words with roots ending in soft **c** (**s** sound) end in **cize**: **criticize, ostracize,** etc. Two other common words in this group are pronounced differently and should pose no problems: **concise** and **precise**. The **ise** in these two words has a hissing **s**, not the **z**, sound.

guise

disguise

guise

mise

compromise
demise*

premise (prem'-is)
surmise*

prise

apprise*
comprise

enterprise
reprise*

surprise

Note	The word **prize**, the reward given to the winner of a contest, is unrelated to these words.

rise

arise	rise	uprise
moonrise	sunrise	

vise

advise	improvise*	supervise
devise	revise	

wise

contrariwise	likewise	sidewise
lengthwise	otherwise	wise

Exceptions The following words do not fall into any group. Study them carefully.

advertise	despise	merchandise
chastise*	franchise*	

Rule 3

All of the more than 400 words that remain end in **ize**.

Here is a list of frequently used words with the **ize** suffix.

agonize	harmonize	philosophize
alphabetize	humanize	plagiarize*
amortize*	hypnotize	pulverize
antagonize	idolize	rationalize
apologize	immunize	realize
atomize	individualize	recognize
authorize	italicize	revolutionize
baptize	itemize	scandalize
brutalize	jeopardize*	scrutinize
capitalize	legalize	specialize
characterize	liberalize	stabilize
circularize	localize	standardize
civilize	magnetize	sterilize
colonize	mechanize	subsidize*
criticize	minimize	symbolize
crystallize	mobilize	synchronize*
demoralize	modernize	synthesize*
dramatize	monopolize*	systematize
economize	moralize	tantalize*
emphasize	nationalize	terrorize
epitomize*	naturalize	utilize
equalize	neutralize	vandalize
familiarize	organize	verbalize
fertilize	ostracize*	visualize
fraternize	particularize	vocalize
galvanize	pasteurize	vulcanize*
generalize	patronize	
glamorize	penalize	

NAME	CLASS	DATE	SCORE

Spelling Assignments

A. Insert **ise, ize,** or **yze** (whichever is correct) in the spaces in the following words. Then rewrite the complete word on the line to the right.

1.	merchand_ise_	_____	16.	surpr _ise_	_____
2.	chast _ise_	_____	17.	equal _ize_	_____
3.	desp _ize_	_____	18.	econom _ize_	_____
4.	apolog _ize_	_____	19.	modern _ise_	_____
5.	dev _ise_	_____	20.	surm _ize_	_____
6.	anal _yze_	_____	21.	harmon _ize_	_____
7.	adv _ise_	_____	22.	emphas _ile_	_____
8.	superv _ise_	_____	23.	otherw _ise_	_____
9.	civil _ize_	_____	24.	ar _ise_	_____
10.	sunr _ise_	_____	25.	mechan _ise_	_____
11.	enterpr _ize_	_____	26.	improv _ize_	_____
12.	comprom _ise_	_____	27.	compr _ize_	_____
13.	exerc _ise_	_____	28.	disgu _ise_	_____
14.	critic _ize_	_____	29.	exc _ise_	_____
15.	paral _yze_	_____	30.	advert _ise_	_____

B. Underline the misspelled word or words in each of the following groups of three. Spell the word or words correctly in the space at the right. If there are no errors in the group, write C.

1.	comprise	surmise	economize	1._____
2.	exercize	despise	paralize	2._____
3.	demise	emphasise	localize	3._____
4.	minimize	franchise	generalise	4._____
5.	legalize	itemise	moralize	5._____
6.	harmonize	sidewise	verbalize	6._____

7.	crystallise	vocalize	mechanize	7. _____
8.	circularize	analize	terrorize	8. _____
9.	hypnotise	nationalize	rationalize	9. _____
10.	visualize	synchronize	vitalise	10. _____
11.	magnetize	civilise	naturalize	11. _____
12.	stigmatize	amortise	alphabetize	12. _____
13.	immunize	recognize	sterilize	13. _____
14.	ostracyze	plagiarize	arise	14. _____
15.	tantalize	sensitise	disguise	15. _____
16.	pasteurize	realize	excize	16. _____
17.	apprize	serialize	incize	17. _____
18.	equalize	penalize	compromize	18. _____
19.	summarize	modernize	lengthwise	19. _____
20.	atomyze	specialise	otherwise	20. _____

Words Often Confused

conscience	a knowledge of the difference between right and wrong and the feeling that one should do right: *Thelma's conscience would not allow her to keep the purse, so she turned it in to the Lost and Found Department.*
conscious	being aware of, able to feel: *A good salesperson is always conscious of the customer's needs and desires.*
console	(kən sōl') (verb) to make someone feel less sad or disappointed, to comfort: *Nothing could console Mr. Levine over the death of his wife.* (kän'sōl) (noun) a cabinet: *Kathleen preferred a stereo console to a stereo component system.*
consul	(kän'səl) an official appointed by a government to live in a foreign city and look after his or her country's business interests and citizens there: *Most foreign countries send a consul to New York. These consuls reside in consulates.*
continual	repeated often, happening over and over again: *Mr. Shaw reprimanded his assistant for her continual lateness.*
continuous	happening without interruption, unceasing: *The strike was averted after twelve hours of continuous negotiations.*
cooperation	acting or working together: *The cooperation of all employees is needed to reduce our high electric bills.*
corporation	a type of business organization: *For tax purposes we have decided to form a corporation.*
costume	(käs'tōōm) style of dress peculiar to a nation, class, or historical period or appropriate to a particular time or occasion; garment worn on the stage or at a masquerade: *Have you selected a costume for the Halloween party?*
custom	(kus'təm) the usual way of acting in given circumstances: *It is our custom to take up a collection for anyone who retires from the company.*
credible	believable, reliable, trustworthy: *If these endorsements are not credible, the consumer will not buy the product.*
creditable	worthy of credit, honorable, respectable: *Marlene did not win the election, but she ran a creditable campaign.*
deceased	(dē sēst') (noun) a dead person: *The deceased had been known in his youth for his musical talent;* (adjective) dead: *Her mother is deceased.*
diseased	(di zēzd') sick, unhealthy: *One diseased chicken can infect a whole brood.*
decent	(dē'sənt) proper, right, respectable, in good taste: *The union struck for a decent wage for its members.*
descent	(dē sent') a coming down from a higher to a lower place: *The hiking party found the descent into the valley quite difficult.*

dissent (verb) to differ in belief or opinion, disagree: *Ms. Gaines was the only person to dissent from the committee's recommendations*; (noun) disagreement: *When the committee's recommendations were announced, one member voiced his dissent.*

defer (dē fur') to put off to a future time, delay: *The committee voted to defer any decision on the matter pending further study*; to yield courteously to the wish or judgment of another: *I will defer to you because of your experience.*

differ (dif'ər) to vary or disagree: *She and Don differ as to the best way to invest the money.*

deference (def'ər əns) a courteous yielding to the wishes or judgment of someone else: *In deference to the wishes of its customers, the bank opened its drive-in window at 7 a.m.*

difference (dif'ər əns) the state of being different, unalike, dissimilar: *There is no major difference between these two videocassette recorders.*

deprecate to express disapproval: *Mr. Gonzalez has a tendency to deprecate any proposal coming out of this office*; to belittle: *Jo-El will always deprecate her own abilities.*

depreciate to lower in value: *A new car depreciates rapidly during the first year.*

desert (dez'ərt) a dry, barren, sandy, treeless region: *Our California offices are only ten miles from the desert*; (verb) (di zurt') to abandon, leave behind: *He planned to desert the Army rather than be shipped overseas.*

dessert (di zurt') course served at the end of a meal: *I never eat dessert after lunch.*

detract to take away, diminish, reduce: *These typographical errors detract from the letter's appearance.*

distract to sidetrack, to divert: *The noise of the traffic outside did not distract us.*

device (di vīs') machine, piece of mechanical apparatus: *Earlier models of the device failed factory tests*; plan, scheme, or trick: *I have a device that could save us money.*

devise (di vīz') to plan, invent, think out: *Our engineers may devise an improved process that will speed production.*

NAME	CLASS	DATE	SCORE

Words Often Confused Assignments

A. Select from the following words the one that correctly fits the blank in each of the sentences below. Then write the word in the answer space.

conscience	costume	dissent	distract
conscious	custom	deference	device
console	credible	difference	devise
consul	creditable	deprecate	
continual	decent	depreciate	
continuous	descent	detract	

1. The uniform was so gaudy that it looked almost like a
   _____ .   1._____

2. On the witness stand, Martin gave a _____ account of the events he saw.   2._____

3. Some new anesthetics enable patients to remain _____ throughout operations.   3._____

4. Our long-standing _____ has been to hold an orientation meeting for our new salespersons.   4._____

5. We watched eagerly as the plane made its _____ onto the runway.   5._____

6. This new _____ seems to be compatible with your other equipment.   6._____

7. The office was open one evening a week in _____ to its customers' wishes.   7._____

8. The _____ between the two plans was minimal.   8._____

9. The _____ sound of the breaking waves lulled her to sleep.   9._____

10. Ursula received a _____ settlement for the injuries that she suffered.   10._____

11. Naturally, Barbara resented any remarks that she felt would _____ her abilities.   11._____

12. Lack of careful grooming can _____ from your overall personal appearance.   12._____

13. In times of inflation, money deposited in savings accounts seems to _____ quickly.

13. _____

14. His _____ nagging irritated me.

14. _____

15. When Greg was reading, even the noisy equipment did not _____ his attention.

15. _____

B. In some of the following sentences, an incorrect word is used. Underline the incorrect word, and write the correct word in the space provided. Where there is no error, write C in the answer space.

1. During my recent vacation in Arizona, I had occasion to drive through the dessert in 110°F temperature.

1. _____

2. Diana was pleased with the creditable performance evaluation she received.

2. _____

3. The motion passed with two descending votes.

3. _____

4. It is not our costume to give credit to new customers.

4. _____

5. Maurice was particularly self-conscience about his accent.

5. _____

6. Her continual lying caused even her best friends to distrust her.

6. _____

7. The noisy air conditioner was very detracting.

7. _____

8. A collection was taken for the family of the deceased.

8. _____

9. Her conscience bothered her so much that she had to tell someone what she had seen.

9. _____

10. Descent working conditions are important for every worker.

10. _____

11. Choosing a dessert was the hardest part of planning the luncheon menu.

11. _____

12. After 5:15 p.m. the building was desserted.

12. _____

13. The story about his decent from power was almost as interesting as the one that explains his ascent to power.

13. _____

14. The fund-raiser was to provide funds for a charity that tried to devise cures for deceased animals.

14. _____

15. Tran invented a custom-made devise to help handicapped people.

15. _____

C. Read the definition, and select the correct word from the second column to match that description. Write the word you selected in the answer space.

Definition	**Word Choice**	
1. to belittle or express disapproval	deprecate, depreciate	1._____
2. unceasing, happening without interruption	continual, continuous	2._____
3. to abandon or leave behind	desert, dessert	3._____
4. to sidetrack or divert	detract, distract	4._____
5. to put off or delay	defer, differ	5._____
6. being aware of	conscience, conscious	6._____
7. sick, unhealthy	deceased, diseased	7._____
8. believable, trustworthy	credible, creditable	8._____
9. a way of acting in given circumstances	costume, custom	9._____
10. to plan, invent, think out	device, devise	10._____

D. Complete each of the following sentences.

1. Distracting noises _____

   _____

2. My conscience tells me _____

   _____

3. The dessert _____

   _____

4. It was the custom_____

   _____

5. Is the device _____

   _____

6. My costume _____

   _____

7. Diseased animals _____

   _____

8. Can you devise _____

_____

9. What is the difference _____

_____

10. The consul _____

_____

NAME	CLASS	DATE	SCORE

Review Exercises

A. There are misspelled words in some of the following sentences. Underline each misspelled word, and write the correct spelling in the space provided. If there are no misspelled words, write C in the space next to the sentence.

1. We disaprove of any practices that might cast discredit upon our product line.

    1._____

2. Our firm provides for substantial insurence payments to the benficiaries of deceased employees.

    2._____

3. A hard disk drive on a computer can capture an apprecible amount of information.

    3._____

4. Are you familiar with the circular sent by the burser of the college?

    4._____

5. The lawyer tried to arbitrate the differences between the laborers and the management.

    5._____

6. We count among our subscribers many aviaters, actors, stenographers, doctors, and editers.

    6._____

7. You will shortly recieve a franchise that will permit you to sell our merchandize in your area.

    7._____

8. Persistance and independance are likely to lead people to success in their chosen careers.

    8._____

9. Ms. Baldwin was arrogent, violent, and ignorant.

    9._____

10. It is important that you recognize the need for more maintenance and inheritance insurance.

    10._____

11. To get desired results, you need to present your grievances and annoyences to the proper authorities.

    11._____

12. We believe that the council will modify its stand and ratify the contract.

    12._____

13. Employees with affable mannerisms are likable.

    13._____

14. The terrible ordeal she experienced left an indelible impression on her.

    14._____

15. As a member of the wrestling team, Dave renched his rist in a recent match.

    15._____

16. We are reluctant to reccommend this man to you because we have serious doubts about his competence.

16. _____

17. If you encounter any resistence or interferance, call the main office immediately.

17. _____

18. Since we have trained all our employees to write in a legable manner, the number of complaints we now receive is negligible.

18. _____

19. You'll find the dictionary very valuable in your vocabulary study.

19. _____

20. We understand that you have a preference for an early conference this year.

20. _____

21. We are now using our last box of stationary.

21. _____

22. You have our assurence that our consultants will give you intelligent and relible assistence.

22. _____

23. The Board of Directors is looking for a successor for the position of Vice President of Internel Affairs.

23. _____

24. We wish to reiterate that we refuze to compromise our principles.

24. _____

25. It is a desirable practice to familiarize yourself with the organization and information that can be found in the typical company manuel.

25. _____

B. Underline each error in the following memos, and write the correct spelling or usage in the space provided to the right of the line. If there are no errors in the line, write C in the space.

MEMO TO: All Department Supervisors

FROM: Robert L. McCloskey, Administrative Services

DATE: October 4, 19--

SUBJECT: Meeting of Office Supervisors, October 21

1 In order to familiarize the supervisery staff with the expanded
2 secretarial services availible as a result of our purchase of
3 three text-editing units, I have skeduled a special meeting of all
4 department supervisors. This meeting will be held on Monday,
5 October 21, at 9 a.m. in the Reference Libery.

6 The new equipment will enable us to systemetize and better
7 equalise the workload. It will also enable us to economize as
8 well as increase our productivity. Machine dictation useage and
9 form letter capabilities will be expanded. All departments should
10 surely benefit from the explanations that will be pervided at this
11 important meeting, which is likely to have far-reaching results
12 that all our employees will appreciate.

13 Your attendance, therefore, is of utmost importance. If--for some
14 reason--you cannot be presant, please let me know who will be
15 representing you and you're department.

db

1. _____
2. _____
3. _____
4. _____
5. _____
6. _____
7. _____
8. _____
9. _____
10. _____
11. _____
12. _____
13. _____
14. _____
15. _____

MEMO TO: Robert L. McCloskey, Administrative Services

FROM: Marcia Redford, Accounting Department

DATE: October 6, 19--

SUBJECT: Meeting of Office Supervisors, October 21

16 Upon checking my calender, I find that I have a prior commitment
17 for October 21. I am scheduled to be out of town at a computor
18 seminar; therefore, I will be unable to attend the meeting
19 regarding the new text-editting equipment.

20 Peter Atkins, senior accountent, will attend the meeting as the
21 representertive from the Accounting Department. I will brief
22 Mr. Atkins concerning our special paperwork problems prier to the
23 meeting. From his report following the meeting, I look foreward
25 to learning how the new equiptment can help our department better
25 solve our paperwork problums.

    jr

16. _____

17. _____

18. _____

19. _____

20. _____

21. _____

22. _____

23. _____

24. _____

25. _____

Final **y**

Chapter 17

In previous chapters you have seen how the addition of a suffix may affect the root. For example, in Chapter 4 you saw that most words that end in a vowel and single consonant double that consonant when suffixes beginning with a vowel are added (for example, **allot—allotting—allotted,** but **allotment**). In Chapter 5 you saw that most words that end in **e** drop the **e** when a suffix beginning with a vowel is added (for example, **complete—completed—completing—completion,** but **completely**).

In this chapter you are going to study how to add suffixes to words ending in **y**. Here, too, sometimes the form of the root is affected, but sometimes it is not.

Take this brief test. Add the indicated suffixes to the words below, and write the correct answers in the spaces provided.

1. obey + ing
2. obey + s
3. obey + ed
4. classify + able
5. day + ly
6. dry + ly
7. happy + ness
8. justify + cation
9. lonely + est
10. try + ed
11. try + ing
12. try + s

The correct answers are as follows: 1. **obeying,** 2. **obeys,** 3. **obeyed,** 4. **classifiable,** 5. **daily,** 6. **dryly,** 7. **happiness,** 8. **justification,** 9. **loneliest,** 10. **tried,** 11. **trying,** 12. **tries.**

Did you notice that in some cases the final **y** changed to **i** and that in other cases it did not? If you know a few simple rules, you will know when to change the **y** to **i** and when not to.

> ### Rule 1
>
> Words that end in **y** preceded by a consonant usually change the **y** to **i** before the addition of any suffix except one beginning with the letter **i**.

Hence **try** + **s** = **tries**, **try** + **ed** = **tried**, **try** + **ing** = **trying**. (If you changed the **y** to **i** when adding **ing**, you would have **triing**, a very awkward combination. Only two common English words contain this double **i** combination—**skiing** and **taxiing**.)

Here is a list of some common words that follow this rule.

accompany	accompanies	accompanied	accompanying
	accompaniment	accompanyist or	accompanist
ally	allies	allied	allying
	alliance		
angry	angrier	angriest	angrily
apply	applies	applied	applying
	application	applicable	
beauty	beautiful	beautify	beautification
bury	buries	buried	burying
	burial		
busy	busier	busiest	business
	busily		
carry	carries	carried	carrying
	carrier		
ceremony	ceremonies	ceremonious	ceremonial
classify	classifies	classified	classification
comply	complies	complied	complication
copy	copies	copied	copying
	copier	copious	
cry	cries	cried	crying
defy*	defies	defied	defying
	defiant		
deify	deifies	deified	deifying
	deification		
deny	denies	denied	denying
	deniable		
early	earlier	earliest	
easy	easier	easiest	easily
edify	edifies	edified	edifying
	edification		
envy	envies	envied	envying
	envious		

fancy	fancies	fancied	fancying
	fanciful		
fortify	fortifies	fortified	fortifying
	fortification		
glory	glories	glorious	
happy	happier	happiest	happiness
harmony	harmonies	harmonious	
heavy	heavier	heaviest	
identify	identifies	identified	identifying
	identification		
ignominy*	ignominies	ignominious	
industry	industries	industrious	industrial
injury	injuries	injurious	
justify	justifies	justified	justifying
	justifiable	justification	
likely	likelier	likeliest	likelihood
lonely	lonelier	loneliest	loneliness
luxury	luxuries	luxurious	luxuriate
marry	marries	married	marrying
	marriage		
mercy	mercies	merciful	merciless
modify	modifies	modified	modifying
	modification		
multiply	multiplies	multiplied	multiplying
	multiplication	multiplicity	
notify	notifies	notified	notifying
	notification		
pacify	pacifies	pacified	pacifying
	pacification		
perfidy*	perfidies	perfidious	
pity	pities	pitied	pitying
	pitiful	pitiless	pitiable
ply	plies	plied	plying
	pliable		
purify	purifies	purified	purifying
	purification		
qualify	qualifies	qualified	qualifying
	qualification		
ratify*	ratifies	ratified	ratifying
	ratification		
rectify	rectifies	rectified	rectifying
	rectification		
rely	relies	relied	relying
	reliable		
remedy	remedies	remedied	remedying
	remedial		
reply	replies	replied	replying
	replication		

sanctify	sanctifies	sanctified	sanctifying
	sanctification		
sanctimony*	sanctimonies	sanctimonious	
satisfy	satisfies	satisfied	satisfying
signify	signifies	signified	signifying
	signification		
silly	sillier	silliest	silliness
simplify	simplifies	simplified	simplifying
	simplification		
specify	specifies	specified	specifying
	specification		
study	studies	studied	studying
	studious		
try	tries	tried	trying
vary	varies	varied	varying
	various		
verify*	verifies	verified	verifying
	verifiable	verification	
victory	victories	victorious	
weary	wearies	wearied	wearying
	weariness		
worry	worries	worried	worrying

Note   Numbers ending in **y** also follow this rule.

twenty	twenties	twentieth
thirty	thirties	thirtieth
forty	forties	fortieth
fifty	fifties	fiftieth
sixty	sixties	sixtieth
seventy	seventies	seventieth
eighty	eighties	eightieth
ninety	nineties	ninetieth

Exceptions   Words ending in consonant + **y** may be exceptions.

Most of the words in this list have a final **y** that sounds like long **e** (**busy, happy, marry**). In some (**justify, rely**) the final **y** has the sound of long **i**. The following five words end with the long **i** sound: **dry, shy, sly, spry, wry**. When **er** or **est** is added to these words, they follow the basic rule and change the **y** to an **i**: **dry, drier, driest**; **shy, shier, shiest**; **sly, slier, sliest**; **spry, sprier, spriest**; **wry, wrier, wriest**. However, while these are the more common spellings, the following spellings are also considered acceptable: **dry, dryer, dryest**; **shy, shyer, shyest**; **sly, slyer, slyest**; **spry, spryly, spryness**; **wry, wryly, wryness**.

Here are these five words in all their forms:

dry	drier or dryer driest or dryest	dryly	dryness
shy	shier or shyer shiest or shyest	shyly	shyness
sly	slier or slyer sliest or slyest	slyly	slyness
spry	sprier or spryer spriest or spryest	spryly	spryness
wry*	wrier or wryer wriest or wryest	wryly	wrynes

Exceptions	A few other common words are also exceptions to the rule. Here the **y** does not change to **i**: **baby** + **hood** = **babyhood** and **lady** + **like** = **ladylike**.

Exceptions	Occasionally the **y** changes to **e** rather than **i**.

beauty + ous = beauteous   (*but* beautiful)
pity + ous = piteous   (*but* pitiful)
plenty + ous = plenteous   (*but* plentiful)

Rule 2

Words that end in **y** preceded by a vowel do not change the **y** to **i** when a suffix is added.

Thus **obey + s = obeys, obey + ed = obeyed, obey + ing = obeying.**

Here is a list of some common words that follow this rule.

allay	allays	allayed	allaying
annoy	annoys annoyance	annoyed	annoying
betray	betrays betrayal	betrayed	betraying
buy	buys	buying	buyer
convey*	conveys conveyor	conveyed	conveying
decay	decays	decayed	decaying

delay	delays	delayed	delaying
destroy	destroys	destroyed	destroying
disobey	disobeys	disobeyed	disobeying
display	displays	displayed	displaying
employ	employs	employed	employing
	employment	employable	employer
	employee		
enjoy	enjoys	enjoyed	enjoying
	enjoyment		
journey	journeys	journeyed	journeying
obey	obeys	obeyed	obeying
play	plays	played	playing
portray	portrays	portrayed	portraying
	portrayal		
prey*	preys	preyed	preying
spray	sprays	sprayed	spraying
stay	stays	stayed	staying
stray	strays	strayed	straying
survey	surveys	surveyed	surveying
sway	sways	swayed	swaying

Exceptions   Some words ending in a vowel + **y** are also exceptions.

day + ly = daily
gay + ety = gaiety
gay + ly = gaily
lay + d = laid
pay + d = paid
say + d = said
slay + n = slain

Other words formed by adding prefixes to these words are also exceptions: **mislaid, over-laid, overpaid, prepaid, repaid, underpaid, unpaid**.

NAME	CLASS	DATE	SCORE

Spelling Assignments

A. Each column contains a word and a suffix. Mentally add the suffix to the word. Then write the complete word in the space provided.

1.	edify + ed	_____	16.	plenty + ful	_____
2.	shy + er	_____	17.	survey + ed	_____
3.	accompany + es	_____	18.	classify + cation	_____
4.	copy + er	_____	19.	ski + ing	_____
5.	ratify + ing	_____	20.	fifty + eth	_____
6.	happy + est	_____	21.	luxury + es	_____
7.	play + ed	_____	22.	sly + ly	_____
8.	rely + ed	_____	23.	industry + ous	_____
9.	heavy + er	_____	24.	ply + ing	_____
10.	dry + ly	_____	25.	lady + like	_____
11.	baby + hood	_____	26.	envy + ous	_____
12.	prepay + ed	_____	27.	luxury + ous	_____
13.	multiply + ing	_____	28.	gay + ly	_____
14.	portray + al	_____	29.	reply + es	_____
15.	pity + ous	_____	30.	pity + ful	_____

B. Underline the misspelled word or words in each of the following groups of three. Spell the word or words correctly in the space at the right. If there are no errors in the group, write C.

1.	denies	dignified	ceremonies	1.	_____
2.	accompanyist	suppling	alliance	2.	_____
3.	delayed	icier	gaiety	3.	_____
4.	angryly	slayn	wryness	4.	_____
5.	mercyful	buying	betraying	5.	_____
6.	deniable	applys	occupys	6.	_____

7.	paid	prettiest	simplifying	7. _____
8.	justifyable	studies	frying	8. _____
9.	beauteous	wearying	emploiable	9. _____
10.	multiplys	annoyance	verification	10. _____
11.	notified	slyest	ratifing	11. _____
12.	trying	business	rectifying	12. _____
13.	driest	injuryous	decays	13. _____
14.	destroyed	pacifies	luckyer	14. _____
15.	reliable	studyous	beautify	15. _____
16.	notification	pityless	heartier	16. _____
17.	enjoyment	obeys	sillyness	17. _____
18.	purifyed	fortyeth	thirtys	18. _____
19.	costlier	shiness	greedier	19. _____
20.	emptyed	dissatisfying	carrys	20. _____

Words Often Confused

dairy	(der´ ē) farm, building, store, or business establishment where milk, cream, and milk products are kept, stored, produced, or sold: *The Ralston Dairy has opened a plant store featuring discount prices.*
diary	(dī´ə rē) a periodic (daily, weekly, etc.) written account of what one has felt, thought, or experienced; the book in which this account is written: *Many executives find it most useful to keep a full and accurate diary of their business day.*
disapprove	(dis´ə proov´) to dislike, consider wrong, reject: *Mr. Blandings is sure to disapprove of your expense budget.*
disprove	(dis proov´) to prove that something is false or incorrect: *We must disprove the rumor that we are planning to relocate.*
disburse	to pay out, to expend: *The auditor told the paymaster to disburse the funds.*
disperse	to break up and scatter in all directions, distribute widely: *The police ordered the crowd to disperse.*
discussed	past tense of *discuss,* to talk or write about: *Ed and Fran discussed the qualifications of the applicants for the new position.*
disgust	a sickening distaste or dislike, revulsion: *The smell from the rotting vegetables filled us with disgust.*
elicit	to draw forth: *This letter should elicit a reply. I'd like to elicit your opinion about this matter.*
illicit	forbidden by law, improper: *Mr. Ponzi was imprisoned for his illicit stock market transactions.*
emanate	to flow forth from a source: *The Mississippi emanates from the Great Divide. These new proposals emanate from the president's office.*
eminent	distinguished, important, exalted, noteworthy: *Ms. Buckley is an eminent scholar and historian.*
imminent	likely or about to happen: *Many economists believe that a recession is imminent.*
envelop	(en vel´əp) to wrap up or cover, to surround completely: *The fog envelops the harbor every morning.*
envelope	(än´və lōp´) wrapper or covering, a folded paper container for letters, etc.: *Please enclose a self-addressed, stamped envelope with your order.* (*Spelling Aid:* An envelopE is made of papEr.)
era	(ir´ə, er´ə) a historical period distinguished by certain important or unusual happenings, a period of time starting from some significant happening or date, or one of five extensive periods in the development of the earth: *The launching of the first earth satellite ushered in the new space era.*
error	(er´ər) a mistake: *Check your inventory again to find the error.*

errand   a short trip taken to deliver a message or perform a task, the purpose of such a trip: *Sally completed several personal errands during her lunch hour.*

errant   roving, wandering: *Ted fancied himself an errant knight in search of adventure;* straying from the proper standards: *If Molly does not correct her errant behavior, she will be dismissed.*

exalt   to raise high or elevate, to praise or glorify: *The people will exalt their new monarch.*

exult   to rejoice: *Mr. DuBois exulted in his election victory.*

exceptionable   debatable, objectionable: *Joe was fired because of his exceptionable behavior.*

exceptional   uncommon, extraordinary: *June is an exceptional secretary.*

executioner   (ek′si kyōō′shən ər) one who carries out a death sentence: *Anne Boleyn died at the hands of the executioner.*

executor   (eg zek′yōō tər) a person named in a will to carry out the provisions of the will: *Joan Mason named Sidney Hobson as the executor of her estate.*

expand   to make larger: *Studying this book will help you expand your vocabulary.*

expend   to use up, to spend: *Do not expend all your energy on this one assignment.*

expansive   having a free and generous nature, sympathetic, demonstrative: *The new department head has an expansive personality;* broad, extensive, comprehensive: *An expansive new shopping mall is planned for this location.*

expensive   high-priced, costly: *This sales campaign has been very expensive.*

NAME	CLASS	DATE	SCORE

Words Often Confused Assignments

A. Select from the following words the one that correctly fits the blank in each of the sentences below. Then write the word in the answer space.

dairy	disperse	imminent	errand	expensive
diary	elicit	envelop	errant	
disapprove	illicit	envelope	executioner	
disprove	emanate	era	executor	
disburse	eminent	error	expansive	

1. We _____ of any practices that might cast discredit on our product or policies.

    1._____

2. We are entering a new _____ in our trade relationships with foreign markets.

    2._____

3. The lawyer could not _____ a response from the sullen witness.

    3._____

4. Mr. Hodges was named _____ of his wife's estate.

    4._____

5. The post office requests that all _____ addresses bear a two-letter state abbreviation and a ZIP Code.

    5._____

6. Dr. Conte was a(n) _____ surgeon.

    6._____

7. The quality of an item is not always determined by how _____ it is.

    7._____

8. Everyone hoped that a reduction in the prime lending rate was _____.

    8._____

9. He felt a little like a(n) _____ after he gave the truthful but damaging testimony on the witness stand.

    9._____

10. Our cafeteria orders its fresh eggs and milk from a _____ farm nearby.

    10._____

11. From what source did your idea _____?

    11._____

12. She was out of the office on a(n) _____ for her employer.

    12._____

13. Every day new things are discovered that _____ what once was regarded as true.

13. _____

14. We must determine whether the amount of money we _____ exceeds the amount budgeted.

14. _____

15. The crowds _____ quickly as they leave the office building at closing time.

15. _____

B. In some of the following sentences, an incorrect word is used. Underline the incorrect word, and write the correct word in the space provided. Where there is no error, write C in the answer space.

1. Because of his errant behavior, he was not considered for the new position.

1. _____

2. Aileen made exceptionable progress in learning to operate the new equipment.

2. _____

3. The smell of gas seemed to envelope the area very quickly.

3. _____

4. The workers were fearful that a layoff was eminent.

4. _____

5. She was aggressive in attempting to illicit information on the confidential project.

5. _____

6. We are in an expanding and highly technical era.

6. _____

7. I did not follow through on the purchase because I thought that it would be too expansive.

7. _____

8. Paul kept track of his auto mileage in his pocket dairy.

8. _____

9. The two sides disgust the terms of the agreement.

9. _____

10. Kent was able to make friends easily because of his expansive manner.

10. _____

11. I exulted when no errors were found in my work.

11. _____

12. Mr. Gordon was fired for his elicit handling of company funds.

12. _____

13. Part of her job was to disperse funds from the petty cash drawer.

13. _____

14. I completed an errant at the bank before returning to the office.

14. _____

15. Pat's exceptionable behavior was the cause of much dissension in the office.

15. _____

C. Read the definition, and select the correct word from the second column to match that description. Write the word you selected in the answer space.

Definition	Word Choice	
1. roving, wandering	errand, errant	1._____
2. debatable, objectionable	exceptionable, exceptional	2._____
3. forbidden by law	elicit, illicit	3._____
4. sickening distaste or dislike	discussed, disgust	4._____
5. distinguished, important, noteworthy	emanate, eminent, imminent	5._____
6. to pay out, expend	disburse, disperse	6._____
7. to rejoice	exalt, exult	7._____
8. to surround completely	envelop, envelope	8._____
9. a person named in a will to carry out its provisions	executioner, executor	9._____
10. a historical period distinguished by certain important or unusual happenings	era, error	10._____

D. Compose a meaningful sentence for each of the following words.

1. errand _____

   _____

2. elicit _____

   _____

3. imminent _____

   _____

4. expensive _____

   _____

5. error_____

   _____

6. diary_____

   _____

7. disprove _____

_____

8. disperse _____

_____

9. exceptional _____

_____

10. expand _____

_____

Plurals 1: Basic Rules

When a noun refers to one person or thing, it is *singular;* when it refers to more than one, it is *plural.* Sometimes spelling problems arise in forming the plurals of singular nouns.

For example, do you know how to spell the plural of **attorney**? of **solo**? of **brother-in-law**? It is really quite easy, if you learn a few simple rules.

Rule 1

Most nouns form their plurals by adding **s** to the singular.

Singular	Plural	Singular	Plural
barrack	barracks	receipt	receipts
camera	cameras	relationship	relationships
desk	desks	screen	screens
development	developments	stenographer	stenographers
employee	employees	terminal	terminals
herd	herds	typewriter	typewriters
piece	pieces	umbrella	umbrellas

This rule also applies to proper names:

Kathleen	Kathleens	Slocum	Slocums

Rule 2	

Most nouns ending in **ch** (as in **itch**), **s, sh, ss, x,** and **z** add **es** to the singular to form their plural.

Singular	Plural	Singular	Plural
annex	annexes	kiss	kisses
boss	bosses	lens	lenses
box	boxes	loss	losses
brush	brushes	lunch	lunches
bush	bushes	mass	masses
business	businesses	patch	patches
buzz	buzzes	tax	taxes
catch	catches	waltz	waltzes
dress	dresses	wish	wishes

This rule also applies to proper names:

Fox	Foxes	Cavendish	Cavendishes
Bench	Benches	Rodriguez	Rodriguezes

Exceptions	There are two notable exceptions to the basic rule:

quiz   quizzes (note the double **z**)

When the final **ch** is pronounced like **k,** just add **s** to form the plural.

Bach   Bachs   stomach   stomachs

For nouns ending in **y,** the same rules you studied in Chapter 17 regarding changing the final **y** to **i** when a suffix is added apply to the formation of plurals.

Rule 3	

When the **y** is preceded by a *consonant*, change the **y** to **i** and add **es**.

Singular: **lady**— consonant **d** before **y**
Plural: **lad + i** (**y** changes to **i**) + **es** = **ladies**

Singular	Plural	Singular	Plural
accessory	accessories	fly	flies
activity	activities	patty	patties
authority	authorities	quality	qualities
category	categories	secretary	secretaries
city	cities	sky	skies
company	companies	specialty	specialties
country	countries	study	studies
courtesy	courtesies	vacancy	vacancies
currency	currencies	variety	varieties
fifty	fifties		

Rule 4

When the **y** is preceded by a *vowel,* add **s** to the singular to form the plural.

Singular: **bay**— vowel **a** before **y**
Plural: **bay** + **s** = **bays**

Singular	Plural	Singular	Plural
alley	alleys	monkey	monkeys
alloy	alloys	play	plays
attorney	attorneys	ray	rays
boy	boys	survey	surveys
chimney	chimneys	trolley	trolleys
day	days	turkey	turkeys
delay	delays	valley	valleys
essay	essays	volley	volleys
journey	journeys	way	ways
joy	joys	whiskey	whiskeys
key	keys	whiskey	whiskies
money	moneys		
money	monies		

Exception			
	colloquy	colloquies	
	soliloquy	soliloquies	

Note	*Proper names* ending in **y**, preceded by a vowel or consonant, add **s** to form the plural.

| Kay | Kay<u>s</u> | Henry | Henry<u>s</u> |
| McCauley | McCauley<u>s</u> | Kennedy | Kennedy<u>s</u> |

Rule 5

A few Old English nouns either add **en** to the singular to form the plural or make other changes within the word.

Singular	Plural	Singular	Plural
child	child<u>ren</u>	man	m<u>en</u>
foot	f<u>eet</u>	mouse	m<u>ice</u>
gentleman	gentlem<u>en</u>	ox	ox<u>en</u>
goose	g<u>ee</u>se	tooth	t<u>ee</u>th
louse	l<u>ice</u>	woman	wom<u>en</u>

NAME CLASS DATE SCORE

Spelling Assignments

A. For each word shown, write the plural form in the space provided.

1.	office		26.	waltz
2.	goose		27.	place
3.	attorney		28.	foot
4.	courtesy		29.	ox
5.	Nanassy		30.	bus
6.	woman		31.	apartment
7.	baby		32.	company
8.	wall		33.	Betty
9.	fifty		34.	barrel
10.	valley		35.	stock
11.	man		36.	buzz
12.	ally		37.	pass
13.	catch		38.	push
14.	stitch		39.	playwright
15.	mass		40.	stomach
16.	child		41.	business
17.	thirty		42.	box
18.	enemy		43.	carton
19.	tax		44.	dress
20.	Walsh		45.	file
21.	lunch		46.	boss
22.	fly		47.	piece
23.	play		48.	camera
24.	gentleman		49.	loss
25.	day		50.	variety

B. For each word shown, write the plural form in the space provided.

1.	trolley	_____	26.	ax	_____
2.	tally	_____	27.	recommendation	_____
3.	party	_____	28.	group	_____
4.	overtone	_____	29.	debt	_____
5.	receipt	_____	30.	soliloquy	_____
6.	typist	_____	31.	act	_____
7.	secretary	_____	32.	heir	_____
8.	screen	_____	33.	forty	_____
9.	mouse	_____	34.	desk	_____
10.	cigarette	_____	35.	economy	_____
11.	terminal	_____	36.	hope	_____
12.	machine	_____	37.	neighbor	_____
13.	waltz	_____	38.	lady	_____
14.	crutch	_____	39.	desire	_____
15.	dish	_____	40.	color	_____
16.	house	_____	41.	country	_____
17.	hose	_____	42.	Marinsulich	_____
18.	industry	_____	43.	quiz	_____
19.	flea	_____	44.	ray	_____
20.	gas	_____	45.	essay	_____
21.	stenographer	_____	46.	one	_____
22.	glass	_____	47.	turkey	_____
23.	duty	_____	48.	activity	_____
24.	accessory	_____	49.	accountant	_____
25.	umbrella	_____	50.	bill	_____

Words Often Confused

explicit	clearly stated: *All employees were given explicit instructions on what to do in case of fire.*
implicit	suggested, not plainly expressed, implied: *The real reasons for Mr. Muhammad's decision to retire are implicit in his memo of last week.*
extant	(eks′tənt) still in existence: *Shakespeare's original manuscripts are no longer extant.*
extent	(ek stent′) area, scope, range, size, space, length, amount: *No one knew the real extent of Mr. Marlow's financial holdings and influence.*
extinct	(ek stiŋkt′) no longer in existence: *If whaling is not abolished, whales may soon become extinct.*
facet	(fas′it) one of the small, polished surfaces of a cut gem: *Every facet of this diamond is perfect;* a phase or aspect: *These television spots are a new facet of our marketing campaign.*
faucet	(fô′sit) a device controlling the flow of water from a pipe: *The plumber fixed the leaky faucet.*
facilitate	to make something easy or easier, to lessen the labor of: *This new computer will facilitate your staff's clerical work.*
felicitate	to express good wishes formally, to congratulate: *As president, I felicitate you on your fifteenth year with our company.*
finale	(fə nal′ē) the last part of a piece of music or a play: *The finale of Beethoven's Ninth Symphony features Schiller's "Ode to Joy."*
finally	(fīn′əl ē) at last: *Finally, Burckhardt agreed to install the new heating system.*
finely	(fīn′lē) delicately, elegantly: *The antique chess set was made of finely crafted ivory.*
flagrant	outrageous, scandalous, notorious, glaring: *Mr. Benson was convicted for flagrant mismanagement of his company's funds.*
fragrant	having a pleasing odor, sweet-smelling: *Roses are fragrant flowers.*
flaunt	to wave or display gaudily or ostentatiously, to show off: *Gaby flaunted her knowledge at every opportunity;* to flutter or wave freely: *The flags flaunted in the breeze in front of the United Nations headquarters.*
flout	to treat contemptuously, to show contempt for, scorn, scoff: *Naomi seemed determined to flout the rules of acceptable behavior in everything she did.*
formally	in accordance with certain rules, forms, procedures, regulations: *At the last meeting of the stockholders, Selma Harris was formally presented as the next director of publicity.*

formerly in the past, some time ago: *Jimmy Carter was formerly President of the United States.*

healthful good for the health, producing or contributing to being hale or sound: *Arizona has a healthful climate.*

healthy having or showing good health, well: *Claudell looks healthy because he eats healthful foods.*

historical providing evidence for a fact of history: *While researching her book, Ms. Oskar discovered a significant historical document*; based on people or events of the past: *Sir Walter Scott wrote many historical novels.*

hysterical wildly excited, subject to uncontrollable fits of laughter or crying: *Denise became hysterical at the news of her husband's death.*

hospitable (häs′pit ə bəl) giving welcome, food, or shelter to guests or strangers: *The motel manager was hospitable to all her guests*; favorable, receptive: *Her business grew and prospered because she was hospitable to new ideas.*

hospital (häs′pit″l) place where sick or injured people or animals are cared for: *The people were taken to Roosevelt Hospital.*

human (hyo͞o′mən) having the form and qualities natural to or characteristic of human beings or people: *To err is human. Selfishness is a human weakness.*

humane (hyo͞o mān′) kind, merciful, compassionate: *People will always remember Dr. Schweitzer for his many humane acts.*

humidity (hyo͞o mid′ə tē) dampness, the amount of moisture in the air: *The summer has been especially uncomfortable because of the high humidity.*

humility (hyo͞o mil′ə tē) humbleness, a modest sense of one's own importance: *Though he was a great scientist, Albert Einstein always accepted praise with deep humility.*

illegible very hard or impossible to read: *Careless handwriting is usually illegible.*

ineligible not suitable, not qualified: *Part-time employees are ineligible for certain employee benefits.*

NAME	CLASS	DATE	SCORE

Words Often Confused Assignments

A. Select from the following words the one that correctly fits the blank in each of the sentences below. Then write the word in the answer space.

extant	faucet	finally	flaunt	healthful
extent	facilitate	finely	flout	healthy
extinct	felicitate	flagrant	formally	human
facet	finale	fragrant	formerly	humane

1. To what _____ have you been affected by the personnel changes?

   1._____

2. This is an important _____ of our employee training program.

   2._____

3. _____ we employed four people to do the job that now requires only three.

   3._____

4. Automation in our shipping department helps us _____ the handling of orders.

   4._____

5. After the _____, the audience in the theater was buzzing with glowing comments.

   5._____

6. We have never before seen an example of such _____ disregard for the law.

   6._____

7. At the next meeting, Risa will be _____ inducted as an officer.

   7._____

8. His co-workers gathered to _____ him on his successful sales campaign.

   8._____

9. A medical examination is usually required before an insurance policy is issued to determine that the person who is to be covered is _____.

   9._____

10. Mechanical calculators are virtually _____ in today's offices.

    10._____

11. Because she waved her hand to _____ it, everyone readily noticed her new ring.

    11._____

12. Many laws have been enacted to enforce the
    _____ treatment of those in our labor force.   12. _____

13. Do not _____ my attempts to give you advice.   13. _____

14. I like to spend my vacation at a resort where the
    climate is _____.   14. _____

15. It was only _____ that Louis should feel hurt
    after the quarrel.   15. _____

B. In some of the following sentences, an incorrect word is used. Underline the incorrect word, and write the correct word in the space provided. Where there is no error, write C in the answer space.

1. The famous lighthouse was eventually declared a historical site.   1. _____

2. The recipe called for finally chopped onions.   2. _____

3. Fred's tan made him look really healthful.   3. _____

4. The hospital manner of the owners and their staff
   made the restaurant one of our favorites.   4. _____

5. Rosita was hysterical with glee when she heard her
   name called as the winner of the jackpot.   5. _____

6. The hospitable coverage on my insurance plan allowed
   $120 per day for a semiprivate room.   6. _____

7. Every faucet of a secretary's duties requires attention.   7. _____

8. We lost the sale because of his flagrant mishandling of
   the situation.   8. _____

9. Their humane response to our request for help was appreciated.   9. _____

10. Ellie finale finished typing the report.   10. _____

11. The disaster was attributed to humane error.   11. _____

12. Our office was formally located in the building that was
    destroyed by fire.   12. _____

13. The union contract is an implicit statement of policies
    to be followed.   13. _____

14. He flaunted his position to the extent that he made
    enemies.   14. _____

15. It was hard to determine the correct spelling of Dana's
    last name because her handwriting was ineligible.   15. _____

C. Read the definition, and select the correct word from the second column to match that description. Write the word you selected in the answer space.

	Definition	Word Choice	
1.	having or showing good health	healthful, healthy	1._____
2.	dampness	humidity, humility	2._____
3.	not plainly expressed	explicit, implicit	3._____
4.	favorable, receptive	hospitable, hospital	4._____
5.	having the form and qualities natural to people	human, humane	5._____
6.	still in existence	extant, extent, extinct	6._____
7.	in the past	formally, formerly	7._____
8.	a phase or aspect	facet, faucet	8._____
9.	outrageous, scandalous	flagrant, fragrant	9._____
10.	to make something easier	facilitate, felicitate	10._____

D. Compose five two-line rhymes. Use the words (or derivatives of the words) given in the list below. Underline the word used in your rhyme. Study the examples below before you begin. As you will see, the vocabulary word may or may not be the word that rhymes.

healthy *In order to be healthy,*
you need not be wealthy.

fragrant *The flower I chose*
was the fragrant rose.

1. humidity _____

_____

2. finally _____

_____

3. human _____

_____

4. faucet _____

_____

5. healthful _____

_____

Plurals 2: Nouns Ending in **f—fe—ff—o**

While the letters **s** and **es** are also used to form the plurals of nouns ending in **f, fe, ff,** and **o,** some of these nouns also require additional changes. Others have more than one acceptable plural form. Study the following groups of nouns carefully.

Rule 1

Some nouns ending in **f** or **fe** form their plurals by changing **f** or **fe** to **ves**.

Singular	Plural	Singular	Plural
calf	calves	loaf	loaves
elf	elves	self	selves
half	halves	shelf	shelves
knife	knives	thief	thieves
leaf	leaves	wife	wives
life	lives	wolf	wolves

Rule 2

Some other nouns ending in **f, fe,** or **ff** simply add **s** to the singular to form the plural.

Singular	Plural	Singular	Plural
bailiff	bailiffs	plaintiff	plaintiffs
belief	beliefs	proof	proofs
brief	briefs	reef	reefs
chef	chefs	roof	roofs
chief	chiefs	safe	safes
cliff	cliffs	serf	serfs
cuff	cuffs	sheriff	sheriffs
grief	griefs	strife	strifes
handkerchief	handkerchiefs	tariff*	tariffs

Rule 3

A few other nouns ending in **f** have two acceptable ways to form the plural.

Singular	Plural
beef	beefs or beeves[1]
dwarf	dwarfs[1] or dwarves
hoof	hoofs[1] or hooves
scarf	scarfs[1] or scarves
staff	[2]staffs or staves
wharf	wharfs or wharves[1]

Rule 4

Nouns ending in a *vowel* plus **o** add **s** to the singular to form the plural.

Singular	Plural	Singular	Plural
cameo	cameos	portfolio	portfolios
curio	curios	radio	radios
duo	duos	ratio	ratios
embryo	embryos	studio	studios
folio	folios	tattoo	tattoos
patio	patios		

[1]This is the more common plural.

[2]When **staff** refers to a pole or a music staff, the correct plural form is **staves**. When **staff** refers to a group of assistants, employees, etc., the correct plural form is **staffs**.

Rule 5

Most nouns ending in a *consonant* plus **o** add **es** to the singular to form the plural.

Singular	Plural	Singular	Plural
buffalo	buffaloes	mosquito	mosquitoes
calico	calicoes	motto	mottoes
cargo	cargoes	potato	potatoes
domino	dominoes	tomato	tomatoes
echo	echoes	tornado	tornadoes
embargo*	embargoes	torpedo	torpedoes
grotto	grottoes	veto	vetoes
hero	heroes	volcano	volcanoes
innuendo*	innuendoes		

Note Many of the words on this list also form the plural by adding only an **s**: **buffalos, calicos, cargos, dominos, innuendos, mosquitos, mottos, tornados,** and **volcanos** are all considered acceptable spellings. For the other words, only **es** is correct. Hence we have listed all these words with only the **es** plural form, which is always the correct or more common way to form the plural.

Rule 6

Most musical terms that end in **o** add **s** to the singular to form the plural.

Singular	Plural	Singular	Plural
alto	altos	piano	pianos
banjo	banjos	piccolo	piccolos
basso	bassos	solo	solos
cello	cellos	soprano	sopranos
concerto	concertos	virtuoso	virtuosos
contralto	contraltos		

> ## Rule 7
>
> A few other words that end in a *consonant* plus **o** add **s** to the singular to form the plural.

Singular	Plural	Singular	Plural
auto	autos	kimono	kimonos
casino	casinos	memento*	mementos
commando	commandos	memo	memos
dynamo*	dynamos	tobacco	tobaccos
Eskimo	Eskimos	zero	zeros
halo	halos		

Note   Some of the words on this list also form the plural by adding **es: commandoes, haloes, mementoes,** and **zeroes.**   While either spelling is acceptable for these four words, for all the rest only the **s** is correct.   Thus we have listed all these words with only the **s** plural form, which is always the correct or more common way to form the plural.

NAME	CLASS	DATE	SCORE

Spelling Assignments

A. For each word shown, write the plural form in the space provided.

1.	belief	_____	11.	loaf	_____
2.	calf	_____	12.	self	_____
3.	chief	_____	13.	plaintiff	_____
4.	cliff	_____	14.	wife	_____
5.	grief	_____	15.	thief	_____
6.	half	_____	16.	brief	_____
7.	handkerchief	_____	17.	wolf	_____
8.	knife	_____	18.	proof	_____
9.	leaf	_____	19.	reef	_____
10.	life	_____	20.	roof	_____

B. For each word shown, write the plural form in the space provided.

1.	auto	_____	12.	mosquito	_____
2.	piano	_____	13.	potato	_____
3.	casino	_____	14.	veto	_____
4.	dynamo	_____	15.	shelf	_____
5.	elf	_____	16.	embargo	_____
6.	Eskimo	_____	17.	innuendo	_____
7.	tobacco	_____	18.	radio	_____
8.	wharf	_____	19.	echo	_____
9.	motto	_____	20.	concerto	_____
10.	zero	_____	21.	dwarf	_____
11.	studio	_____	22.	tariff	_____

23. memento _____
24. folio _____
25. safe _____
26. scarf _____

27. hoof _____
28. sheriff _____
29. memo _____
30. ratio _____

Words Often Confused

immigrate	to come into a country of which one is not a native: *Mr. Riccardi's grandparents immigrated to America in the early 1900s.*
emigrate	to leave a country for residence in another: *Ms. Schniller's great-grandparents emigrated from Germany.*
imply	to suggest without stating, express indirectly: *Judy didn't say so directly, but she implied that she would be leaving the company soon. What do you mean to imply by that statement?*
infer	to deduce, conclude from evidence: *I inferred from what Judy said that she would be leaving the company soon. What should I infer from that remark?*
incite	(in sīt') to urge to action, to arouse: *Brenda worked hard to incite the other union members to strike.*
insight	(in'sīt) ability to see and understand clearly the nature of things: *Effective advertisers need clear insight into the desires of the consumer.*
incredible	too unusual or improbable to be possible, unbelievable: *The increase in sales of our new soft drink from last year to this year is incredible.*
incredulous	unwilling or unable to believe, doubting, skeptical: *Mr. Yang looked incredulous when he heard the latest sales figures.*
indigent	poor, needy, destitute: *His parents were indigent migrant workers.*
indignant	feeling or expressing anger or scorn: *Sandra became highly indignant at his insulting behavior.*
ingenious	(in jēn'yəs) clever, skillful at inventing, resourceful, cleverly made and planned: *The phonograph is an ingenious invention. Edison had an ingenious mind.*
ingenuous	(in jen'yoo̅ əs) sincere, open, honest; unsophisticated, unworldly, innocent in a childlike way, naive: *Although Frank was nearly thirty, his outlook on life was remarkably ingenuous.*
intelligent	able to learn quickly, alert, wise: *Ms. Mazzo is an intelligent young woman who should advance rapidly in the organization.*
intelligible	capable of being understood: *If you wish your speech to be intelligible, speak clearly, distinctly, and slowly.*
interstate	existing between states: *The Interstate Commerce Act covers all transactions taking place from state to state.*
intestate	having made no valid will: *Serious legal complications can result when a person dies intestate.*
intrastate	existing within a single state: *Each state has exclusive control over its intrastate affairs.*

later (lāt′ər) at a future time, after an occurrence: *I'll meet you later in the day.*

latter (lat′ər) the second of two persons or things mentioned: *Sue and Jane are both excellent employees, but the latter is more dependable;* being near the end or close: *I will visit your region the latter part of next month.*

leased past tense of *lease,* to rent property for a specified period of time: *All the office space in the new building has been leased.*

least (adverb) smallest in degree or size, lowest in position or importance: *The least expensive product is usually not the best buy;* (noun) smallest amount, degree, etc.: *Meeting tomorrow's deadline is the least of my worries.*

lest for fear that: *I'm worried lest we fail to meet tomorrow's deadline.*

legislator lawmaker or elected member of a lawmaking body: *Senators, representatives, and members of the city council are legislators.*

legislature lawmaking body: *The Kansas Legislature convenes next week following the Easter recess.*

liable (lī′ə bəl) responsible, legally obligated: *We are liable for all expenses incurred by our employees;* likely to occur, particularly danger or risk: *Mr. Nemerov is liable to have a heart attack if he doesn't slow down.*

libel (lī′bəl) (noun) oral, written, or printed statement that injures a person's reputation: *Mr. Toomer sued the magazine's owners for libel;* (verb) to make or publish a libel against: *The magazine article on dishonesty in government libeled an innocent legislator.*

lifelong continuing through life: *Ms. Kumin has had a lifelong interest in consumer protection.*

livelong (liv′lôŋ) whole, entire: *We worked on that project the livelong day.*

lightening (līt′'n iŋ) making lighter or brighter, reducing the load: *The Senate is now considering laws for lightening our tax burden.*

lightning (līt′niŋ) discharge or flash of electricity in the sky: *Lightning struck a tree outside our window.*

NAME	CLASS	DATE	SCORE

Words Often Confused Assignments

A. Select from the following words the one that correctly fits the blank in each of the sentences below. Then write the word in the answer space.

immigrate	incredible	interstate	latter	liable
emigrate	incredulous	intestate	leased	libel
imply	ingenious	intrastate	least	lifelong
infer	ingenuous	later	lest	livelong

1. The car that was involved in the accident was one that had been _____ by the company.

    1._____

2. The invention of the airplane was a(n) _____ idea in its time.

    2._____

3. All trading between states is controlled by federal regulations affecting _____ commerce.

    3._____

4. Many people had a good reason to _____ from Europe to America in the late 1800s.

    4._____

5. Martina was _____ when she learned that she had been selected for the award.

    5._____

6. Though his manner appeared _____, he was actually a very sophisticated and worldly man.

    6._____

7. The New Jersey Legislature passed new laws for the state concerning _____ commerce.

    7._____

8. They arrived _____ than we expected.

    8._____

9. I recently completed courses in transcription and Speedwriting—the _____ I enjoyed immensely.

    9._____

10. What did you _____ from her actions?

    10._____

11. I have written the date in my appointment book _____ I forget.

    11._____

12. The proprietor was _____ for the damages caused by his negligence.

    12._____

13. _____ job placement was guaranteed to all graduates of the private business school.

    13._____

14. Of all the candidates, I felt that Gene was the
    _____ impressive.

14. _____

15. The newspaper was sued for _____ by the
    Senator.

15. _____

B. In some of the following sentences, an incorrect word is used. Underline the incorrect word, and write the correct word in the space provided. Where there is no error, write C in the answer space.

1. His remarks were unintelligible because of his heavy accent.

1. _____

2. The summer storm frightened us with its dramatic flashes of lightning.

2. _____

3. The fact that Ben died intrastate affected the distribution of his estate.

3. _____

4. The jury in the liable suit is due to present its verdict soon.

4. _____

5. Silence does not necessarily infer consent.

5. _____

6. Selected happenings at today's meeting of the legislator were reported on the television.

6. _____

7. Tina showed remarkable incite into politics for someone so young.

7. _____

8. Lightening their load made it easier for the pack animals to climb the trail.

8. _____

9. Mrs. Bingham was assured of livelong possession of the property.

9. _____

10. Latter incidents proved that our thoughts were correct.

10. _____

11. Chan's lack of enthusiasm caused us to infer that he was not happy with the arrangements we made for him.

11. _____

12. In the summer months, many people from the cities immigrate to the shore on weekends.

12. _____

13. Firms involved in intrastate highway building have to observe federal specifications.

13. _____

14. The customer became indigent when the clerk refused to cash her check.

14. _____

15. As a result of implementing his ingenuous idea, our production has increased tremendously.

15. _____

C. Read the definition, and select the correct word from the second column to match that description. Write the word you selected in the answer space.

	Definition	Word Choice	
1.	to deduce	imply, infer	1._____
2.	whole, entire	lifelong, livelong	2._____
3.	oral, written, or printed statement that injures a person's reputation	liable, libel	3._____
4.	reducing the load	lightening, lightning	4._____
5.	lawmaker or member of a lawmaking body	legislator, legislature	5._____
6.	within a single state	interstate, intestate, intrastate	6._____
7.	capable of being understood	intelligent, intelligible	7._____
8.	sincere, open, honest; naive	ingenious, ingenuous	8._____
9.	ability to see clearly the nature of things	incite, insight	9._____
10.	the second of two	later, latter	10._____

D. Complete each of the following sentences.

1. When the lightning_____

_____

2. Jerome was indignant _____

_____

3. We inferred _____

_____

4. Lest we forget,_____

_____

5. If a person dies intestate, _____

_____

6. An example of an ingenious device_____

_____

7. She was so intelligent that _____

_____

8. The legislature _____

_____

9. Who was liable _____

_____

10. Later in the day, _____

_____

NAME	CLASS	DATE	SCORE

Vocabulary Enrichment

Chapters 16–19

A. You should now be familiar with the meaning of each of the words below. In the space provided to the right, write the word that best completes the meaning of the sentence. Cross out each word in the list as you use it.

amortize	embargo	innuendo	prey	synthesize
apprise	epitomize	jeopardize	ratify	tantalize
chastise	excise	memento	reprise	tariff
defy	franchise	monopolize	subsidize	verify
demise	improvise	ostracize	surmise	vulcanize
dynamo	incise	plagiarize	synchronize	wry

1. Carvel, Burger King, and Pizza Hut are examples of
   _____ businesses.   1._____

2. His guilt was not firmly established; instead, it was im-
   plied by _____.   2._____

3. After learning more about the facts of the case, I was
   able to _____ what the next move should be.   3._____

4. My company's tuition aid program helped to
   _____ the cost of my college education.   4._____

5. If we do not get full cooperation from all departments,
   we will _____ our plan's chances for success.   5._____

6. A tactic used in foreign diplomacy is to threaten a(n)
   _____.   6._____

7. The increase in the price of gasoline helped to bring
   about the _____ of larger automobiles.   7._____

8. One of Hilda's faults was that whenever she was in a
   group, she tried to _____ the conversation.   8._____

9. Mr. Lane asked me to _____ the accuracy of the
   report by recalculating the data.   9._____

10. Her rapid rise up the career ladder seemed to
    _____ success.   10._____

11. Our new projector can automatically _____ both
    the audio and the visual.   11. _____

12. In the conclusion of the report, I tried to _____ all
    the reactions affecting the proposal.   12. _____

13. It takes much self-discipline to avoid falling
    _____ to laziness.   13. _____

14. In contrast with our former president, who had a slow
    and casual style, our new president is a(n)
    _____.   14. _____

15. The author insists that he did not _____ any
    material from another book.   15. _____

B. For this exercise you must refer to the list of words for assignment A above. Select any
ten words that you did not use in completing assignment A. For each of the ten words
you selected, compose a meaningful sentence on a separate sheet of paper.

C. Choose the word from the list below that is closest in meaning to the numbered word or
words in the paragraphs on pages 311–312. Write the word you selected from the list in
the answer space. Use each word only once.

bank	**program**
cycle	**protect**
destruction	**quantity**
dispose	**resource**
effects	**retained**
haphazardly	**specialized**
hardware	**standard**
interfacing	**storage**
listing	**systematized**
monitor	**ultimate**
off-site	**unnecessary**
operation	**usefulness**
organized	

Managing Information

Records are the memory 1. REPOSITORY of an organization,
and an inadequate program of managing records can have
disastrous 2. CONSEQUENCES for any business or organization.

Just like human beings, records have a life 3. SPAN. As
surely as a record is created—whether in hard copy (paper),
microfilm, or computer-oriented format—some provision must be
made for its storage and use. But good records management does
not stop there. Some provision must be made to 4. GET RID of
records when they are no longer useful, and this is a pitfall of many
existing record systems.

Managing information is, therefore, an organization-wide 5. SYSTEM
that provides for the 6. PLANNED control of records, including their
creation, maintenance, storage, transfer, and disposition—that is, from
"creation to 7. DISPOSITION."

Some of the 8. SPECIFIC areas of concern to those who
handle information include the following:

Files management and retrieval, which provides for the use
of 9. ROUTINE storage and retrieval procedures as well as the
careful selection and use of equipment and supplies.

Records retention, which recognizes the need to develop a
10. ROSTER of all types of records needed by a firm, including
the length of time each record is to be 11. KEPT and how it is
to be stored during its period of 12. FUNCTIONALITY.

Vital records retention, providing for special storage
procedures that 13. SAFEGUARD those records which are
critical to the continued 14. FUNCTION of the firm.

1. _____

2. _____

3. _____

4. _____

5. _____

6. _____

7. _____

8. _____

9. _____

10. _____

11. _____

12. _____

13. _____

14. _____

Inactive records management, providing for the 15. REMOTE   15. _____

maintenance and 16. STOWING of records not readily needed as   16. _____

well as for their eventual 17. SYSTEMATIC destruction.   17. _____

Forms management, providing for an ongoing program

designed to 18. EVALUATE and control the quantity, quality, and   18. _____

content of forms used within an organization—especially

striving to dispose of 19. UNWANTED forms in order to effect   19. _____

cost savings.

Correspondence and report management, which gives

attention to the quality and 20. AMOUNT of correspondence and   20. _____

report preparation with the 21. FINAL goal of assuring   21. _____

cost-effective preparation and distribution.

Microfilm and optical information system management, which

requires unique systems, formats, and 22. EQUIPMENT.   22. _____

These concerns—among others—clearly indicate that

efficient information management cannot be accomplished

23. ACCIDENTALLY. In order to meet the challenges posed by   23. _____

24. INTERACTING technologies, information management is   24. _____

destined to grow into an organization-wide program that will

manage a 25. SUBSTANCE as important as humans, machines,   25. _____

money, and materials.

Plurals 3: Compound Words, Letters, Numerals, Titles, Etc.

The compound words and other special types of nouns presented in this chapter form their plurals in a variety of ways. Study them carefully.

A compound word is a word that is composed of two or more words linked together: **copyright, trademark, brother-in-law**.

Rule 1

When a compound noun is written as one complete word, without hyphens, form the plural by making the last part plural.

Singular	Plural	Singular	Plural
blackboard	blackboards	letterhead	letterheads
bookcase	bookcases	middleman	middlemen
bookshelf	bookshelves	mousetrap	mousetraps
bylaw	bylaws	stepchild	stepchildren
bystander	bystanders	stockholder	stockholders
classmate	classmates	stopover	stopovers
copyright	copyrights	takeoff	takeoffs
courthouse	courthouses	toothbrush	toothbrushes
database	databases	trademark	trademarks
grandchild	grandchildren	understanding	understandings
headwaiter	headwaiters	undertaking	undertakings
homecoming	homecomings	weekday	weekdays

Exception   There is one notable exception.

passerby	passersby

313

Rule 2

When a compound noun is written as two or more separate words or with one or more hyphens, form the plural by making the principal, or most important, word plural.

For example, in **mother-in-law** the principal, or most important, part of the word is **mother**. In forming the plural of **mother-in-law**, only **mother** changes to plural.

mother-in-law   mothers-in-law

The same holds true for the following:

Singular	Plural
attorney at law	attorneys at law
attorney general	attorneys general
bill of lading	bills of lading
bill of sale	bills of sale
board of education	boards of education
brother-in-law	brothers-in-law
commander in chief	commanders in chief
consul general	consuls general
court-martial	courts-martial
editor in chief	editors in chief
hanger-on	hangers-on
leave of absence	leaves of absence
maid in waiting	maids in waiting
maid of honor	maids of honor
man-of-war	men-of-war
notary public	notaries public
runner-up	runners-up
sister-in-law	sisters-in-law

Rule 3

Words of measure ending in **ful** add **s** to the singular to form the plural.

armful	armfuls
basketful	basketfuls
bucketful	bucketfuls
cupful	cupfuls
handful	handfuls
spoonful	spoonfuls

Rule 4

Titles form their plurals in the regular manner.

Captain	Captains Hold and Brown
Judge	Judges Hare and Hotchkiss
Master	Masters Harry and Tom
Miss	Misses Jane and Mary
President	Presidents Monroe and Madison
Professor	Professors Howard and Lau

Rule 5

The plurals of most capital letters, numerals, signs, symbols, abbreviations, and words referred to as words are formed by adding **s** or **es** to the singular. To avoid possible confusion, the plurals of all lowercase letters and the capital letters **A, I, M,** and **U** are formed by adding **'s**.

The following examples will make this clearer.

Jill received all Bs and Cs on her report card.
Your 5s look like 3s.
Odets was much admired in the 1930s.
There are *s throughout this book.
You use too many etcs. in your correspondence.
On the final ballot the yeses outnumbered the noes almost 2 to 1.
The M's on these pages are blurred.
Be sure to dot your *i's* and cross your *t's*.

Rule 6

The following abbreviations do not follow any set rule in forming their plurals.

Singular	Plural
Dr.	Drs.
Mr.	Messrs. *This abbreviation is derived from the French word* **Messieurs.**
Mrs.	Mmes. *This abbreviation is derived from the French word* **Mesdames.**
Ms.	Mses.

Rule 7

The following nouns are almost *always* used in the singular, even though they end in **s** and seem to have a plural "feeling" or meaning.

aeronautics	measles
arthritis	molasses
civics	mumps
economics	news
ethics	phonetics
genetics	physics *the science*
logistics*	politics
mathematics	rickets

Rule 8

The following nouns are rarely or never used in the singular. They are almost invariably plural.

acoustics*	goods	scissors
annals*	headquarters	shears
auspices	odds	statistics
barracks	pants *trousers*	suds
belongings	pliers	tactics
cattle	premises	thanks
clothes	proceeds	trousers
contents	remains	tweezers
credentials	riches	winnings
earnings		

Rule 9

Some nouns have the same form in the singular and the plural.

chassis	grouse	series
Chinese	herd *of cattle*	sheep
corps	Japanese	species
deer	means *methods*	trout
fish	moose	vermin
gross	salmon	Vietnamese

Rule 10

Foreign and scientific words often take foreign plural endings. Some of these words also have more conventional English plural endings.

Singular	Foreign Plural	English Plural
addendum	addenda	
alga	algae	
alumna *feminine*	alumnae	
alumnus *masculine*	alumni	
analysis	analyses	
antithesis*	antitheses	
appendix	appendices	appendixes
automaton	automata	automatons
axis	axes	
bacillus*	bacilli	
bacterium*	bacteria	
basis	bases	
cactus	cacti	cactuses
crisis	crises	
criterion	criteria	criterions
curriculum	curricula	curriculums
datum	data	datums
diagnosis	diagnoses	
erratum*	errata	
focus	foci	focuses
formula	formulae	formulas
fungus	fungi	funguses
graffito	graffiti	
hypothesis	hypotheses	
index	indices	indexes
larva	larvae	
libretto	libretti	librettos
maximum	maxima	maximums
medium	media	mediums
memorandum	memoranda	memorandums
minimum	minima	minimums
neurosis*	neuroses	
oasis	oases	
parenthesis	parentheses	
phenomenon*	phenomena	phenomenons
psychosis	psychoses	
radius	radii	radiuses
stimulus*	stimuli	
stratum*	strata	
synopsis*	synopses	
synthesis*	syntheses	
thesis	theses	

NAME	CLASS	DATE	SCORE

Spelling Assignments

A. For each word, number, etc., shown, write the plural form in the space provided. If the item has no plural form or is given in its plural form, put a check ✓ in the space.

1. Jack-of-all-trades _____
2. editor in chief _____
3. runner-up _____
4. handful _____
5. captain _____
6. 5 _____
7. S _____
8. Mr. _____
9. Mrs. _____
10. medium _____
11. ethic _____
12. mumps _____
13. cattle _____
14. sheep _____
15. fish _____

16. economics _____
17. mathematics _____
18. civics _____
19. corps _____
20. Vietnamese _____
21. deer _____
22. front _____
23. physics _____
24. molasses _____
25. measles _____
26. judge _____
27. middleman _____
28. Ms. _____
29. news _____
30. tactic _____

B. For each word or abbreviation shown, write the singular form in the space provided. If the item has no singular form or is given in its singular form, put a check ✓ in the space.

1. hangers-on _____
2. courts-martial _____
3. annals _____
4. proceeds _____
5. links _____
6. stockholders _____

7. spoonfuls _____
8. remains _____
9. pants _____
10. tactics _____
11. clothes _____
12. men-of-war _____

13.	goods	_____	20.	gross	_____
14.	shears	_____	21.	fives	_____
15.	scissors	_____	22.	Messrs.	_____
16.	tweezers	_____	23.	takeoffs	_____
17.	pliers	_____	24.	politics	_____
18.	trousers	_____	25.	fish	_____
19.	grouse	_____			

C. For each word, abbreviation, etc., shown, write the plural form in the space provided. If the item has no plural form or is given in its plural form, put a check ✓ in the space. If you are in doubt, look up the plural in your dictionary.

1.	maximum	_____	14.	phenomenon	_____
2.	criterion	_____	15.	index	_____
3.	alumnus	_____	16.	medium	_____
4.	alumna	_____	17.	occurrence	_____
5.	cargo	_____	18.	sister-in-law	_____
6.	crisis	_____	19.	bill of sale	_____
7.	formula	_____	20.	spoonful	_____
8.	boss	_____	21.	A	_____
9.	Mr.	_____	22.	Miss	_____
10.	sheep	_____	23.	roommate	_____
11.	appendix	_____	24.	passerby	_____
12.	deer	_____	25.	corps	_____
13.	minimum	_____			

D. For each word or abbreviation shown, write the singular form in the space provided. If the item has no singular form or is given in its singular form, put a check ✓ in the space.

1.	data	_____	7.	crises	_____
2.	salmon	_____	8.	gross	_____
3.	geese	_____	9.	headquarters	_____
4.	Mesdames	_____	10.	wolves	_____
5.	editors in chief	_____	11.	alumni	_____
6.	hangers-on	_____	12.	alumnae	_____

13. indices   _____   17. Drs.   _____

14. Misses   _____   18. harnesses   _____

15. tallies   _____   19. mice   _____

16. tales   _____   20. goods   _____

E. For each word, abbreviation, etc., shown, write the plural form in the space provided. If the item has no plural form or is given in its plural form, put a check ✓ in the space.

1.	typist	_____	21.	twenty	_____
2.	envelope	_____	22.	address	_____
3.	choice	_____	23.	chief	_____
4.	freeman	_____	24.	warranty	_____
5.	specialty	_____	25.	CPA	_____
6.	means	_____	26.	delay	_____
7.	half	_____	27.	courtesy	_____
8.	beneficiary	_____	28.	man	_____
9.	parenthesis	_____	29.	bookshelf	_____
10.	library	_____	30.	proof	_____
11.	ratio	_____	31.	scarf	_____
12.	banjo	_____	32.	veto	_____
13.	species	_____	33.	facility	_____
14.	news	_____	34.	Mary	_____
15.	hypothesis	_____	35.	bus	_____
16.	basis	_____	36.	Bush	_____
17.	annuity	_____	37.	leave of absence	_____
18.	memorandum	_____	38.	1980	_____
19.	absence	_____	39.	Ms.	_____
20.	ten	_____	40.	Chinese	_____

F. Insert **is** or **are** (whichever is correct) in the following sentences. Then rewrite the word on the line to the right.

1. Mathematics _____ difficult for most students.   1. _____

2. Our facilities _____ new.   2. _____

3. The criteria _____ not easy to identify.

3. _____

4. Her credentials _____ very impressive.

4. _____

5. Good news _____ always welcome.

5. _____

6. The Wilsons _____ our neighbors.

6. _____

7. Ethics _____ the study of the motives and values in human conduct.

7. _____

8. The safes _____ locked.

8. _____

9. Boards of education _____ quite often elected by taxpayers.

9. _____

10. The remains of the fire _____ in the process of being appraised.

10. _____

Words Often Confused

local	(lō'kəl) having to do with a certain place, not far-reaching: *The local news is broadcast at 6 p.m. and 11 p.m.*; making all or almost all stops: *The local train stops here; the express train does not.*
locale	(lō kal') a place where something specific occurred or will occur, a setting: *The locale of the new motion picture is the Pyrenees Mountains.*
loose	(loōs) not tight: *One of my front teeth is loose;* not bound together or fastened down: *These loose boards are dangerous*; careless about morals or conduct: *He is known to have a loose character.*
lose	(loōz) to mislay or be deprived of: *When did you lose your pocketbook?* Unless sales improve soon, many people may lose their jobs.*
magnate	an important or influential person in any field of activity, especially in a large business: *Aristotle Onassis was a shipping magnate.*
magnet	a person or thing that attracts: *This paper clip dispenser contains a magnet. Professor Turner was a magnet for the university, attracting graduate students who wished to study with her.*
marital	(mar'i təl) pertaining to marriage: *Most people no longer indicate their marital status on their résumés.*
marshal	(mär'shəl) (noun) a law officer: *Wyatt Earp was a famous marshal*; (verb) to arrange in order: *We must first marshal all the facts in the case.* (*Note:* Marshall Plan—the plan for aid to Europe after World War II, named after General George C. Marshall.)
martial	(mär'shəl) pertaining to or suitable for war or the military: *The new government declared a state of martial law until order could be restored.*
may be	a verb form expressing possibility: *It may be that I'll see you at the meeting. The rest of the order may be included in a separate shipment.*
maybe	perhaps: *Maybe I'll see you at the meeting.*
mode	(mōd) prevailing style, fashion, or custom: *Short skirts became the mode around 1920.*
mood	(moōd) state of mind or feeling: *Ms. Moritake is in a good mood today.*
moral	(môr'əl) (adjective) good or virtuous in character or conduct: *She is known by everyone as a moral person*; according to civilized standards of right and wrong: *I believe it is a moral act to admit our country's mistakes*; dealing with the difference between right and wrong: *Whether we should return the money is a moral question*; (noun) the lesson or inner meaning of a story, fable, or event: *The moral of the story is that you should be happy with what you have.*
morale	(məral') mental or emotional condition of courage, confidence, enthusiasm, etc.: *Good working conditions produce good morale among employees.*

ordinance law, rule, regulation: *Our factory complies with every local safety ordinance as well as with the requirements of the state and federal governments.*

ordnance military supplies: *During World War II this factory was converted for the manufacture of ordnance for the military.*

partition (noun) something that separates or divides: *A wooden partition divided the room*; (verb) to divide or separate into parts: *We can partition this large room into four offices.*

petition (noun) a formal request to one or more people capable of granting some privilege, right, or benefit: *We signed the petition that was being circulated at work*; (verb) to make a formal request to another: *The people must petition their representatives to make the change.*

persecute to bring undeserved suffering or unhappiness upon someone, to plague, oppress, hunt down: *Throughout history individuals have been persecuted for unorthodox opinions.*

prosecute to bring before a court of law: *Shoplifters will be prosecuted to the full extent of the law.*

personal (pŭr′sə nəl) done in person directly by oneself: *The president made a personal visit to the assembly line*; pertaining to the body or bodily appearance: *Ms. Robarts always stressed the importance of personal hygiene*; offensively relating to a person: *Those remarks were highly personal.*

personnel (pŭr′sə nel′) persons employed in any work, business, or service: *Our employment director personally selects the personnel for our office.*

perspective the art of drawing objects as they appear to the eye with respect to relative depth and distance: *The artist sketched the main entrance using linear perspective*; a point of view or opinion based on certain factors: *Our losses are not too severe if seen from the proper perspective.*

prospective looking to the future, expected, likely: *The prospective upturn in business encouraged many people to invest in the market.*

picture an image or likeness of something produced by painting, drawing, or photography: *Mr. Andres keeps a picture of his family on his desk.*

pitcher a container with a handle and lip for holding and pouring liquids: *There were glasses and a pitcher of water near the podium*; in baseball, the player who pitches the ball to the opposing batters: *Babe Ruth started his baseball career as a pitcher.*

plaintiff one who brings a suit into a court of law: *The plaintiff accused the defendant of breach of contract.*

plaintive sad, melancholy: *Someone in the other room uttered a plaintive sigh.*

NAME   **CLASS**   **DATE**   **SCORE**

Words Often Confused Assignments

A. Select from the following words the one that correctly fits the blank in each of the sentences below. Then write the word in the answer space.

local	magnate	may be	moral	picture
locale	magnet	maybe	morale	pitcher
loose	marital	mode	partition	plaintiff
lose	martial	mood	petition	plaintive

1. The bar chart gave a graphic _____ of the operating expenses.

   1._____

2. If you do not treat your customers fairly, you will _____ them.

   2._____

3. Mr. Haskins is a man of fine _____ character.

   3._____

4. Donald Trump is a real estate _____ and an entrepreneur.

   4._____

5. The machine failed to operate properly because a bolt was _____.

   5._____

6. The Atlanta area was the _____ for the training film.

   6._____

7. The _____ police were unable to cope with the rise in crime in the town.

   7._____

8. _____ status must be declared for tax deduction purposes.

   8._____

9. An employee's _____ is usually high after she or he receives a raise or a promotion.

   9._____

10. Offices with a modern design often provide for an attractive, movable _____ between workstations.

    10._____

11. The _____ in the lawsuit accused our Accounting Department of negligence.

    11._____

12. About sixty employees signed the _____.

    12._____

13. _____ we can come to an agreement soon.

    13._____

14. It _____ necessary to rewrite this policy.   14. _____

15. I was not impressed with her _____ of operation. 15. _____

B. In some of the following sentences, an incorrect word is used. Underline the incorrect word, and write the correct word in the space provided. Where there is no error, write C in the answer space.

1. The verdict was in favor of the plaintive.   1. _____

2. Working conditions affect a worker's moral.   2. _____

3. The ordnance did not apply to commercial property.   3. _____

4. Any attempt to prosecute a minority group constitutes a danger to all citizens.   4. _____

5. The prospective buyer's offer was much too low.   5. _____

6. The morale of the story is always to be prompt.   6. _____

7. The sign warned that all offenders would be per-secuted to the full extent of the law.   7. _____

8. May be I can be of help to you.   8. _____

9. Soundproof petitions are very popular in the design of modern offices.   9. _____

10. The high inflation rate affects the mood and actions of consumers.   10. _____

11. What mode of transportation does your firm use most for shipping?   11. _____

12. Employees should not make personnel phone calls during work hours.   12. _____

13. Several military officers were in charge of ordering and storing ordinance.   13. _____

14. I may be the one who will be given that assignment next.   14. _____

15. Erika shopped for just the right picture to decorate the wall in her office.   15. _____

C. Read the definition, and select the correct word from the second column to match that description. Write the word you selected in the answer space.

Definition	**Word Choice**	
1. military supplies	ordinance, ordnance	1. _____
2. perhaps	may be, maybe	2. _____

3. to make a formal request
   to another   partition, petition   3._____

4. to bring undeserved
   suffering or unhappiness
   upon someone   persecute, prosecute   4._____

5. sad   plaintiff, plaintive   5._____

6. place where something
   specific occurred   local, locale   6._____

7. to mislay or be deprived of   loose, lose   7._____

8. pertaining to marriage   marital, martial   8._____

9. good or virtuous in
   character   moral, morale   9._____

10. prevailing style, fashion,
    or custom   mode, mood   10._____

D. Compose a meaningful sentence for each of the following words.

1. prosecute_____

   _____

2. morale _____

   _____

3. ordinance_____

   _____

4. petition_____

   _____

5. may be_____

   _____

6. locale _____

   _____

7. loose _____

   _____

8. personnel_____

   _____

9. mode _____

_____

10. perspective _____

_____

NAME CLASS DATE SCORE

Review Exercises

A. Underline any errors in the following letter, and write the corrected item in the answer space. If there are no errors in the line, write C in the space.

165 Merrill Avenue
Lowell, MA 01850
January 10, 19--

1 Ms. Janice Darden, Presdent
2 Phi Theta Gamma Fraternity
3 Algonquin Colege
4 McClees Hall
5 New York, NY 10020

6 Dear Ms. Darden:

7 You're invitation to serve as a guest speaker at your Annual Spring
8 Convocation comes as a delightful serprise. I am very happy to be
9 able to except your invitation to speak with the members of your
10 group who are interested in journalism as a carreer.

11 I vividly recal my undergraduate and graduate days in college, and
12 I wellcome this opportunity to reminisce. My background, of which
13 you are well aware, is one of "raising from the ranks," and I find
14 that it is always a pleasure to be able to shair my experiences
15 with others.

16 There are so many career opportunitys in journalism and in its
17 allyed career options--radio and television broadcasting and
18 communications, to name but a few--that I plan to give a talk that
19 will enspire as well as inform.

20 As I plan to use some handout matereals, I would appreciate
21 knowing the approximate number you aspect in the audience. An
22 overhead projecter will also be necessary.

23 I plan to drive to your campus; therefore, please supply me with
24 specific directions to the facilite where my talk will be given.

25 I look foreward to Saturday, May 3, at 3 p.m.

Sincerely,

J. R. Reynolds

eck

1._____
2._____
3._____
4._____
5._____
6._____
7._____
8._____
9._____
10._____
11._____
12._____
13._____
14._____
15._____
16._____
17._____
18._____
19._____
20._____
21._____
22._____
23._____
24._____
25._____

B. Underline any errors, and write the corrected item in the answer space. If there are no errors in the line, write C in the space.

```
1                       AN INTRODUCTION
                             to
2                       J. R. Reynolds
3                   Editer, High Tech World


4        In the paste five years Ms. J. R. Reynolds has been
5  involved in conducting over 30 workshops and seminars for
6  journalists, educators, and business office personal in the
7  subject areas of communications, creative writting, career
8  oppertunities, and media systems.

9        Virtually every office worker--from clerk to executive--
10 is familar with High Tech World, and Ms. Reynolds is in her
11 nineth year as editor of this widely read publication.  She
12 is the author of more than fourty articles in professional
13 journals.  Currently she is in the proccess of authoring a
14 text on writting for business and media.  In addition, she
15 has taught journalism as an adjunct instructor at Longacre
16 College, Bronx, New York.

17       In her presentation today Ms. Reynolds will address the
18 topic "Goals for Self-Development:  Perk Up!  Bone Up!  Move
19 Up!"  Her presentation will involve the use of a number of
20 dyhamic consciousness-raising strategies in the areas of
21 assertiveness, skill development, and career concerns.  She
22 will present a welth of suggestions that participants in
23 today's workshop can use to work toward farther improvement
24 on an individual bases in order to get ready for a move up
25 the career lader.
```

1. _____

2. _____

3. _____

4. _____

5. _____

6. _____

7. _____

8. _____

9. _____

10. _____

11. _____

12. _____

13. _____

14. _____

15. _____

16. _____

17. _____

18. _____

19. _____

20. _____

21. _____

22. _____

23. _____

24. _____

25. _____

The Apostrophe

POSSESSIVES

The possessive form of a noun shows ownership or possession. All nouns, singular or plural, regular or irregular, are made possessive through the addition of an apostrophe (') or 's. If you are familiar with a few simple rules and apply them carefully, you will have no difficulty in forming the possessive of any noun.

The singular possessive

Rule 1

Form the possessive of a singular noun that does not end in **s** by adding **'s**.

boy	boy's coat
child	child's toy
employee	employee's keys
fox	fox's den
Fran	Fran's car
man	man's hat

Rule 2

Form the possessive of a singular noun that ends in **s** by adding **'s** unless pronunciation is awkward. If the addition of **'s** makes pronunciation awkward, add only an apostrophe.

boss	boss's desk
Charles	Charles's résumé
Keats	Keats's poems

BUT

Ms. Simons	Ms. Simons' application
Sophocles	Sophocles' plays
Mr. Fields	Mr. Fields' office
Genesis	Genesis' new album

The plural possessive

Rule 1

Form the possessive of a plural noun that ends in **s** by adding only the apostrophe (').

boys	boys' hats
employees	employees' cafeteria
girls	girls' coats
ladies	ladies' scarves

Rule 2

Form the possessive of a plural noun that does not end in **s** by adding **'s**.

alumni	alumni's donations
children	children's playroom
people	people's rights
women	women's apparel

Abbreviations

Rule 1

Form the possessive of a singular abbreviation by adding **'s**.

CEO's decision   NAACP's position
M.D.'s diagnosis   YMCA's building fund

Rule 2

Form the possessive of plural abbreviations ending in **s** by adding only an apostrophe.

all RNs' reports   both CPAs' recommendations

Pronouns

Rule 1

Form the possessive of indefinite pronouns by adding **'s**.

Singular	**Singular Possessive**
anyone	anyone's clothing
everyone	everyone's affairs
no one	no one's fault
one	one's possessions
someone	someone's wallet

Rule 2

Never use an apostrophe with possessive pronouns.

mine   yours   his   hers   theirs   ours   its   whose

Compound words

> ### Rule
>
> Form the possessive case of a compound word by putting the *last element* in the compound in the possessive case.

Singular	Singular Possessive
attorney general	attorney general's
editor in chief	editor in chief's
father-in-law	father-in-law's
stockholder	stockholder's

Plural	Plural Possessive
attorneys general	attorneys general's
editors in chief	editors in chief's
fathers-in-law	fathers-in-law's
stockholders	stockholders'

Inanimate objects

> ### Rule
>
> The possessive case for inanimate objects can be formed by using **'s**.

At one time the possessive case of inanimate objects was generally shown by using a phrase beginning with **of** instead of **'s**:

The corner of the street—(*not* the street's corner)
The sleeve of my jacket—(*not* my jacket's sleeve)

This usage is no longer held by all authorities. Certainly, all agree on the use of the following possessives with expressions of time, measurement, and personification.

a day's trip	an hour's ride	for goodness' sake
a moment's notice	a week's delay	for pity's sake
a month's journey	a year's salary	sixty days' notice
your money's worth		

Joint and separate ownership

Rule 1

To show *joint* ownership or authorship by two or more individuals, put *only the last named person* in the possessive case.

Robertson and Smith's new market closed last week.
Robertson and Smith are partners.

Smith, Dutton, and Randle's *Modern Democracy* is widely used in American schools.
Refers to one book.

Rule 2

To show *separate* ownership or authorship, put each name in the possessive case.

The American Steel Company's and the Graybar Corporation's new plants were opened a week ago.
Here there are two plants, each separately owned.

CONTRACTIONS

When you speak, you quite naturally follow certain shortcuts. You say:

could've	for	could have
don't	for	do not
I'd	for	I had *or* I would *or* I should
I'll	for	I will *or* I shall

When you run words together, such as **I'll** (**I will**), you create *contractions*. Since contractions are generally informal in tone, at one time it was considered poor usage to use contractions in any kind of written business communication. Today, however, while contractions may still be avoided in formal reports, they appear regularly in advertising and in other forms of business writing. Hence it is important to know how to use and spell contractions correctly.

When you write contractions, you must be careful to indicate what words you have run together and what letter or letters you have left out. The apostrophe (') does the job.

aren't   for   are not

The apostrophe shows us that a letter (**o**) has been omitted.

I've   for   I have

The apostrophe shows us that the letters **h** and **a** have been left out.

The following list contains the most common contractions. Look at each of these very carefully. Note where the apostrophe is placed. Note, too, what letter or letters have been omitted.

aren't	are not	she'll	she will *or* she shall
can't	cannot	she's	she is *or* she has
couldn't	could not	shouldn't	should not
could've	could have	should've	should have
doesn't	does not	there's	there is *or* there has
don't	do not	they'd	they had *or* they would
hadn't	had not	they'll	they will *or* they shall
hasn't	has not	they're	they are
haven't	have not	they've	they have
he'd	he had *or* he would	we'd	we had *or* we would
he'll	he will *or* he shall	we'll	we will *or* we shall
he's	he is *or* he has	weren't	were not
I'd	I had *or* I would *or* I should	who's	who is *or* who has
I'll	I will *or* I shall	won't	will not
I'm	I am	wouldn't	would not
isn't	is not	would've	would have
it's	it is	you'd	you had *or* you would
I've	I have	you'll	you will *or* you shall
let's	let us	you're	you are
mustn't	must not	you've	you have
she'd	she had *or* she would		

NAME   **CLASS**   **DATE**   **SCORE**

Spelling Assignments

A. For each word or abbreviation shown, write the possessive form in the space provided.

1.	woman	_____	26.	lady	_____
2.	firm	_____	27.	committee	_____
3.	employees	_____	28.	editor in chief	_____
4.	men	_____	29.	it	_____
5.	month	_____	30.	everyone	_____
6.	U.S.A.	_____	31.	someone	_____
7.	secretaries	_____	32.	ladies	_____
8.	sister-in-law	_____	33.	our	_____
9.	Charles	_____	34.	notary public	_____
10.	notebooks	_____	35.	typists	_____
11.	winners	_____	36.	cargo	_____
12.	days	_____	37.	Cavendish	_____
13.	oxen	_____	38.	classmate	_____
14.	U.C.L.A.	_____	39.	beneficiary	_____
15.	offices	_____	40.	magazines	_____
16.	General Motors	_____	41.	representative	_____
17.	week	_____	42.	patio	_____
18.	children	_____	43.	advisor	_____
19.	attorneys general	_____	44.	directors	_____
20.	typewriter	_____	45.	territory	_____
21.	manager	_____	46.	employee	_____
22.	Oldfields	_____	47.	company	_____
23.	authors	_____	48.	Gus	_____
24.	telephones	_____	49.	chairperson	_____
25.	CEOs	_____	50.	participants	_____

B. In some of the following sentences, the possessive form is incorrectly written. Underline each error, and write the correct form in the space provided. If the sentence has no errors, write C in the space.

1. In business, as elsewhere, there is no such thing as beginner's luck.

1. _____

2. There will be a sensational mens clothing sale at Bob Harris store in the Overbrook Mall.

2. _____

3. You will have ten days notice before we ship your order.

3. _____

4. The supply's you ordered have arrived.

4. _____

5. The corner desk was her's.

5. _____

6. We have written to Marshalls New York office to let them know that the responsibility is not ours.

6. _____

7. The contribution we received recently was theirs'.

7. _____

8. Taylor and Stone's fall clothing line is refreshingly original.

8. _____

9. Bannion Corporations net profit for the first quarter of the year was up.

9. _____

10. Tonys father's-in-law investments proved very profitable.

10. _____

11. Pennys store and Stuarts store are in the same shopping center.

11. _____

12. I don't like it's design.

12. _____

13. There will be a months delay in filling your order.

13. _____

14. He used one of the visitors parking spaces.

14. _____

15. Nashville is just a days trip from Mr. Flores home.

15. _____

16. She feels it is all citizens duty to support their governments position at home and abroad.

16. _____

17. "For goodness sake," Linda exclaimed with surprise.

17. _____

18. We discovered that the errors were our's, not your's.

18. _____

19. No employee may be discharged unless at least two weeks notice has been given.

19. _____

20. Men's clothing tends to be more conservative than womens' wear.

20. _____

C. Supply the missing apostrophes in the following sentences. Underline the word or words that are incorrect, and write them correctly in the space provided. If the answer is correct, write C in the space.

1. If youll look in the drawer, youll find what youre searching for.

   1._____

2. Hes taking his and Joes files with him.

   2._____

3. Ms. Baxter said she wouldnt and couldnt do the job for only one weeks salary.

   3._____

4. Your 6s look like Os.

   4._____

5. You've spelled too many words incorrectly to earn a passing grade on this paper.

   5._____

6. Shes not interested in anybodys money—not yours, mine, or Steves.

   6._____

7. It's James opinion that it's not easy to get your moneys worth these days.

   7._____

8. Jack and Eddie's new restaurant is a flourishing business.

   8._____

9. The editor in chiefs office will be the site of future executive meetings.

   9._____

10. The governments transportation improvement program will eventually cost billions of our taxpayers dollars.

   10._____

D. There are words in the following sentences that should be written with an apostrophe. Underline these words, and write them correctly in the space provided.

1. The banks arent as generous with credit as they were last year.

   1._____

2. Ive told you that I cant possibly open the store before weve taken our inventory.

   2._____

3. Couldnt you tell us what we shouldve done?

   3._____

4. Im sure Ron doesn't know what hes supposed to do.

   4._____

5. We wont guarantee this fabric against shrinkage.

   5._____

6. Werent you aware that you hadnt enclosed the order blank?

   6._____

7. Ill agree with you that there isnt anything Mark won't do to win his point.

   7._____

8. Dont you think shed have been more willing to talk if shed known wed listen sympathetically?

8. _____

9. Lets be frank with our employees and tell them what they mustnt do.

9. _____

10. If I haven't heard from you by noon, I'll call you and let you know whether theres any point in waiting for the plan.

10. _____

E. Underline any errors in spelling or in the use of the apostrophe in the following sentences. Write the correct words in the space provided. If the sentence is correct, write C in the space.

1. The five creditors accounts were found in the files.

1. _____

2. Yours is the first of our customers names listed.

2. _____

3. James Wilson and Companys address is 54 Worth Street.

3. _____

4. There's the report I have been trying to locate.

4. _____

5. Smiths and Grahams names are both on the policy as beneficiaries.

5. _____

6. The warranties terms provide for one years coverage.

6. _____

7. Bill Ryan's book and Sue Foxs book were the major textbooks in the career orientation field.

7. _____

8. Are the supply's in the cabinet properly arranged?

8. _____

9. The job description's for the computer operator positions A and B were recently rewritten.

9. _____

10. I referred to last years' departmental report's for additional information.

10. _____

Words Often Confused

poplar	a type of tree: *A tulip tree is a kind of poplar.*
popular	liked by many or most people: *A popular actor appeared at the store to promote his new book;* accepted among people in general, common: *There are several popular misconceptions about insurance.*

portion	a part of anything: *She was dissatisfied with her portion of the estate.*
potion	drink, especially of medicine or poison: *Socrates drank a potion made from hemlock bark.*

practicable	(prak'ti kə bəl) workable, possible, theoretically capable of being put into practice: *Earlier in this century television did not seem practicable.*
practical	(prak'ti kəl) useful, having to do with action or practice rather than theory: *Edison's approach to science was always a practical one.*

precede	to be or go before in importance, position, or time: *A buffet luncheon will precede the awards ceremony.*
proceed	to go forward, to carry on after having been stopped: *The defense lawyer protested, but the witness was told to proceed with her testimony.*
proceeds	(always used as a plural form) money received from the sale of merchandise: *The proceeds from today's sales will be donated to charity.*

precedent	(pres'ə dənt) a case or instance that may serve as an example or reason for a later case: *If we permit overtime pay on this job, we will set a precedent for the future.*
president	(prez'ə dənt) the elected head of a nation, firm, association: *The president will attend an international business conference next month.*

premise	a prior statement or assertion that serves as the basis for an argument: *Bart began every discussion with the premise that he was right and everyone else was wrong.*

> **Note** The plural form, **premises**, also has a separate meaning: a piece of real estate; a house or building and its land: *The sign posted on the door read "Keep off the premises."*

promise	(noun) a vow, pledge, or agreement: *In law the person to whom a promise is made is called the promisee;* (verb) to vow or pledge, assure: *I promise to repay the loan with interest by the end of the year.*

preposition	a part of speech that shows a relationship between other words, e.g., *on, with, at, in: Some people consider it improper style to end a sentence with a preposition.*
proposition	a proposal: *We discussed a business proposition during lunch.*

prescribe to order as a remedy: *The doctor prescribed a mild sedative to help her patient sleep*; to set down as a rule: *The restaurant manager prescribed certain standards of conduct and dress for all employees.*

proscribe to forbid or prohibit: *The restaurant manager proscribed jeans and T-shirts for all the employees.*

prophecy (präf′ə sē) (noun) a prediction, a foretelling of future events: *Economists ventured a prophecy that we would have an economic recession within a year.*

prophesy (präf′ə sī′) (verb) to predict, to foretell the future: *Some economists prophesy that there will be an economic boom within a year.*

propose to suggest: *I propose that we relocate our central offices from New York to Chicago*; to make plans, intend: *I propose to offer Julie a joint partnership next week.*

purpose aim, intention: *What is your purpose in suggesting that we relocate?*

quiet (adjective) calm, still, peaceful: *Matsuo needed absolutely quiet surroundings in order to concentrate*; (noun) state of stillness: *He needed the quiet*; (verb) to make quiet; calm or pacify: *The candidate walked forward and raised her hand to quiet the crowd.*

quit to stop, leave: *Ralph plans to quit his job next week.*

quite completely: *We were quite satisfied with his performance*; very: *Our plant is located quite close to public transportation.*

raise to lift: *Raise your hand if you wish to ask a question.*

rise to get up: *Everyone should rise when the president enters the room.*

Note **Rise (rose, risen)** is an intransitive verb; that is, it does not take an object. **Raise (raised, raised)** is a transitive verb; it takes an object. *Rise from your chair if you wish to raise an objection.*

read (rēd) to understand something written or printed: *I seldom have time to read a book*; (red) past tense of *read: Have you read the annual report?*

reed (rēd) a kind of tall grass: *The dock is surrounded by reeds*; part of a wind instrument: *The reed for the clarinet is made of special bamboo.*

red a color: *The decorating scheme was built around red and gray*; showing a financial loss: *On a balance sheet the losses are shown in red ink. Our company has been in the red for three straight quarters.*

reality that which is real: *Neil could not accept the reality that his proposed mortgage payments were more than he could afford.*

realty real estate: *Ms. Murdoch works part time as an agent for a local realty company.*

NAME	CLASS	DATE	SCORE

Words Often Confused Assignments

A. Select from the following words the one that correctly fits the blank in each of the sentences below. Then write the word in the answer space.

portion	proceeds	proposition	prophesy	quit	red
potion	precedent	prescribe	propose	quite	reality
precede	president	proscribe	purpose	read	realty
proceed	preposition	prophecy	quiet	reed	

1. The class was asked to _____ Chapter 6 for homework.

   1. *read*

2. A _____ company can help you find out what your property is worth.

   2. *realty*

3. The company _____ called the meeting to order.

   3. *president*

4. Time proved that her _____ was correct.

   4. *prophesy*

5. Phil made me an attractive _____ for the sale of the property.

   5. *pr*

6. The word *to* is usually a _____.

   6. _____

7. If the motion is passed, it will set a _____ for future actions.

   7. _____

8. _____ to the corner; then turn left.

   8. _____

9. His conduct was not according to the behavior that the teachers _____.

   9. _____

10. All the _____ were donated to charity.

    10. _____

11. A _____ of every paycheck is withheld for taxes.

    11. _____

12. I was worried that they would _____ to change my role in the new organizational structure.

    12. _____

13. Usually, I am too _____ at meetings.

    13. _____

14. The work of the surveyors had to _____ the work of the builders.

    14. _____

15. Deena's face turned _____ when her name was called.

    15. _____

B. In some of the following sentences, an incorrect word is used. Underline the incorrect word, and write the correct word in the space provided. Where there is no error, write C in the answer space.

1. Of all the proposals submitted, Mr. Baldwin's seems to be the most practicable.

    1. _____

2. If you red the instructions carefully, you should be able to do it.

    2. _____

3. I am not qualified to prophecy on that subject.

    3. _____

4. What do you purpose as an alternative?

    4. _____

5. After she said she would quit, she was sorry.

    5. _____

6. The acoustical hood quieted some of the machine noise.

    6. _____

7. Each of us had a quiet different view of the situation.

    7. _____

8. The safety issue was rised in the campaign.

    8. _____

9. The verdict in the case will set a president for the future.

    9. _____

10. Bill proposed his brother for membership.

    10. _____

11. The realty of the situation was that she could not afford the rent.

    11. _____

12. Television is a result of the practical application of the science of electronics.

    12. _____

13. Much discussion proceeded the merger.

    13. _____

14. The partnership agreement clearly defined what portion of the profits each partner would receive.

    14. _____

15. Mildred reed the classified ads to look for a job.

    15. _____

C. Read the definition, and select the correct word from the second column to match the description. Write the word you selected in the answer space.

Definition	Word Choice	
1. to go before	precede, proceed, proceeds	1. _____
2. a type of tree	poplar, popular	2. _____
3. drink, especially of medicine or poison	portion, potion	3. _____
4. a prediction	prophecy, prophesy	4. _____
5. to forbid or prohibit	prescribe, proscribe	5. _____

6. real estate	reality, realty	6._____
7. having to do with action rather than theory	practicable, practical	7._____
8. a kind of tall grass	read, reed, red	8._____
9. a proposal	preposition, proposition	9._____
10. calm, still, peaceful	quiet, quit, quite	10._____

D. Complete each of the following sentences.

1. One premise is _____

_____

2. A very popular _____

_____

3. Our proposition _____

_____

4. The president_____

_____

5. How will the proceeds _____

_____

6. The reality is _____

_____

7. It was quite _____

_____

8. My portion _____

_____

9. They needed to raise_____

_____

10. The purpose _____

_____

Capitalization

Like correct spelling, the correct use of capitals is a matter of following agreed-upon conventions. Many people feel that to make a mistake in the use of capitals is as serious an error as to misspell the word itself. Certainly, standard business writing demands that words not only be spelled correctly but also be capitalized where appropriate. The precise business writer knows what words to capitalize and when.

In this chapter you will review the rules governing the use of capitals. Many of these rules you already know. Concentrate on those with which you are less familiar.

FIRST WORDS

Rule 1

Capitalize the first word of every sentence (including this one).

Rule 2

Capitalize the first word of an independent phrase functioning as a sentence.

Now, back to business.   No, not really.

Rule 3

Capitalize the first word of a direct quotation that is a complete sentence.

Ms. O'Keefe said, "Unless working conditions improve, I will be forced to resign."

Note Do not capitalize the first word of a quotation that is not a complete sentence.

She said she would resign "unless working conditions improve."

Rule 4

Capitalize the first word after a colon when it introduces a complete sentence, two or more complete sentences, or a vertical listing.

She issued an ultimatum: "Unless working conditions improve, I will be forced to resign."

Howard conducted his business on the basis of a single guiding principle: Always place the needs of the customer first.

Ms. Fisahn said there were two important questions we had to address: What factors caused the sharp drop in sales during the last quarter? What steps can we take to reverse our declining sales?

On your résumé include the following information for each employer:

1. Name and address of employer
2. Your job title
3. How long you worked there
4. Your responsibilities and accomplishments

Rule 5

Capitalize the first word of each line in a poem.

My mind to me a kingdom is;
Such present joys therein I find
That it excels all other bliss
That earth affords or grows by kind.
     —Sir Edward Dyer

Rule 6

Capitalize the first word plus all nouns and titles in the salutation of a letter.

Dear Ms. Jiminez: My fellow Americans: Dear Sam,
Ladies and Gentlemen: Dear Dr. Alfred and Professor Fry:

Rule 7

Capitalize the first word in the complimentary closing of a letter plus all nouns and titles in the writer's identification line.

Cordially,   Gerald Shapiro
                         Director of Permissions
Sincerely,

Very truly yours,   Linda A. Smigelski
                         Assistant to the President

TITLES OF LITERARY AND ARTISTIC WORKS

Rule

Capitalize the important words in titles of books, magazines, songs, articles, paintings, etc. Do not capitalize articles (**a, an, the**), conjunctions of fewer than four letters, and short prepositions that appear in the middle of the title.

Business Spelling and Word Power
The Saturday Evening Post
Winning Through Intimidation
"How to Invest Wisely in the Stock Market"
How to Succeed in Business Without Really Trying
The Last Supper
"Battle Hymn of the Republic"

NOUNS WITH NUMBERS OR LETTERS

Rule

Capitalize a noun followed by a number or letter, but do not capitalize the nouns **line, note, page, paragraph, size,** and **verse**.

Appendix C	line 25
Chapter 22	note 2
Figure 4	page 17
Flight 172	paragraph 4
Gate 16	size 16
Model K57a12	verse 3
Policy 654321	
Volume III	

Note The abbreviation for **Number (No.)** is also capitalized. It is usually not necessary to include the abbreviation **No.** when an identifying noun precedes the figure. However, **No.** is used in the following:

License No. S5506 96554 39852
Patent No. 727,943
Social Security No. 123 45 6789

LETTERS AND ABBREVIATIONS

Rule 1

Capitalize the following letters and abbreviations:

1. College degrees such as **B.A., M.A., Ph.D.**
2. Radio and television stations such as **WNCN** and **WNET**
3. Initials standing for proper names such as **J.F.K.** and **F.D.R.**
4. Abbreviations for proper nouns such as **D.C.** (District of Columbia) and **USC** (University of Southern California)

Do not capitalize abbreviations if the words they represent are not capitalized. For example:

8 a.m.	p. 42	6 doz.
6:30 p.m.	pp. 42–46	c.o.d.

Rule 2

Capitalize the pronoun **I** and the interjection **O**. (In business writing, you will seldom if ever have the occasion to use **O** unless you are writing advertising copy.) **O** is usually found in poetry.

So strong you thump O terrible drums—so loud you bugles blow.
(from "Beat! Beat! Drums!"—Walt Whitman)

PROPER NOUNS

Capitalize all proper nouns. Recall that a proper noun refers to a specific person, place, or thing.

Ronald Reagan	Canada	Chrysler

The derivatives of proper nouns are also capitalized.

Canadian border	Shakespearean drama	Victorian England

Since company names, product names, and trade names are all proper nouns, business correspondence is full of proper nouns. While you should have no difficulty knowing when to capitalize most of them, some of the rules are a bit tricky. The following rules should help you. Study them carefully.

Titles of people

Rule 1

Capitalize a person's title when it comes directly before his or her name.

Budget Director Schwartz   Professor Ortiz
Mayor Washington   Sales Manager Nguyen
President Murphy   Sergeant York

Rule 2

Do not capitalize the title when it follows a person's name, is used instead of a person's name, or is followed by an appositive. (Recall that an appositive renames or explains a previously mentioned noun or pronoun.)

Marilyn Murphy, president of Busico, spoke to reporters.
The president and chairman of the board conferred frequently during the meeting.
Our sales manager, Mr. Nguyen, has just returned from a three-day conference.

Exceptions

1. The titles of high-ranking government officials or religious leaders are capitalized when they precede, follow, or replace a name.
   The President of the United States
   an audience with the Pope
   Diana, Princess of Wales
   the Senator from New Hampshire
   Henry Kissinger, the former Secretary of State
   our Governor, James Florio

2. The titles of company officials are capitalized in that organization's formal minutes, rules, or bylaws.
   The Treasurer's report was submitted and approved.
   The Secretary is responsible for the timely distribution of minutes.

Family relationships

Rule

Capitalize words that show family relationships when the word precedes the person's name or is used in place of the person's name. Do not capitalize such a word when it is preceded by a possessive pronoun.

Uncle George   my uncle   We sent Uncle a card.
My mother is visiting us this week.   Is Father coming?

Organizations

Rule 1

Capitalize the principal words in the names of all organizations.

American Cancer Society
American Federation of Teachers
Illinois Department of Motor Vehicles
Junior Chamber of Commerce
National Business Association
National Park Service

Rule 2

Do not capitalize words like **company, association, society,** and **board** when they are used to replace the full name of the organization.

The company has its main offices in Pittsburgh.
The board meets every Wednesday.

Exceptions These shortened names may be capitalized in formal or legal documents.

The Treasurer of the Association is responsible for the collection of dues.

The shortened names of national government bodies are capitalized.

The House adjourned at midnight. (House of Representatives)

When will Congress consider this new legislation? (U.S. Congress)

Rule 3

Capitalize the names of departments, divisions, and committees in your own company. Capitalize only the names of specific departments, divisions, or committees outside of your organization.

The Claims Department is on the third floor.
Mr. Fowler is the new director of the Northwest Division of Bellco Labs.
Your applications will be kept on file in the Personnel Department.
Dr. Butterfield chairs the Business Department Personnel Advisory Committee.
Send your application to their personnel department.
Please have a member of your advertising department contact us.
Please forward my request to your Department of Information Services.

Trade names and registered trademarks

Rule

Capitalize brand names or registered trademarks, but do not capitalize former trademarks that have become common nouns through general usage. When in doubt, consult your dictionary.

Celluloid	aspirin
Paper-Mate	cellophane
Pepsi-Cola	nylon
Vaseline	thermos bottle

Directions and points of the compass

Rule 1

Capitalize directions when they refer to specific sections of the country or the world. Names derived from such geographical locations are also capitalized.

The Middle East is a site of international tensions.
The Southwest is a rapidly growing region of the country.
While most of our products are manufactured in the South, they are primarily distributed in the North.
Do you consider yourself a Southerner or Northerner?

Note	Do not capitalize points of the compass.

Our plant is southwest of the airport.
The Mississippi flows from north to south.

Rule 2

Capitalize **Eastern, Western, Northern,** and **Southern** when they are used as part of the proper name of a major world division (hemisphere, continent, country.) Do not capitalize them when they are used as part of the name of a minor world division (state, county, city).

Most peoples of the world live in the Northern Hemisphere.
Mr. O'Reilly feels that the troubles in Northern Ireland will never be resolved.
He commutes daily from eastern Pennsylvania to southern Connecticut.

Geographical locations and landmarks

Rule 1

Capitalize the names of specific places such as continents, countries, states, cities, mountains, valleys, oceans, rivers, and lakes.

Africa	Mount Rainier
Italy	Death Valley
North Dakota	Indian Ocean
St. Louis	Missouri River
Rocky Mountains	Lake Ontario

Rule 2

Capitalize a geographical term when it is used as part of the name of a particular geographical place and when it is used in the plural form with the names of specific places. Do not capitalize such terms when they precede the names of specific places.

Fox River	the river Jordan
Fox River Valley	the valley of the river Nile
Hudson River	Hudson and St. Lawrence Rivers
Pacific Ocean	Atlantic and Pacific Oceans

Rule 3

Capitalize the names of buildings, highways, tunnels, monuments, parks, streets, and other landmarks.

Park Plaza Hotel	Vietnam Memorial	Maple Avenue
McCarter Highway	Central Park	

Note   Also capitalize the terms **buildings, highways, tunnels, monuments, parks, streets,** etc., when they are used in the plural.

Empire State and Chrysler Buildings
Park Plaza and Century Tower Hotels
Lincoln and Holland Tunnels

Political designations

Rule

Capitalize political designations like **state, city,** and **county** when they are part of the specific name of the area, but not when they appear before the name.

New York State	the state of Alaska
Salt Lake City	the city of London
Bergen County	

Government terms

Rule 1

Capitalize the names of specific government agencies, departments, bureaus, and divisions plus the names of political parties.

United States Supreme Court
Bureau of the Census
Department of Health and Human Services
Office of Management and Budget
Republican Party   Democratic Party

Rule 2

The words **federal, state, government,** and **nation** are not capitalized unless they are part of a specific title.

Federal Trade Commission
New Jersey Association of State College Faculty
The federal government and state government disagree about who has jurisdiction in the matter.

Dates, periods, and events

Rule 1

Capitalize the months of the year, days of the week, and holidays, as well as historic events and periods.

This year classes begin on the first Tuesday in September, nearly one week before Labor Day.
the Great Depression   the Renaissance
the Industrial Revolution   the Revolutionary War

Rule 2

Do not capitalize the names of decades and centuries.

in the sixties
during the eighteenth century

Rule 3

Do not capitalize the names of the seasons unless the season is being personified (that is, referred to as though it were a living being).

Is your house protected from Winter's icy breath?
It was nearly winter before our fall shipment arrived.

Academic subjects

Rule

Capitalize the names of numbered courses and specific course titles. Do not capitalize the names of academic subject areas (except for any proper nouns in such names).

In the fall I plan to take refresher courses in shorthand and typing.
I am enrolled in Shorthand II and Typing II this fall.
Both sections of English 206: Business English are closed.
Next semester I plan to study English grammar and accounting.

Note   Capitalize the words **high school** and **college** only if the specific name of a particular school is used.

I went to Elgin High School before entering college.

Ethnic references

Rule

Capitalize terms that relate to a particular culture, language, or race.

Afro-American	Chinese	Hebrew
Chicanos	German	Oriental

Religious references

Rule 1

Capitalize all nouns and pronouns that refer to a supreme being, as well as personal pronouns that stand alone, without an antecedent nearby.

God, the Father   the Trinity

Give thanks to the Lord, for he is good.
Give thanks to Him.

Rule 2

Capitalize books of the Bible and other sacred works.

Book of Job	Koran
Ecclesiastes	Talmud

NAME	CLASS	DATE	SCORE

Spelling Assignments

A. Below is a series of "sentence starters." Study the word or words that are underlined in each example. If the capitalization is correct as it appears, write C in the answer space. If the capitalization is incorrect, write the word or words as they should be capitalized in the answer space.

<u>my</u> skill in. . .   *My*

The <u>Bureau of The Census</u>. . .   *the*

<u>Will</u> you please. . .   *C*

1. Our <u>winter</u> line of coats. . .   1. _____

2. The <u>treasurer</u> of our organization, Phil Roberts,. . .   2. _____

3. The <u>constitution</u> defers that right. . .   3. _____

4. The <u>aircraft carrier Constellation</u>. . .   4. _____

5. If the <u>Federal Government</u> can. . .   5. _____

6. The search narrowed to the <u>U.S. Pacific Northwest</u> after the informant. . .   6. _____

7. The <u>white house staff</u>. . .   7. _____

8. The <u>President</u> of Braniff Airlines. . .   8. _____

9. Frank Dobish, our <u>Director of Publicity</u>,. . .   9. _____

10. When <u>Northern</u> New Jersey colleges are considered. . .   10. _____

11. Letter formats are described in <u>appendix C</u>. . .   11. _____

12. Ed Watkins, <u>Co-Host of WSIM-TV's</u> nightly. . .   12. _____

13. The <u>Personnel department</u> is located. . .   13. _____

14. The new <u>College President</u> will. . .   14. _____

15. The <u>senator's</u> friends in. . .   15. _____

16. Changes after <u>world war II</u>. . .   16. _____

17. She said, "<u>the</u> report grossly exaggerated. . ."   17. _____

18. She said that the report "<u>grossly</u> exaggerated. . ."   18. _____

19. The neo-roman arches. . .   19. _____

20. My studies in accounting, physics, and Western
    Civilization I. . .   20. _____

21. In Chicago the Sears tower. . .   21. _____

22. The Northeastern part of the United States. . .   22. _____

23. Former press secretary James Brady was. . .   23. _____

24. On a recent trip, president Bush. . .   24. _____

25. One of the most influential Roman Catholic Priests. . .   25. _____

B. In the examples below, phrases have been extracted from sentences. Study the word or words that are underlined in each example. If the capitalization is correct as it appears, write C in the answer space. If the capitalization is incorrect, write the word or words as they should be capitalized in the answer space.

. . .my Spanish, English, and Algebra I books so that. . .   _____ *C* _____

. . .on the Secretary's desk to. . .   *secretary's*

. . .for aunt Mary's benefit when. . .   *Aunt*

1. . . .1920s comedy *Beggar On Horseback* is. . .   1. _____

2. . . .trip to Key west, Florida, was. . .   2. _____

3. . . .explained: "first, let me say. . ."   3. _____

4. . . .professor John Herrera lectured. . .   4. _____

5. . . .recently earned her Pilot's License. . .   5. _____

6. . . . a Salt Lake city detective. . .   6. _____

7. . . .the study of Keynesian Economics is. . .   7. _____

8. . . .the convention of the democratic party. . .   8. _____

9. . . .members of the Board voted to. . .   9. _____

10. . . .took over as chairman of the firm when. . .   10. _____

11. . . .in my High School yearbook. . .   11. _____

12. . . .each Business School graduate. . .   12. _____

13. . . .to my Brother Bob. . .   13. _____

14. . . .asked God to help us. . .   14. _____

15. . . .vacationing in the Far East. . .   15. _____

16. . . .started rumors on capitol hill that. . .   16. _____

17. . . .in the Roaring twenties. . .   17. _____

18. . . .for which <u>japanese workers</u> get. . .   18._____

19. . . .the <u>Fourth sunday</u> in May. . .   19._____

20. . . .the <u>federal</u> Rehabilitation Act of 1973. . .   20._____

21. . . .down New York's <u>fifth avenue</u>. . .   21._____

22. . . .the <u>fourth</u> of July holiday. . .   22._____

23. . . .was on <u>Page</u> 12 and . . .   23._____

24. . . .asked: <u>Was</u> it accurate? <u>Was</u> it complete? <u>Did</u> it
     have. . .?   24._____

25. . . .to the Mississippi and St. Lawrence <u>Rivers</u>. . .   25._____

Words Often Confused

receipt	a written acknowledgment that money or goods have been received: *No refunds or exchanges will be made without a receipt.*
recipe	a list of materials and directions for preparing or achieving something: *It is always advisable to read through a recipe first before beginning to prepare a dish.*
recent	(rē'sənt) done or made not long ago, modern: *A recent magazine article discussed the problems confronting savings and loan institutions.*
resent	(ri zent') to feel insulted, indignant: *We resent the distorted image of our company that you convey in your article.*
respectably	in a decent or acceptable fashion: *We have behaved respectably throughout this ordeal. Roberto dressed respectably for the interview.*
respectfully	in a manner showing respect or honor: *He spoke respectfully to the minister. Della signed all her letters, "Respectfully yours."*
respectively	a number of items taken as individual units in the order named: *Jackson, Abel, and Wilkins were elected respectively president, secretary, and treasurer of the company.* (In the order named: Jackson—president; Abel—secretary; Wilkins—treasurer.)
root	(rō͞ot) the part of a plant that grows in the ground: *The roots of this tree are cracking the sidewalk. Potatoes are a root vegetable.*
rote	(rōt) a fixed, mechanical way of doing something: *Most students learn the multiplication tables by rote*; by memory alone, without thought or understanding: *The tour guide gave rote answers to all our questions.*
rout	(rout) to disperse in disorderly defeat, to defeat completely: *The British routed the French in the Battle of Waterloo.*
route	(rō͞ot) (noun) a road: *I use Route 80 to commute to work*; (verb) to send by way of a certain road or route: *Because the bridges were down, all traffic was routed through Centerdale. Route all requests through the Purchasing Department.*
salvage	(sal'vij) to recover property from wreckage; to restore property damaged by fire or some other disaster: *We could salvage very little from the fire.*
selvage	(sel'vij) woven edge that prevents cloth or fabric from raveling: *Cheap cloth often has no selvage.*
statue	a carved or cast image: *We took the ferry to the Statue of Liberty.*
stature	natural height of a person: *The other athletes were envious of Barton's stature*; quality or status attained by growth or development: *Because of his wise investments, he grew in stature as an investment counselor.*
statute	law: *The Governor has just signed the latest statute designed to control the sale of securities in this state.*

suit　(sōot) (noun) a set of outer garments: *Janet bought a new winter suit for her baby daughter;* act of bringing legal action: *Mr. Atkins asked his lawyer to file suit against the Jamison Corporation;* one of four sets of cards (clubs, diamonds, hearts, or spades): *In bridge the highest-ranking suit is spades;* (verb) to satisfy or please: *The new designs suit my taste.*

suite　(swēt) series of connected rooms: *We stayed in the bridal suite;* a set of matching furniture: *The new living room suite arrived this afternoon;* a musical composition: *The orchestra performed the* Grand Canyon Suite.

sweet　pleasant-tasting, opposite of sour: *This wine is too sweet for my taste.*

tenant　a person who pays rent to occupy or use property: *A new tenant just moved into the apartment at the end of the hall.*

tenet　a principle, doctrine, or belief held as truth: *Her principal tenet for consumers was that you get what you pay for.*

than　a conjunction used to indicate a comparison: *Myra earns more money than I do. Our quarterly profits are smaller than I had expected.*

then　at that time: *I'll see you then. Wait until then before responding;* next, soon afterward: *Kristin finished her breakfast and then left for work.*

thorough　complete: *Nathan saw the doctor for a thorough physical examination last week;* very exact and painstaking: *All our products are subjected to thorough research and testing to ensure their safety.*

though　in spite of the fact that: *Even though she studied for hours, Emily failed the chemistry exam.*

through　in one side and out the other: *His engine stalled while he was driving through the Lincoln Tunnel;* by way or means of: *We have compiled this information through the results of numerous opinion surveys.*

threw　the past tense of *throw,* to toss or hurl: *Fawzia took off her coat and threw it on the couch.*

treaties　(trēt′ēz) plural of *treaty,* formal agreement between nations: *The United States has special treaties with most of the nations of the world.*

treatise　(trēt′is) systematic essay or book on some subject: *Bertrand Russell has written a famous treatise on philosophy.*

urban　relating to a city: *We are especially interested in developing and expanding the urban market.*

urbane　suave, polished: *Allison was urbane in both speech and manner.*

want　(verb) to wish or desire: *I want to congratulate you on a fine job;* (noun) lack: *The want of work has been bad for them.*

wont　(adjective) accustomed, used: *Mr. Jenkins is wont to get his way on important matters;* (noun) habit: *It is my wont to go to bed early and to rise early.*

won't　contraction for *will not: I won't be able to keep my 3 p.m. appointment.*

were　form of the verb *be,* to exist: *Were you able to attend the conference? We were delighted to read your progress report.*

we're　contraction for *we are: We're going to the conference next year.*

where　(adverb) at or in what place?: *Where are you going? Where is it?;* (conjunction) at or in what place: *I know where we are.*

NAME	CLASS	DATE	SCORE

Words Often Confused Assignments

A. Select from the following words the one that correctly fits the blank in each of the sentences below. Then write the word in the answer space.

recent	root	suit	thorough	wont
resent	rout	suite	though	won't
respectably	route	sweet	through	were
respectfully	salvage	than	threw	we're
respectively	selvage	then	want	where

1. Traffic on his normal _____ was delayed.

1._____

2. The auditor was _____ in her investigation.

2._____

3. Contrary to his belief, I did not _____ the criticism.

3._____

4. The conference will be held in the president's _____.

4._____

5. The _____ of the plant draws water and nourishment from the soil.

5._____

6. Janet was able to use less material to make the dress because she used the _____ for the hem.

6._____

7. The most _____ census figures showed an increase in population.

7._____

8. The proposed marketing plan didn't quite _____ me.

8._____

9. Williams, Starns, and Walters were presidents in 1980, 1981, and 1982, _____.

9._____

10. We were unable to _____ much after the fire.

10._____

11. Doug is _____ to have his way—or else!

11._____

12. Can you tell me _____ you put the Morrison file?

12._____

13. _____ you please try to join us for dinner?

13._____

14. She finished the typing; _____ she did the proofreading.

14._____

15. I learned more at the seminar _____ I thought I
    would.   15. _____

B. In some of the following sentences, an incorrect word or incorrect words are used. Underline the incorrect word, and write the correct word in the space provided. Where there is no error, write C in the answer space.

1. Wear were you just a few minutes ago when I called?   1. _____

2. The number of years covered by the statue of limitations varies from state to state.   2. _____

3. It is unfortunate that some office employees recent some of the resent technological advances.   3. _____

4. In spite of his small statute, he was physically powerful.   4. _____

5. Carol counted on support from the urban voters to help her win the election.   5. _____

6. Wilma's urbane manner was an appealing personal characteristic.   6. _____

7. We planned to raise funds though a telephone campaign.   7. _____

8. If it is a challenge, than I am interested.   8. _____

9. Better understanding among people can ensure world peace more than formal treatises.   9. _____

10. "Let the buyer beware" is a realistic tenant.   10. _____

11. The route of a plant is usually below the ground and holds the plant in position.   11. _____

12. A prominent sculptor was commissioned to create a fitting statute of our deceased founder.   12. _____

13. Phong always dresses respectably for work.   13. _____

14. It is good practice to save sales recipes.   14. _____

15. Jim always spoke respectively about his parents.   15. _____

C. Read the definition, and select the correct word from the second column to match that description. Write the word you selected in the answer space.

Definition	Word Choice	
1. to disperse in disorderly defeat	root, rote, rout, route	1. _____
2. conjunction used to indicate comparison	than, then	2. _____

3. series of connected rooms	suit, suite, sweet	3._____
4. a fixed, mechanical way of doing something	root, rote, rout, route	4._____
5. to feel insulted, indignant	recent, resent	5._____
6. suave, polished	urban, urbane	6._____
7. a written acknowledgment that money or goods have been received	receipt, recipe	7._____
8. systematic essay or book on some subject	treaties, treatise	8._____
9. law	statue, stature, statute	9._____
10. in a manner showing respect or honor	respectably, respectfully, respectively	10._____

D. Compose ten newspaper headlines. Use the words (or derivatives of the words) listed below. Try to keep your headlines informative but brief (4 to 8 words). They can represent real or fictitious events. Underline the vocabulary word in each headline

rout _____ *Blaze Routs Two Families* _____

respectably _____ *Incumbent Wins Respectably* _____

1. receipt _____

2. urban _____

3. won't _____

4. statue _____

5. tenant _____

6. root _____

7. rote _____

8. recent _____

_____

9. treaties _____

_____

10. statute _____

_____

Spelling Demons and Word Division

SPELLING DEMONS

Here is a list of about 350 words frequently misspelled all the way from first grade through college—words frequently misspelled in the business office too. Because these words bother so many people, we have called them *spelling demons*. And yet, as you examine these words, you will be struck with the fact that they are all very simple—so simple that you will wonder why people should be baffled by them.

Lists of demons are generally presented alphabetically or in approximate order of difficulty. To make this list more *useful* to you, we have *grouped* the words according to the *special problems* they present. In most cases the heading refers you to the chapter in this book where the particular spelling problem is treated in detail. Do not be surprised if you have already studied some of these words elsewhere in the book. They are repeated here for special emphasis.

Pronunciation—Chapter 3

accept	February	perform	strict
accurate	forward	prejudice	surprise
athlete	government	probably	temperament
disastrous	hindrance	quantity	temperature
environment	hundred	recognize	tragedy
except	irrelevant	remembrance	tremendous
experiment	laboratory	similar	undoubtedly
familiar			

Doubling the final consonant—Chapter 4

admitted	admitting	occurred	occurring
beginner	beginning	planned	planning
bigger	biggest	preferred	preferring
controlled	controlling	referred	referring
dropped	dropping	stepped	stepping
equipped	equipping	transferred	transferring

Adding suffixes to words ending in silent e—Chapter 5

advantageous	becoming	losing	shining
advertisement	changeable	ninety	using
arguing	changing	ninth	writing
argument	coming	noticeable	

Words with ei—ie—Chapter 6

achieve	field	leisure	receive
achievement	financier	mischief	relieve
belief	foreign	niece	seize
believe	friend	piece	weird
conceive	height	receipt	yield
deceive			

Double letters—Chapter 7

cc

accident	accomplish	accuse	occasion
acclaim	accuracy	accustom	occur
accompany	accurate		

ff

difference	different	difficult	sufficient

gg

aggravate	aggressive	exaggerate

ll

alleviate	challenge	fallacy	intellect
allot	collect	illusion	parallel
allowed			

mm

commercial	dilemma	immense	roommate
committee	immediate	recommend	summary
Communism			

nn

annual	connote	manner	tyranny

pp

apparatus	appreciate	approximate	oppose
appear	approach	opportunity	opposite
applies			

rr

arrange	curriculum	surrounding
correlate	irritable	warrant

Silent letters—Chapter 8

playwright	psychology	rhythm	subtle

Prefixes—Chapter 9

disappoint	dissatisfied	interrupt	unnecessary
disillusioned			

Suffixes—Chapter 10

accidentally	cruelly	financially	morally
actually	evidently	generally	really
annually	extremely	ideally	sincerely
basically	finally	incidentally	wholly
completely			

Words ending in cede—ceed—sede—Chapter 11

accede	precede	succeed
concede	proceed	supersede

Words ending in ance—ence—Chapter 15

appear<u>ance</u>	exist<u>ence</u>	magnific<u>ence</u>	pres<u>ence</u>
conven<u>ience</u>	guid<u>ance</u>	occurr<u>ence</u>	sent<u>ence</u>
dilig<u>ence</u>	independ<u>ence</u>		

Words ending in ant—ent—Chapter 15

abund<u>ant</u>	differ<u>ent</u>	excell<u>ent</u>	persist<u>ent</u>
conven<u>ient</u>	domin<u>ant</u>	magnific<u>ent</u>	promin<u>ent</u>
depend<u>ent</u>	effici<u>ent</u>		

Words ending in yze—Chapter 16

anal<u>yze</u>   paral<u>yze</u>

Homonyms

its	there	too	whose
it's	they're	two	your
their	to	who's	you're

Words often confused

advice—advise	ingenious—ingenuous
affect—effect	later—latter
all ready—already	lead—led
all together—altogether	loose—lose
breath—breathe	may be—maybe
choose—chose	moral—morale
conscience—conscious	personal—personnel
desert—dessert	prophecy—prophesy
device—devise	quiet—quite

Tough spots

The demons in this final group refuse to be classified. So we call them *tough spots*. The particular letters that cause the most trouble are underlined in the words. For example, **fascinate** is frequently misspelled because people have difficulty with the **sc**. So the word is printed as follows:

fascinate

We know from experience that this is where the problem is likely to be. The letter or letters are underlined so it becomes clear at once that this is the spot on which you should concentrate.

absence	curtain	gaiety	particular
absurd	dealt	genius	persuade
acquaint	definite	genuine	pleasant
acquire	describe	grammar	prestige
adequate	description	humor	prevalent
afraid	desire	humorous	privilege
against	despair	influential	pursue
amateur	destruction	ingredient	recipe
article	disciple	initiative	recognize
author	discipline	inquisitive	resources
bargain	discuss	interest	ridiculous
benefit	disease	interpret	schedule
boundary	disgusted	irrelevant	separate
brilliant	divide	knowledge	sergeant
Britain	divine	length	shoulder
calendar	eighth	likelihood	significance
captain	eliminate	liveliest	speech
certain	endeavor	livelihood	strength
character	entirely	loneliness	symbol
cigarette	escape	luxury	synonym
comparative	expense	maintenance	technique
concentrate	facilitate	marriage	thorough
concern	fascinate	meant	tragedy
criticism	favorite	minute	villain
criticize	felicitate	paid	woman (sing.)
cruel	fictitious	parliament	women (plural)
curious			

NAME   **CLASS**   **DATE**   **SCORE**

Spelling Assignments

A. In the following list, some words are misspelled. Underline each misspelled word, and write the correct spelling in the space provided. If the printed word is correctly spelled, write C in the space.

1.	incidently	_____	24.	certain _____
2.	finaly	_____	25.	ninty _____
3.	disastrous	_____	26.	irrevelant _____
4.	generaly	_____	27.	strenth _____
5.	envirment	_____	28.	rememberance _____
6.	temperment	_____	29.	sacrafice _____
7.	sieze	_____	30.	likelihood _____
8.	probaly	_____	31.	accurate _____
9.	knowlege	_____	32.	falasy _____
10.	dissapoint	_____	33.	ilusion _____
11.	precede	_____	34.	dilema _____
12.	rythm	_____	35.	tremendous _____
13.	vacum	_____	36.	roomate _____
14.	separate	_____	37.	suprise _____
15.	criticizm	_____	38.	basicaly _____
16.	definate	_____	39.	minature _____
17.	grammer	_____	40.	ideally _____
18.	facinate	_____	41.	accross _____
19.	predjudice	_____	42.	supercede _____
20.	column	_____	43.	noticeable _____
21.	privelege	_____	44.	agravate _____
22.	humerous	_____	45.	fourty _____
23.	judgement	_____	46.	prevelent _____

47. disguize _____   49. attendence _____

48. competiter _____   50. terible _____

B. In each of the following words, one or more key letters have been omitted. Insert the proper letters. Then rewrite the complete word on the line to the right.

1. arg_____ment _____   26. r_____culous _____

2. advantag__us _____   27. parti_____ar _____

3. refe _____ ing _____   28. counter _____it _____

4. contro ____ed _____   29. corres ____ce _____

5. bel_____ve _____   30. ac _____odate _____

6. h _____ ght _____   31. consc ____ce _____

7. occu ___ence _____   32. defic _____nt _____

8. dec _____ve _____   33. crit_____on _____

9. para_____el _____   34. d ____cription _____

10. benefi ____ed _____   35. phen _____on _____

11. indep____nce _____   36. techn_____ue _____

12. inciden ____ly _____   37. ach ____ment _____

13. finan _____er _____   38. becom____ng _____

14. dis ____lusion _____   39. undou _____ly _____

15. inter_____pt _____   40. dis _____tisfy _____

16. ad ____quate _____   41. oc _____sion _____

17. bound _____y _____   42. bril_____nt _____

18. compar __tive _____   43. mis___atement _____

19. ficti _____ous _____   44. p _____sue _____

20. init_____tive _____   45. in _____endo _____

21. p _____suade _____   46. effici_____ly _____

22. signif ____nce _____   47. justi _____y _____

23. im ____iately _____   48. indisc_____t _____

24. profe _____al _____   49. maint_____ce _____

25. aud _____nce _____   50. adver___ment _____

WORD DIVISION

The trend in letter writing in business today is to avoid the use of word divisions whenever possible. Lines without divided words are easier to type and to read. They are also more attractive. When it is absolutely necessary to divide a word in order to maintain a reasonably even right margin, the word is begun at the end of one line and completed on the next line. The two parts are separated by a hyphen (-) placed at the end of the first line.

When you are typing copy, observe the following guidelines governing the hyphenation of words.

What to do

Rule 1

Divide words only between syllables. Consult your dictionary to see how words are properly divided (syllabicated).

con-fer-ence   pro-por-tion   cou-ra-geous

Rule 2

Divide words after prefixes and before suffixes if possible.

trans-portation   vaca-tion
inter-fere   employ-ment
dis-approval   adapt-able

Rule 3

Divide words after a single vowel except when that vowel is part of a suffix.

hesi-tate   vulner-able
bene-fit   secur-ity
accompani-ment   divis-ible

Rule 4

Divide words between two vowels that are pronounced separately.

continu-ation	radi-ator
depreci-ation	valu-able

Rule 5

Divide words between double consonants unless the root word ends with these double consonants.

excel-lent	bill-ing
run-ning	small-est
neces-sary	install-ing
embar-rass	sell-ers

Rule 6

Divide hyphenated words at the point of the hyphen and compound words between the parts of the compound.

brother-/in-law	sales/person
self-/control	copy/right
court-/martial	letter/head

What Not To Do

Rule 1

Do not divide a word of one syllable.

The following words, for example, may not be divided.

thought	strength	planned
through	shipped	strained

Rule 2

Do not divide a word of five or fewer letters.

The following words, for example, may not be divided.

again	allot	begin
ago	also	retry

Note It is also preferable not to divide a word of six letters unless failure to do so would result in a very uneven right margin.

Rule 3

Do not set off a syllable of a single letter at either the beginning or the end of a word.

The following divisions are unacceptable.

a-rouse	e-nough
a-warded	health-y

Rule 4

Do not set off a syllable of two letters at the end of a word.

Correct	**Incorrect**
briefly	brief-ly
monthly	month-ly
pre-sented	present-ed
com-pany	compa-ny
con-sumer	consum-er
prop-erty	proper-ty

Note Authorities are divided about whether it is acceptable to separate a two-letter prefix from the rest of the word. Our advice is to divide words in this fashion if absolutely necessary but to avoid doing so whenever possible.

Acceptable	**Preferable**
be-neath	beneath
re-lieve	relieve
de-cline	decline
un-selfish	unselfish

Rule 5

Do not divide proper nouns, titles, contractions, numerals, or abbreviations.

None of the following items, for example, may be divided.

Richard	shouldn't	11,423,778,569
Chicago	could've	UNESCO
Governor	$25,000.00	ILGWU

Note If an abbreviation contains a hyphen (for example, **AFL-CIO**), it may be divided after the hyphen.

Rule 6

Do not divide the last word of more than two consecutive lines.

Rule 7

Do not divide the last word of the last full line in a paragraph or the last word on a page.

Word groups

Do not separate certain kinds of word groups that need to be read as a unit—for example, page and number, month and day, month and year, number and abbreviation, number and unit of measure, model number.

page 86	6:30 a.m.
May 24	15 feet
November 1988	Model K5A

Longer word groups may be separated only in specific places, as shown in the following sections.

Dates. Dates may be separated between the day and the year, not between the month and the day.

Correct	**Incorrect**
August 16,/1977	August/16, 1977

Street addresses. Street addresses may be broken between the name of the street and the street designation. If the street name has more than one word, the address may also be broken between words in the street name.

Correct	**Incorrect**
1263 Ocean/Boulevard	1263/Ocean Boulevard
452 59th/Street	452/59th Street
826 North Mountain/Avenue	826/North Mountain Avenue
826 North/Mountain Avenue	

Names of places. Names of places should be separated between the city and the state, or between the state and ZIP Code.

Correct	**Incorrect**
Clifton,/New Jersey 07013	Clifton, New/Jersey 07013
Mission Hills, CA/91345	Mission/Hills, CA 91345

Names of people. Names of people may be broken directly before the surname. Names preceded by long titles may be separated between the title and the given name.

Correct	**Incorrect**
Mr. John Q./Public	Mr. John/Q. Public
Lieutenant/Ed Kowalski	Lieutenant Ed/Kowalski

Names may also be broken between words in the title.

Vice/President Albert Bennett
Professor/Emeritus Barbara Andrews

Word Division Assignments

A. Underline any word or words in each of the following groups of three that are incorrectly divided or that do not follow preferred word division style. Write the correct version for the division of each word you underlined in the answer space. If there are no errors in the group, write C. The / indicates where the hyphen should be placed. *DO NOT GUESS: Use a dictionary to verify syllabication.*

1.	adminis/tration	accept/able	employ/er	1._____
2.	confi/dent	ef/fect	indeb/tedness	2._____
3.	cur/rent	e/quipped	coopera/tive	3._____
4.	hei/ght	ap/proval	volun/teer	4._____
5.	bul/letin	ac/cess	antici/pate	5._____
6.	bus/iness	u/nique	per/sonal	6._____
7.	pro/gress	an/nul	question/naire	7._____
8.	alumi/num	mor/tgage	bu/reau	8._____
9.	ap/point	al/ready	conven/ience	9._____
10.	adequ/ate	th/rough	recog/nize	10._____
11.	ship/ped	doc/ument	occa/sion	11._____
12.	manage/ment	grad/uate	cour/tesy	12._____
13.	differ/ence	ter/ritory	no/tice	13._____
14.	corpor/ation	physi/cian	proce/dural	14._____
15.	represen/tative	recom/mendation	begin/ning	15._____
16.	hap/py	condi/tion	con/nection	16._____
17.	demon/strative	safe/ty	mod/ern	17._____
18.	cas/ual	tele/graph	impor/tant	18._____
19.	father-/in-law	rota/tion	record/ing	19._____
20.	defi/nite	demo/cratic	lei/sure	20._____
21.	stan/dard	dis/advantage	tremen/dous	21._____
22.	com/municate	jam/med	re/ceipt	22._____
23.	perman/ent	mes/sage	pri/vate	23._____

24.	over/lap	neces/sary	vand/alize	24. _____
25.	modi/fication	agreea/ble	multi/ply	25. _____
26.	dis/charge	subsi/dize	practi/cal	26. _____
27.	remit/tance	expos/ure	strate/gic	27. _____
28.	of/fice	ma/chine	histo/ry	28. _____
29.	econ/omical	en/deavor	hop/ping	29. _____
30.	self-/awareness	des/cription	hop/ing	30. _____
31.	hur/ricane	sug/gest	edit/or in chief	31. _____
32.	natu/ral	extrav/agant	specif/ic	32. _____
33.	expens/ive	intel/ligible	regrett/able	33. _____
34.	prop/erly	ordi/narily	relaxa/tion	34. _____
35.	satis/fy	overstep/ping	imag/ination	35. _____

B. Rewrite each item to show the preferred end-of-line word or word division ending. If the item cannot be divided, rewrite the item in full.

December   *December*

Miami, Florida   *Miami,*

1.	October 23, 1984	1. _____
2.	Mr. John H. Regensberg	2. _____
3.	specialized (last word on a page)	3. _____
4.	131-55-8789	4. _____
5.	satisfaction (last word of last full line in a paragraph)	5. _____
6.	wouldn't	6. _____
7.	Minneapolis	7. _____
8.	typewriting (the previous two lines already end with divided words)	8. _____
9.	58 Main Street	9. _____
10.	UNICEF	10. _____
11.	8:30 p.m.	11. _____
12.	Atlanta, GA 30390	12. _____
13.	164 South State Street	13. _____
14.	President Lois Grant	14. _____
15.	pages 15–19	15. _____

Vocabulary Enrichment

Choose the word from the list below that is closest in meaining to the numbered word or words in the paragraphs on pages 388–390. Write the word you selected from the list in the answer space. Use each word only once.

accommodations	luggage
agent	major
beforehand	mode
chains	option
clothing	passengers
comfort	pertinent
confirmation	place
constraints	preparing
daily	rates
decision	record
deluxe	reservations
departure	resort
destination	seasoned
duties	short
expenses	substantiate
expensive	tablets
factors	taxicab
fares	timetable
files	toll-free
frustrate	undesirable
frustrating	unexpected
group	unrealistic
incidental	useful
knowledgeable	valuable
limousine	wardrobe

Making Travel Arrangements

Being 1. ENLIGHTENED about travel arrangements can be very
useful if you are arranging for your own travel or making travel
plans for someone else as part of your job's 2. RESPONSIBILITIES.
This exercise will review some of the basic 3. ITEMS that need to be
covered when you are making travel arrangements.

The most important step in making travel arrangements is
planning. "Failure to plan is planning to fail" when it comes to
4. ARRANGING for a successful travel experience, whether it
is for business or for pleasure.

Choosing the 5. MANNER of transportation is the first critical
6. JUDGMENT that must be made. Some factors to consider
when you plan to travel by air, bus, train, or car are the distance to
be traveled, the time 7. LIMITATIONS, and the 8. COSTS involved.
Contacting a travel 9. REPRESENTATIVE is the fastest way to get
information about travel by air or train. A road map and a road atlas
are 10. HANDY guides when you plan to travel by car.

Since time is probably the most 11. PRECIOUS commodity when
you plan a business trip, and since most business trips are scheduled
to 12. PRINCIPAL cities, air travel is normally the mode of travel
selected. Air 13. FEES are based on the time of 14. TAKEOFF and
the class of service selected. First-class service is the most
15. COSTLY, while coach service costs the least. Charter flights
are inexpensive because they are based on rates for a
16. LARGE NUMBER OF PEOPLE. Usually, 17. TRAVELERS on a
charter flight are members of a particular group or organization.

One concern of the air traveler is getting from the airport to the hotel
or other meeting 18. SITE. Some hotels provide their own airport
19. LARGE, LUXURIOUS CAR service, especially in
20. VACATION areas. In larger cities the traveler can take a
21. CAR IN WHICH A PASSENGER PAYS A FARE or a minibus or

1. _____

2. _____

3. _____

4. _____

5. _____

6. _____

7. _____

8. _____

9. _____

10. _____

11. _____

12. _____

13. _____

14. _____

15. _____

16. _____

17. _____

18. _____

19. _____

20. _____

21. _____

van, which carries a large number of passengers to a variety of
destinations at comparatively low 22. FARES. Another
23. ALTERNATIVE is to rent a car. In order to do this, planning
is critical because 24. PRIOR GUARANTEED REQUESTS are
often necessary 25. AHEAD OF TIME.

22._____

23._____

24._____

25._____

Hotel 26. LODGINGS vary from standard to 27. ELEGANT,
and it is best to reserve a room in advance. Most hotel/motel
28. FRANCHISES provide 29. NO-CHARGE telephone numbers
that can be used to make reservations in distant cities. If time
permits, you will usually receive a 30. VERIFICATION form to
31. CORROBORATE the reservation.

26._____

27._____

28._____

29._____

30._____

31._____

A detailed listing that shows a 32. DAY-BY-DAY schedule of
the traveler's flights, meetings, overnight accommodations,
contact telephone numbers, and other 33. RELEVANT information
is called an itinerary. This is a helpful 34. DOCUMENT for the
traveler, the office staff, and the family as a means of keeping in
touch should the need arise.

32._____

33._____

34._____

Some 35. MINOR BUT ASSOCIATED items that add to the
traveler's 36. WELL-BEING should be thought about in advance too.
For example, any medicine, air sickness 37. PILLS, eyeglasses,
or other special prescription items should be taken along. For
38. BRIEF trips, an under-the-seat suitcase prevents the bother of
39. BAGGAGE checking and retrieval.

35._____

36._____

37._____

38._____

39._____

Finally, comfortable 40. APPAREL should be worn for the trips, with
an equally appropriate 41. COLLECTION OF GARMENTS planned
for the climate of the 42. PLACE WHERE YOU ARE GOING. Time
zone changes will also affect a traveler's well-being and should be
considered in planning the 43. SCHEDULE of events.

40._____

41._____

42._____

43._____

Some special problems that 44. HINDER THE SUCCESS OF   44. _____
the traveler include scheduling too much in one day or
scheduling 45. IMPRACTICAL travel time from one place to   45. _____
another; arriving at the destination without the important
business 46. PAPERS that are needed to conduct business;   46. _____
finding out that 47. UNFORESEEN circumstances have   47. _____
caused a change in plans; and, finally, having to put up with
48. OBJECTIONABLE accommodations or facilities.   48. _____

Whether you are planning your first trip or whether you are a
49. VETERAN traveler, it is a fact that with appropriate   49. _____
planning, traveling can be an exciting experience rather than
a 50. VERY DISCOURAGING one.   50. _____

Summary Review Exercises

We have come a long way together. In addition to becoming familiar with the use of the dictionary, you have mastered the basic rules governing the spelling of words; the correct usage of homonyms and words often confused; the forming of plurals, possessives, and contractions; the proper styles of capitalization; and the correct rules for dividing words.

You have learned a great deal—but the most important step is yet to come. You must now apply what you have learned toward everything you do in order to retain and profit from what you have studied. The following assignments will help you get started by enabling you to apply what you have learned in a business setting.

As administrative assistant to J. R. Reynolds, editor in chief of *High Tech World,* you must, as one of your responsibilities, check carefully any written work that will go out from Ms. Reynold's office. Twelve such items are presented in this part of the text, representing a variety of materials typically reviewed by you as the administrative assistant. You will be proofreading letters, form letters, a memorandum, a bibliography, and several galley proof columns. Galley proof columns represent the narrow columns of print usually found in magazines and newspapers, and you will be making the final check in order to indicate any changes necessary before the actual printing takes place.

Use the knowledge you have acquired through *Business Spelling and Word Power* as you proceed. If you are not sure, refer back to the text or check the dictionary. Whether transcribing or proofreading, be aware that accuracy is the primary requirement. The degree to which you are accurate is your autograph of excellence. Starting with these exercises, strive to autograph each piece of work assigned to you with your imprint of excellence!

NAME	CLASS	DATE	SCORE

Summary Review Exercises

Underline any errors in the following documents, and write the corrected item in the answer space. If there are no errors in the line, write C in the space.

SUMMARY REVIEW 1

1 Febuary 14, 19--

2 Mr. Christopher Onderko
3 Apartmint 5G
4 991 Westover Court
5 New York, NY 10020

6 Dear Mr. Onkerko:

7 Thank you for sending us you're manuscript for publication
8 consideration in <u>High Tech World</u>.

9 After carefully reviewing your work, our editorial board is happy
10 to inform you that your article has been excepted for publication
11 in the August issue. Congradulations!

12 We are confident that the informative and practicle suggestions
13 given in your article will be of great value to our many reader's
14 in technical ocupations.

15 An honorarium will be fowarded to you upon publication.
16 Concurrently, six complimentary copies of the August issue will be
17 sent too you.

18 You can be proud of your achievment, Mr. Onderko! Your article,
19 "Suggestions for Writting Documentation," is a fine effort, and it
20 will make a sustantial contribution to others in the field. We
21 are happy too publish your work, and we encourage you to send us
22 more articles in the future..

23 Very sincerely yours,

24 J. R. Reynolds
25 Editor in Chief

eok

1. _____
2. _____
3. _____
4. _____
5. _____
6. _____
7. _____
8. _____
9. _____
10. _____
11. _____
12. _____
13. _____
14. _____
15. _____
16. _____
17. _____
18. _____
19. _____
20. _____
21. _____
22. _____
23. _____
24. _____
25. _____

SUMMARY REVIEW 2

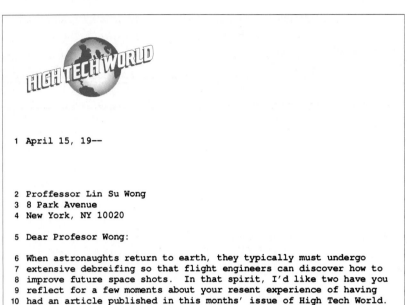

1 April 15, 19--

2 Proffessor Lin Su Wong
3 8 Park Avenue
4 New York, NY 10020

5 Dear Profesor Wong:

6 When astronaughts return to earth, they typically must undergo
7 extensive debreifing so that flight engineers can discover how to
8 improve future space shots. In that spirit, I'd like two have you
9 reflect for a few moments about your resent experience of having
10 had an article published in this months' issue of <u>High Tech World</u>.

11 I would apreciate it if you would share whatever recommendations
12 you may have to improve our system. As you undoutedly know,
13 producing a monthly periodcal is the work of many people. Even
14 though we try to do our very best, some times there are slip-ups,
15 or there may be even better weighs of doing things that we have
16 not taught of.

17 To get your comments, I am purposely not enclosing a questionaire
18 to fill out. I would rather have you present the impressions that
19 you feel are most relevent.

20 Be candit. I assure you that your responses will be held in the
21 strickest confidence. May I hear from you within the next two
22 week's. Many thanks.

23 Sincerely yours,

24 J. R. Reynolds
25 Editor in Cheif

 eok

1. _____
2. _____
3. _____
4. _____
5. _____
6. _____
7. _____
8. _____
9. _____
10. _____
11. _____
12. _____
13. _____
14. _____
15. _____
16. _____
17. _____
18. _____
19. _____
20. _____
21. _____
22. _____
23. _____
24. _____
25. _____

SUMMARY REVIEW 3

HIGH TECH WORLD

May 18, 19--

Dr. Elaine Griffin
62 Rushingbrook Drive
Raleigh, NC 27612

Dear Ms. Griffin:

1 As an auther of a number of articles on office automation, you
2 have excellant credentials to bring to <u>High Tech World</u> if you were
3 to submit a article for publication consideration.

4 Our editoral staff is always interested in obtaining interesting
5 and informertive manuscripts that reflect current trends from the
6 practionners perspective; therefore, we invite you to submit a
7 manuscript for publication.

8 Manuscript topics related to current technology's are always
9 welcome. Our readers want to learn more about successfull
10 practices in useing technologies such as electronic mail,
11 facsimile, micrographics, desktop publishing, an local area
12 networks, as exampels.

13 Manuscripts submitted for review must confirm to the following
14 guidelines: Manuscripts must be typed with double spacing and
15 1-inch margins on 8 1/2- by 11 inch bond paper. Manuscripts
16 containning 2000 to 3000 words are preferred, and all artwork
17 submitted must be camera-ready.

18 Our editorial board reads and evaluates all manuscripts and makes
19 publication deciseons. The board also reserves the right to edit
20 manuscripts excepted for publication. Manuscripts not selected
21 for publication will be returned too the author.

22 I look foreword to receiving a manuscript from you. If you need
23 additional information, telephone me any time at 555-4141,
24 Extention 23.

25 Very truely yours,

J. R. Reynolds
Editor in Chief

eok

1. _____
2. _____
3. _____
4. _____
5. _____
6. _____
7. _____
8. _____
9. _____
10. _____
11. _____
12. _____
13. _____
14. _____
15. _____
16. _____
17. _____
18. _____
19. _____
20. _____
21. _____
22. _____
23. _____
24. _____
25. _____

SUMMARY REVIEW 4

1 GETTING READY FOR THE EMERGING TECHNOLOGIES

2 By Sandy L. Homer

3 Office professionals are continualy facing the prospect of
4 technological innovation that is designed to improof worker
5 productivity. The personal computer is a major alement in the
6 office technology revolution.

7 A portable personal computer today can due more than the
8 computers that weighted more and cost more ten years ago. And
9 the forcast is that in the future computers will continue to
10 become smaller, less expensive, more powerful, and even more
11 prevalant.

12 The roll of the computer is to process information. It is a
13 tool that can perform a wealth of marvalous applications, such as
14 word procesing, spreadsheets, database management, graphics, and
15 other specialised tasks. Probably the greatest technological
16 contribution effecting the computer is the innovation in
17 telecommunications that enables computers to be lincked across the
18 room, across the miles, and even across continants. This truly
19 facilitates communication between workers in remote locations.

20 Dispite the number of technological advances, however, it
21 takes more than automation to enhance job perfromance. It will
22 take more than an expenditure of money and user-friendly personnel
23 computers to do it. Ultimately, the way people relates to the
24 new technologies will determine weather productivity will be
25 improved.

1. _____
2. _____
3. _____
4. _____
5. _____
6. _____
7. _____
8. _____
9. _____
10. _____
11. _____
12. _____
13. _____
14. _____
15. _____
16. _____
17. _____
18. _____
19. _____
20. _____
21. _____
22. _____
23. _____
24. _____
25. _____

SUMMARY REVIEW 5

1 GETTING READY FOR THE EMERGING TECHNOLOGIES Page 2	1._____
	2._____
2 To involv people successfully, the automation of selected	3._____
3 office functions that are redundent and laborious is the first	4._____
4 step. In this way, individuals can be involved in tasks that	5._____
5 require judgment, initiative, incite, and imaginative problem	6._____
6 solving--all qualities and activities that engender pride and	7._____
7 enhance self esteem.	8._____
8 Change Management	9._____
9 Just as change is a natural occurrence in the office setting,	10._____
10 so, too, is resistance to change it's natural counterpart. It is	11._____
11 true that no matter how well you manage the change process, their	12._____
12 will always be some resistance.	13._____
13 It is said that there are five phases in implamenting change	14._____
14 in office automation. These phases are initiation, acclimination,	15._____
15 reluctant acceptance, acceptance, and effective operation. Now	16._____
16 without positive user participation at each step, the promises an	17._____
17 rewards of automation can not be achieved.	18._____
18 Managers must plane to involve users in the change process at	19._____
19 the very begining so that the users will be less inclined to fear	20._____
20 change. Instead, they will become apart of the change process by	21._____
21 providing input from there perspective.	22._____
22 If managers first recognise that resistance is a predictable	23._____
23 response to empending change, they will address the problem ahead	24._____
24 of time so that the symptoms of resistance--defiance, withdrawl,	25._____
25 and contrary behavior--will not appear.	

SUMMARY REVIEW 6

GETTING READY FOR THE EMERGING TECHNOLOGIES   Page 3

<u>Converging Technologies</u>

1   It has been said that office automation system's have been

2 designed primarily to make the workers jobs easier and more

3 efficient. As a result, a number of discreet technologies--such

4 as word processing, facsimile transmission, and micrographics, as

5 examples--were developed to meat specific needs. Today the

6 computer serves as the nerve center for integrating technological

7 developements.

8   At many work sights, the "automated office" is not yet a

9 reality because the trully automated office is not characterized

10 by a single system or piece of equiptment but exists only when

11 several technologies are integrated into a functionning system

12 and are interconnected electronically.

13   Automation in the office implies a change in both the weigh

14 the office is run and the way managers and users perform there

15 jobs. At managerial or user workstations, information is input,

16 processed, stored, and distributed. Electronic file's and

17 electronic person-to person communication replace the previous

18 dependance on paper and oral communication.

19   As technology advances, it always illicits its price. In

20 solveing one problem, it creates others. The shift from discrete

21 to integrated technological systems has grate consequences for the

22 future. One factor is certain, however, and that is that success

23 in office automation can be acheived only if the office

24 professional is viewed as the most important component in the

25 change process.

1. _____

2. _____

3. _____

4. _____

5. _____

6. _____

7. _____

8. _____

9. _____

10. _____

11. _____

12. _____

13. _____

14. _____

15. _____

16. _____

17. _____

18. _____

19. _____

20. _____

21. _____

22. _____

23. _____

24. _____

25. _____

SUMMARY REVIEW 7

GETTING READY FOR THE EMERGING TECHNOLOGIES   Page 28

1   BIOGRAPHY

2   Arnoudse, Donald M, L. Paul Oullette, and John D. Whalen, "When
3   users Resist Change," Information Center, August 6, 1988,
4   pp. 44-46, 48.

5   Buzawa, Dorothy J., "working With Difficult People," Management
6   World, July/August 2988, pp. 17-19.

7   Doktar, Ralph, "Implementation of Information Sience," Inform,
8   Novamber 12, 1933, pp. 46-62.

9   Finlay, Douglas, "Dont Wait Until You Get Burned," Administrative
10   Management, March 1988, pp. 16-22.

11 Grushanta, Vigi, "IRM and Innovation," Inform, Aprile 16, 1988,
12   pp. 20-21, 23.

13 Izzo, Joseph E., "Planing and Creating an Information System,"
14   Information Center, september 1987, pp. 38-45.

15 Li, Penelope, "Software Engineerring," Journal of Science and
16   Technology, January 1989, pp. 22-36.

17 Menkus, Belden, "How Voice Messageing Is Used," Modren Office
18   Technology, Augurst 1988, p. 74.

19 Perrone, giovanni, "Primary Product in the Development Life
20   Cycle," Software Magezine, August 1988, pp. 35-38, 40-41.

21 Walter, Gerry, "Interactive Dokument Processing Systems," Journal
22   of Infomation and Image Management, May 1986, pp. 9-11, 13.

23 Zeeman, Steven R., Paul H. Murphy, and Rebecca M. Chast, "Computer
24   Applications in the Modern Offise," Modern Office Technology,
25   February 1989, pp. 11-22.

1. _____
2. _____
3. _____
4. _____
5. _____
6. _____
7. _____
8. _____
9. _____
10. _____
11. _____
12. _____
13. _____
14. _____
15. _____
16. _____
17. _____
18. _____
19. _____
20. _____
21. _____
22. _____
23. _____
24. _____
25. _____

SUMMARY REVIEW 8

1 Octobre 14, 19--

2 Miss Elizabeth Martin
3 Superviser of Information Systems
4 Williams Pharmeceutical Company
5 1214 Avenue Of the Americas
6 New York, NY 10017

7 Dear Miss. Martin:

8 In only five short years, you have played a remarkable roll in
9 the strides toward word processing development at Williams
10 Pharmeceutical! Thank you for hosting such an interesting and
11 informative trip for those of us from High Tech World on Wedesday,
12 October 10. We are planing a seminar for other staff members at
13 our offices so that we can share what we learned at Williams.

14 I enjoyed hearing you trace William's many developments in word
15 processing in you're introductory presentation and was especially
16 impressed with your preceptive feedback during the concluding
17 question-and-answer session. Your handouts, to, have potential
18 for possible future aplication. Would it be possible for you to
19 send me aditional handouts for the seminar planned for the staff
20 at High Tech World?

21 Once again, many thanks to you and your Staff for your combined
22 efforts in making our visit such a rewording one.

23 Sincerely yours,

24 J. R. Reynolds
25 Editor in Cheif
   eok

1. _____
2. _____
3. _____
4. _____
5. _____
6. _____
7. _____
8. _____
9. _____
10. _____
11. _____
12. _____
13. _____
14. _____
15. _____
16. _____
17. _____
18. _____
19. _____
20. _____
21. _____
22. _____
23. _____
24. _____
25. _____

SUMMARY REVIEW 9

(FORM LETTER to be sent to a
selected group of publishers

1 Ladies and Gentleman:

2 As in the preceeding two years, High Tech World will publish--in
3 its Feburary issue--a listing of publications of interest to
4 comtemporery office personnel.

5 We are presently compiling a biography of books that have a
6 copywrite during this current year, and we invite you to
7 supply us with a complete listing of any idems you publish that
8 would be of interest to our readers--primarily administrative,
9 tecknical, and operative office workers.

10 To facilitate processing this information, please include the
11 following date for each title you wish to submit that bears the
12 current years copyright:

13   Authors last name, first name, initial

14   Complete title of book, including addition

15   Total number of pages

16   List price

17   One sentence--no more than 20 words--discribing the
18   focus of the book

19 I would appreciate recieving the above data by December 15. Your
20 cooperation will be appreciated and will also issure you that the
21 information you submit will be encluded in our listing this
22 comming February.

23 Very truly yours,

24 J. R. reynolds
25 Editor In Chief

   eok

1._____
2._____
3._____
4._____
5._____
6._____
7._____
8._____
9._____
10._____
11._____
12._____
13._____
14._____
15._____
16._____
17._____
18._____
19._____
20._____
21._____
22._____
23._____
24._____
25._____

SUMMARY REVIEW 10

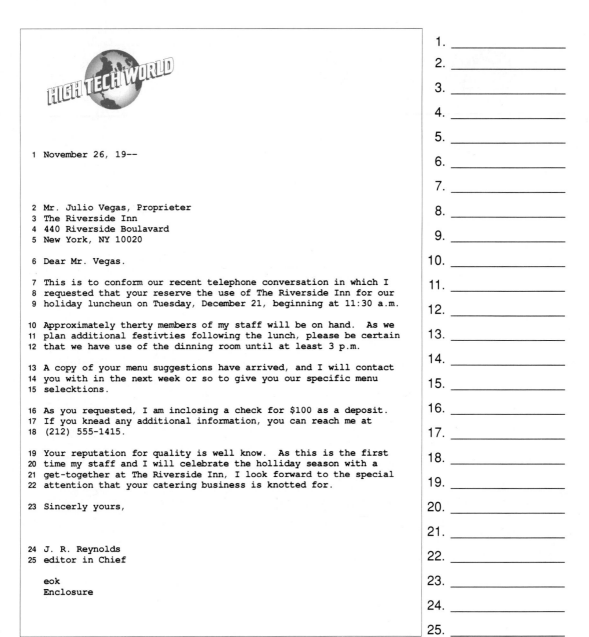

1 November 26, 19--

2 Mr. Julio Vegas, Proprieter
3 The Riverside Inn
4 440 Riverside Boulavard
5 New York, NY 10020

6 Dear Mr. Vegas.

7 This is to conform our recent telephone conversation in which I
8 requested that your reserve the use of The Riverside Inn for our
9 holiday luncheun on Tuesday, December 21, beginning at 11:30 a.m.

10 Approximately therty members of my staff will be on hand. As we
11 plan additional festivties following the lunch, please be certain
12 that we have use of the dinning room until at least 3 p.m.

13 A copy of your menu suggestions have arrived, and I will contact
14 you with in the next week or so to give you our specific menu
15 selecktions.

16 As you requested, I am inclosing a check for $100 as a deposit.
17 If you knead any additional information, you can reach me at
18 (212) 555-1415.

19 Your reputation for quality is well know. As this is the first
20 time my staff and I will celebrate the holliday season with a
21 get-together at The Riverside Inn, I look forward to the special
22 attention that your catering business is knotted for.

23 Sincerly yours,

24 J. R. Reynolds
25 editor in Chief

   eok
   Enclosure

1. _____
2. _____
3. _____
4. _____
5. _____
6. _____
7. _____
8. _____
9. _____
10. _____
11. _____
12. _____
13. _____
14. _____
15. _____
16. _____
17. _____
18. _____
19. _____
20. _____
21. _____
22. _____
23. _____
24. _____
25. _____

SUMMARY REVIEW 11

1 MEMO TO: All Staff Members

2 FROM: J. R. Reynolds, Editor in Chief

3 DATE: Deceber 2, 19--

4 SUBJECT: Anual Christmas Luncheon

5 The Annual Christmas Luncheon will be held on Tuesday, December
6 21, at The Riverside inn, 440 Riverside Boulevard, New York,
7 begining at 11:30 a.m. All current staff members are invited to
8 join us at that time. The Luncheon menu will include a choice of
9 either hot turkey or hot Roast beef sandwiches with all the tasty
10 trimings. The cost will be $5 per person.

11 Please set this time a side for pleasure and festivities at this
12 traditional end-of-the-year evant. To plan this get-together
13 effectivelly, we need to know exactly how many people will be
14 present. Please reserve your place by completeing the attached
15 reservation form and sending it to me with your check maid payable
16 to "High Tech World Staff Account."

17 The closing date for Reservations is Tuesday, December 14. Hope
18 you will be able to join us!

   eok/rmc

- -

RESERVATION FORM

19 I plan to attend the Annual Christmas luncheon on Tuesday,
20 December 21. My check for $5 is inclosed. The item that is
21 checked below is my luncheon selection.

22 _____ Hot turkey sanwich
23 _____ Hot roast beef sanwich

24 NAME _____

25 DEPARMENT _____

   (Please return this form to J. R. Reynolds, C-302.)

1. _____
2. _____
3. _____
4. _____
5. _____
6. _____
7. _____
8. _____
9. _____
10. _____
11. _____
12. _____
13. _____
14. _____
15. _____
16. _____
17. _____
18. _____
19. _____
20. _____
21. _____
22. _____
23. _____
24. _____
25. _____

SUMMARY REVIEW 12

(FORM LETTER to be sent to all
subscribors. Inside addresses will
be individually typed.)

December 15, 19--

1 Dear Subscribor:

2 Letters from our readers confirm that they find the monthly issues
3 of High Tech World enjoyible, entertaining, and informative.

4 We want to continue to keep our subscribors happy; and in order
5 to do this, we have devised a short yet comprehensive questionaire
6 for use in analyzing subscriber preferances. So that we can learn
7 more about you and the types of articles and features you perfer,
8 please fill out the enclosed survay, and mail it back to us in the
9 postpaid envelop that is also enclosed.

10 Tabulated results of the survey will be published in a forthcoming
11 issue, and we hope to gear the contents of future issues to the
12 types of coverage and special intrests indicated by our readers.

13 Don't be reluctant to participate. You'll find that it will take
14 only a few minutes of your time. Every completed questionnaire is
15 important to us and will help to assure us of the relevence of our
16 publication. Seize this opportunity to formerly share all of your
17 preferences, reactions, and idears with us.

18 To acknowledge your response, we have a special bonus planned. By
19 return mail, we will send you a ticket for our annual drawing,
20 which is discribed in detail in the enclosed folder. Enter our
21 annual sweepstakes drawing now by completeing and returning the
22 survey form today.

23 Very truely yours,

24 J. R. Reynolds
25 Editor in Cheef

eok
Enclosures

1. _____
2. _____
3. _____
4. _____
5. _____
6. _____
7. _____
8. _____
9. _____
10. _____
11. _____
12. _____
13. _____
14. _____
15. _____
16. _____
17. _____
18. _____
19. _____
20. _____
21. _____
22. _____
23. _____
24. _____
25. _____

Appendix

Numbers
Common prefixes
Common suffixes
Foreign words and phrases in common use
Common abbreviations
    States and territories
    Canadian provinces
    Months of the year
    Compass directions
    Units of measure
    Standard business terms

Numbers

Rule 1

As a rule in business writing, both approximate numbers and specific numbers are usually expressed in figures.

Nearly 300 people attended the conference.
There were 295 people at the conference.

Rule 2

Express numbers from 1 through 10 in words. Express numbers higher than 10 in figures.

There are five people on the township committee, three Republicans and two Democrats.
Our company now has 21 branch offices.

Exception   Page numbers in a book are always expressed in figures: p. 5, pp. 43–47.

Rule 3

Numbers that begin a sentence should be spelled out, even if they would normally be written as figures.

Forty-eight employees were promoted last year.

If the number is long, reword the sentence to avoid awkwardness.

Awkward. Two hundred thirty-four people attended the banquet.
Revised. There were 234 people in attendance at the banquet.

Rule 4

When several related numbers appear in the same sentence or paragraph, they should all be expressed the same way.

Of the 241 full-time and 135 part-time employees, only 6 failed to report because of the storm.

When numbers are performing different or unrelated functions, a mixed style is acceptable.

They employed 241 full-time and 135 part-time employees in their six stores.

Rule 5

Percentages are usually expressed as figures, with the word **percent** spelled out.

The merger was approved by 83 percent of the stockholders.

Rule 6

Both approximate and exact amounts of money are expressed in figures.

Yesterday our sales totaled over $5000.
Yesterday our sales totaled $5134.

Rule 7

Write the time in figures when **a.m.** or **p.m.** follows, but when **o'clock** follows, use figures for emphasis or words for formality.

11:45 a.m.   4:30 p.m.   4 o'clock (for emphasis)   four o'clock (for formality)

Rule 8

Building numbers are normally written as figures. Street names of 10 and below are spelled out; street names above 10 are written in figures.

We moved our offices from 134 Second Street to 431 34th Street.

Common Prefixes

	Meaning	Examples
a, **ab**	from, away	*avert, absent*
ad	to, toward	*adhere, adverb*
ante	before	*antecedent, antedate*
anti	against, opposite	*antidote, antitoxin*
circum	around	*circumference, circumscribe*
com, **con**	with, very	*commit, confide*
de	away, down	*decline, depressed*
di, **dis**	separation, reversal, apart	*divert, disappoint*
e, **ex**	out of, former	*elect, exclude*
hyper	over, above	*hyperactive, hypercritical*
il	not	*illegal, illiterate*
im	not	*immoral, impatient*
in	in, into	*inspect, invert*
in	not	*inappropriate, invalid*
inter	between	*interstate, intervene*
ir	not	*irregular, irresponsible*
mis	wrong, bad	*misconduct, mistake*
non	not, not one	*non-American, nonrefundable*
ob	against	*object, obstruct*
over	above, excessive	*overlook, overpaid*
poly	many	*polygamy, polytechnic*
post	after, behind	*postpone, postscript*
pre	before	*predict, prepare*
pro	forward	*proceed, promote*
re	again, back	*repay, restore*
retro	backward, behind	*retroactive, retrogress*
sub	under	*submarine, subscribe*
super	above, over	*superfluous, superhuman*
trans	across	*transfer, transport*
ultra	beyond	*ultramodern, ultraviolet*
un	not	*unhappy, unpleasant*
under	beneath	*underneath, underpaid*

Common Suffixes

	Meaning	Examples
able, **ible**	able to be	*adaptable, flexible*
acy	quality of being or having	*accuracy, inadequacy*
al (**eal**, **ial**)	pertaining to	*verbal, vocal*
ance, **ancy**, **ence**, **ency**	quality of _____ing	*hesitancy, influence*
ant, **ent** (**ient**)	has, shows, or does	*hesitant, fluent*
archy	rule by	*anarchy, monarchy*
cracy	rule by	*aristocracy, democracy*
efy, **fy**, **ify**	to make	*classify, rectify*
ety, **ity**, **ty**	quality of	*novelty, sanity*
gram	thing written	*diagram, telegram*
graph	writing, instrument for writing	*photograph, telegraph*
graphy	writing, art or science of writing	*biography, photography*
ian	specialist in	*politician, technician*
ic	pertaining to	*classic, rustic*
ics, **tics**	art, science, or study of	*physics, politics*
il, **ile**	pertaining to	*civil, juvenile*
ine	pertaining to	*feminine, masculine*
ion	act of	*completion, production*
ism	belief in	*atheism, communism*
ist	one who believes in	*atheist, communist*
ive	tending to	*active, effective*
ize	to make, do something with, subject to	*Americanize, criticize*
logy	science of	*psychology, theology*
ment	result of, state of	*excitement, settlement*
meter	measure	*diameter, speedometer*
metry	art or science of measuring	*geometry, trigonometry*
nomy	science of	*astronomy, economy*
ous (**eous**, **ious**)	full of, pertaining to, like	*curious, famous*
ure	act of, result of	*fracture, puncture*
y	quality of, state of, act of, result of	*custody, perjury*

Foreign Words and Phrases in Common Use

	Pronunciation	Meaning
a la carte	ä′lə kärt′	according to the bill of fare
a la mode	ä′lə mōd′	after the fashion
apropos	ap′rə pō′	with respect to
au revoir	ō′rə vwär′	until we meet again
blasé	blä zā′	bored
bona fide	bō′nə fīd′	in good faith, authentic
bourgeois	boor zhwä′	a person of the middle class, characteristic of the middle class
carte blanche	kärt′ blänsh′	unlimited authority
chic	shēk	smart elegance of style
coiffure	kwä fyoor′	style of arranging the hair
connoisseur	kän′ə sur′	one who has expert knowledge in a field
coterie	kōt′ər ē	a clique
coup de grâce	koo′də gräs′	decisive finishing blow or event
debris	də brē′	rubble, litter
debut	dā byoo′	first appearance
de facto	dē fak′tō	in reality
de jure	dē joor′ē	by right or legal establishment
de trop	də trō′	too much, unwanted
dilettante	dil′ə tant′	an admirer of fine arts
elite	ā lēt′	the select part
en route	en root′	on the way
entourage	än′too räzh′	a group of attendants or associates
entree	än′trā	access; main dish of a meal
entre nous	än′trə noo′	between ourselves, confidentially
ex officio	eks′ə fish′ō′	by virtue of one's office
exposé	eks′pō zā′	public disclosure of a crime or scandal
ex post facto	eks′pōst fak′tō	after the fact, retroactively
fait accompli	fāt′ə käm′plē′	an accomplished fact
faux pas	fō pä′	a social error
finesse	fə nes′	cunning, artfulness
gratis	grāt′is	free
habeas corpus	hā′bē əs kôr′pəs	a writ to produce a person before a court
interim	in′tər im	the period of time between
laissez faire	les′ā fer′	noninterference
modus operandi	mō′dəs ō′pə rän′dē	manner of operating, procedure
naive	nä ēv′	childlike, unsophisticated
nee	nā	born (used to indicate the maiden name of a married woman)
nom de plume	näm′də ploom′	pen name
non sequitur	nän′sek′wi tər	it does not follow

passé	pä sā′	behind the times
per capita	pər kap′i tə	for each person
per diem	pər dē′əm	daily
per se	pʉr sā′	by (or in) itself
petite	pə tēt′	small
piquant	pē′kənt	pleasantly sharp or biting to the taste, pungent
première	pri myer′	the first performance
prestige	pres tēzh′	influence derived from success, renown
prima facie	prī′mə fā′shē ē′	at first sight
prospectus	prō spek′təs	a statement outlining the main features of a new work or enterprise
protégé	prōt′ə zhā′	a person helped and guided in his or her career by another
pro tempore (pro tem.)	prō tem′pə rē′	temporary
regime	rə zhēm′	system of management or government
rendezvous	rän′dā vōō′	meeting place
repertoire	rep′ər twär′	list of songs, roles, plays, etc., a singer, actor, or company is ready to perform
résumé	rez′ə mā′	a summary
revue	ri vyōō′	musical show
savoir-faire	sav′wär fer′	tact; knowing what to do and say or when and how to do or say it
sine qua non	sī′nē kwā nän′	absolutely indispensable thing
status quo	stat′əs kwō′	the existing condition
table d′hôte	tä′bəl dōt′	a complete meal, with specified courses, at a fixed price
tête-à-tête	tāt′ə tāt′	private conversation between two people
vis-à-vis	vē′zə vē′	face to face with, in comparison with

Common Abbreviations

States and Territories

	ZIP		ZIP		ZIP
Alabama	AL	Kentucky	KY	Oklahoma	OK
Alaska	AK	Louisiana	LA	Oregon	OR
Arizona	AZ	Maine	ME	Pennsylvania	PA
Arkansas	AR	Maryland	MD	Puerto Rico	PR
California	CA	Massachusetts	MA	Rhode Island	RI
Colorado	CO	Michigan	MI	South Carolina	SC
Connecticut	CT	Minnesota	MN	South Dakota	SD
Delaware	DE	Mississippi	MS	Tennessee	TN
District of		Missouri	MO	Texas	TX
Columbia	DC	Montana	MT	Utah	UT
Florida	FL	Nebraska	NE	Vermont	VT
Georgia	GA	Nevada	NV	Virgin Islands	VI
Guam	GU	New Hampshire	NH	Virginia	VA
Hawaii	HI	New Jersey	NJ	Washington	WA
Idaho	ID	New Mexico	NM	West Virginia	WV
Illinois	IL	New York	NY	Wisconsin	WI
Indiana	IN	North Carolina	NC	Wyoming	WY
Iowa	IA	North Dakota	ND		
Kansas	KS	Ohio	OH		

Canadian Provinces

Alberta	AB	Newfoundland	NF	Quebec	PQ
British Columbia	BC	Nova Scotia	NS	Saskatchewan	SK
Manitoba	MB	Ontario	ON		
New Brunswick	NB	Prince Edward Island	PE		

Months of the Year

January	Jan.	May	May	September	Sept.
February	Feb.	June	June	October	Oct.
March	Mar.	July	July	November	Nov.
April	Apr.	August	Aug.	December	Dec.

Compass Directions

East	E	Northwest	NW	Southwest	SW
North	N	South	S	West	W
Northeast	NE	Southeast	SE		

Units of Measure

Length		**Weight**		**Time**		**Electronic**	
centimeter	cm	centigram	cg	day	d	ampere	a
foot, feet	ft	grain	gr	hour	hr	cycle	c
inch	in	gram	gm	minute	min	kilocycle	kc
meter	m	kilogram	kg	month	mo	kilovolt	kv
mile	mi	milligram	mg	second	sec	kilowatt	kw
millimeter	mm	ounce	oz	year	yr	megacycle	mc
yard	yd	pound	lb	before noon	a.m.	volt	v
				noon	m.	watt	w
				afternoon	p.m.		

Standard Business Terms

abbreviated, abbreviation	abbr.	board	bd.
absolute	abs.	bill of lading	B/L
account	acct.	bills payable	B.P.
acknowledged	ack'd	bills receivable	B.R.
acre	a	bill of sale	B/S
additional	addl.	Boulevard	Blvd.
adjective	adj.	branch office	B.O.
ad libitum (at pleasure)	ad lib.	Brother	Bro.
administration	adm.	Brothers	Bros.
Administrative Management		brought forward	b.f.
Society	AMS	building	bldg.
Administrator	Admr.	Bureau	Bu., Bur.
adverb	adv.	bushel	bu
affidavit	afft.	by way of	via
against	vs.		
agent	agt.	capital	cap.
agreement	agmt.	Captain	Capt.
also known as	a.k.a.	carbon copy	cc, c.c.
America, American	Am.	care of	c/o
American Automobile		carton	ctn.
Association	AAA	catalog	cat.
American Bankers Association	ABA	cathode-ray tube	CRT
amount	amt.	Centigrade	C
and	&	cents	cts.
and others	et al.	certificate	cert., ct., ctf.
and the following pages	ff.	certificate of deposit	CD
anno Domini		Certified Administrative Manager	CAM
(in the year of our Lord)	A.D.	Certified Financial Planner	CFP
anonymous	anon.	Certified Professional Secretary	CPS
apartment	apt.	Certified Public Accountant	CPA, C.P.A.
appendix	app.	chapter	chap., ch., C.
as soon as possible	ASAP	charge	chg.
Associated Press	AP	chief executive officer	CEO
association	assn.	Christmas	Xmas
assorted	astd.	circa (about)	ca.
at	@	collect, or cash, on delivery	c.o.d., COD
Attention	Attn., Atten.	Colonel	Col.
Attorney	Atty.	commerce	com.
Avenue	Av., Ave.	commission	comm.
average	av., avg.	Company	Co.
		compare	cf.
Bachelor of Arts	A.B., B.A.	continued	contd., cont., con.
Bachelor of Laws	LL.B.	copyright	©
Bachelor of Science	B.S.	Corporation	Corp.
balance	bal.	correct	OK
banking	bkg.	cost, insurance and freight	c.i.f., CIF
barrel	bbl	cost-of-living adjustment	COLA
before Christ	B.C.	credit	cr.

creditor	cr.	figure	fig.
		first	1st (no period)
debit	dr.	first class	A-1
degree	deg., °	footnote	fn., ftnt.
department	dept.	for example	e.g.
destination	dstn.	for your information	FYI
direct current	d.c., dc	Fort	Ft.
Director	Dir.	forward	fwd.
discount	dis.	fourth	4th (no period)
distributor, distribution	distr.	free alongside ship	f.a.s., FAS
division	div.	free on board	f.o.b., FOB
Doctor	Dr.	freight	frt.
Doctor of Dental Surgery	D.D.S.	from	fr., fm.
Doctor of Divinity	D.D.doz.		
Doctor of Laws	LL.D.	gallon	gal
Doctor of Medicine	M.D.	General	Gen.
Doctor of Philosophy	Ph.D.	General Headquarters	GHQ
doing business as	d.b.a.	general mortgage	gm
dollars	dls., dols.	good	gds.
dozen	doz.	government	govt.
		Governor	Gov.
each	ea.	gram	g
Editor	Ed.	gross	gr.
electric	elec.	gross national product	GNP
employment	empl.	guaranteed	gtd.
enclosure	enc., encl.		
end of month	e.o.m., EOM	half	hf.
envelope	env.	hardware	hdw.
Environmental Protection Agency	EPA	Headquarters	HQ, Hq.
equal	eq.	health maintenance organization	HMO
Equal Employment Opportunity		height	ht.
Commission	EEOC	Highway	Hwy., Hy.
errors and omissions expected	E. & O.E.	history	hist.
Esquire	Esq.	Honorable	Hon.
established	est.	horsepower	hp., hp, HP
estimated time of arrival	ETA	hospital	hosp.
et cetera, and so forth	etc.	hundred	C
example	ex.	hundredweight	cwt.
exchange	exc., exch.		
Executive	Exec.	I owe you	IOU
expense, express	exp.	illustration, illustrated	ill., illus.
extension	ext.	in the place cited	loc. cit.
		in the same place	ib., ibid.
Fahrenheit	F, Fahr.	in the work cited	op. cit.
Federal	Fed.	inches	in., in
Federal Bureau of Investigation	FBI	inclusive	incl.
Federal Communications		Incorporated	Inc.
Commission	FCC	Individual Retirement Account	IRA
Federal Deposit Insurance		industrial, independent	ind.
Corporation	FDIC	inferior	inf.
Federal Insurance Contributions		in regard to	re
Act	FICA	insurance	ins.
Federal Reserve Board	FRB	intelligence quotient	IQ, I.Q.
Federal Trade Commission	FTC	interest	int.
feminine	fem., f.	International	Intl., Int.

International Business Machines	IBM		medium	med.
Interstate Commerce Commission	ICC		memorandum	memo
inventory	invt.		merchandise	mdse.
invoice, investment	inv.		Mesdames	Mmes.
Invoice Book	I.B.		Messieurs	Messrs., MM.
Island, Isle	I.		metropolitan	met.
italic	ital.		midnight	mid., mdnt.
			miscellaneous	misc.
joint	jt.		Miss or Mrs.	Ms.
Journal	J., Jr., Jour.		Mister	Mr.
Junior	Jr.		Mistress	Mrs.
Justice of the Peace	J.P.		money order	m.o.
			Monsieur	M.
karat	k., kt.		mortgage	mtg.
			mount	Mt.
laboratory	lab.		municipal	mun.
language	lang.			
large	la.,lg.		namely	viz.
latitude	lat.		namely or to wit	sc., scil., sct.
ledger folio	L.F.		national	Nat., Natl.
Legislature	Leg.		net in 30 days	n/30
less-than-carload lot	l.c.l., LCL		no good	n.g.
let it stand	stet		not available, not applicable	NA
letter	ltr.		not sufficient funds	N.S.F.
letter of credit	L.C.		Notary Public	N.P.
library	lib.		note well	n.b., N.B.
Lieutenant	Lieut., Lt.		number	no., #
limited	Ltd.			
list price	L.P.		obituary	obit.
liter	L		obsolete	obs.
literature	lit.		Occupational Safety and Health	
location, local	loc.		Administration	OSHA
longitude	long.		opened	opd.
lumber	lbr.		opposite	opp.
			optional	opt.
machine	mch., mach.		ordinance	ord.
Madame	Mme.		organization	org.
Mademoiselle	Mlle.		original	orig.
magazine	mag.		out of stock	OS
mail order, money order	MO			
Major	Maj.		Pacific	Pac.
Manager	Mgr.		package	pkg.
manufacture, manufacturer	mfr.		page	p.
manufactured	mfd.		pages	pp.
manufacturing	mfg.		paid	pd.
manuscript(s)	ms., MS., mss., MSS.		pair	pr.
mark	mk.		paragraph	¶ , par.
market	mkt., mar.		parcel post	PP
masculine	m., mas., masc.		parenthesis	paren., par.
Master of Arts	M.A.		parkway	Pkwy.
Master of Business Administration	M.B.A.		part	pt.
Master of Ceremonies	M.C.		patent	pat.
Master of Science	M.S.		payment	payt.
mathematics	math.		per annum	per an.
maximum	max.		percent	%, pct.

piece	pc.	Secretary	Sec., Secy.
pint	pt	section	sec.
plaintiff	Plf.	Securities and Exchange	
population	pop.	Commission	SEC
port of entry	p.o.e., POE	Senate, Senator	Sen.
post exchange	PX	Senior	Sr.
postmaster	PM.	shipment	shpt.
post office	P.O.	shipping order	SO
postpaid	ppd.	signature	sig.
postscript	PS., PS	signed	/S/
pounds, shillings, pence	£ s. d.	singular	sing.
pound sterling	£	so written, thus	sic
power of attorney	P/A	square	sq
preferred	pfd.	standard	std.
premium	pm., prem.	Street	St.
President	Pres.	subsidiary	subs.
principal	prin.	Superintendent	Supt.
private branch exchange	PBX	supplement	supp.
problem	prob.	syndicate	synd.
Professor	Prof.		
profit and loss	P & L	tablespoon	tbsp., T.
pronoun	pron.	teaspoon	tsp., t.
public, publishing,		telephone	tel.
publisher	pub.	temporarily	pro tem.
purchase order	PO	Territory	Ter.
		that is	i.e.
quality	qly.	the following	seq.
quantity	qty.	the same	id.
quart	qt	thousand	M
quarter, quire	qr.	township	Twp.
question	q.	Treasurer	Treas.
		trial balance	T. B.
railroad	RR.	trust, trustee	tr.
ream, room	rm.		
receipt	rect.	United Nations	U.N., UN
receivable	rec.	United Press International	UPI
received	recd., rcd.	University	Univ.
reference	ref.		
registered	®, rg., reg.	very important person	VIP
Registered Nurse	R.N.	vice president	V.P.
regular	reg.	video display terminal	VDT
Reply, if you please	R.S.V.P.	volume	vol.
report	rept.		
returned	rtd.	warehouse receipt	W.R.
Reverend	Rev.	waybill	WB
revised	rev.	week, work	wk.
right	rt.	weight	wt.
road	rd.	which see	q.v.
Route	Rte., Rt.	which was to be proved	Q.E.D.
rural free delivery	R.F.D.	wholesale	whsle.
rural route	R.R.	Wide-Area Telecommunications	
		Service	WATS
Saint (female)	Ste.		
Savings	Sav.	zero-base budgeting	ZBB
school	sch.		

Dictionary Section

a|bey·ance (ə bā′əns) *n.* ⟦Anglo-Fr *abeiance* < OFr *abeance,* expectation < *a-,* to, at + *bayer,* to gape, wait expectantly: see BAY² ⟧ **1** temporary suspension, as of an activity or function **2** *Law* a state of not having been determined or settled, as of lands the present ownership of which has not been established

ab·hor (ab hôr′, əb-) *vt.* **-horred′, -hor′ring** ⟦ME *abhorren* < L *abhorrere* < *ab-,* away, from + *horrere,* to shudder: see HORRID⟧ to shrink from in disgust or hatred; detest **—SYN.** HATE **—ab·hor′rer** *n.*

ab·hor·rence (-hôr′əns, -här′-) *n.* **1** an abhorring; loathing; detestation **2** something abhorred; something repugnant **—SYN.** AVERSION

ab·hor·rent (-ənt) *adj.* ⟦L *abhorrens,* prp. of *abhorrere,* ABHOR⟧ **1** causing disgust, hatred, etc.; detestable *[an abhorrent crime]* **2** feeling abhorrence **3** opposed or contrary (*to*) *[abhorrent to his principles]* **—SYN.** HATEFUL **—ab·hor′rently adv.**

a|bridge (ə brij′) *vt.* **a|bridged′, a|bridg′ing** ⟦ME *abregen* < OFr *abregier* < LL *abbreviare,* ABBREVIATE⟧ **1** to reduce in scope, extent, etc.; shorten **2** to shorten by using fewer words but keeping the main contents; condense **3** to lessen or curtail (rights, authority, etc.) **4** [Rare] to deprive (*of* rights, privileges, etc.) **—SYN.** SHORTEN **—a|bridg′a|ble** or **a|bridge′a|ble** *adj.* **—a|bridg′er** *n.*

ab·sti·nence (ab′stə nəns) *n.* ⟦ME < OFr < L *abstinentia* < prp. of *abstinere:* see ABSTAIN⟧ **1** the act of voluntarily doing without some or all food, drink, or other pleasures **2** *R.C.Ch.* abstention from flesh meat on certain designated days **—ab′sti·nent** *adj.* **—ab′sti·nently adv.**

ac·cess (ak′ses′) *n.* ⟦ME & OFr *acces* < L *accessus,* pp. of *accedere,* ACCEDE⟧ **1** the act of coming toward or near to; approach **2** a way or means of approaching, getting, using, etc. **3** the right to enter, approach, or use; admittance **4** increase or growth **5** an outburst; paroxysm *[an access of anger]* **—vt.** to gain or have access to; esp., to retrieve data from, or add data to, a database *[branch officials can access the central database]*

ac·cu·mu·late (ə kyōōm′yōō lāt′, -yə-) *vt., vi.* **-lat′ed, -lat′ing** ⟦< L *accumulatus,* pp. of *accumulare* < *ad-,* to + *cumulare,* to heap: see CUMULUS⟧ to pile up, collect, or gather together, esp. over a period of time **—ac·cu′mu·la|ble** (-lə bəl) *adj.*

a|cous·tics (ə kōōs′tiks) *n.pl.* **1** the qualities of a room, theater, etc. that have to do with how clearly sounds can be heard or transmitted in it **2** [*with sing. v.*] the branch of physics dealing with sound, esp. with its transmission

ac·quit·tal (ə kwit′'l) *n.* ⟦ME *aquital* < Anglo-Fr *aquitaille:* see prec.⟧ **1** an acquitting; discharge (of duty, obligation, etc.) **2** *Law* a setting free or being set free by judgment of the court

ac·tu·ary (ak′chōō er′ē) *n., pl.* **-ies** ⟦L *actuarius,* clerk < *actus:* see ACT⟧ a person whose work is to calculate statistically risks, premiums, life expectancies, etc. for insurance

a|cu·men (ə kyōō′mən; *often,* ak′yə-) *n.* ⟦L, a point, sting, mental acuteness < *acuere,* to sharpen < IE base **ak-:* see ACID⟧ keenness and quickness in understanding and dealing with a situation; shrewdness

Ad·dis A|ba·ba (ad′is ab′ə bə) capital of Ethiopia, in the central part; pop. 1,413,000

ad·ja·cent (ə jā′sənt) *adj.* ⟦L *adjacens,* prp. of *adjacere,* to lie near < *ad-,* to + *jacere,* to lie, throw: see JET¹⟧ near or close (*to* something); adjoining **—ad·ja′cently adv.**
SYN.—adjacent things may or may not be in actual contact with each other, but they are not separated by things of the same kind *[adjacent angles, adjacent farmhouses];* that which is **adjoining** something else touches it at some point or along a line *[adjoining rooms];* things are **contiguous** when they touch along the whole or most of one side *[contiguous farms];* **tangent** implies contact at a single, nonintersecting point with a curved line or surface *[a line tangent to a circle];* **neighboring** things lie near to each other *[neighboring villages]*

ad·ver·sary (ad′vər ser′ē) *n., pl.* **-saries** ⟦ME < OFr *adversarie* < L *adversarius* < *adversus,* ADVERSE⟧ a person who opposes or fights against another; opponent; enemy **—SYN.** OPPONENT **—the Adversary** Satan

ae|gis (ē′jis) *n.* ⟦L < Gr *aigis,* shield of Zeus, goatskin < ? *aix* (gen. *aigos*), goat, hence ? orig. the short goatskin cloak of Zeus⟧ **1** *Gr. Myth.* a shield borne by Zeus and, later, by his daughter Athena and occasionally by Apollo **2** a protection **3** sponsorship; auspices

af·fa|ble (af′ə bəl) *adj.* ⟦ME *affabyl* < L *affabilis* < *ad-,* to + *fari,* to speak: see FAME⟧ **1** pleasant and easy to approach or talk to; friendly **2** gentle and kindly *[an affable smile]* **—SYN.** AMIABLE **—af′fa|bil′ity** (-bil ə tē) *n.* **—af′fa|bly adv.**

af·fi·da·vit (af′ə dā′vit; *occas.,* -vid′) *n.* ⟦ML, he has made oath; perf. tense of *affidare:* see AFFIANCE⟧ *Law* a written statement made on oath before a notary public or other person authorized to administer oaths

af·fil·i·ate (ə fil′ē āt′; *for n., usually,* -it) *vt.* **-at′ed, -at′ing** ⟦< ML *affiliatus,* pp. of *affiliare,* to adopt as a son < L *ad-* + *filius,* son⟧ **1** to take in as a member or branch **2** to connect or associate (oneself *with*) **3** to trace the origins or source of; specif., to determine legally the paternity of **—vi.** to associate oneself; join **—n.** an affiliated individual or organization; member **—SYN.** RELATED

af·fix (ə fiks′, a-; *for n.,* af′iks′) *vt.* ⟦< L *affixus,* pp. of *affigere,* to fasten to < *ad-,* to + *figere,* FIX⟧ **1** to fasten; attach *[to affix a label to a bottle]* **2** to add at the end; append **—n.** ⟦Fr *affixe* < L *affixus:* see the *v.*⟧ **1** a thing affixed **2** *Linguis.* a prefix, suffix, or infix **—af·fix|al** (af′iks əl) *adj.*

af·flu·ent (-ənt) *adj.* ⟦ME < L *affluens,* prp. of *affluere:* see prec.⟧ **1** flowing freely **2** plentiful; abundant **3** wealthy; prosperous; rich *[the affluent society]* **—n.** **1** a tributary stream: opposed to EFFLUENT **2** an affluent person **—SYN.** RICH **—af′flu·ently adv.**

ag·gre·gate (ag′rə git, ag′rə-; *for v.,* -gāt′) *adj.* ⟦L *aggregatus,* pp. of *aggregare,* to lead to a flock, add to < *ad-,* to + *gregare,* to herd < *grex* (gen. *gregis*), a herd⟧ **1** gathered into, or considered as, a whole; total *[the aggregate number of unemployed]* **2** *Bot. a)* massed into a dense head or cluster, as a flower *b)* formed of closely clustered carpels, as the raspberry **3** *Geol.* made up of a mixture of mineral fragments, crystals, or similar materials *[an aggregate rock]* **—n.** **1** a group or mass of distinct things gathered into, or considered as, a total or whole **2** the sand or pebbles added to cement in making concrete or mortar **3** an aggregate rock **—vt.** **-gat′ed, -gat′ing** **1** to gather into a whole or mass **2** to amount to; total **—SYN.** SUM **—in the aggregate** taken all together **—ag′gre·gate|ly adv.**

ag·grieve (ə grēv′) *vt.* **-grieved′, -griev′ing** ⟦ME *agreven* < OFr *agrever,* to aggravate < L *aggravare,* AGGRAVATE⟧ **1** to cause grief or injury to; offend **2** to injure in one's legal rights **—SYN.** WRONG

al|ien (āl′yən, āl′ē ən) *adj.* ⟦ME & OFr < L *alienus* < *alius,* other: see ELSE⟧ **1** belonging to another country or people; foreign **2** strange; not natural *[cruel words alien to his lips]* **3** opposed or repugnant *[beliefs alien to one's religion]* **4** of aliens **—n.** **1** a foreigner **2** a foreign-born resident in a country who has not become a naturalized citizen **3** an outsider **4** a hypothetical being in or from outer space, as in science fiction, that may visit or invade the earth **—vt.** ⟦ME *alienen* < OFr *aliener* < L *alienare*⟧ to transfer (land, property, etc.)
SYN.—alien is applied to a resident who bears political allegiance to another country; **foreigner,** to a visitor or resident from another country, esp. one with a different language, cultural pattern, etc.; **stranger,** to a person from another region who is unacquainted with local people, customs, etc.; **immigrant,** to a person who comes to another country to settle; **émigré,** to a citizen of one country who has left it to take political refuge in another See also EXTRINSIC **—ANT.** citizen, subject, national

a|lign (ə lin′) *vt.* ⟦Fr *aligner* < *a-,* to + *ligner* < *ligne,* LINE¹⟧ **1** to bring into a straight line; adjust by line **2** to bring (parts or components, as the wheels of a car) into proper coordination **3** to bring into agreement, close cooperation, etc. *[he aligned himself with the liberals]* **—vi.** to come or fall into line; line up

al·lege (ə lej′) *vt.* **-leged′, -leg′ing** ⟦ME *aleggen,* to produce as evidence; form < OFr *esligier* < VL **exlitigare* < L *ex-,* out of + *litigare* (see LITIGATE); meaning infl. by OFr *alleguer,* declare on oath < L *allegare,* to send, mention, adduce < *ad-,* to + *legare,* to send: see LEGATE⟧ **1** to assert positively, or before; affirm; esp., to assert without proof **2** to offer as a plea, excuse, etc. *[in his defense he alleged temporary insanity]* **3** [Archaic] to cite as an authority (*for* or *against*) **—al·lege′a|ble adj.**

al·le·vi·ate (ə lē′vē āt′) *vt.* **-at′ed, -at′ing** ⟦ME *alleviaten* < LL *alleviatus,* pp. of *alleviare,* for L *allevare* < *ad-,* to + *levis,* LIGHT²⟧ **1** to make less hard to bear; lighten or relieve (pain, suffering, etc.) **2** to reduce or decrease *[to alleviate poverty]* **—SYN.** RELIEVE **—al·le′vi|a·tor** *n.* **—al·le′vi|a·tive** or **al·le′vi|a·to′ry** (-ə tôr′ē) *adj.*

al·lo·cate (al′ō kāt′, al′ə-) *vt.* **-cat′ed, -cat′ing** ⟦< ML *allocatus,* pp. of *allocare* < L *ad-,* to + *locare,* to place < *locus:* see LOCUS⟧ **1** to set apart for a specific purpose *[to allocate funds for housing]* **2** to distribute in shares or according to a plan; allot **3** to fix the location of; locate **—SYN.** ALLOT **—al·lo·ca|ble** (al′ə kə bəl) or **al′lo·cat′·a|ble** *adj.*

a|me·na|ble (ə mē′nə bəl, -men′ə-) *adj.* ⟦Anglo-Fr < OFr *amener,* to bring about, lead in < *a-,* to + *mener,* to lead < L *minare,* to drive (animals) < *minari,* to threaten: see MENACE⟧ **1** responsible or answerable **2** able to be controlled or influenced; responsive; submissive *[a person amenable to suggestion; an illness amenable to treatment]* **3** that can be tested by (with *to*) *[amenable to the laws of physics]* **—SYN.** OBEDIENT **—a|me′na|bil′ity** (-bil′ə tē) *n.* **—a|me′na|bly adv.**

am·i·ca·ble (am′i kə bəl) *adj.* ⟦LL *amicabilis*: see AMIABLE⟧ friendly in feeling; showing good will; peaceable /an *amicable* discussion/ — **am′i·ca·bil′i·ty** (-bil′ə tē) *n.* —**am′i·ca·bly** *adv.*

am·or·tize (am′ər tiz′, ə môr′-) *vt.* **-tized′, -tiz′ing** ⟦ME *amortisen* < extended stem of OFr *amortir*, to extinguish, sell in mortmain (< ML *amortire*); or < ML *amortizare*; both ML forms < L *ad-*, to + *mors*, death: see MORTAL⟧ **1** to put money aside at intervals, as in a sinking fund, for gradual payment of (a debt, etc.) either at or before maturity **2** *Accounting* to write off (expenditures) by prorating over a fixed period **3** *Law* to reduce, transfer, or sell (property) in mortmain —**am′or·tiz′a·ble** *adj.*

am·pli·fi·er (am′plə fī′ər) *n.* **1** a person or thing that amplifies **2** *Electronics* a device, esp. one with electron tubes or semiconductors, used to increase the strength of an electric signal

an·nals (an′əlz) *n.pl.* ⟦L *annalis*, pl. *annales* < *annus*, year: see ANNUAL⟧ **1** a written account of events year by year in chronological order **2** historical records or chronicles; history **3** any journal containing reports of discoveries in some field, meetings of a society, etc.

an·nu·i·ty (ə nō̄o′ə tē, -nyō̄o′-) *n., pl.* **-ties** ⟦ME & OFr *annuite* < ML *annuitas* < L *annuus*, annual < *annus*: see ANNUAL⟧ **1** a payment of a fixed sum of money at regular intervals of time, esp. yearly **2** an investment yielding periodic payments during the annuitant's lifetime, for a stated number of years, or in perpetuity

an·nul (ə nul′) *vt.* **-nulled′, -nul′ling** ⟦ME *annullen* < OFr *anuller* < LL(Ec) *annullare*, to bring to nothing < L *ad-*, to + *nullum*, nothing, neut. of *nullus*: see NULL⟧ **1** to do away with; put an end to **2** to make no longer binding under the law; invalidate; cancel —**SYN.** ABOLISH

a·non (ə nän′) *adv.* ⟦ME < OE *on an* acc., into one, together, straightway⟧ **1** [Archaic] immediately; at once **2** *a)* soon; shortly *b)* at another time: now nearly archaic or a self-conscious usage — **ever and anon** now and then

Anon or **anon** *abbrev.* anonymous

an·thol·o·gy (an thäl′ə jē) *n., pl.* **-gies** ⟦Gr *anthologia*, a garland, collection of short poems < *anthologos*, gathering flowers < *anthos* (see ANTHO-) + *legein*, to gather (see LOGIC)⟧ a collection of poems, stories, songs, excerpts, etc., chosen by the compiler —**an·tho·log·i·cal** (an′thə läj′i kəl) *adj.*

an·tith·e·sis (an tith′ə sis) *n., pl.* **-ses** (-sēz′) ⟦ME *antitesis* < LL *antithesis* < Gr < *antithenai* < *anti-*, against + *tithenai*, to place: see DO¹⟧ **1** a contrast or opposition of thoughts, usually in two phrases, clauses, or sentences (Ex.: you are going; I am staying) **2** the second part of such an expression **3** a contrast or opposition: see also DIALECTIC (sense 3) **4** the exact opposite /joy is the *antithesis* of sorrow/

ap·prais·al (ə prāz′əl) *n.* **1** an appraising or being appraised **2** an appraised value or price; esp., an expert valuation for taxation, tariff duty, sale, etc.; estimate Also **ap·praise′ment**

ap·prise or **ap·prize** (ə prīz′) *vt.* **-prised′** or **-prized′, -pris′ing** or **-priz′ing** ⟦Fr *appris*, pp. of *apprendre*, to teach, inform < L *apprehendere*, APPREHEND⟧ to inform or notify —**SYN.** NOTIFY

ar·rears (ə rirz′) *n.pl.* ⟦ME *arrers* < *arrere* < OFr *ariere* < VL *aretro* < L *ad-*, to + *retro*, behind⟧ **1** unpaid and overdue debts **2** any obligation not met on time; unfinished business, work, etc. —**in arrears** (or **arrear**) behind in paying a debt, doing one's work, etc.

as·sail (ə sāl′) *vt.* ⟦ME *assailen* < OFr *asaillir* < VL *assalire*, for L *assilire*, to leap on < *ad-*, to + *salire*, to leap: see SALIENT⟧ **1** to attack physically and violently; assault **2** to attack with arguments, questions, doubts, etc. **3** to begin working on (a task, problem, etc.) with vigor and determination **4** to have a forceful effect on /a loud noise *assailed* their ears/ —**SYN.** ATTACK —**as·sail′a·ble** *adj.* —**as·sail′er** *n.* —**as·sail′ment** *n.*

as·sess·ment (-mənt) *n.* **1** the act of assessing **2** an amount assessed See also SPECIAL ASSESSMENT

as·sim·i·late (ə sim′ə lāt′) *vt.* **-lat′ed, -lat′ing** ⟦ME *assimilaten* < L *assimilatus*, pp. of *assimilare* < *ad-*, to + *similare*, make similar < *similis*, like: see SAME⟧ **1** to change (food) into a form that can be taken up by, and made part of, the body tissues; absorb into the body **2** to absorb and incorporate into one's thinking **3** to absorb (groups of different cultures) into the main cultural body **4** to make like or alike; cause to resemble: with *to* **5** [Now Rare] to compare or liken **6** *Linguis.* to cause to undergo assimilation —*vi.* **1** to become like or alike **2** to be absorbed and incorporated **3** *Linguis.* to undergo assimilation —**as·sim′i·la·ble** (-ə lə bəl) *adj.*

au·di·tor (ô′dit ər) *n.* ⟦ME < L < *audire*: see AUDIENCE⟧ **1** a hearer or listener **2** a person who is authorized to audit accounts ☆**3** a person who audits classes

ba·cil·lus (bə sil′əs) *n., pl.* **-cil′li** (-ī) ⟦ModL < LL, little rod < L *bacillum*, dim. of *baculus*, var. of *baculum*, a stick < IE base *bak-*, staff > PEG, Gr *baktron*⟧ **1** any of a genus (*Bacillus*) of rod-shaped bacteria that occur in chains, produce spores, and are active only in the presence of oxygen **2** any rod-shaped bacterium: distinguished from COCCUS, SPIRILLUM **3** [*usually pl.*] loosely, any of the bacteria, esp. those causing disease

bac·te·ri·a (bak tir′ē ə) *n.pl., sing.* **-ri·um** (-əm) ⟦ModL, pl. of *bacterium* < Gr *baktērion*, dim. of *baktron*, a staff: see BACILLUS⟧ any of a division (Bacteria) of typically one-celled microorganisms which have no chlorophyll, multiply by simple division, and can be seen only with a microscope: they occur in three main forms, spherical (cocci), rod-shaped (bacilli), and spiral (spirilla); some bacteria cause diseases such as pneumonia, tuberculosis, and anthrax, and others are necessary for fermentation, nitrogen fixation, etc. —**bac·te′ri·al** *adj.* —**bac·te′ri·al·ly** *adv.*

bank·rupt (baŋk′rupt′, -rəpt) *n.* ⟦Fr *banqueroute* < It *banca rotta* < *banca*, bench (see BANK¹) + *rotta*, broken < L *rupta*, fem. pp. of *rumpere*, to break: see RUPTURE⟧ **1** a person legally declared unable to pay his or her debts: the property of a bankrupt is administered for the benefit of his or her creditors and divided among them **2** anyone unable to pay his or her debts **3** a person who lacks a certain quality or has failed completely in some way /a political *bankrupt*/ —*adj.* **1** that is a bankrupt; insolvent **2** lacking in some quality; destitute /morally *bankrupt*/ **3** that has failed completely /a *bankrupt* foreign policy/ —*vt.* to cause to become bankrupt

bank·rupt·cy (-rupt′sē, -rəp sē) *n., pl.* **-cies** **1** the state or an instance of being bankrupt **2** complete failure; ruin

bel·lig·er·ent (bə lij′ər ənt) *adj.* ⟦L *belligerans*, prp. of *belligerare*, to wage war < *bellum*, war (see BELLICOSE) + *gerere*, to carry on⟧ **1** at war; designating or of a state recognized under international law as being engaged in a war **2** of war; of fighting **3** seeking war; warlike **4** showing a readiness to fight or quarrel /a *belligerent* gesture or tone/ —*n.* a belligerent person, group, or nation —**bel·lig′er·ent·ly** *adv.*

SYN.—**belligerent** implies a taking part in war or fighting or in actions that are likely to provoke fighting /*belligerent* nations/; **bellicose** implies a warlike or hostile nature, suggesting a readiness to fight /a *bellicose* mood/; **pugnacious** and **quarrelsome** both connote aggressiveness and a willingness to initiate a fight, but **quarrelsome** more often suggests pettiness and eagerness to fight for little or no reason; **contentious** suggests an inclination to argue or quarrel, usually with annoying persistence —**ANT.** peaceful, friendly

ben·e·fi·cial (ben′ə fish′əl) *adj.* ⟦ME < OFr < LL *beneficialis* < L *benefacere*: see BENEFACTION⟧ **1** producing benefits; advantageous; favorable **2** receiving benefit **3** *Law* for one's own benefit /*beneficial* interest/ —**ben·e·fi′cial·ly** *adv.*

be·nev·o·lent (-lənt) *adj.* ⟦ME & OFr < L *benevolens* < *bene*, well + *volens*, prp. of *velle*, to wish: see WILL¹⟧ **1** doing or inclined to do good; kindly; charitable **2** characterized by or resulting from benevolence —**SYN.** KIND —**be·nev′o·lent·ly** *adv.*

be·nign (bi nīn′) *adj.* ⟦ME & OFr *benigne* < L *benignus*, good, lit., well-born < *bene*, well (cf. sense development of GENTLE)⟧ **1** good-natured; kindly **2** favorable; beneficial **3** *Med.* doing little or no harm; not malignant —**SYN.** KIND —**be·nign′ly** *adv.*

bi·en·ni·al (bī en′ē əl) *adj.* ⟦< L *biennium*, period of two years < *bi-*, BI-¹ + *annus*, year + -AL⟧ **1** happening every two years **2** lasting or living two years —*n.* **1** a biennial event or occurrence **2** *Bot.* a plant that lasts two years, usually producing flowers and seed the second year —**bi·en′ni·al·ly** *adv.*

bur·sar (bur′sər) *n.* ⟦ML *bursarius*, treasurer < *bursa*: see PURSE⟧ **1** a treasurer, as of a college or similar institution **2** in Scotland, a university student who has a scholarship

busi·ness (biz′niz, -nis) *n.* ⟦ME *bisinesse* < OE *bisignes*: see BUSY & -NESS⟧ **1** one's work, occupation, or profession **2** a special task, duty, or function **3** rightful concern or responsibility /no one's *business* but his own/ **4** a matter, affair, activity, etc. /the *business* of packing for a trip/ **5** the buying and selling of commodities and services; commerce; trade **6** a commercial or industrial establishment; store, factory, etc. **7** the trade or patronage of customers **8** commercial practice or policy **9** a bit of action in a drama, as pouring a drink, intended to establish character, take up a pause in dialogue, etc. —*adj.* **1** of or for business **2** *Bridge* designating a double intended to penalize one's opponents: cf. TAKEOUT (*adj.* 2) — **business is business** sentiment, friendship, etc. cannot be allowed to interfere with profit making —**do business with 1** to engage in commerce with **2** to have dealings with —☆**give** (or **get**) **the business** [Slang] to subject (or be subjected) to rough treatment, practical joking, etc. —**mean business** [Colloq.] to be in earnest

SYN.—**business**, in this comparison, refers generally to the buying and selling of commodities and services and connotes a profit motive; **commerce** and **trade** both refer to the distribution or exchange of commodities, esp. as this involves their transportation, but **commerce** generally implies such activity on a large scale between cities, countries, etc.; **industry** refers chiefly to the large-scale manufacture of commodities

ca·reer (kə rir′) *n.* ⟦Fr *carrière*, road, racecourse < It *carriera* < VL *carraria (via)*, carriage (road) < L *carrus*, CAR⟧ **1** orig., a racing course **2** a swift course, as of the sun through the sky **3** one's progress through life or in a particular vocation **4** a profession or occupation which one trains for and pursues as a lifework —☆*adj.* pursuing a normally temporary activity as a lifework *[a career soldier]* —*vi.* to move at full speed; rush wildly —**in full career** at full speed

car·pe di·em (kär′pē dī′em) ⟦L, seize the day⟧ make the most of present opportunities

cen·sure (sen′shər) *n.* ⟦L *censura* < *censor*, CENSOR⟧ **1** a condemning as wrong; strong disapproval **2** a judgment or resolution condemning a person for misconduct; specif., an official expression of disapproval passed by a legislature —*vt.* **-sured, -sur·ing** to express strong disapproval of; condemn as wrong —**SYN.** CRITICIZE —**cen′sur·er** *n.*

cen·sus (sen′səs) *n.* ⟦L, orig., pp. of *censere*, to assess: see CENSOR⟧ **1** in ancient Rome, the act of counting the people and evaluating their property for taxation **2** an official, usually periodic, count of population and recording of economic status, age, sex, etc.

cen·ten·ni·al (sen ten′ē əl, -yəl) *adj.* ⟦< L *centum*, HUNDRED + *annus*, year (see ANNUAL) + -AL⟧ **1** of 100 years **2** happening once in 100 years **3** lasting 100 years **4** of a 100th anniversary —*n.* a 100th anniversary or its commemoration —**cen·ten′ni·al·ly** *adv.*

chas·tise (chas tīz′, chas′tīz′) *vt.* **-tised′, -tis′ing** ⟦ME *chastisen* < extended stem of OFr *chastier*: see prec.⟧ **1** to punish, esp. by beating **2** to scold or condemn sharply **3** [Archaic] to chasten —**SYN.** PUNISH —**chas·tise·ment** (chas′tīz mənt; chas tīz′-) *n.* —**chas·tis′er** *n.*

chau·vin·ism (shō′vin iz′əm) *n.* ⟦Fr *chauvinisme*, after N. *Chauvin*, soldier of Napoleon I, notorious for his bellicose attachment to the lost imperial cause⟧ **1** militant, unreasoning, and boastful devotion to one's country; fanatic patriotism; jingoism **2** unreasoning devotion to one's race, sex, etc. with contempt for other races, the opposite sex, etc. *[male chauvinism]* —**chau′vin·ist** *n., adj.* —**chau′vin·is′tic** *adj.* —**chau·vin·is′ti·cal·ly** *adv.*

☆**civ·ics** (siv′iks) *n.pl.* [*with sing. v.*] the branch of political science that deals with civic affairs and the duties and rights of citizenship

CO·BOL (kō′bôl′) *n.* ⟦*co(mmon) b(usiness-)o(riented) l(anguage)*⟧ a computer language employing English words, used in business applications Also written **Cobol**

co·in·ci·den·tal (kō in′sə dent′'l) *adj.* characterized by coincidence —**co·in′ci·den′tal·ly** *adv.*

col·lat·er·al (kə lat′ər əl) *adj.* ⟦ME < ML *collateralis* < L *com-*, together + *lateralis*, LATERAL⟧ **1** side by side; parallel **2** parallel in time, rank, importance, etc.; corresponding **3** accompanying or existing in a subordinate, corroborative, or indirect relationship **4** descended from the same ancestors but in a different line *[a cousin is a collateral relative]* **5** *a*) designating or of security given as a pledge for the fulfillment of an obligation *b*) secured or guaranteed by property, as stocks, bonds, etc. *[a collateral loan]* —*n.* **1** a collateral relative ☆**2** anything, such as stocks or bonds, that insures or guarantees the discharge of an obligation —**col·lat′er·al·ly** *adv.*

col·league (käl′ēg′) *n.* ⟦Fr *collègue* < L *collega*, one chosen along with another < *com-*, with + *legare*, to appoint as deputy: see LEGATE⟧ a fellow worker in the same profession; associate —**SYN.** ASSOCIATE

com·mence (kə mens′) *vi., vt.* **-menced′, -menc′ing** ⟦ME *commencen* < OFr *comencier* < VL **cominitiare*, orig., to initiate as priest, consecrate < L *com-*, together + *initiare*, to INITIATE⟧ to begin; start; originate —**SYN.** BEGIN —**com·menc′er** *n.*

com·pen·sate (käm′pən sāt′) *vt.* **-sat′ed, -sat′ing** ⟦< L *compensatus*, pp. of *compensare*, to weigh one thing against another < *com-*, with + *pensare*, freq. of *pendere*, to weigh: see PENDANT⟧ **1** to make up for; be a counterbalance to in weight, force, etc. **2** to make equivalent or suitable return to; recompense; pay *[to compensate an owner for land taken by a city]* **3** *Mech.* to counteract or make allowance for (a variation) —*vi.* **1** to make or serve as compensation or amends *(for)* **2** *Psychol.* to engage in compensation —**SYN.** PAY[1] —**com·pen·sa·tive** (kəm pen′sə tiv, käm′pən sāt′iv) *adj.* —**com·pen·sa·to·ry** (kəm pen′sə tôr′ē) *adj.*

com·pli·ant (-ənt) *adj.* complying or tending to comply; yielding; submissive —**SYN.** OBEDIENT —**com·pli′ant·ly** *adv.*

comp·trol·ler (kən trō′lər) *n.* ⟦altered (infl. by Fr *compte*, an account) < CONTROLLER⟧ CONTROLLER (sense 1, esp. in government usage) —**comp·trol′ler·ship** *n.*

con·cede (kən sēd′) *vt.* **-ced′ed, -ced′ing** ⟦L *concedere* < *com-*, with + *cedere*, to go, grant, CEDE⟧ **1** to admit as true or valid; acknowledge *[to concede a point in argument]* **2** to admit as certain or proper *[to concede victory to an opponent]* **3** to grant as a right or privilege —*vi.* **1** to make a concession ☆**2** to acknowledge defeat in an election —**con·ced′er** *n.*

con·coct (kən käkt′) *vt.* ⟦< L *concoctus*, pp. of *concoquere*, to boil together, prepare < *com-*, together + *coquere*, COOK⟧ **1** to make by combining various ingredients; compound **2** to devise, invent, or plan —**con·coct′er** *n.* —**con·coc′tion** *n.* —**con·coc′tive** *adj.*

con·di·tion·al (kən dish′ən əl) *adj.* **1** *a*) containing, implying, or dependent on a condition or conditions; qualified; not absolute *[a conditional award]* *b*) *Logic* designating or including a compound proposition that has the form "if p, then q," in which *p* and *q* are two different propositions **2** expressing a condition *[a conditional clause]* —*n. Gram.* a word, clause, mood, or tense expressing a condition —**con·di′tion·al′i·ty** (-al′ə tē) *n.* —**con·di′tion·al·ly** *adv.*

con·do·lence (kən dō′ləns) *n.* ⟦< LL(Ec) *condolens*: see prec.⟧ [*often pl.*] expression of sympathy with another in grief Also **con·dole′ment** —**SYN.** PITY

con·stit·u·ent (kən stich′ōō ənt) *adj.* ⟦< L *constituens*, prp. of *constituere*: see fol.⟧ **1** necessary in forming or making up a whole; component *[a constituent part]* **2** that can or does appoint or vote for a representative **3** authorized to make or revise a political constitution or establish a government *[a constituent assembly]* —*n.* **1** a person who appoints another to act as agent or representative **2** a member of a constituency, esp. any of the voters represented by a particular official **3** a necessary part or element; component **4** an element of a word or construction: in "they painted signs" the main elements *they* and *painted signs* are called *immediate constituents*; the further morphologically indivisible elements *they, paint, -ed, sign,* and *-s* are called *ultimate constituents* —**SYN.** ELEMENT —**con·stit′u·ent·ly** *adv.*

con·triv·ance (kən trī′vəns) *n.* **1** the act, way, or power of contriving **2** something contrived, as an invention, mechanical device, or ingenious plan

con·trive (kən trīv′) *vt.* **-trived′, -triv′ing** ⟦ME *contreven* < OFr *controver*, to find out, contrive, imagine < VL *contropare*, to compare < *com*, COM- + *tropus*, TROPE⟧ **1** to think up; devise; scheme; plan *[to contrive a way to help]* **2** to construct skillfully or ingeniously; fabricate **3** to bring about, as by a scheme; manage *[he contrived to get in]* **4** to scheme for evil purposes —*vi.* to form plans; scheme —**con·triv′a·ble** *adj.* —**con·triv′er** *n.*

con·vey (kən vā′) *vt.* ⟦ME *conveien* < Anglo-Fr *conveier* (OFr *convoier*), to escort, convoy < VL **conviare*, to accompany on the way < L *com-*, together + *via*, way: see VIA⟧ **1** to take from one place to another; transport; carry *[a chimney conveys smoke to the outside]* **2** to serve as a channel or medium for; transmit **3** to make known; communicate in words, actions, appearance, etc. **4** to transfer, as property or title to property, from one person to another **5** [Obs.] *a*) to take away secretly *b*) to steal —**SYN.** CARRY —**con·vey′a·ble** *adj.*

con·vey·ance (kən vā′əns) *n.* ⟦ME *conveiaunce*⟧ **1** the act of conveying **2** a means of conveying; conveying device, esp. a vehicle **3** *a*) the transfer of the ownership of real property from one person to another *b*) the document by which this is effected; deed

cor·pu·lence (kôr′pyōō ləns, -pyə-) *n.* ⟦< L *corpulentia*: see fol.⟧ fatness or stoutness of body; obesity Also **cor′pu·len·cy**

cor·rob·o·rate (kə räb′ə rāt′) *vt.* **-rat′ed, -rat′ing** ⟦< L *corroboratus*, pp. of *corroborare*, to strengthen < *com-*, intens. + *roborare* < *robur*, strength: see ROBUST⟧ **1** orig., to strengthen **2** to make more certain the validity of; confirm; bolster; support *[evidence to corroborate his testimony]* —**SYN.** CONFIRM —**cor·rob′o·ra′tion** *n.* —**cor·rob′o·ra′tor** *n.*

coun·ter·feit (kount′ər fit′) *adj.* ⟦ME *countrefete* < OFr *contrefait*, pp. of *contrefaire*, to make in opposition, imitate < *contre-*, counter- + *faire* < L *facere*, to make, DO[1]⟧ **1** made in imitation of something genuine so as to deceive or defraud; forged *[counterfeit money]* **2** pretended; sham; feigned *[counterfeit sorrow]* —*n.* **1** *a*) an imitation made to deceive; forgery *b*) something that so closely resembles something else as to mislead **2** [Obs.] an impostor; cheat —*vt., vi.* **1** to make an imitation of (money, pictures, etc.), usually in order to deceive or defraud **2** to pretend; feign **3** to resemble (something) closely —**SYN.** FALSE, ARTIFICIAL —**coun′ter·feit′er** *n.*

coun·ter·sign (kount'ər sin'; *for v., also* kount'ər sin') *n.* **1** a signature added to a document previously signed by another, for authentication or confirmation **2** a secret sign or signal in answer to another, as in a secret society **3** *Mil.* a secret word or signal which must be given to a guard or sentry by someone wishing to pass; password —*vt.* to authenticate (a previously signed document) by adding one's own signature —**coun'ter·sig'na·ture** (-sig'nə chər) *n.*

-cra|cy (krə sē) [Fr *-cracie* < ML *-cratia* < Gr *-kratia*, rule < *kratos*, rule, strength: see HARD] *combining form* a (specified) type of government; rule by [*autocracy, theocracy*]

cre·den·tial (kri den'shəl) *adj.* [ME *credencial* < ML *credentialis*: see CREDENCE] [Rare] entitling to credit, confidence, etc.; accrediting —*n.* **1** that which entitles to credit, confidence, etc. **2** [*usually pl.*] a letter or certificate given to a person to show that he has a right to confidence or to the exercise of a certain position or authority; specif., LETTERS OF CREDENCE —*vt.* **-tialed, -tial·ing** to furnish with credentials

cred·i·ble (kred'ə bəl) *adj.* [ME < L *credibilis* < *credere*: see CREED] that can be believed; believable; reliable —*SYN.* PLAUSIBLE —**cred'·i|bil'i|ty** or **cred'i·ble·ness** *n.* —**cred'i|bly** *adv.*

cred|it (kred'it) *n.* [Fr *crédit* < It *credito* < L *creditus*, pp. of *credere*: see CREED] **1** belief or trust; confidence; faith **2** [Rare] the quality of being credible or trustworthy **3** *a)* the favorable estimate of a person's character; reputation; good name *b)* one's influence based on one's reputation **4** praise or approval to which one is entitled; commendation [*to deserve credit* for trying] **5** a person or thing bringing approval or honor [*a credit* to the team] **6** *a)* acknowledgment of work done or assistance given *b)* [*pl.*] a list of such acknowledgments in a motion picture, television program, book, etc. **7** *a)* the amount of money remaining in a bank account, etc. *b)* a sum of money made available by a bank, on which a specified person or firm may draw *c)* such sums collectively **8** *Accounting a)* the acknowledgment of payment on a debt by entry of the amount in an account *b)* the right-hand side of an account, where such amounts are entered *c)* an entry on this side *d)* the sum of such entries *e)* sum deducted (from an amount owed) or added (as to a bank account) in making an adjustment **9** *Business a)* trust in one's integrity in money matters and one's ability to meet payments when due *b)* one's financial reputation or status *c)* the time allowed for payment ☆**10** *Educ. a)* the certification of a student's successful completion of a unit or course of study *b)* a unit of work so certified —*vt.* **1** to believe in the truth, reliability, etc. of; trust **2** to give credit to or deserved commendation for **3** to give credit in a bank account, charge account, etc. **4** [Rare] to bring honor to **5** *Accounting* to enter on the credit side ☆**6** *Educ.* to enter a credit or credits on the record of (a student) —*SYN.* ASCRIBE —**credit someone with 1** to believe that someone has or is responsible for; ascribe to one —**do credit to** to bring approval or honor to —**give credit to 1** to have confidence or trust in; believe **2** to commend —**give one credit for 1** to commend one for **2** to believe or recognize that one has —**on credit** with the agreement that payment will be made at a future date —**to one's credit** bringing approval or honor to one

cred·i·tor (kred'it ər) *n.* [ME *creditour* < L *creditor*: see CREDIT] a person who extends credit or to whom money is owed

deb|it (deb'it) *n.* [LME & OFr *debite* < L *debitum*, what is owing; debt; neut. pp. of *debere*: see DEBT] **1** *Accounting a)* the left-hand side of an account, where entries are made showing an increase in assets, a decrease in liabilities, etc. *b)* such an entry *c)* the sum of such entries *d)* a sum deducted from one's bank account, as for a check **2** a disadvantage or shortcoming —*vt.* to enter as a debit or debits; enter on the left-hand side of an account

debt|or (det'ər) *n.* [altered (after L) < ME *dettur* < OFr *detor* < L *debitor* < *debitus*, pp. of *debere*: see DEBT] a person, company, nation, etc. that owes something to another or others

de·fer[1] (dē fur', di-) *vt., vi.* **-ferred', -fer'ring** [ME *differren* < OFr *differer*: see DIFFER] **1** to put off to a future time; postpone; delay **2** to postpone the induction of (a person) into compulsory military service —*SYN.* YIELD —**de·fer'ra·ble** *adj.* —**de·fer'rer** *n.*

de·fer[2] (dē fur', di-) *vi.* **-ferred', -fer'ring** [ME *deferen* < OFr *deferer*, to yield, pay deference to < L *deferre* < *de-*, down + *ferre*, to BEAR[1]] to give in to the wish or judgment of another, as in showing respect; yield with courtesy (*to*)

def·er·ence (def'ər əns) *n.* [Fr *déférence* < L *deferens*, prp. of DEFER[1]] **1** a yielding in opinion, judgment, or wishes **2** courteous regard or respect —*SYN.* HONOR —**in deference to** out of regard or respect for (a person or the person's position or wishes)

de·fy (dē fī', di-; *also, for n.,* dē'fī) *vt.* **-fied', -fy'ing** [ME *defien* < OFr *defier*, to distrust, repudiate, defy < LL **disfidare* < *dis-*, from + **fidare*, to trust < *fidus*, faithful: see FAITH] **1** to resist or oppose boldly or openly **2** to resist completely in a baffling way [the puzzle *defied* solution] **3** to dare (someone) to do or prove something **4** [Archaic] to challenge (someone) to fight —*n., pl.* **-fies** a defiance or challenge

deign (dān) *vi.* [ME *deignen* < OFr *deignier* < L *dignare, dignari*, to deem worthy < *dignus*, worthy: see DIGNITY] to condescend to do something thought to be slightly beneath one's dignity [the duchess *deigned* to shake my hand] —*vt.* to condescend to give [to *deign* no answer] —*SYN.* STOOP[1]

de·lete (dē lēt', di-) *vt.* **-let'ed, -let'ing** [< L *deletus*, pp. of *delere*, to blot out, destroy < *de-*, from + base of *linere*, to daub, rub over (writing on a wax table with the blunt end of the style) < IE base **lei-*, viscous, smooth > LIME[1]] to take out (a printed or written letter, word, etc.); cross out —*SYN.* ERASE

de·mise (dē mīz', di-) *n.* [Fr *démise*, fem. pp. of OFr *démettre*, to dismiss, put away < L *demittere*: see DEMIT] **1** *Law* a transfer of an estate by lease, esp. for a fixed period **2** the transfer of sovereignty by death or abdication **3** a ceasing to exist; death —*vt.* **-mised', -mis'ing 1** to grant or transfer (an estate) by lease, esp. for a fixed period **2** to transfer (sovereignty) by death or abdication

de·pre·ci·ate (dē prē'shē āt', di-) *vt.* **-at'ed, -at'ing** [ME *depreciaten* < LL *depretiatus*, pp. of *depretiare*, to lower the price of (in LL(Ec), to make light of) < L *de-*, from + *pretiare*, to value < *pretium*, PRICE] **1** to reduce in value or price **2** to make seem less important; belittle; disparage —☆*vi.* to drop in value or price —*SYN.* DISPARAGE —**de·pre'cia·to'ry** (-shē ə tôr'ē, -shē ə tôr'ē) or **de·pre'ci·a'tive** (-shē āt'iv, -shə tiv) *adj.*

des·pi·ca·ble (des'pi kə bəl, des'pik'ə-; di spik'ə-, de-) *adj.* [LL *despicabilis*: see fol.] deserving to be despised; contemptible —**des'·pi·ca·ble·ness** *n.* —**des'pi·ca·bly** *adv.*

de·ter (dē tur', di-) *vt.* **-terred', -ter'ring** [L *deterrere* < *de-*, from + *terrere*, to frighten: see TERROR] to keep or discourage (a person, group, or nation) from doing something by instilling fear, anxiety, doubt, etc. —**de·ter'ment** *n.*

de·vel·op (di vel'əp) *vt.* [Fr *développer* < OFr *desveloper* < *des-* (L *dis-*), apart + *voloper*, to wrap, prob. OIt *viluppo*, a bundle < ? *faluppa*, bundle of straw; infl. by L *volvere*, to roll] I. *to cause to grow gradually in some way* **1** to build up or expand (a business, industry, etc.) **2** to make stronger or more effective; strengthen (muscles) **3** to bring (something latent or hypothetical) into activity or reality **4** to cause (one's personality, a bud, etc.) to unfold or evolve gradually **5** to make (housing, highways, etc.) more available or extensive **6** *Music* to elaborate (a theme) as by rhythmic or melodic changes **7** *Photog. a)* to immerse (an exposed film, plate, or printing paper) in various chemical solutions in order to make the picture visible *b)* to make (a picture) visible by doing this II. *to show or work out by degrees* **1** to make (a theme or plot) known gradually **2** to explain more clearly; enlarge upon **3** *Geom.* to change the form of (a surface); esp., to flatten out (a curved surface) **4** *Math.* to work out in detail or expand (a function or expression) —*vi.* **1** to come into being or activity; occur or happen **2** to become larger, fuller, better, etc.; grow or evolve, esp. by natural processes **3** to become known or apparent; be disclosed **4** to progress economically, socially, and politically from an underdeveloped condition [the *developing* nations] —**de·vel'op·a·ble** *adj.*

dif·fi·dent (-dənt) *adj.* [L *diffidens*: see prec.] full of diffidence; lacking self-confidence; timid; shy —*SYN.* SHY[1] —**dif'fi·dent|ly** *adv.*

dili·gence[1] (dil'ə jəns) *n.* [ME < OFr < L *diligens*, prp. of *diligere*, to esteem highly, select < *di-*, apart + *legere*, to choose, collect: see LOGIC] **1** the quality of being diligent; constant, careful effort; perseverance **2** [Obs.] speed; haste **3** *Law* the degree of attention or care expected of a person in a given situation

dili·gence[2] (dil'ə jəns; *Fr* dē lē zhäns') *n.* [Fr < *carrosse de diligence*, lit., coach of diligence, i.e., fast coach < *faire diligence*, to hurry] a public stagecoach, esp. as formerly used in France

dis·as·trous (-trəs) *adj.* [Fr *désastreux*] of the nature of a disaster; causing great harm, damage, grief, etc.; calamitous —**dis·as'trous|ly** *adv.*

dis·burse (dis burs') *vt.* **-bursed', -burs'ing** [OFr *desbourser* < *des-*, DIS- + *bourse, borse*, purse: see DIS- & BOURSE] to pay out; expend —**dis·burs'a·ble** *adj.* —**dis·burs'er** *n.*

dis·cern (di zʉrn′, -sʉrn′) **vt.** ║ME *discernen* < OFr *discerner* < L *discernere* < *dis-*, apart + *cernere*, to separate: see HARVEST║ **1** to separate (a thing) mentally from another or others; recognize as separate or different **2** to perceive or recognize; make out clearly — **vi.** to perceive or recognize the difference —**dis·cern′i·ble** *adj.* — **dis·cern′i·bly** *adv.*

SYN.—*discern* implies a making out or recognizing of something visually or mentally *[to discern one's motives]*; **perceive** implies recognition by means of any of the senses, and, with reference to mental apprehension, often implies keen understanding or insight *[to perceive a change in attitude]*; **distinguish**, in this connection, implies a perceiving clearly or distinctly by sight, hearing, etc. *[he distinguished the voices of men down the hall]*; **observe** and **notice** both connote some measure of attentiveness and usually suggest use of the sense of sight *[to observe an eclipse, to notice a sign]*

dis·cre·tion (di skresh′ən) **n.** ║ME *discrecioun* < OFr *discrecion* < L *discretio*, separation (in LL, discernment) < *discretus*: see DIS-CREET║ **1** the freedom or authority to make decisions and choices; power to judge or act **2** the quality of being discreet, or careful about what one does and says; prudence **3** [Archaic] the action or power of discerning; judgment —**at one's discretion** as one wishes

dis·cre·tion·ar·y (-er′ē) *adj.* left to one's discretion; regulated by one's own choice Also **dis·cre′tion‖al**

dis·pel (di spel′) **vt. -pelled′, -pel′ling** ║ME *dispellen* < L *dispellere* < *dis-*, apart + *pellere*, to drive: see FELT║ to scatter and drive away; cause to vanish; disperse —**SYN.** SCATTER

dis·sect (di sekt′; *also* di sekt′, dī′sekt′) **vt.** ║< L *dissectus*, pp. of *dissecare*, to cut apart < *dis-*, apart + *secare*, to cut: see SAW[1]║ **1** to cut apart piece by piece; separate into parts, as a body for purposes of study; anatomize **2** to examine or analyze closely

dis·sem·ble (di sem′bəl) **vt. -bled, -bling** ║ME *dissemblen* < OFr *dessembler* < *des-*, DIS- + *sembler* < L *simulare*: see SIMULATE║ **1** to conceal under a false appearance; disguise *[to dissemble fear by smiling]* **2** [Obs.] to pretend to be in a state of; simulate; feign *[to dissemble innocence]* **3** [Obs.] to pretend not to notice; ignore —**vi.** to conceal the truth, or one's true feelings, motives, etc., by pretense; behave hypocritically —**dis·sem′blance n.** —**dis·sem′bler n.**

dis·sem·i·nate (di sem′ə nāt′) **vt. -nat′ed, -nat′ing** ║< L *disseminatus*, pp. of *disseminare*, lit., to scatter seed, hence disseminate < *dis-*, apart + *seminare*, to sow < *semen*, SEED║ to scatter far and wide; spread abroad, as if sowing; promulgate widely —**dis·sem′i·na′tion n.** —**dis·sem′i·na′tive adj.** —**dis·sem′i·na′tor n.**

dis·ser·ta·tion (dis′ər tā′shən) **n.** ║LL *dissertatio* < L *dissertare*, to discuss, argue, freq. of *disserere* < *dis-*, apart + *serere*, to join: see SERIES║ a formal and lengthy discourse or treatise on some subject, esp. one based on original research and written in partial fulfillment of requirements for a doctorate: see THESIS

dis·sim‖u·late (di sim′yoō lāt′) **vt., vi. -lat′ed, -lat′ing** ║ME *dissimulaten* < pp. of L *dissimulare*: see DIS- & SIMULATE║ to hide (one's feelings, motives, etc.) by pretense; dissemble —**dis·sim′u·la′tion n.** —**dis·sim′u·la′tor n.**

dis·si·pate (dis′ə pāt′) **vt. -pat′ed, -pat′ing** ║< L *dissipatus*, pp. of *dissipare*, to scatter < *dis-*, apart + supine to throw < IE base *swep- > Sans *svapū*, broom, LowG *swabbeln*, to SWAB║ **1** to break up and scatter; dispel; disperse **2** to drive completely away; make disappear **3** to waste or squander —**vi.** **1** to be dissipated; disperse or vanish **2** to spend much time and energy on indulgence in pleasure, esp. drinking, gambling, etc., to the point of harming oneself —**SYN.** SCATTER —**dis′si·pat′er** or **dis′si·pa′tor n.** —**dis′si·pa′tive adj.**

dis·sol·u·ble (di säl′yoō bəl, dis′ə lə bəl) *adj.* ║L *dissolubilis* < *dissolvere*: see DISSOLVE║ that can be dissolved —**dis·sol′u·bil′i·ty n.**

dis·so·lu·tion (dis′ə loō′shən) **n.** ║ME *dissolucioun* < L *dissolutio*║ a dissolving or being dissolved; specif., *a)* a breaking up or into parts; disintegration *b)* the termination, as of a business, association, or union *c)* the ending of life; death *d)* the dismissal of an assembly or adjournment of a meeting

dis·so·nance (dis′ə nəns) **n.** ║ME *dissonaunce* < LL *dissonantia* < L *dissonans*, prp. of *dissonare*, to be discordant < *dis-*, apart + *sonus*, a SOUND[1]║ **1** an inharmonious sound or combination of sounds; discord **2** any lack of harmony or agreement; incongruity **3** *Music* a chord that sounds incomplete or unfulfilled until resolved to a harmonious chord

dis·trib‖u·tor (di strib′yoot ər) **n.** a person or thing that distributes; specif., ☆*a)* an agent or business firm that distributes goods to consumers or dealers ☆*b)* a device for distributing electric current to the spark plugs of a gasoline engine so that they fire in proper order —**dis·trib′u·tor·ship′ n.**

du·ress (dooo̅ res′, dyoō′-; doo̅ res′, dyoō-) **n.** ║ME *dures* < OFr *durece* < L *duritia*, hardness, harshness < *durus*, hard < IE base *deru-*, tree, oak (orig. ? hard) > TREE║ **1** imprisonment **2** the use of force or threats; compulsion *[a confession signed under duress]*

dy·na‖mo (di nə mō′) **n., pl. -mos′** ║< *dynamoelectric machine*║ **1** early term for GENERATOR (sense 1b) **2** a forceful, dynamic person

ec·cen·tric (ək sen′trik, ik-) *adj.* ║ME *eccentrik* < ML *eccentricus* < LL *eccentros*, out of the center, eccentric < Gr *ekkentros* < *ek-*, out of (see EX-[1]) + *kentron*, CENTER║ **1** not having the same center, as two circles one inside the other: opposed to CONCENTRIC: see CONCENTRIC, illus. **2** not having the axis exactly in the center; off-center *[an eccentric wheel]* **3** not exactly circular in shape or motion **4** deviating from the norm, as in conduct; out of the ordinary; odd; unconventional —**n.** **1** a disk set off center on a shaft and revolving inside a strap that is attached to one end of a rod, thereby converting the circular motion of the shaft into back-and-forth motion of the rod **2** an odd or unconventional person —**ec·cen′tri·cal‖ly adv.**

ec·lec·tic (ek lek′tik) *adj.* ║Gr *eklektikos* < *eklegein*, to select, pick out < *ek-*, out + *legein*, to choose, pick: see LOGIC║ **1** selecting from various systems, doctrines, or sources **2** composed of material gathered from various sources, systems, etc. —**n.** a person who uses eclectic methods in philosophy, science, or art —**ec·lec′ti·cal‖ly adv.**

ec‖o·nom·ics (ek′ə näm′iks, ē′kə-) **n.pl.** [*with sing. v.*] **1** the science that deals with the production, distribution, and consumption of wealth, and with the various related problems of labor, finance, taxation, etc. **2** economic factors

ed·i·fy (ed′i fī′) **vt. -fied′, -fy′ing** ║ME *edifien* < OFr *edifier* < L *aedificare*, to build, construct (in LL(Ec) to edify) < *aedes*, a dwelling, house, temple, orig., hearth, fireplace < IE base *ai-dh-*, to burn (> Gr *aithein*, to burn, OE *ad*, pyre) + *-ficare* < *facere*, to make, DO[1]║ **1** to instruct, esp. so as to instruct, improve, enlighten, or uplift morally or spiritually **2** [Archaic] to build; establish —**ed′i·fi‖er n.**

em·bar‖go (em bär′gō, im-) **n., pl. -goes** ║Sp < *embargar* < VL *imbarricare* < L *in-*, in, on + ML *barra*, BAR[1]║ **1** a government order prohibiting the entry or departure of commercial ships at its ports, esp. as a war measure **2** any restriction or restraint, esp. one imposed on commerce by law; specif., *a)* a prohibition of trade in a particular commodity *b)* a prohibition or restriction of freight transportation —**vt. -goed, -go·ing** to put an embargo upon

em·bez·zle (em bez′əl, im-) **vt. -zled, -zling** ║ME *embesilen* < Anglo-Fr *enbesiler* < OFr *embesillier* < *en-* (see EN-[1]) + *besillier*, to destroy║ to steal (money, etc. entrusted to one's care); take by fraud for one's own use —**em·bez′zle·ment n.** —**em·bez′zler n.**

em·i·nent (em′ə nənt) *adj.* ║ME < L *eminens*: see EMINENCE║ **1** rising above other things or places; high; lofty **2** projecting; prominent; protruding **3** standing high by comparison with others, as in rank or achievement; renowned; exalted; distinguished **4** outstanding; remarkable; noteworthy *[a man of eminent courage]* —**SYN.** FAMOUS —**em′i·nent‖ly adv.**

em·is·sar‖y (em′i ser′ē) **n., pl. -sar·ies** ║L *emissarius* < pp. of *emittere*: see EMIT║ a person or agent, esp. a secret agent, sent on a specific mission —*adj.* of, or serving as, an emissary or emissaries

e‖nu·mer·ate (ē noō′mər āt′, -nyoō′-; i-) **vt. -at‖ed, -at′ing** ║< L *enumeratus*, pp. of *enumerare* < *e-*, out + *numerare*, to count < *numerus*, NUMBER║ **1** to determine the number of; count **2** to name one by one; specify, as in a list —**e‖nu′mer·a‖ble** (-mər ə bəl) *adj.* —**e‖nu·mer‖a′tion n.** —**e‖nu·mer‖a′tive adj.** —**e‖nu·mer‖a′tor n.**

en·vi·ron·ment (en vī′rən mənt, in-; *often*, -vī′ərn-) **n.** [prec. + -MENT] **1** [Rare] a surrounding or being surrounded **2** something that surrounds; surroundings **3** all the conditions, circumstances, and influences surrounding, and affecting the development of, an organism or group of organisms —**en·vi·ron·men·tal** (-ment′'l) *adj.* —**en·vi·ron·men′tal‖ly adv.**

e‖pit‖o·me (ē pit′ə mē′, i-) **n., pl. -mes** ║L < Gr *epitomē*, abridgment < *epitemnein*, to cut short < *epi-*, upon + *temnein*, to cut: see -TOMY║ **1** a short statement of the main points of a book, report, incident, etc.; abstract; summary **2** a person or thing that is representative or typical of the characteristics or general quality of a whole class —**SYN.** ABRIDGMENT

e‖pit‖o·mize (-mīz′) **vt. -mized′, -miz′ing** to make or be an epitome of —**e‖pit′o·miz‖er n.**

eq‖ui·ta·ble (ek′wit ə bəl) *adj.* ║Fr *équitable* < *équité*║ **1** characterized by equity; fair; just: said of actions, results of actions, etc. **2** *Law a)* having to do with equity, as distinguished from common or statute law *b)* valid in equity —**eq′ui·ta·ble·ness n.** —**eq′ui·ta·bly adv.**

er·ra·tum (er rät′əm, -rät′-) **n., pl. -ta** (-ə) ║L, neut. of *erratus* < pp. of *errare*: see ERR║ an error discovered in a work already printed: see ERRATA

erst (ʉrst) *adv.* ‖ME *erest* < OE *ǣrest*, superl. of *ǣr*: see ERE ‖ **1** [Obs.] at first; originally **2** [Archaic] formerly —*adj.* [Obs.] first

er·u·dite (er'yōo dīt', er'ōo-; er'yə-, er'ə-) *adj.* ‖ME *erudit* < L *eruditus*, pp. of *erudire*, to instruct, lit., free from roughness < *e-*, out + *rudis*, RUDE ‖ having or showing a wide knowledge gained from reading; learned; scholarly —**er'u·dite'ly** *adv.*

es·chew (es chōo') *vt.* ‖ME *eschewen* < Anglo-Fr *eschuer* < OHG *sciuhan*, to fear: akin to SHY¹ ‖ to keep away from (something harmful or disliked); shun; avoid; abstain from —**es·chew'al** *n.*

eth·i·cal (eth'i kəl) *adj.* ‖ME *ethik* (< L *ethicus* < Gr *ēthikos* < *ēthos*, character, custom < IE base *swedh-*, essential quality, own character > Goth *swes*, L *suus*, one's own & *suescere*, to become accustomed) + -AL ‖ **1** having to do with ethics or morality; of or conforming to moral standards **2** conforming to the standards of conduct of a given profession or group **3** designating or of a drug obtainable only on a doctor's prescription —*SYN.* MORAL —**eth'i·cal'i·ty** (-kal'ə tē) or **eth'i·cal·ness** *n.* —**eth'i·cal·ly** *adv.*

ex·cise¹ (ek'sīz' *also*, -sīs') *n.* ‖altered (after fol.) < earlier *accise* < MDu *accijs*, earlier *assijs* < OFr *assise*: see ASSIZE ‖ **1** orig., any tax **2** a tax or duty on the manufacture, sale, or consumption of various commodities within a country, as liquor, tobacco, etc.: also **excise tax 3** a fee paid for a license to carry on certain occupations, sports, etc. —*vt.* **-cised', -cis'ing** to put an excise on

ex·cise² (ek sīz', ik-) *vt.* **-cised', -cis'ing** ‖ < L *excisus*, pp. of *excidere*: see EXCIDE ‖ to remove (a tumor, organ, etc.) by cutting out or away —**ex·ci'sion** (-sizh'ən) *n.*

ex·em·pla·ry (eg zem'plə rē, ig-; eg'zem plər'ē) *adj.* ‖LL *exemplaris*: see prec. ‖ **1** serving as a model or example; worth imitating *[exemplary behavior]* **2** serving as a warning or deterrent *[exemplary punishment]* **3** serving as a sample, instance, type, etc.; illustrative *[exemplary extracts]* —**ex·em'pla·ri·ly** *adv.* —**ex·em'pla·ri·ness** *n.*

ex·on·er·ate (eg zän'ər āt', ig-) *vt.* **-at'ed, -at'ing** ‖ < L *exoneratus*, pp. of *exonerare*, to disburden < *ex-*, out + *onerare*, to load < *onus* (gen. *oneris*), a burden: see ONUS ‖ **1** orig., to relieve of (a burden, obligation, etc.); unload **2** to free from a charge or the imputation of guilt; declare or prove blameless; exculpate —*SYN.* ABSOLVE —**ex·on·er·a'tion** *n.* —**ex·on'er·a'tive** *adj.* —**ex·on'er·a'tor** *n.*

ex·or·bi·tant (-tənt) *adj.* ‖ME < L *exorbitans*, prp. of *exorbitare*, to go out of the track < *ex-*, out + *orbita*, a track, ORBIT ‖ going beyond what is reasonable, just, proper, usual, etc.; excessive; extravagant: said esp. of charges, prices, etc. —*SYN.* EXCESSIVE —**ex·or'bi·tant·ly** *adv.*

ex·pe·di·ent (ek spē'dē ənt, ik-) *adj.* ‖ME < OFr < L *expediens*, prp. of *expedire*: see EXPEDITE ‖ **1** useful for effecting a desired result; suited to the circumstances or the occasion; advantageous; convenient **2** based on or offering what is of use or advantage rather than what is right or just; guided by self-interest; politic —*n.* **1** an expedient thing; means to an end **2** a device used in an emergency; makeshift; resource —*SYN.* RESOURCE —**ex·pe'di·ent·ly** *adv.*

ex·u·ber·ant (-ənt) *adj.* ‖ME < L *exuberans*: see prec. ‖ **1** growing profusely; luxuriant or prolific *[exuberant vegetation]* **2** characterized by good health and high spirits; full of life; uninhibited **3** overly elaborate; flowery **4** very great; extreme —**ex·u'ber·ant·ly** *adv.*

fa·cil·i·tate (fə sil'ə tāt') *vt.* **-tat'ed, -tat'ing** ‖ < Fr *faciliter* < It *facilitare* < L *facilis* (see prec.) + -ATE¹ ‖ to make easy or easier —**fa·cil'i·ta'tor** *n.*

fal·li·ble (fal'ə bəl) *adj.* ‖ME < ML *fallibilis* < L *fallere*, to deceive: see FAIL ‖ **1** liable to be mistaken or deceived **2** liable to be erroneous or inaccurate —**fal'li·bil'i·ty** or **fal'li·ble·ness** *n.* —**fal'li·bly** *adv.*

fea·si·ble (fē'zə bəl) *adj.* ‖ME *faisible* < OFr < stem of *faire*, to do < L *facere*: see DO¹ ‖ **1** capable of being done or carried out; practicable; possible *[a feasible scheme]* **2** within reason; likely; probable *[a feasible story]* **3** capable of being used or dealt with successfully; suitable *[land feasible for cultivation]* —*SYN.* POSSIBLE —**fea·si·bil'i·ty**, *pl.* **-ties**, *n.* —**fea'si·ble·ness** *n.* —**fea'si·bly** *adv.*

fluc·tu·ate (fluk'chōo āt', -chə wāt') *vi.* **-at'ed, -at'ing** ‖ < L *fluctuatus*, pp. of *fluctuare* < *fluctus*, a flowing, wave < pp. stem of *fluere*, to flow < IE *bhleu-*, to swell up, flow (> BLUSTER) < base *bhel-*, to swell up > BALL¹ ‖ **1** to move back and forth or up and down; rise and fall; undulate, as waves **2** to be continually changing or varying in an irregular way *[fluctuating prices]* —*vt.* to cause to fluctuate —*SYN.* SWING —**fluc'tu·ant** *adj.* —**fluc'tu·a'tion** *n.*

for·bear·ance (fôr ber'əns) *n.* **1** the act of forbearing **2** the quality of being forbearing; self-control; patient restraint **3** *Law* the act by which a creditor extends time for payment of a debt or forgoes for a time the right to enforce legal action on the debt —*SYN.* PATIENCE

Ford (fôrd) **1 Ford Ma·dox** (mad'əks) (born *Ford Madox Hueffer*) 1873-1939; Eng. writer & editor **2 Gerald R(udolph), Jr.** (born *Leslie Lynch King, Jr.*) 1913- ; 38th president of the U.S. (1974-77) **3 Henry** 1863-1947; U.S. automobile manufacturer **4 John** 1586-c. 1639; Eng. dramatist **5 John** (born *Sean O'Feeney*) 1895-1973; U.S. motion-picture director

fore·cas·tle (fōk's'l, fôr'kas'əl) *n.* ‖FORE + CASTLE: from the foremost of the two castlelike structures on the hull of a medieval vessel ‖ **1** the upper deck of a ship in front of the foremast **2** the front part of a merchant ship, where the crew's quarters are located

fore·close (fôr klōz', fôr'-) *vt.* **-closed', -clos'ing** ‖ME *forclosen* < OFr *forclos*, pp. of *forclore*, to exclude < *fors* (< L *foris*: see DOOR), outside + *clore* (< L *claudere*), CLOSE³ ‖ **1** to shut out; exclude; bar **2** to extinguish the right to redeem (a mortgage) by foreclosure **3** to deprive (a mortgagor) of this right by foreclosure **4** to hinder or prevent **5** to claim exclusively —*vi.* to foreclose a mortgage —**fore·clos'a·ble** *adj.*

for·feit (fôr'fit) *n.* ‖ME *forfet* < OFr *forfait*, pp. of *forfaire*, to transgress < ML *forisfacere*, to do wrong, lit., to do beyond < L *foris*, *foras*, out-of-doors, beyond (see FOREIGN) + *facere* (see FACT) ‖ **1** something that one loses or has to give up because of some crime, fault, or neglect of duty; specif., a fine or penalty **2** *a)* a thing taken away as a penalty for making some mistake in a game, and redeemable by a specified action *b)* [*pl.*] any game in which such forfeits are taken **3** the act of forfeiting; forfeiture —*adj.* lost, given up, or taken away as a forfeit —*vt.* to lose, give up, or be deprived of as a forfeit for some crime, fault, etc. —**for'feit·a·ble** *adj.* —**for'feit·er** *n.*

for·mi·da·ble (fôr'mə də bəl) *adj.* ‖ME < OFr < L *formidabilis* < *formidare*, to fear, dread < *formido*, fear < IE *mormo-*, to feel horror > Gr *mormoros*, fear ‖ **1** causing fear or dread **2** hard to handle or overcome **3** awe-inspiring in size, excellence, etc.; strikingly impressive —**for'mi·da·bil'i·ty** or **for'mi·da·ble·ness** *n.* —**for'mi·da·bly** *adv.*

fran·chise (fran'chīz') *n.* ‖ME < OFr < *franc*, free: see FRANK¹ ‖ **1** orig., freedom from some restriction, servitude, etc. **2** any special right, privilege, or exemption granted by the government, as to be a corporation, operate a public utility, etc. **3** the right to vote; suffrage: usually preceded by *the* **4** *a)* the right to market a product or provide a service, often exclusive for a specified area, as granted by a manufacturer or company *b)* a business granted such a right ☆**5** *a)* the right to own a member team as granted by a league in certain professional sports *b)* such a member team —*vt.* **-chised', -chis'ing** to grant a franchise to

fraud (frôd; *also* fräd) *n.* ‖ME *fraude* < OFr < L *fraus* (gen. *fraudis*) < IE base *dhwer-*, to trick > Sans *dhvárati*, (he) injures ‖ **1** *a)* deceit; trickery; cheating *b)* *Law* intentional deception to cause a person to give up property or some lawful right **2** something said or done to deceive; trick; artifice **3** a person who deceives or is not what he pretends to be; impostor; cheat —*SYN.* DECEPTION

fraud·u·lent (frô'jə lənt; frôd'yōo lənt, -yə-) *adj.* ‖ME < OFr < L *fraudulentus* < *fraus*, prec. ‖ **1** acting with fraud; deceitful **2** based on or characterized by fraud **3** done or obtained by fraud —**fraud'u·lence** or **fraud'u·len·cy** *n.* —**fraud'u·lent·ly** *adv.*

GMAT Graduate Management Admission Test

gnarled (närld) *adj.* ‖ult. < ME *knorre*, a knot: see KNUR ‖ **1** knotty and twisted, as the trunk of an old tree **2** roughened, hardened, sinewy, etc., as hands that do rough work Also **gnarl'y, gnarl'i·er**, or **gnarl'i·est**

goof (gōof) *n.* ‖prob. < dial. *goff* < Fr *goffe*, stupid < It *goffo* ‖ **1** a stupid, silly, or credulous person **2** a mistake; blunder —*vi.* [Slang] **1** to make a mistake; blunder, fail, etc. **2** to waste time, shirk one's duties, etc.: (usually with *off* or *around*)

griev·ous (grēv'əs) *adj.* ‖ME *grevous* < OFr < *grever*: see prec. ‖ **1** causing grief **2** showing or characterized by grief *[a grievous cry]* **3** causing suffering; hard to bear; severe *[grievous pain]* **4** very serious; deplorable *[a grievous fault]* **5** atrocious; heinous *[a grievous crime]* —**griev'ous·ly** *adv.* —**griev'ous·ness** *n.*

gul·li·ble (gul'ə bəl) *adj.* ‖GULL², v. + -IBLE ‖ easily cheated or tricked; credulous Also [Rare] **gul'la·ble** —**gul'li·bil'i·ty** *n.* —**gul'li·bly** *adv.*

hag·gard (hag'ərd) *adj.* ‖MFr *hagard*, untamed, untamed hawk ‖ **1** *Falconry* designating a hawk captured after reaching maturity **2** untamed; unruly; wild **3** *a)* wild-eyed *b)* having a wild, wasted, worn look, as from sleeplessness, grief, or illness; gaunt; drawn —*n. Falconry* a haggard hawk —**hag'gard·ly** *adv.* —**hag'gard·ness** *n.*

har·ass (hə ras', har'əs) *vt.* ‖Fr *harasser* < OFr *harer*, to set a dog on < *hare*, cry to incite dogs < OHG *harēn*, to call, cry out ‖ **1** to trouble, worry, or torment, as with cares, debts, repeated questions, etc. **2** to trouble by repeated raids or attacks; harry —**har·ass'er** *n.* —**har·ass'ment** *n.*

haugh·ty (hôt′ē) *adj.* **-ti·er, -ti·est** ⟦ME *haut*, high, haughty < OFr *high < altus* (with *h-* after Frank **hoh*, high) + -Y³: *gh* prob. inserted by analogy with NAUGHTY⟧ **1** having or showing great pride in oneself and disdain, contempt, or scorn for others; proud; arrogant; supercilious **2** [Archaic] lofty; noble —*SYN.* PROUD —**haugh′ti·ly** *adv.* —**haugh′ti·ness** *n.*

hei·nous (hā′nəs) *adj.* ⟦ME *hainous* < OFr *hainös* (Fr *haineux*) < *haine*, hatred < *hair*, to hate < Frank **hatjan*, akin to Ger *hassen*, HATE⟧ outrageously evil or wicked; abominable *[a heinous crime]* —*SYN.* OUTRAGEOUS —**hei′nous·ly** *adv.* —**hei′nous·ness** *n.*

hi·er·ar·chy (hi′ər är′kē; *often* hi′rär-) *n.*, *pl.* **-chies** ⟦altered (modeled on Gr) < ME *ierarchie* < OFr *jerarchie* < ML(Ec) *hierarchia* < LGr(Ec), power or rule of a hierarch < Gr *hierarchēs*: see HIERARCH⟧ **1** a system of church government by priests or other clergy in graded ranks **2** the group of officials, esp. the highest officials, in such a system **3** a group of persons or things arranged in order of rank, grade, class, etc.

HIEROGLYPHICS
One cannot attain the limit of craftsmanship,
And there is no craftsman who acquires his total mastery.
—Ptahhotep, *c.* 2350 B.C.

hi·er·o·glyph·ic (hi′ər ō′glif′ik, -ər ə-; *often* hi′rō-, -rə-) *adj.* ⟦Fr *hiéroglyphique* < LL *hieroglyphicus* < Gr *hieroglyphikos* < *hieros*, sacred (see HIERO-) + *glyphein*, to carve, hollow out: see GLYPH⟧ **1** of, or having the nature of, hieroglyphics **2** written in hieroglyphics **3** hard to read or understand Also **hi·er·o·glyph′i·cal** —*n.* **1** a picture or symbol representing a word, syllable, or sound, used by the ancient Egyptians and others, instead of alphabetical letters **2** [*usually pl.*] a method of writing using hieroglyphics; picture writing **3** a symbol, sign, etc. hard to understand **4** [*pl.*] writing hard to decipher —**hi′er·o·glyph′i·cal·ly** *adv.*

hin·drance (hin′drəns) *n.* ⟦ME *hinderaunce*⟧ **1** the act of hindering **2** any person or thing that hinders; obstacle; impediment; obstruction —*SYN.* OBSTACLE

hos·pi·ta·ble (häs′pit ə bəl; *often* häs pit′-) *adj.* ⟦MFr < ML *hospitabilis* < *hospitare*, to receive as a guest < *hospes*: see prec.⟧ **1** *a)* friendly, kind, and solicitous toward guests *b)* prompted by or associated with friendliness and solicitude toward guests *[a hospitable act]* **2** favoring the health, growth, comfort, etc. of new arrivals; not adverse *[a hospitable climate]* **3** receptive or open, as to new ideas —**hos′pi·ta·bly** *adv.*

ig·no·min·y (ig′nə min′ē) *n.*, *pl.* **-min·ies** ⟦Fr *ignominie* < L *ignominia* < *in-*, no, not + *nomen*, NAME⟧ **1** loss of one's reputation; shame and dishonor; infamy **2** disgraceful, shameful, or contemptible quality, behavior, or act

il·leg·i·ble (il lej′ə bəl, i lej′-) *adj.* ⟦< IN-² + LEGIBLE⟧ very difficult or impossible to read because badly written or printed, faded, etc. —**il·leg′i·bil′i·ty** *n.* —**il·leg′i·bly** *adv.*

il·lic·it (il lis′it, i lis′-) *adj.* ⟦Fr *illicite* < L *illicitus*, not allowed: see IN-² & LICIT⟧ not allowed by law, custom, rule, etc.; unlawful; improper; prohibited; unauthorized —**il·lic′it·ly** *adv.* —**il·lic′it·ness** *n.*

im·mi·nent (im′ə nənt) *adj.* ⟦L *imminens*, prp. of *imminere*, to project over, threaten < *in-*, on + *minere*, to project: see MENACE⟧ likely to happen without delay; impending; threatening: said of danger, evil, misfortune —**im′mi·nent·ly** *adv.*

im·pro·vise (im′prə viz′) *vt.*, *vi.* **-vised′, -vis′ing** ⟦Fr *improviser* < It *improvvisare* < *improvviso*, unprepared < L *improvisus*, unforeseen < *in-*, not + *provisus*, pp. of *providere*, to foresee, anticipate: see PROVIDE⟧ **1** to compose, or simultaneously compose and perform, on the spur of the moment and without any preparation; extemporize **2** *a)* to bring about, make, or do on the spur of the moment *[to improvise a solution to a problem]* *b)* to make, provide, or do with the tools and materials at hand, usually to fill an unforeseen and immediate need *[to improvise a bed out of leaves]* —**im′pro·vis′er,** **im′pro·vi′sor,** or **im·prov′i·sa·tor** (-präv′i zāt′ər) *n.*

im·pu·dent (im′pyōō dənt) *adj.* ⟦ME < L *impudens* < *in-*, not + *pudens*, modest, orig. prp. of *pudere*, to feel shame⟧ **1** orig., immodest; shameless **2** shamelessly bold or disrespectful; saucy; insolent —*SYN.* IMPERTINENT —**im′pu·dent·ly** *adv.*

in·can·des·cent (in′kən des′ənt) *adj.* ⟦L *incandescens*, prp. of *incandescere*: see IN-¹ & CANDESCENT⟧ **1** glowing with intense heat; red-hot or, esp., white-hot **2** very bright; shining brilliantly; gleaming —**in′can·des′cence** *n.* —**in′can·des′cent·ly** *adv.*

in·cin·er·ate (in sin′ər āt′) *vt.* **-at·ed, -at·ing** ⟦< ML *incineratus*, pp. of *incinerare*, to burn to ashes < L *in*, in, to + *cinis* (gen. *cineris*), ashes < IE **kenis* < base **ken-*, to scratch, rub > Gr *konis*, dust, ashes⟧ to burn to ashes; burn up; cremate —**in·cin′er·a′tion** *n.*

in·cin·er·a·tor (-ər āt′ər) *n.* a person or thing that incinerates; esp., a furnace or other device for incinerating trash

in·cise (in siz′) *vt.* **-cised′, -cis′ing** ⟦Fr *inciser* < L *incisus*, pp. of *incidere*, to cut into < *in-*, into + *caedere*, to cut: see -CIDE⟧ **1** to cut into with a sharp tool; specif., to cut (designs, inscriptions, etc.) into (a surface); engrave; carve

in·co·her·ent (in′kō hir′ənt; *also*, -her′-) *adj.* not coherent; specif., *a)* lacking cohesion; not sticking together *b)* not logically connected; disjointed; rambling *c)* characterized by incoherent speech, thought, etc. —**in′co·her′ent·ly** *adv.*

in·com·pre·hen·si·ble (in′käm′prē hen′sə bəl, -pri-) *adj.* ⟦ME < OFr or L: OFr *incompréhensible* < L *incomprehensibilis*⟧ **1** not comprehensible; that cannot be understood; obscure or unintelligible **2** [Archaic] illimitable —**in′com·pre·hen′si·bil′i·ty** *n.* —**in′com·pre·hen′si·bly** *adv.*

in·cor·ri·gi·ble (in kôr′ə jə bəl, -kär′-) *adj.* ⟦ME *incorygibile* < OFr < LL *incorrigibilis*⟧ not corrigible; that cannot be corrected, improved, or reformed, esp. because firmly established, as a habit, or because set in bad habits, as a child —*n.* an incorrigible person —**in·cor′ri·gi·bil′i·ty** or **in·cor′ri·gi·ble·ness** *n.* —**in·cor′ri·gi·bly** *adv.*

in·cum·bent (in kum′bənt) *adj.* ⟦L *incumbens*, prp. of *incumbere*, to recline or rest on < *in-*, on + *cubare*, to lie down: see CUBE¹⟧ **1** lying, resting, or pressing with its weight on something else **2** currently in office —*n.* the holder of an office or benefice —**incumbent on** (or **upon**) resting upon as a duty or obligation

in·de·fat·i·ga·ble (in′di fat′i gə bəl) *adj.* ⟦MFr *indéfatigable* < L *indefatigabilis* < *in-*, not + *defatigare*, to tire out, weary: see DE- & FATIGUE⟧ that cannot be tired out; not yielding to fatigue; untiring —**in′de·fat′i·ga·bil′i·ty** *n.* —**in′de·fat′i·ga·bly** *adv.*

in·del·i·ble (in del′ə bəl) *adj.* ⟦L *indelibilis* < *in-*, not + *delibilis*, perishable < *delere*, to destroy: see DELETE⟧ **1** that cannot be erased, blotted out, eliminated, etc.; permanent; lasting **2** leaving an indelible mark *[indelible ink]* —**in·del′i·bil′i·ty** *n.* —**in·del′i·bly** *adv.*

in·dict (in dit′) *vt.* ⟦altered (infl. by L) < ME *enditen*, to write down, accuse < Anglo-L *indictare* < LL **indictare* < L *in*, against + *dictare*: see DICTATE⟧ to charge with the commission of a crime; esp., to make a formal accusation against on the basis of positive legal evidence: usually said of the action of a grand jury —*SYN.* ACCUSE —**in·dict·ee′** *n.* —**in·dict′er** or **in·dict′or** *n.*

in·dom·i·ta·ble (in däm′i tə bəl) *adj.* ⟦LL *indomitabilis* < L *indomitus*, untamed < *in-*, not + *domitus*, pp. of *domitare*, to tame, intens. < *domare*, to TAME⟧ not easily discouraged, defeated, or subdued; unyielding; unconquerable —**in·dom′i·ta·bil′i·ty** or **in·dom′i·ta·ble·ness** *n.* —**in·dom′i·ta·bly** *adv.*

in·duce (in dōōs′, -dyōōs′) *vt.* **-duced′, -duc′ing** ⟦ME *enducen* < L *inducere* < *in-*, in + *ducere*, to lead: see DUCT⟧ **1** to lead on to some action, condition, belief, etc.; prevail on; persuade **2** to bring on; bring about; cause; effect *[to induce vomiting with an emetic]* **3** to draw (a general rule or conclusion) from particular facts; infer by induction **4** *Physics* to bring about (an electric or magnetic effect) in a body by exposing it to the influence or variation of a field of force —**in·duc′er** *n.* —**in·duc′i·ble** *adj.*

in·ex·o·ra·ble (in eks′ə rə bəl) *adj.* ⟦L *inexorabilis*: see IN-² & EXORABLE⟧ **1** that cannot be moved or influenced by persuasion or entreaty; unrelenting **2** that cannot be altered, checked, etc. *[their inexorable fate]* —**in·ex′o·ra·bil′i·ty** *n.* —**in·ex′o·ra·bly** *adv.*

in·fer (in fur′) *vt.* **-ferred′, -fer′ring** ⟦L *inferre*, to bring or carry in, infer < *in-*, in + *ferre*, to carry, BEAR¹⟧ **1** orig., to bring on or about; cause; induce **2** to conclude or decide from something known or assumed; derive by reasoning; draw as a conclusion **3** *a)* to lead to as a conclusion; indicate *b)* to indicate indirectly; imply (in this sense, still sometimes regarded as a loose usage) —*vi.* to draw inferences —**in·fer·a·ble** (in′fər ə bəl, in fur′-) *adj.* —**in′fer·a·bly** *adv.* —**in·fer′rer** *n.*

SYN.—**infer** suggests the arriving at a decision or opinion by reasoning from known facts or evidence *[from your smile, I infer that you're pleased]*; **deduce**, in strict discrimination, implies inference from a general principle by logical reasoning *[the method was deduced from earlier experiments]*; **conclude** strictly implies an inference that is the final logical result in a process of reasoning *[I must, therefore, conclude that you are wrong]*; **judge** stresses the careful checking and weighing of premises, etc. in arriving at a conclusion; **gather** is an informal substitute for **infer** or **conclude** *[I gather that you don't care]*

in·i·tial (i nish′əl) *adj.* ⟦< Fr or L: Fr < L *initialis* < *initium*, a beginning < *inire*, to go into, enter upon, begin < *in-*, into, in + *ire*, to go < IE base **ei-* > Goth *iddja*⟧ having to do with, indicating, or occurring at the beginning *[the initial stage of a disease, the initial letter of a word]* —*n.* **1** a capital, or uppercase, letter; specif., *a)* an extra-large capital letter at the start of a printed paragraph, chapter, etc. *b)* the first letter of a name **2** *Biol.* a primordial cell that determines the basic pattern of derived tissues; specif., a meristematic cell —*vt.* **-tialed** or **-tialled, -tial·ing** or **-tial·ling** to mark or sign with an initial or initials

in·no·va·tion (in′ə vā′shən) *n.* ⟦LL *innovatio*⟧ **1** the act or process of innovating **2** something newly introduced; new method, custom, device, etc.; change in the way of doing things —**in′no·va′tion·al** *adj.*

in·nu·en·do (in′yoo en′dō) *n., pl.* **-does** or **-dos** ⟦L, by nodding to, abl. of ger. of *innuere*, to nod to, hint < *in-*, in + *-nuere*, to nod < IE base **neu-*, to jerk, beckon, nod > Sans *návatē*, (he) turns, L *numen*, a nod⟧ **1** *Law* explanatory material set forth in the complaint in an action for libel or slander which explains the expressions alleged to be libelous or slanderous **2** an indirect remark, gesture, or reference, usually implying something derogatory; insinuation

in·nu·mer·a·ble (in noo′mər ə bəl, i noo′-; -nyoo′-) *adj.* ⟦ME < L. *innumerabilis*: see IN-² & NUMERABLE⟧ too numerous to be counted; very many; countless Also [Old Poet.] **in·nu′mer·ous** —**in·nu′mer·a·bil′i·ty** or **in·nu′mer·a·ble·ness** *n.* —**in·nu′mer·a·bly** *adv.*

in·scru·ta·ble (in skroot′ə bəl) *adj.* ⟦ME < LL(Ec) *inscrutabilis* < L *in-*, not + *scrutari*, to search carefully, examine: see SCRUTINY⟧ that cannot be easily understood; completely obscure or mysterious; unfathomable; enigmatic —**SYN.** MYSTERIOUS —**in·scru′ta·bil′i·ty** *n.* —**in·scru′ta·bly** *adv.*

in·sin·u·ate (in sin′yoo āt′) *vt.* **-at′ed, -at′ing** ⟦< L *insinuatus*, pp. of *insinuare*, to introduce by windings and turnings, insinuate < *in-*, in + *sinus*, curved surface⟧ **1** to introduce or work into gradually, indirectly, and artfully *[to insinuate oneself into another's favor]* **2** to hint or suggest indirectly; imply —*vi.* to make insinuations —**SYN.** SUGGEST —**in·sin′u·at′ing·ly** *adv.* —**in·sin′u·a′tive** *adj.* —**in·sin′u·a′tor** *n.*

in·so·lent (in′sə lənt) *adj.* ⟦ME < L *insolens* < *in-*, IN-² + *solens*, prp. of *solere*, to be accustomed⟧ **1** boldly disrespectful in speech or behavior; impertinent; impudent **2** [Now Rare] arrogantly contemptuous; overbearing —**SYN.** IMPERTINENT, PROUD —**in′so·lence** *n.* —**in′so·lent·ly** *adv.*

in·sol·vent (in säl′vənt) *adj.* **1** not solvent; unable to pay debts as they become due; bankrupt **2** not enough to pay all debts *[an insolvent inheritance]* **3** of insolvents or insolvency —*n.* an insolvent person

in·still or **in·stil** (in stil′) *vt.* **-stilled′, -still′ing** ⟦MFr *instiller* < L *instillare* < *in-*, in + *stillare*, to drop < *stilla*, a drop⟧ **1** to put in drop by drop **2** to put (an idea, principle, feeling, etc.) in or into little by little; impart gradually —**in·stil·la′tion** *n.* —**in·still′er** *n.* —**in·still′ment** or **in·stil′ment** *n.*

in·ter·cede (in′tər sēd′) *vi.* **-ced′ed, -ced′ing** ⟦L *intercedere* < *inter-*, between + *cedere*, to go: see CEDE⟧ **1** to plead or make a request in behalf of another or others *[to intercede with the authorities for the prisoner]* **2** to intervene for the purpose of producing agreement; mediate

in·ter·mit·tent (in′tər mit′'nt) *adj.* ⟦L *intermittens*, prp. of *intermittere*: see prec.⟧ stopping and starting again at intervals; pausing from time to time; periodic —**in′ter·mit′tence** *n.* —**in′ter·mit′tent·ly** *adv.*

SYN.—intermittent and **recurrent** both apply to something that stops and starts, or disappears and reappears, from time to time, but the former usually stresses the breaks or pauses, and the latter, the repetition or return *[an intermittent fever, recurrent attacks of the hives]*; **periodic** refers to something that recurs at more or less regular intervals *[periodic economic crises]*; **alternate** is usually used of two recurrent things that follow each other in regular order *[a life of alternate sorrow and joy]* —**ANT.** continued, continuous

in·ter·ro·gate (in ter′ə gāt′) *vt.* **-gat′ed, -gat′ing** ⟦< L *interrogatus*, pp. of *interrogare*, to ask < *inter-*, between + *rogare*, to ask: see ROGATION⟧ to ask questions of formally in examining *[to interrogate a witness]* —*vi.* to ask questions —**SYN.** ASK

ir·rel·e·vant (ir rel′ə vənt, i rel′-) *adj.* not relevant; not pertinent; not to the point; not relating to the subject —**ir·rel′e·vance** or **ir·rel′e·van·cy**, *pl.* **-cies**, *n.* —**ir·rel′e·vant·ly** *adv.*

ir·rev·o·ca·ble (ir rev′ə kə bəl, i rev′-) *adj.* ⟦ME < MFr *irrévocable* < L *irrevocabilis*⟧ that cannot be revoked, recalled, or undone; unalterable —**ir·rev′o·ca·bil′i·ty** or **ir·rev′o·ca·ble·ness** *n.* —**ir·rev′o·ca·bly** *adv.*

i·tal·ic (i tal′ik; *also* ī-) *adj.* ⟦see fol.: so called because first used in an Italian edition of Virgil (1501)⟧ designating or of a type in which the characters slant upward to the right, used variously, as to emphasize words, indicate foreign words, set off book titles, etc. (Ex.: *this is italic type*) —*n.* **1** an italic letter or other character **2** [*usually pl., sometimes with sing. v.*] italic type or print

I·tal·ic (i tal′ik; *also* ī-) *n.* ⟦L *Italicus*⟧ a subfamily of languages within the Indo-European language family, including Latin, the Romance languages, Oscan, Imbrian, and other languages of ancient Italy —*adj.* **1** designating or of these languages **2** of ancient Italy, or its peoples or cultures

i·tal·i·cize (i tal′ə sīz′, ī-) *vt.* **-cized′, -ciz′ing** **1** to print in italics **2** to underscore (handwritten or typed matter) with a single line to indicate that it is to be printed in italics —**i·tal′i·ci·za′tion** *n.*

jeop·ard·ize (jep′ər dīz′) *vt.* **-ized′, -iz′ing** to put in jeopardy; risk loss, damage, or failure of; endanger

ju·di·ci·ar·y (joo dish′ē er′ē, -dish′ər ē, -ē ə rē) *adj.* ⟦L *judiciarius* < *judicium*, judgment, court of justice < *judex*: see JUDGE⟧ of judges, law courts, or their functions —*n., pl.* **-ar′ies** **1** the part of government whose work is the administration of justice **2** a system of law courts **3** judges collectively

lam·en·ta·ble (lam′ən tə bəl; *often* lə men′tə bəl) *adj.* ⟦ME < MFr < L *lamentabilis*⟧ **1** to be lamented; grievous; deplorable; distressing **2** [Now Rare] expressing sorrow; mournful —**lam′en·ta·bly** *adv.*

le·ni·ent (lēn′yənt, lē′nē ənt) *adj.* ⟦L *leniens*, prp. of *lenire*, to soften, alleviate < *lenis*, smooth, soft, mild < IE base **lei-*: see LATE⟧ **1** not harsh or severe in disciplining, punishing, judging, etc.; mild; merciful; clement **2** [Archaic] soothing —**le′ni·en·cy**, *pl.* **-cies**, or **le′ni·ence** *n.* —**le′ni·ent·ly** *adv.*

li·en (lēn, lē′ən) *n.* ⟦Fr < L *ligamen*, a band < *ligare*, to bind, tie: see LIGATURE⟧ *Law* a claim on the property of another as security for the payment of a just debt

liq·ue·fy (lik′wi fī′) *vt., vi.* **-fied′, -fy′ing** ⟦Fr *liquefier* < L *liquefacere*: see LIQUID & -FY⟧ to change into a liquid —**SYN.** MELT —**liq′ue·fi′a·ble** *adj.* —**liq′ue·fi′er** *n.*

liq·ui·date (lik′wi dāt′) *vt.* **-dat′ed, -dat′ing** ⟦< ML *liquidatus*, pp. of *liquidare*, to make liquid or clear < L *liquidus*, LIQUID⟧ **1** to settle by agreement or legal process the amount of (indebtedness, damages, etc.) **2** to settle the accounts of (a bankrupt business firm that is closing, etc.) by apportioning assets and debts **3** to pay or settle (a debt) **4** to convert (holdings or assets) into cash **5** to dispose of or get rid of, as by killing —*vi.* to liquidate debts, accounts, etc.

lo·gis·tics (-tiks) *n.pl.* ⟦Fr *logistique* < *logis*, lodgings (< *loger*, to quarter: see LODGE): form as if < ML *logisticus*: see prec.⟧ **1** the branch of military science having to do with procuring, maintaining, and transporting materiel, personnel, and facilities **2** the managing of the details of an undertaking

lu·mi·nar·y (loo′mə ner′ē) *n., pl.* **-nar·ies** ⟦OFr *luminarie* < LL(Ec) *luminarium*, < L *luminare*: see ILLUMINATE⟧ **1** a body that gives off light, such as the sun or moon **2** *a)* a person who sheds light on some subject or enlightens mankind; famous intellectual *b)* any famous or well-known person

ma·lign (mə līn′) *vt.* ⟦ME *malignen* < OFr *malignier*, to plot, deceive < LL *malignare* < LL *malignus*, wicked, malicious < *male*, ill (see MAL-) + base of *genus*, born: see GENUS⟧ to speak evil of; defame; slander; traduce —*adj.* **1** showing ill will; malicious **2** evil; baleful *[a malign influence]* **3** very harmful; malignant —**SYN.** SINISTER —**ma·lign′er** *n.*

mal·le·a·ble (mal′ē ə bəl) *adj.* ⟦ME *malliable* < ML *malleabilis* < L *malleare*, to beat with a hammer < *malleus*, a hammer < IE base **mel-*, to grind, beat > MILL¹⟧ **1** that can be hammered, pounded, or pressed into various shapes without breaking: said of metals **2** capable of being changed, molded, trained, etc.; adaptable —**SYN.** PLIABLE —**mal′le·a·bil′i·ty** or **mal′le·a·ble·ness** *n.*

me·men·to (mə men′tō) *n., pl.* **-tos** or **-toes** ⟦L, imper. of *meminisse*, to remember: for IE base see MIND⟧ **1** [M-] *R.C.Ch.* either of two prayers in the Canon of the Mass, one for the living and one for the dead, beginning "Memento" **2** anything serving as a reminder or warning **3** a souvenir

mis·chie·vous (mis′chə vəs) *adj.* ⟦ME *mischevous* < Anglo-Fr⟧ **1** causing mischief; specif., *a)* injurious; harmful *b)* prankish; teasing; full of tricks **2** inclined to annoy or vex with playful tricks; naughty: said esp. of a child —**mis′chie·vous·ly** *adv.* —**mis′chie·vous·ness** *n.*

mis·de·mean·or (mis′di mēn′ər) *n.* ⟦MIS-¹ + DEMEANOR⟧ **1** [Rare] the act of misbehaving **2** *Law* any minor offense, as the breaking of a municipal ordinance, for which statute provides a lesser punishment than for a felony: the penalty is usually a fine or imprisonment for a short time (usually less than one year) in a local jail, workhouse, etc.: Brit. sp. **mis′de·mean′our**

mis·hap (mis'hap') *n.* ‖ME (see MIS-¹ & HAP¹), prob. after OFr *mescheance,* mischance‖ **1** an unlucky or unfortunate accident **2** [Now Rare] bad luck; misfortune

Mo·liè·re (mōl yer', mō'lē er'; *Fr* mô lyer') (born *Jean Baptiste Poquelin*) 1622-73; Fr. dramatist

mol·li·fy (mäl'ə fī') *vt.* **-fied', -fy'ing** ‖ME *molifien,* MFr *mollifier* < LL *mollificare,* to soften (< L *mollis,* soft (< IE *mldu-,* soft < base *mel-,* to crush > MILL¹) + *facere,* to make, DO¹‖ **1** to soothe the temper of; pacify; appease **2** to make less intense, severe, or violent —**SYN.** PACIFY —**mol'li·fi·ca'tion** *n.* —**mol'li·fi'er** *n.*

mo·nop·o·lize (mə näp'ə līz') *vt.* **-lized', -liz'ing 1** to get, have or exploit a monopoly of **2** to get full possession or control of; dominate completely *[to monopolize a conversation]* —**mo·nop'o·li·za'tion** *n.* —**mo·nop'o·liz'er** *n.*

mo·nop·o·ly (mə näp'ə lē) *n., pl.* **-lies** ‖L *monopolium* < Gr *monopōlion,* right of exclusive sale, *monopōlia,* exclusive sale < *monos,* single (see MONO-) + *pōlein,* to sell < IE base *pel-* > Lith *pelnas,* wages‖ **1** exclusive control of a commodity or service in a given market, or control that makes possible the fixing of prices and the virtual elimination of free competition **2** an exclusive privilege of engaging in a particular business or providing a service, granted by a ruler or by the state **3** exclusive possession or control of something **4** something that is held or controlled as a monopoly **5** a company or combination that has a monopoly *6* [M-] a game played on a special board by two or more players: they move according to the throw of dice, engaging in mock real estate transactions with play money

SYN.—**monopoly** applies to the exclusive control of a commodity, etc., as defined above; a **trust** is a combination of corporations, organized for the purpose of gaining a monopoly, in which stock is turned over to trustees who issue stock certificates to the stockholders: trusts are now illegal in the U.S.; **cartel,** the European term for a trust, now usually implies an international trust; a **syndicate** is now usually a group of bankers, corporations, etc. organized to buy large blocks of securities, afterward selling them in small parcels to the public at a profit; a **corner** is a temporary speculative monopoly of some stock or commodity for the purpose of raising the price

neg·li·gence (neg'lə jəns) *n.* ‖ME *neglygence* < OFr *négligence* < L *negligentia*‖ **1** the quality or condition of being negligent; specif., *a)* habitual failure to do the required thing *b)* carelessness in manner or appearance; indifference **2** an instance of such failure, carelessness, or indifference **3** *Law* failure to use a reasonable amount of care when such failure results in injury or damage to another

neu·ro·sis (noo rō'sis, nyoo-) *n., pl.* **-ses'** (-sēz') ‖ModL: see NEUR- & -OSIS‖ any of various mental functional disorders characterized by anxiety, compulsions, phobias, depression, dissociations, etc.

New Jersey ‖after JERSEY (the Channel Island)‖ Eastern State of the U.S. on the Atlantic: one of the 13 original States; 7,836 sq. mi. (20,296 sq. km); pop. 7,364,000; cap. Trenton: abbrev. *NJ* or *N.J.* —**New Jer'sey·ite'**

no·ta·ry (nōt'ə rē) *n., pl.* **-ries** ‖ME *notarye* < OFr *notaire* < L *notarius* < *notare,* to NOTE‖ *short for* NOTARY PUBLIC

notary public *pl.* **notaries public** or **notary publics** an official authorized to certify or attest documents, take depositions and affidavits, etc.

nul·li·fy (nul'ə fī') *vt.* **-fied', -fy'ing** ‖LL(Ec) *nullificare,* to despise < L *nullus,* none (see NULL) + *facere,* to make, DO¹‖ **1** to make legally null; make void; annul **2** to make valueless or useless; bring to nothing **3** to cancel out —*nul'li·fi'er n.*

ob·fus·cate (äb fus'kāt', äb'fəs kāt') *vt.* **-cat'ed, -cat'ing** ‖< L *obfuscatus,* pp. of *obfuscare,* to darken < *ob-* (see OB-) + *fuscare,* to obscure < *fucus,* dark < IE base *dhus-* > DUSK, DOZE, DUST‖ **1** to cloud over; obscure; make dark or unclear **2** to muddle; confuse; bewilder —**ob'fus·ca'tion** *n.*

ob·so·les·cent (äb'sə les'ənt) *adj.* ‖L *obsolescens*‖ in the process of becoming obsolete —**ob'so·les'cence** *n.* —**ob'so·les'cent·ly** *adv.*

ob·so·lete (äb'sə lēt', äb'sə lēt') *adj.* ‖L *obsoletus,* pp. of *obsolescere,* to go out of use < *ob-* (see OB-) + *-solescere* (< *exolescere,* to grow out of use < *ex-,* EX-¹ + ? *alescere,* to increase: see ADOLESCENT‖ **1** no longer in use or practice; discarded **2** no longer in fashion; out-of-date; passé **3** *Biol.* rudimentary or poorly developed as compared with its counterpart in other individuals of a related species, the opposite sex, etc.; vestigial: said of an organ, etc. —*vt.* **-let'ed, -let'ing** to make obsolete, as by replacing with something newer —**SYN.** OLD —**ob'so·lete'ly** *adv.* —**ob'so·lete'ness** *n.*

*☆***OK** or **O.K.** (ō kā'; ō'kā', ō'kā') *adj., adv., interj.* ‖orig. U.S. colloq.: first known use (March 23, 1839) by C. G. Greene, editor, in the Boston *Morning Post,* as if abbrev. for "oll korrect," facetious misspelling of *all correct*; ? altered < Scot dial. *och aye,* ah yes, oh yes < Gael *och,* ah, oh + AYE²‖ all right; correct —*n., pl.* **OK's** or **O.K.'s** approval; endorsement —*vt.* **OK'd** or **O.K.'d, OK'ing** or **O.K.'ing** to put an OK on; approve; endorse

ope (ōp) *adj., vt., vi.* **oped, op'ing** ‖ME < *open(en)*‖ *old poet. var. of* OPEN

os·ten·si·ble (ä sten'sə bəl) *adj.* ‖Fr < ML *ostensibilis* < L *ostendere,* to show < *ob(s)-,* against (see OB-) + *tendere,* to stretch: see THIN‖ **1** apparent; seeming; professed **2** [Rare] clearly evident —**os·ten'si·bly** *adv.*

os·tra·cize (äs'trə sīz') *vt.* **-cized', -ciz'ing** ‖Gr *ostrakizein,* to exile by votes written on tiles or potsherds < *ostrakon,* a shell, potsherd, akin to *osteon,* bone: see OSSIFY‖ to banish, bar, exclude, etc. by ostracism —**SYN.** BANISH

pac·i·fy (pas'ə fī') *vt.* **-fied', -fy'ing** ‖ME *pacifien* < OFr *pacefier* < L *pacificare* < *pax* (gen. *pacis*), PEACE + *facere,* to make, DO¹‖ **1** to make peaceful or calm; appease; tranquilize **2** *a)* to establish or secure peace in (a nation, etc.) *☆b)* to seek to neutralize or win over (people in occupied areas) —**pac'i·fi'able** *adj.*

SYN.—**pacify** implies a making quiet and peaceful that which has become noisy or disorderly *[to pacify* a crying child*];* **appease** suggests a pacifying by gratifying or giving in to the demands of *[to appease* one's hunger*];* **mollify** suggests a soothing of wounded feelings or an allaying of indignation *[his* compliments failed to *mollify* her*];* **placate** implies the changing of a hostile or angry attitude to a friendly or favorable one *[to placate* an offended colleague*];* **propitiate** implies an allaying or forestalling of hostile feeling by winning the good will of *[to propitiate* a deity*];* **conciliate** implies the use of arbitration, concession, persuasion, etc. in an attempt to win over —**ANT.** anger, enrage

pal·pa·ble (pal'pə bəl) *adj.* ‖ME < LL *palpabilis* < L *palpare,* to touch, prob. < IE base *pel-,* to make move, shake > FEEL‖ **1** that can be touched, felt, or handled; tangible **2** easily perceived by the senses; audible, recognizable, perceptible, noticeable, etc. **3** clear to the mind; obvious; evident; plain —**SYN.** EVIDENT, PERCEPTIBLE —**pal'pa·bil'i·ty** *n.* —**pal'pa·bly** *adv.*

par·al·lel (par'ə lel', -ləl) *adj.* ‖Fr *parallèle* < L *parallelus* < Gr *parallēlos* < *para-,* side by side (see PARA-¹) + *allēlos,* one another < *allos,* other: see ELSE‖ **1** extending in the same direction and at the same distance apart at every point, so as never to meet, as lines, planes, etc. **2** having parallel parts or movements, as some machines, tools, etc. **3** *a)* closely similar or corresponding, as in purpose, tendency, time, or essential parts *b)* characterized by a balanced or coordinated arrangement of syntactic elements, esp. of phrases or clauses *[*"I came, I saw, I conquered" is an example of *parallel* structure*]* **4** *Elec.* designating, of, or pertaining to a circuit in parallel **5** *Music* having consistently equal intervals in pitch, as two parts of harmony, a series of chords, etc. —*adv.* in a parallel manner —*n.* **1** something parallel to something else, as a line or surface **2** any person or thing essentially the same as, or closely corresponding to, another; counterpart **3** the condition of being parallel; conformity in essential points **4** any comparison showing the existence of similarity or likeness **5** *a)* any of the imaginary lines parallel to the equator and representing degrees of latitude on the earth's surface *b)* such a line drawn on a map or globe: see LATITUDE, illus.: in full **parallel of latitude 6** *[pl.]* a sign (‖) used in printing as a reference mark **7** *Elec.* a method of circuit interconnection in which two or more components in the system have their negative terminals joined to one conductor and their positive to another, so that an identical potential difference is applied to each component: usually in the phrase **in parallel** —*vt.* **-leled** or **-lelled, -lel'ing** or **-lel'ling 1** *a)* to make (one thing) parallel to another *b)* to make parallel to each other **2** to be parallel with; extend parallel to *[a* road that *parallels* the river*]* **3** to compare (things, ideas, etc.) in order to show similarity or likeness **4** to be or find a counterpart for; match; equal

part·ner (pärt'nər) *n.* ‖ME *partener,* altered (by assoc. with *part,* PART) < *parcener:* see PARCENER‖ **1** a person who takes part in some activity in common with another or others; associate; specif., *a)* one of two or more persons engaged in the same business enterprise and sharing its profits and risks: each is an agent for the other or others and is liable, except when limited to his or her own investment, for the debts of the firm *b)* a husband or wife *c)* either of two persons dancing together *d)* either of two players on the same side or team playing or competing against two others, as in bridge or tennis **2** *[usually pl.]* *Naut.* a framework, as of timbers, for supporting a mast, capstan, etc. where it passes through the deck —*vt.* **1** to join (others) as partners **2** to be or provide a partner for

pat·ent (*for adj. 1 & 5-7* pat'nt; *for adj. 2-4 & 8* pāt'nt, pat'-; *for n. & v.,* pat'nt; *for most uses, Brit usually* pāt'nt) *adj.* ‖ME < MFr & L: MFr *patent* < L *patens,* prp. of *patere,* to be open: see PATELLA‖ **1** *a)* open to examination by the public (said of a document granting some right or rights, as to land, a franchise, an office, or, now esp., an invention) *[letters patent] b)* granted or appointed by letters patent **2** open to all; generally accessible or available **3** obvious; plain; evident *[a patent* lie*]* **4** open or unobstructed **5** *a)* protected by a patent; patented *b)* of or having to do with patents or the granting of patents [patent law] **6** produced or sold as a proprietary product: cf. PATENT MEDICINE **7** new, unusual, individual, etc.: also **patented 8** Bot., Zool. spreading out or open; patulous —**n. 1** an official document open to public examination and granting a certain right or privilege; letters patent; esp., a document granting the exclusive right to produce, sell, or get profit from an invention, process, etc. for a specific number of years **2** a) the right so granted b) the thing protected by such a right; patented article or process **3** public land, or title to such land, granted to a person by letters patent **4** any exclusive right, title, or license —**vt. 1** to grant a patent to or for **2** to secure exclusive right to produce, use, and sell (an invention or process) by a patent; get a patent for —**pat·ent·a·ble** (pat′'nt ə bəl) **adj.**

per·ceive (pər sēv′) **vt., vi.** **-ceived′, -ceiv′ing** [ME perceyven < OFr perceivre < L percipere, to take hold of, feel, comprehend < per, through + capere, to take: see HAVE] **1** to grasp mentally; take note (of); observe **2** to become aware (of) through sight, hearing, touch, taste, or smell —**SYN.** DISCERN —**per·ceiv′a·ble adj.** —**per·ceiv′a·bly adv.** —**per·ceiv′er n.**

per·fi·dy (pur′fə dē) **n.**, pl. **-dies** [Fr perfidie < L perfidia < perfidus, faithless < per fidem (decipi), (to deceive) through faith < per (see PER) + fides, FAITH] the deliberate breaking of faith; betrayal of trust; treachery

per·se·ver·ance (pur′sə vir′əns) **n.** [OFr < L perseverantia < perseverans, prp. of perseverare: see fol.] **1** the act of persevering; continued, patient effort **2** the quality of one who perseveres; persistence **3** in Calvinism, the continuance in grace of people elected to eternal salvation —**per′se·ver′ant adj.**

per·se·vere (pur′sə vir′) **vi.** **-vered′, -ver′ing** [ME perseveren < OFr perseverer < L perseverare < perseverus, very severe, strict < per-, intens. + severus, SEVERE] to continue in some effort, course of action, etc. in spite of difficulty, opposition, etc.; be steadfast in purpose; persist —**per′se·ver′ing·ly adv.**

per·sist·ent (pər sist′ənt, -zist′-) **adj.** [L persistens, prp. of persistere: see PERSIST] **1** refusing to relent; continuing, esp. in the face of opposition, interference, etc.; stubborn **2** continuing to exist or endure; lasting without change **3** constantly repeated; continued **4** Bot. remaining attached permanently or for a longer than normal time, as some leaves, perianths, etc. **5** Zool. a) remaining essentially unchanged over a long period of geologic time, as a species b) remaining for life (said of such parts retained in the adult that normally disappear or wither at an early stage) —**per·sist′ent·ly adv.**

per·tain (pər tān′) **vi.** [ME partenen < OFr partenir < L pertinere, to stretch out, reach < per-, intens. + tenere, to hold: see THIN] **1** to belong; be connected or associated; be a part, accessory, etc. [lands pertaining to an estate] **2** to be appropriate or suitable [conduct that pertains to a lady] **3** to have reference or relevance; be related [laws pertaining to the case] —**pertaining to** having to do with; belonging to

pet·u·lant (pech′ə lənt) **adj.** [L petulans (gen. petulantis), forward, petulant < base of petere, to rush at, fall: see FEATHER] **1** [Obs.] a) forward; immodest b) pert; insolent **2** impatient or irritable, esp. over a petty annoyance; peevish —**pet′u·lance** or **pet′u·lan·cy n.** —**pet′u·lant·ly adv.**

phe·nom·e·non (fə näm′ə nən′, -nän) **n.**, pl. **-na** (-nə); also, esp. for 3 and usually for 4, **-nons′** [LL phaenomenon < Gr phainomenon, neut. prp. of phainesthai, to appear, akin to phainein: see FANTASY] **1** any event, circumstance, or experience that is apparent to the senses and that can be scientifically described or appraised, as an eclipse **2** in Kantian philosophy, a thing as it appears in perception as distinguished from the thing as it is in itself independent of sense experience: distinguished from NOUMENON **3** any extremely unusual or extraordinary thing or occurrence **4** [Colloq.] a person with an extraordinary quality, aptitude, etc.; prodigy

phy·sique (fi zēk′) **n.** [Fr: see PHYSIC] the structure, constitution, strength, form, or appearance of the body

piti·a·ble (pit′ē ə bəl) **adj.** [ME piteable < MFr < pitier: see PITY] arousing or deserving pity, sometimes mixed with scorn or contempt —**SYN.** PITIFUL —**pit′i·a·ble·ness n.** —**pit′i·a·bly adv.**

pla·gia·rize (plā′jə rīz′; -jē ə-) **vt., vi.** **-rized′, -riz′ing** [see fol.] to take (ideas, writings, etc.) from (another) and pass them off as one's own —**pla′gia·riz′er n.**

plau·si·ble (plô′zə bəl) **adj.** [L plausibilis < plaudere, to applaud] **1** seemingly true, acceptable, etc.: often implying disbelief **2** seemingly honest, trustworthy, etc.: often implying distrust —**plau·si·bil′i·ty** or **plau′si·ble·ness n.** —**plau′si·bly adv.**
SYN.—**plausible** applies to that which at first glance appears to be true, reasonable, valid, etc. but which may or may not be so, although there is no connotation of deliberate deception [a plausible argument]; **credible** is

used of that which is believable because it is supported by evidence, sound logic, etc. [a credible account]; **specious** applies to that which is superficially reasonable, valid, etc. but is actually not so, and it connotes intention to deceive [a specious excuse] —**ANT.** genuine, actual

pli·a·ble (plī′ə bəl) **adj.** [LME plyable < MFr < plier, to bend, fold < L plicare, to fold, bend: see PLY[1]] **1** easily bent or molded; flexible **2** easily influenced or persuaded; tractable **3** adjusting readily; adaptable —**pli·a·bil′i·ty** or **pli′a·ble·ness n.** —**pli′a·bly adv.**
SYN.—**pliable** and **pliant** both imply capability of being easily bent, suggesting the suppleness of a wooden switch and, figuratively, a yielding nature or adaptability; **plastic** is used of substances, such as plaster or clay, that can be molded into various forms which are retained upon hardening, and figuratively suggests an impressionable quality; **ductile** literally and figuratively suggests that which can be finely drawn or stretched out [copper is a ductile metal]; **malleable** literally or figuratively suggests that which can be hammered, beaten, or pressed into various forms [copper is malleable as well as ductile] —**ANT.** inflexible, rigid, brittle

pneu·mat·ic (nōō mat′ik, nyōō-) **adj.** [L pneumaticus < Gr pneumatikos < pneuma, breath: see prec.] **1** of or containing wind, air, or gases **2** a) filled with compressed air [pneumatic tire] b) worked by compressed air [pneumatic drill] **3** Theol. having to do with the spirit or soul **4** Zool. having hollows filled with air, as certain bones in birds —**pneu·mat′i·cal·ly adv.**

☆**poison pill** Business any defensive measure for preventing the take over of a corporation by making its acquisition prohibitively expensive for the party attempting to acquire it

post·pone (pōst pōn′) **vt.** **-poned′, -pon′ing** [L postponere < post-, POST- + ponere, to put: see POSITION] **1** to put off until later; defer; delay **2** to put at or near the end of the sentence [the German verb is postponed] **3** [Rare] to subordinate —**SYN.** ADJOURN —**post·pon′a·ble adj.** —**post·pone′ment n.** —**post·pon′er n.**

pre·cip·i·tate (for v., prē sip′ə tāt′, pri-; for adj. & n., -tit, also, -tāt′) **vt.** **-tat′ed, -tat′ing** [< L praecipitatus, pp. of praecipitare < praeceps: see PRECIPICE] **1** to throw headlong; hurl downward **2** to cause to happen before expected, warranted, needed, or desired; bring on; hasten [to precipitate a crisis] **3** Chem. a) to cause (a slightly soluble substance) to become insoluble, as by heat or by a chemical reagent, and separate out from a solution b) to cause the separation of a suspended liquid or solid from a gas **4** Meteorol. to condense (water vapor) and cause to fall to the ground as rain, snow, sleet, etc. —**vi. 1** Chem. to be precipitated **2** Meteorol. to condense and fall to the ground as rain, snow, sleet, etc. —**adj.** [L praecipitatus: see the v.] **1** falling steeply, rushing headlong, flowing swiftly, etc. **2** acting, happening, or done very hastily or rashly; impetuous; headstrong **3** very sudden, unexpected, or abrupt —**n.** [ModL praecipitatum] a substance that is precipitated out from a solution or gas —**SYN.** SUDDEN —**pre·cip′i·tate·ly adv.** —**pre·cip′i·tate·ness n.** —**pre·cip′i·ta′tive adj.** —**pre·cip′i·ta′tor n.**

prej·u·dice (prej′ōō dis, - oo-; prej′ə-) **n.** [ME < MFr < L praejudicium < prae-, before (see PRE-) + judicium, judgment < judex (gen. judicis), JUDGE] **1** a judgment or opinion formed before the facts are known; preconceived idea, favorable or, more usually, unfavorable **2** a) a judgment or opinion held in disregard of facts that contradict it; unreasonable bias [a prejudice against modern art] b) the holding of such judgments or opinions **3** suspicion, intolerance, or irrational hatred of other races, creeds, regions, occupations, etc. **4** injury or harm resulting as from some judgment or action of another or others —**vt.** **-diced, -dic·ing 1** to injure or harm, as by some judgment or action **2** to cause to have or show prejudice; bias —**without prejudice 1** without detriment or injury **2** Law without dismissal of or detriment to (a legal right, claim, etc.): often with to
SYN.—**prejudice** implies a preconceived and unreasonable judgment or opinion, usually an unfavorable one marked as by suspicion, fear, or hatred [a murder incited by race prejudice]; **bias** implies a mental leaning in favor of or against someone or something [few of us are without bias of any kind]; **partiality** implies an inclination to favor a person or thing because of strong fondness or attachment [the conductor's partiality for the works of Brahms]; **predilection** implies a preconceived liking, formed as a result of one's background, temperament, etc., that inclines one to a particular preference [he has a predilection for murder mysteries]

prev·a·lent (prev′ə lənt) **adj.** [L praevalens, prp. of praevalere: see PREVAIL] **1** [Rare] stronger, more effective, etc.; dominant **2** a) widely existing b) generally practiced, occurring, or accepted —**SYN.** PREVAILING —**prev′a·lence** (-ləns) **n.** —**prev′a·lent·ly adv.**

prey (prā) **n.** [ME preye < OFr preie < L praeda < base of prehendere, to seize: see PREHENSILE] **1** orig., plunder; booty **2** an animal hunted or killed for food by another animal **3** a person or thing that falls victim to someone or something **4** the mode of living by preying on other animals [a bird of prey] —**vi. 1** to plunder; rob **2** to hunt or kill other animals for food **3** to make profit from a victim as by swindling **4** to have a wearing or harmful influence; weigh heavily Generally used with on or upon —**prey′er n.**

priv·i·lege (priv′ə lij, priv′lij) *n.* ⟦OFr < L *privilegium*, an exceptional law for or against any individual < *privus*, PRIVATE + *lex* (gen. *legis*), law: see LEGAL⟧ **1** a right, advantage, favor, or immunity specially granted to one; esp., a right held by a certain individual, group, or class, and withheld from certain others or all others **2** [Rare] a basic civil right, guaranteed by a government *[the privilege of trial by jury]* **3** an option, as a put or call, to buy or sell a stock —*vt.* **-leged, -leg·ing** to grant a privilege or privileges to

pro·fi·cient (prō fish′ənt, prə-) *adj.* ⟦L *proficiens*, prp. of *proficere*, to advance < *pro-*, forward + *facere*, to make: see PRO-² & DO¹⟧ highly competent; skilled; adept —*n.* an expert —**pro·fi′cien·cy** (-ən sē), *pl.* **-cies,** *n.* —**pro·fi′cient·ly** *adv.*

pro·pel (prō pel′, prə-) *vt.* **-pelled′, -pel′ling** ⟦ME *propellen* < L *propellere* < *pro-*, forward + *pellere*, to drive: see FELT¹⟧ to push, drive, or impel onward, forward, or ahead

proph·et (präf′ət, -it) *n.* ⟦ME *prophete* < OFr < LL *propheta*, soothsayer, in LL(Ec), prophet < Gr *prophētēs*, interpreter of a god's will (in LXX, a Hebrew prophet; in N.T., an inspired preacher) < *pro-*, before + *phanai*, to speak: see BAN¹⟧ **1** a person who speaks for God or a god, or as though under divine guidance **2** a religious teacher or leader regarded as, or claiming to be, divinely inspired **3** a spokesman for some cause, group, movement, etc. **4** a person who predicts future events in any way —**the Prophet** among Muslims, Mohammed ☆**2** among Mormons, Joseph Smith —**the Prophets 1** one of the three major divisions of the Jewish Holy Scriptures, following the Pentateuch and preceding the Hagiographa **2** the authors or subjects of the prophetic books in this division, including Amos, Hosea, Isaiah, Micah, Jeremiah, etc. —**proph′et·ess** *n.fem.*

pro·phet·ic (prō fet′ik, prə-) *adj.* ⟦MFr *prophetique* < LL(Ec) *propheticus* < Gr *prophētikos*⟧ **1** of, or having the powers of, a prophet **2** of, having the nature of, or containing a prophecy *[a prophetic utterance]* **3** that predicts or foreshadows Also **pro·phet′i·cal** —**pro·phet′i·cal·ly** *adv.*

pro·pose (prō pōz′, prə-) *vt.* **-posed′, -pos′ing** ⟦LME < OFr *proposer*, altered (infl. by *poser*: see POSE¹) < L *proponere* (pp. *propositus*), to set forth, display, propose: see PRO-² & POSITION⟧ **1** to put forth for consideration or acceptance **2** to purpose, plan, or intend **3** to present as a toast in drinking **4** to nominate (someone) for membership, office, etc. —*vi.* **1** to make a proposal; form or declare a purpose or design **2** to offer marriage —SYN. INTEND —**pro·pos′er** *n.*

pro·pri·e·tor (prō prī′ə tər, prə-) *n.* ⟦irreg. formation < PROPRIET(ARY) + -OR⟧ **1** a person who has a legal title or exclusive right to some property; owner ☆**2** the owner of a proprietary colony **3** one who owns and operates a business establishment —**pro·pri′e·tor·ship′** *n.* —**pro·pri′e·tress** (-tris) *n.fem.*

pru·dent (prōōd′ nt) *adj.* ⟦OFr < L *prudens*, for *providens*: see PROVIDENT⟧ **1** capable of exercising sound judgment in practical matters, esp. as concerns one's own interests **2** cautious or discreet in conduct; circumspect; not rash **3** managing carefully and with economy —SYN. CAREFUL —**pru′dent·ly** *adv.*

pseu·do·nym (sōō′də nim′, sōōd′n im′) *n.* ⟦Fr *pseudonyme* < Gr *pseudōnymos*: see fol.⟧ a fictitious name, esp. one assumed by an author; pen name —**pseu′do·nym′i·ty** *n.*
SYN.—a **pseudonym** is a fictitious name assumed, esp. by a writer, for anonymity, for effect, etc.; **pen name** and **nom de plume** are applied specifically to the pseudonym of a writer; **alias** also refers to an assumed name and, in popular use, is specifically applied to one taken by a criminal to disguise identity; **incognito** is usually applied to a fictitious name temporarily assumed by a famous person, as in traveling, to avoid being recognized

psy·cho·a·nal·y·sis (sī′kō ə nal′ə sis) *n.* ⟦ModL: see PSYCHO- & ANALYSIS⟧ **1** a method, developed by Freud and others, of investigating mental processes and of treating neuroses and some other disorders of the mind: it is based on the assumption that such disorders are the result of the rejection by the conscious mind of factors that then persist in the unconscious as repressed instinctual forces, causing conflicts which may be resolved or diminished by discovering and analyzing the repressions and bringing them into consciousness through the use of such techniques as free association, dream analysis, etc. **2** the theory or practice of this —**psy′cho·an′a·lyt′ic** (-an′ə lit′ik) or **psy′cho·an′a·lyt′i·cal** *adj.* —**psy′cho·an′a·lyt′i·cal·ly** *adv.*

psy·cho·sis (sī kō′sis) *n., pl.* **-cho′ses′** (-sēz′) ⟦ModL: see PSYCHO- & -OSIS⟧ a major mental disorder in which the personality is very seriously disorganized and contact with reality is usually impaired: psychoses are of two sorts, *a*) functional (characterized by lack of apparent organic cause, and principally of the schizophrenic, paranoid, or manic-depressive type), and *b*) organic (characterized by a pathological organic condition such as brain damage or disease, metabolic disorders, etc.) —SYN. INSANITY

pto·maine (tō′mān′) *n.* ⟦It *ptomaina* < Gr *ptōma*, corpse < *piptein*, to fall: see FEATHER⟧ any of a class of alkaloid substances, some of which are poisonous, formed in decaying animal or vegetable matter by bacterial action on proteins

pul·mo·nar·y (pul′mə ner′ē, pool′-) *adj.* ⟦L *pulmonarius* < *pulmo* (gen. *pulmonis*), lung < IE *pleumon*, lung, orig., floater < base *pleu-*, to swim, float > FLOW: for semantic development see LIGHTS⟧ **1** of, like, or affecting the lungs **2** having lungs or lunglike organs **3** designating the artery conveying blood from the right ventricle of the heart to the lungs or any of the veins conveying oxygenated blood from the lungs to the left atrium of the heart

pu·tre·fy (pyōō′trə fī′) *vt., vi.* **-fied′, -fy′ing** ⟦ME *putrifien* < L *putrefacere*: see PUTRID & -FY⟧ to make or become putrid or rotten; decompose —SYN. DECAY —**pu′tre·fi′er** *n.*

Que. Quebec

quell (kwel) *vt.* ⟦ME *quellen* < OE *cwellan*, to kill, akin to *qwalu*, death, Ger *quälen*, torment, afflict < IE base *gwel-*, to stab, pain, death > OIr *at-baill*, (he) dies⟧ **1** to crush; subdue; put an end to **2** to quiet; allay —*n.* [Obs.] a killing; murder —**quell′er** *n.*

quin·tes·sence (kwin tes′əns) *n.* ⟦ME *quyntencense* < MFr *quinte essence* < ML *quinta essentia*⟧ **1** in ancient and medieval philosophy, the fifth essence, or ultimate substance, of which the heavenly bodies were thought to be composed: distinguished from the four elements (air, fire, water, and earth) **2** the pure, concentrated essence of anything **3** the most perfect manifestation of a quality or thing —**quin′tes·sen′tial** (-te sen′shəl) *adj.*

rar·e·fy (rer′ə fī′) *vt., vi.* **-fied′, -fy′ing** ⟦ME *rarefien* < MFr *rarefier* < L *rarefacere* < *rarus*, RARE¹ + *facere*, to make, DO¹⟧ **1** to make or become thin, or less dense *[the rarefied mountain air]* **2** to make or become more refined, subtle, or lofty *[a rarefied sense of humor]* —**rar′e·fac′tion** (-fak′shən) *n.* —**rar′e·fac′tive** *adj.*

rat·a·ble (rāt′ə bəl) *adj.* **1** that can be rated, or estimated, etc. **2** figured at a certain rate; proportional **3** [Brit., etc. (exc. Cdn.)] liable to the payment of taxes (rates) —**rat′a·bly** *adv.*

rat·i·fy (rat′ə fī′) *vt.* **-fied′, -fy′ing** ⟦ME *ratifien* < MFr *ratifier* < ML *ratificare* < L *ratus* (see RATE¹) + *facere*, to make, DO¹⟧ to approve or confirm; esp., to give official sanction to —SYN. APPROVE —**rat′i·fi·ca′tion** *n.*

re·ces·sion¹ (ri sesh′ən) *n.* ⟦L *recessio* < pp. of *recedere*: see RECEDE¹⟧ **1** a going back or receding; withdrawal **2** a procession leaving a place of assembly **3** a receding part, as of a wall **4** *Econ.* a temporary falling off of business activity during a period when such activity has been generally increasing —**re·ces′sion·ar′y** *adj.*

re·ces·sion² (rē′sesh′ən) *n.* ⟦RE- + CESSION⟧ a ceding back, as to a former owner

re·cip·i·ent (ri sip′ē ənt) *n.* ⟦< L *recipiens*, prp. of *recipere*: see RECEIVE⟧ a person or thing that receives —*adj.* receiving, or ready or able to receive —**re·cip′i·ence** or **re·cip′i·en·cy** *n.*

rec·on·cile (rek′ən sīl′) *vt.* **-ciled′, -cil′ing** ⟦ME *reconsilen* < OFr *reconcilier* < L *reconciliare*: see RE- & CONCILIATE⟧ **1** to make friendly again or win over to a friendly attitude **2** to settle (a quarrel or dispute) or compose (a difference) **3** to make (arguments, ideas, texts, accounts, etc.) consistent, compatible, etc.; bring into harmony **4** to make content, submissive, or acquiescent (*to*) *[to become reconciled to one's lot]*

rec·ti·fy (rek′tə fī′) *vt.* **-fied′, -fy′ing** ⟦ME *rectifien* < MFr *rectifier* < LL *rectificare*: see RECTI- & -FY⟧ **1** to put or set right; correct; amend **2** to adjust, as in movement or balance; adjust by calculation **3** *Chem.* to refine or purify (a liquid) by distillation, esp. by fractional or repeated distillations **4** *Elec.* to convert (alternating current) to direct current **5** *Math.* to find the length of (a curve) —**rec′ti·fi·a·ble** *adj.* —**rec′ti·fi·ca′tion** *n.*

re·im·burse (rē′im burs′) *vt.* **-bursed′, -burs′ing** ⟦RE- + archaic *imburse*, to pay, after Fr *rembourser* < *re-*, again + *embourser*, to pay < *en-*, in + *bourse*, PURSE⟧ **1** to pay back (money spent) **2** to repay or compensate (a person) for expenses, damages, losses, etc. —SYN. PAY¹ —**re′im·burs′a·ble** *adj.* —**re′im·burse′ment** *n.*

re·it·er·ate (rē it′ə rāt′) *vt.* **-at′ed, -at′ing** ⟦< L *reiteratus*, pp. of *reiterare*, to repeat: see RE- & ITERATE⟧ to repeat (something done or said); say or do again or repeatedly —SYN. REPEAT —**re·it′er·a′tion** *n.* —**re·it′er·a·tive** (-ə rāt′iv, -ər ə tiv) *adj.* —**re·it′er·a·tive·ly** *adv.*

rel·e·vant (rel′ə vənt) *adj.* ⟦ML *relevans*, prp. of *relevare*, to bear upon < L, to lift up: see RELIEVE⟧ bearing upon or relating to the matter in hand; pertinent; to the point —**rel′e·vance** or **rel′e·van·cy** *n.* —**rel′e·vant·ly** *adv.*
SYN.—**relevant** implies close logical relationship with, and importance to, the matter under consideration *[relevant testimony]*; **germane** implies such close natural connection as to be highly appropriate or fit *[your reminiscences are not truly germane to this discussion]*; **pertinent** implies an immediate and direct bearing on the matter in hand *[a pertinent sugges-*

tion/; **apposite** applies to that which is both relevant and happily suitable or appropriate /an *apposite* analogy/; **applicable** refers to that which can be brought to bear upon a particular matter or problem /your description is *applicable* to several people/; **apropos** is used of that which is opportune as well as relevant /an *apropos* remark/ —**ANT.** inappropriate, extraneous

re·mem·brance (ri mem′brəns) *n.* ‖ME < OFr: see prec. & -ANCE ‖ 1 a remembering or being remembered 2 the power to remember 3 something remembered; memory 4 the extent of time over which one can remember 5 an object that serves to bring to mind or keep in mind some person, event, etc.; souvenir, gift, keepsake, memento, etc. 6 commemoration /in *remembrance* of the deceased/ 7 [*pl.*] greetings

rem·i·nis·cence (-əns) *n.* ‖Fr *réminiscence* < LL *remeniscentia*: see fol. ‖ 1 the act of remembering or recollecting past experiences 2 a memory or recollection 3 [*pl.*] an account, written or spoken, of remembered experiences 4 something that suggests or recalls something else; reminder

re·mit (ri mit′) *vt.* **-mit′ted, -mit′ting** ‖ME *remytten* < L *remittere* (pp. *remissus*), to send back, in LL(Ec), to forgive sin < *re-*, back + *mittere*, to send: see MISSION ‖ 1 to forgive or pardon (sins, etc.) 2 *a)* to refrain from exacting (a payment, tax, etc.) *b)* to refrain from inflicting (a punishment) or enforcing (a sentence or fine); cancel 3 to let slacken; decrease /without *remitting* one's efforts/ 4 *a)* to submit or refer (a matter) for consideration, judgment, etc. *b)* *Law* REMAND (*vt.* 2) 5 to put back, as into a state or position 6 to put off; postpone 7 to send (money) in payment /please *remit* the full amount by the date shown/ 8 [Obs.] to give up; surrender —*vi.* 1 *a)* to become more moderate in force or intensity *b)* to have its symptoms lessen or disappear (said of a disease) 2 to send money, as in payment; pay —*n.* 1 the act or an instance of remitting 2 [Brit.] the area of responsibility, expertise, etc. of a person, agency, etc. — **re·mit′ment** *n.* —**re·mit′ta·ble** *adj.* —**re·mit′ter** *n.*

rep·re·hend (rep′ri hend′) *vt.* ‖ME *reprehenden* < L *reprehendere* < *re-*, back + *prehendere*: see PREHENSILE ‖ 1 to reprimand or rebuke (a person) 2 to find fault with (something done); censure —**SYN.** CRITICIZE

rep·re·sent·a·tive (rep′rə zen′tə tiv) *adj.* ‖ME < MFr or ML: MFr *représentatif* < ML *repraesentativus* ‖ 1 representing or serving to represent; specif., *a)* picturing; portraying; reproducing *b)* acting or speaking, esp. by due authority, in the place or on behalf of another or others; esp., serving as a delegate in a legislative assembly 2 composed of persons duly authorized, as by election, to act and speak for others /a *representative* assembly/ 3 of, characterized by, or based on representation of the people by elected delegates /*representative* government/ 4 being an example or type of a certain class or kind of thing; typical /a building *representative* of modern architecture/ —*n.* 1 a person or thing enough like the others in its class or kind to serve as an example or type 2 a person duly authorized to act or speak for another or others; specif., *a)* a member of a legislative assembly *b)* a salesman or agent for a business firm ☆3 [**R-**] a member of the lower house of Congress (*House of Representatives*) or of a State legislature —**rep′re·sent′a·tive·ly** *adv.* —**rep′re·sent′a·tive·ness** *n.*

re·prieve (ri prēv′) *vt.* **-prieved′, -priev′ing** ‖earlier *repry* < Anglo-Fr *repris* < MFr, pp. of *reprendre*, to take back, prob. altered by assoc. with ME *repreven*, REPROVE ‖ 1 to postpone the punishment of; esp., to postpone the execution of (a person condemned to death) 2 to give temporary relief to, as from trouble or pain —*n.* a reprieving or being reprieved; specif., *a)* postponement of a penalty, esp. that of death; also, a warrant ordering this *b)* a temporary relief or escape, as from trouble or pain

re·prise (ri prīz′; *for n.* 2 & *vt., usually* rə prēz′) *n.* ‖ME < OFr, fem. of *repris*, pp. of *reprendre*, to take back < L *reprehendere*: see REPREHEND ‖ 1 *Eng. Law* a deduction and payment, as for an annuity, out of income from lands: *usually used in pl.* 2 *Music a)* RECAPITULATION *b)* any repetition or copying of a song, part of a song, role, etc. performed earlier —*vt.* **-prised′, -pris′ing** to present a reprise of (a song)

re·pug·nant (-nənt) *adj.* ‖ME < MFr < L *repugnans*: see prec. ‖ 1 contradictory; inconsistent /actions *repugnant* to his words/ 2 offering resistance; opposed; antagonistic /*repugnant* forces/ 3 causing repugnance; distasteful; offensive; disagreeable /a *repugnant* odor/ —**SYN.** HATEFUL —**re·pug′nant·ly** *adv.*

ro·bot (rō′bät′; *also*, -bət, -but′) *n.* ‖ < Czech *robota*, forced labor < OSlav *rabota*, menial labor < *rabu*, servant < IE base *orbho-*: see ORPHAN ‖ 1 *a)* any anthropomorphic mechanical being, as those in Karel Čapek's play *R.U.R.* (Rossum's Universal Robots), built to do routine manual work for human beings *b)* any mechanical device operated automatically, esp. by remote control, to perform in a seemingly human way 2 an automaton; esp., a person who acts or works mechanically and without original thinking —**ro·bot′ic** (rō bät′ik) *adj.* —**ro′bot·ism** *n.*

sanc·ti·mo·ny (saŋk′tə mō′nē) *n.* ‖OFr *sanctimonie* < L *sanctimonia* < *sanctus*, holy: see SAINT ‖ 1 affected piety or righteousness; religious hypocrisy 2 *obs. var.* of SANCTITY

seethe (sēth) *vt.* **seethed, seeth′ing** ‖ME *sethen* < OE *sēothan*, akin to Ger *sieden* < IE base *sew-*, to cook, boil > Sans *hāvayan*, (they) stew ‖ 1 to cook by boiling 2 to soak, steep, or saturate in liquid — *vi.* 1 to boil or to surge, bubble, or foam as if boiling 2 to be violently agitated or disturbed —*n.* the act or condition of seething —**SYN.** BOIL[1]

so·lic·it (sə lis′it) *vt.* ‖ME *soliciten* < MFr *solliciter* < L *sollicitare* < *sollicitus*: see SOLICITOUS ‖ 1 to ask or seek earnestly or pleadingly; appeal to or for /to *solicit* aid, to *solicit* members for donations/ 2 to tempt or entice (someone) to do wrong 3 to approach for some immoral purpose, as a prostitute does —*vi.* to solicit someone or something —**SYN.** BEG —**so·lic′i·tant** (-i tənt) *n., adj.* —**so·lic′i·ta′-tion** *n.*

SOS (es′ō′es′) *n.* 1 a signal of distress in code (. . . .- - -. . .) used internationally in wireless telegraphy, as by ships 2 [Colloq.] any call for help

sov·er·eign (säv′rən, -ər in; *occas.* suv′-) *adj.* ‖ME *soveraine* < OFr < VL *superanus* < L *super*, above, OVER ‖ 1 above or superior to all others; chief; greatest; supreme 2 supreme in power, rank, or authority 3 of or holding the position of ruler; royal; reigning 4 independent of all others /a *sovereign* state/ 5 excellent; outstanding 6 very effectual, as a cure or remedy —*n.* 1 a person who possesses sovereign authority or power; specif., a monarch or ruler 2 a British gold coin valued at 20 shillings or one pound sterling, no longer minted for circulation —**sov′er·eign·ly** *adv.*

stim·u·lus (-ləs) *n., pl.* **-u·li** (-lī′) ‖L, a goad, sting, torment, pang, spur, incentive: see STYLE ‖ 1 something that rouses or incites to action or increased action; incentive 2 *Physiol., Psychol.* any action or agent that causes or changes an activity in an organism, organ, or part, as something that excites an end organ, starts a nerve impulse, activates a muscle, etc.

stra·te·gic (strə tē′jik) *adj.* 1 of or having to do with strategy 2 characterized by sound strategy; favorable; advantageous 3 *a)* essential to effective military strategy ☆*b)* operating or designed to operate directly against the military, industrial, etc. installations of an enemy /the *Strategic* Air Command/ 4 required for the effective conduct of a war /*strategic* materials/ Also **stra·te′gi·cal** —**stra·te′gi·cal·ly** *adv.*

stra·tum (strāt′əm, strat′-) *n., pl.* **stra′ta** (-ə) or **-tums** ‖ModL < L, a covering, blanket < *stratus*, pp. of *sternere*, to spread, stretch out, cover: for IE base see STREW ‖ 1 a horizontal layer or section of material, esp. any of several lying one upon another; specif., *a) Biol.* a layer of tissue *b) Geol.* a single layer of sedimentary rock 2 a section, level, or division, as of the atmosphere or ocean, regarded as like a stratum 3 any of the socioeconomic groups of a society as determined by birth, income, education, etc.

stub·born (stub′ərn) *adj.* ‖ME *stoburn*, prob. < OE *stubb*, var. of *stybb*, STUB ‖ 1 refusing to yield, obey, or comply; resisting doggedly or unreasonably; resolute or obstinate 2 done or carried on in an obstinate or doggedly persistent manner /a *stubborn* campaign/ 3 hard to handle, treat, or deal with; intractable /a *stubborn* cold/ — **stub′born·ly** *adv.* —**stub′born·ness** *n.*
SYN.—**stubborn** implies an innate fixedness of purpose, course, condition, etc. that is strongly resistant to change, manipulation, etc. /a *stubborn* child, belief, etc./; **obstinate** applies to one who adheres persistently, and often unreasonably, to a purpose, course, etc., against argument or persuasion /a panel hung by an *obstinate* juror/; **dogged** implies thoroughgoing determination or, sometimes, sullen obstinacy /the *dogged* pursuit of a goal/; **pertinacious** implies a strong tenacity of purpose that is regarded unfavorably by others /a *pertinacious* critic/ —**ANT.** compliant, tractable

stu·pe·fy (stōo′pə fī′, styōo′-) *vt.* **-fied′, -fy′ing** ‖Fr *stupéfier* < L *stupefacere* < *stupere*, to be stunned (see STUPID) + *facere*, to make, DO[1] ‖ 1 to bring into a state of stupor; stun; make dull or lethargic 2 to astound, amaze, or bewilder —**stu′pe·fi′er** *n.*

sub·si·dize (sub′sə dīz′) *vt.* **-dized′, -diz′ing** ‖ < fol. + -IZE ‖ 1 to support with a subsidy 2 to buy the aid or support of with a subsidy, often as a kind of bribe —**sub′si·di·za′tion** *n.* —**sub′si·diz′er** *n.*

sub·si·dy (sub′sə dē) *n., pl.* **-dies** ‖ME < Anglo-Fr *subsidie* < L *subsidium*, auxiliary forces, reserve troops, aid, support < *subsidere*, to sit down, remain: see SUBSIDE ‖ a grant of money; specif., *a)* a grant of money from one government to another, as for military aid *b)* a government grant to a private enterprise considered of benefit to the public *c)* [Historical] in England, money granted by Parliament to the king

suc·cumb (sə kum′) *vi.* ‖L *succumbere* < *sub-*, SUB- + *cumbere*, nasalized form of *cubare*, to lie: see CUBE[1] ‖ 1 to give way (to); yield; submit /to *succumb* to persuasion/ 2 to die /to *succumb* to a plague/ —**SYN.** YIELD

su·per·sede (-sēd') *vt.* **-sed'ed, -sed'ing** ‖ MFr *superseder,* to leave off, give over < L *supersedere,* lit., to sit over, preside over, forbear: see SUPER- & SIT ‖ **1** to cause to be set aside or dropped from use as inferior or obsolete and replaced by something else **2** to take the place of in office, function, etc.; succeed **3** to remove or cause to be removed so as to make way for another; supplant —**SYN.** REPLACE —**su'per·sed'er** *n.* —☆**su'per·se'dure** (-sē'jər) or **su'per·sed'ence** *n.*

sur·feit (sur'fit) *n.* ‖ ME *surfet* < OFr *sorfait* < *sorfaire,* to overdo < LL *superficere* < L *super* (see SUPER-) + *facere,* to make, DO[1] ‖ **1** too great an amount or supply; excess (*of*) *[a surfeit of compliments]* **2** overindulgence, esp. in food or drink **3** discomfort, disgust, nausea, etc. resulting from any kind of excess; satiety —*vt.* ‖ ME *sorfeten* ‖ to feed or supply to satiety or excess —*vi.* [Now Rare] to indulge or be supplied to satiety or excess; overindulge —**SYN.** SATIATE —**sur'feit·er** *n.*

sur·mise (sər mīz'; *for n., also* sur'mīz) *n.* ‖ ME *surmyse* < OFr *surmise,* accusation, fem. of *surmis,* pp. of *surmettre,* lit., to put upon, hence to accuse < *sur-* (see SUR-) + *mettre,* to put < L *mittere,* to send (see MISSION) ‖ **1** an idea or opinion formed from evidence that is neither positive nor conclusive; conjecture; guess **2** the act or process of surmising; conjecture in general —*vt., vi.* **-mised', -mis'ing** to imagine or infer (something) without conclusive evidence; conjecture; guess —**SYN.** GUESS

sur·veil·lance (sər vā'ləns, -vāl'yəns) *n.* ‖ Fr < *surveiller,* to watch over < *sur-* (see SUR-[1]) + *veiller* < L *vigilare,* to watch, WAKE[1] ‖ **1** *a)* close watch kept over someone, esp. a suspect *b)* constant observation of a place or process **2** supervision or inspection

sus·te·nance (sus'tə nəns) *n.* ‖ ME < OFr *soustenance* < LL *sustinentia,* patience, endurance < L *sustinere:* see SUSTAIN ‖ **1** a sustaining or being sustained **2** one's means of livelihood; maintenance; support **3** that which sustains life; nourishment; food

syn·chro·nize (siŋ'krə nīz', sin'-) *vi.* **-nized', -niz'ing** ‖ Gr *synchronizein,* to be contemporary with < *synchronos,* contemporary < *syn-,* together + *chronos,* time ‖ to move or occur at the same time or rate; be synchronous —*vt.* **1** to cause to agree in time or rate of speed; regulate (clocks, a flash gun and camera shutter, etc.) so as to make synchronous **2** to assign (events, etc.) to the same date or period; represent as or show to be coincident or simultaneous **3** *Film* to align (the picture and soundtrack) —**syn'chro·ni·za'tion** *n.* —**syn'chro·niz'er** *n.*

syn·op·sis (si näp'sis) *n., pl.* **-ses** (-sēz) ‖ LL < Gr < *syn-,* together + *opsis,* a seeing, visual image < *ōps,* EYE ‖ a statement giving a brief, general review or condensation; summary —**SYN.** ABRIDGMENT

syn·the·sis (sin'thə sis) *n., pl.* **-ses** (-sēz') ‖ Gr < *syn-,* together + *tithenai,* to place, DO[1] ‖ **1** the putting together of parts or elements so as to form a whole **2** a whole made up of parts or elements put together **3** *Chem.* the formation of a complex compound by the combining of two or more simpler compounds, elements, or radicals **4** *Philos.* in Hegelian philosophy, the unified whole in which opposites (thesis and antithesis) are reconciled

syn·the·size (-sīz') *vt.* **-sized', -siz'ing 1** to bring together into a whole by synthesis **2** to form by bringing together separate parts **3** *Chem.* to produce by synthesis rather than by extraction, refinement, etc.

tan·gi·ble (tan'jə bəl) *adj.* ‖ LL *tangibilis* < L *tangere,* to touch: see TACT[1] ‖ **1** that can be touched or felt by touch; having actual form and substance **2** corporeal and able to be appraised for value *[tangible assets]* **3** that can be understood; definite; objective —*n.* *[pl.]* property that can be appraised for value; assets having real substance; material things —**SYN.** PERCEPTIBLE —**tan'gi·bil'i·ty** or **tan'gi·ble·ness** *n.* —**tan'gi·bly** *adv.*

tan·ta·lize (tan'tə līz') *vt.* **-lized', -liz'ing** ‖ < TANTALUS + -IZE ‖ to tease or disappoint by promising or showing something desirable and then withholding it —**tan'ta·li·za'tion** *n.* —**tan'ta·liz'er** *n.*

tar·iff (tar'if) *n.* ‖ It *tariffa* < Ar *taʿrīf,* information, explanation < *ʿarafa,* to know, inform ‖ **1** a list or system of taxes placed by a government upon exports or, esp., imports **2** a tax of this kind, or its rate **3** any list or scale of prices, charges, etc. ☆**4** [Colloq.] any bill, charge, fare, etc. —*vt.* **1** to make a schedule of tariffs on; set a tariff on **2** to fix the price of according to a tariff

tele- (tel'i, -ə) *combining form* **1** ‖ Gr *tēle-* < *tēle,* far off < IE base *kwel-,* distant, remote > Welsh *pell,* distant ‖ at, over, from, or to a distance *[telegraph]* **2** ‖ < TELE(VISION) ‖ of, in, or by television *[telecast]*

tem·per·a·ment (tem'pər ə mənt; *often,* -prə-) *n.* ‖ ME < L *temperamentum,* proper mixing < *temperare:* see TEMPER ‖ **1** orig., the act or an instance of tempering; proportionate mixture or balance of ingredients **2** in medieval physiology, any of the four conditions of body and mind, the *sanguine, phlegmatic, choleric* (or *bilious*), and *melancholic temperaments,* attributed to an excess of one of the four

corresponding humors: see HUMOR **3** one's customary frame of mind or natural disposition; nature *[a man of even temperament]* **4** a nature that is excitable, moody, capricious, volatile, etc. *[the temperament of a prima donna]* **5** [Obs.] *a)* climate *b)* temperature **6** *Music* a system of adjustment of the intervals between the tones of an instrument of fixed intonation: it may be **pure temperament,** in which the intervals are set exactly according to theory, or **equal temperament,** as in a piano, in which the pitch of the tones is slightly adjusted to make them suitable for all keys —**SYN.** DISPOSITION

thanks (thaŋks) *n.pl.* ‖ pl. of ME *thank* < OE *thanc,* thanks: see THANK ‖ an expression of gratitude; grateful acknowledgment of something received by or done for one —*interj.* I thank you — **thanks to 1** thanks be given to **2** on account of; because of

tran·sient (tran'shənt, -sē ənt; -zhənt, -zē ənt) *adj.* ‖ L *transiens,* prp. of *transire:* see TRANSIT ‖ **1** *a)* passing away with time; not permanent; temporary; transitory *b)* passing quickly or soon; fleeting; ephemeral ☆**2** staying only for a short time *[the transient population at resorts]* —*n.* ☆**1** a transient person or thing *[transients at a hotel]* **2** *Elec.* a temporary component of a current, resulting from a voltage surge, a change from one steady-state condition to another, etc. —**tran'sience** or **tran'sien·cy** *n.* —**tran'sient·ly** *adv.*
SYN.—**transient** applies to that which lasts or stays but a short time *[a transient guest, feeling, etc.];* **transitory** refers to that which by its very nature must sooner or later pass or end *[life is transitory];* **ephemeral** literally means existing only one day and, by extension, applies to that which is markedly short-lived *[ephemeral glory];* **momentary** implies duration for a moment or an extremely short time *[a momentary lull in the conversation];* **evanescent** applies to that which appears momentarily and fades quickly away *[evanescent mental images];* **fleeting** implies of a thing that it passes swiftly and cannot be held *[a fleeting thought]* —**ANT.** lasting, permanent

trans·pose (trans pōz') *vt.* **-posed', -pos'ing** ‖ ME *transposen* < MFr *transposer* (for L *transponere*): see TRANS- & POSE[1] ‖ **1** to transfer or shift; now, specif., to change the usual, normal, relative, or respective order or position of; interchange *[inadvertently transposed the e and the i in "weird"]* **2** to transfer (an algebraic term) from one side of an equation to the other, reversing the plus or minus value **3** to rewrite or play (a musical composition) in a different key or at another pitch level **4** [Obs.] to transform; convert —*vi.* to play music in a key or at a pitch level different from the one in which it is written —*n. Math.* a matrix obtained by interchanging the rows and columns of a given matrix —**trans·pos'a·ble** *adj.* —**trans·pos'er** *n.*

un·wield·y (-wēl'dē) *adj.* **1** hard to wield, manage, handle, or deal with, as because of large size or weight, or awkward form **2** [Now Rare] awkward; clumsy —**un·wield'i·ness** *n.*

va·grant (vā'grənt) *n.* ‖ ME *vagraunt,* prob. < Anglo-Fr *wacrant, walcrant* < OFr *walcrer,* to wander < Frank *walken* (see WALK): infl. prob. by L *vagari,* to wander ‖ **1** a person who wanders from place to place or lives a wandering life; rover **2** one who wanders from place to place without a regular job, supporting oneself by begging, etc.; idle wanderer; vagabond **3** *Law* a tramp, beggar, prostitute, or similar idle or disorderly persons whose way of living makes them liable to arrest and detention —*adj.* **1** wandering from place to place or living a wandering life; roaming; nomadic **2** living the life of a vagabond or tramp **3** of or characteristic of a vagrant **4** characterized by straggling growth: said of plants **5** following no fixed direction, course, or pattern; random, wayward, fleeting, erratic, etc. —**va'grant·ly** *adv.*
SYN.—**vagrant** refers to a person without a fixed home who wanders about from place to place, gaining support from begging, etc., and in legal usage, implies such a person regarded as a public nuisance, subject to arrest; **vagabond,** orig. implying shiftlessness, rascality, etc., now often connotes no more than a carefree, roaming existence; **bum, tramp,** and **hobo** are informal equivalents for the preceding, but **bum** always connotes an idle, dissolute, often alcoholic person who never works, **tramp** and **hobo** connote a vagrant, whether one who lives by begging or by doing odd jobs; **hobo** now also means a migratory laborer. See also ITINERANT

ven·er·a·ble (ven'ər ə bəl) *adj.* ‖ ME < MFr *vénérable* < L *venerabilis,* to be reverenced < *venerari:* see VENERATE ‖ **1** worthy of respect or reverence by reason of age and dignity, character, or position **2** impressive on account of age or historic or religious associations *[a venerable monument]* **3** [V-] *a) Anglican Ch.* a title of reverence for an archdeacon *b) R.C.Ch.* a title of veneration for a dead person who may later be beatified —**ven'er·a·bil'i·ty** or **ven'er·a·ble·ness** *n.* —**ven'er·a·bly** *adv.*

ve·rac·i·ty (və ras'ə tē) *n., pl.* **-ties** ‖ ML *veracitas,* truthfulness < L *verax:* see prec. ‖ **1** habitual truthfulness; honesty **2** accordance with truth; accuracy of statement **3** accuracy or precision, as of perception **4** that which is true; truth —**SYN.** TRUTH

ver‖i·fy (ver′ə fī′) *vt.* **-fied′, -fy′ing** ⟦ME *verifien* < MFr *verifier* < ML *verificare*, to make true < L *verus*, true (see VERY) + *-ficare*, -FY⟧ **1** to prove to be true by demonstration, evidence, or testimony; confirm or substantiate **2** to test or check the accuracy or correctness of, as by investigation, comparison with a standard, or reference to the facts **3** *Law a*) to add a verification to (a pleading) *b*) to affirm on oath —**SYN.** CONFIRM —**ver′i·fi′er** *n.*

vig‖i·lant (vij′ə lənt) *adj.* ⟦Fr < L *vigilans*, prp. of *vigilare*, to watch < *vigil*, awake: see VIGIL⟧ staying watchful and alert to danger or trouble —**SYN.** WATCHFUL —**vig′i·lant‖ly** *adv.*

vi·gnette (vin yet′) *n.* ⟦Fr, dim. < *vigne*, *vine*, VINE⟧ **1** an ornamental design (orig. one of vine leaves, tendrils, and grapes) or illustration used on a page of a book, magazine, etc., as at the beginning or end of a chapter or section **2** a picture, photograph, film image, etc. with no definite border, shading off gradually at the edges into the background **3** *a*) a short literary sketch or description *b*) a short, delicately memorable scene in a film or play —*vt.* **-gnet′ted, -gnet′-ting** to make a vignette of —**vi·gnet′tist** *n.*

vil‖i·fy (vil′ə fī′) *vt.* **-fied′, -fy′ing** ⟦LL(Ec) *vilificare*: see prec. & -FY⟧ to use abusive or slanderous language about or of; calumniate; revile; defame —**vil′i·fi·ca′tion** *n.* —**vil′i·fi′er** *n.*

vul·cani·za·tion (vul′kən i zā′shən) *n.* ⟦< fol. + -ATION⟧ **1** the process of treating crude rubber with sulfur or its compounds and subjecting it to heat in order to make it nonplastic and increase its strength and elasticity **2** a process somewhat like this, for hardening some substance

vul·can·ize (vul′kən īz′) *vt.* **-ized′, -iz′ing** ⟦VULCAN + -IZE⟧ to subject to vulcanization —*vi.* to undergo vulcanization —**vul′can·iz′er** *n.*

vul·ner‖a·ble (vul′nər ə bəl) *adj.* ⟦LL *vulnerabilis*, wounding, likely to injure (also, in pass. sense, vulnerable) < L *vulnerare*, to wound < *vulnus* (gen. *vulneris*), a wound < IE base *wel- > L *vellere*: see REVULSION⟧ **1** that can be wounded or physically injured **2** *a*) open to criticism or attack *[a vulnerable* reputation] *b*) easily hurt, as by adverse criticism; sensitive *c*) affected by a specified influence, temptation, etc. *[vulnerable* to political pressure] **3** open to attack by armed forces **4** *Bridge* liable to increased penalties and entitled to increased bonuses: said of a team which has won one game —**vul′-ner·a‖bil′i‖ty** *n.* —**vul′ner·a‖bly** *adv.*

war·rant (wôr′ənt, wär′-) *n.* ⟦ME *warant* < NormFr (OFr *garant*), a warrant < Frank *warand* < prp. of *warjan*; akin to OE *werian*, to guard, defend: see WEIR⟧ **1** *a*) authorization or sanction, as by a superior or the law *b*) justification or reasonable grounds for some act, course, statement, or belief **2** something that serves as an assurance, or guarantee, of some event or result **3** a writing serving as authorization or certification for something; specif., *a*) authorization in writing for the payment or receipt of money *b*) a short-term note issued by a municipality or other governmental agency, usually in anticipation of tax revenues *c*) an option issued by a company granting the holder the right to buy certain securities, generally common stock, at a specified price and usually for a limited time *d*) *Law* a writ or order authorizing an officer to make an arrest, seizure, or search, or perform some other designated act *e*) *Mil.* the certifi-

cate of appointment to the grade of warrant officer (cf. WARRANT OFFICER) —*vt.* **1** *a*) to give (someone) authorization or sanction to do something *b*) to authorize (the doing of something) **2** to serve as justification or reasonable grounds for (an act, belief, etc.) *[a remark that did not warrant* such anger] **3** to give formal assurance, or guarantee, to (someone) or for (something); specif., *a*) to guarantee the quality, quantity, condition, etc. of (goods) *b*) to guarantee to (the purchaser) that goods sold are as represented *c*) to guarantee to (the purchaser) the title of goods purchased; assure of indemnification against loss *d*) *Law* to guarantee the title of granted property to (the grantee) **4** [Colloq.] to state with confidence; affirm emphatically *[I warrant* they'll be late] —**SYN.** ASSERT —**war′rant·a‖ble** *adj.*

wry (rī) *vt.*, *vi.* **wried, wry′ing** ⟦ME *wrien*, to twist, bend < OE *wrigian*, to turn, twist, akin to OFris *wrigia*, to bend, stoop < IE *wreik-* (> L *rica*, head veil) < base *wer-*, to turn, bend⟧ to writhe or twist —*adj.* **wri′er** or **wry′er**, **wri′est** or **wry′est 1** turned or bent to one side; twisted; distorted **2** made by twisting or distorting the features *[a wry* face expressing distaste] **3** stubbornly contrary **4** distorted in meaning, interpretation, etc. **5** perverse, ironic, etc. *[wry* humor] —**wry′ly** *adv.* —**wry′ness** *n.*

yield (yēld) *vt.* ⟦ME *yelden* < OE *gieldan*, to pay, give, akin to Ger *gelten*, to be worth < IE base *ghel-tō*, (I) give, pay⟧ **1** to produce; specif., *a*) to give or furnish as a natural process or as the result of cultivation *[an orchard that yielded* a good crop] *b*) to give in return; produce as a result, profit, etc. *[an investment that yielded* high profits] **2** to give up under pressure; surrender: sometimes used reflexively with *up [to yield* oneself up to pleasure] **3** to give; concede; grant *[to yield* the right of way, to *yield* a point] **4** [Archaic] to pay; recompense —*vi.* **1** to produce or bear *[a* mine that has *yielded* poorly] **2** to give up; surrender; submit **3** to give way to physical force *[the gate would not yield* to their blows] **4** to give place; lose precedence, leadership, etc.; specif., *a*) to let another, esp. a motorist, have the right of way *b*) to give up willingly a right, position, privilege, etc.: often with *to* —*n.* **1** the act of yielding, or producing **2** the amount yielded or produced; return on labor, investment, taxes, etc.; product **3** *Finance* the ratio of the annual cash dividends or of the earnings per share of a stock to the market price **4** *Physics, Chem. a*) the total products actually obtained from given raw materials, usually expressed as a percentage of the amount theoretically obtainable *b*) the force in kilotons or megatons of a nuclear or thermonuclear explosion —**yield′er** *n.*

SYN.—**yield** implies a giving way under the pressure or compulsion of force, entreaty, persuasion, etc. *[to yield* to demands]; **capitulate** implies surrender to a force that one has neither the strength nor will to resist further *[to capitulate* to the will of the majority]; **succumb** stresses the weakness of the one who gives way or the power and irresistibility of that which makes one yield *[she succumbed* to his charms]; **relent** suggests the yielding or softening of one in a dominant position who has been harsh, stern, or stubborn *[he relented* at the sight of her grief]; **defer** implies a yielding to another because of respect for his dignity, authority, knowledge, etc. *[to defer* to another's judgment] —**ANT.** resist

Zn *Chem. symbol for* zinc